Writing and Reporting the News

Mitchell Stephens

New York University

Gerald Lanson

Boston University

Holt, Rinehart and Winston
New York   Chicago   San Francisco   Philadelphia
Montreal   Toronto   London   Sydney
Tokyo   Mexico City   Rio de Janeiro   Madrid

Publisher:	Susan Katz
Acquisitions Editor:	Lucy Rosendahl
Senior Project Editors:	Maruta Mitchell
	Kathleen Nevils
Production Manager:	Annette Mayeski
Design Supervisor:	Louis Scardino
Text Designer:	Caliber Design Planning, Inc.
Cover Designer:	Ben Santora
Photo Researcher:	Nicolette Harlin

Library of Congress Cataloging-in-Publication Data

Stephens, Mitchell.
 Writing and reporting the news.

 Includes index.
 1. Reporters and reporting. I. Lanson, Gerald.
II. Title.
PN4781.S775   1986   070.4′3   85–22032
ISBN 0-03-060483-4

CBS COLLEGE PUBLISHING
Holt, Rinehart and Winston
The Dryden Press
Saunders College Publishing

Preface

This is a book about the reporter's craft; its title makes that clear. But we believe it also has value for people who may never find a job in a professional newsroom. Those who read its discussions and tackle its variety of exercises should come away with a clearer sense of the language and how it can be used most effectively. They should also gain a greater understanding of what goes on in the offices, meeting rooms, courtrooms and board rooms where society's decisions are made.

The book is unusual in that it combines thorough instruction in writing and reporting with extensive opportunities to apply that instruction. It is both a text and workbook.

In preparing the text, we have tried to use the techniques it teaches:

• The writing is designed to engage as it informs. We hope the book is, among other things, a good read.

• Each chapter attempts to break sometimes difficult procedures into their component parts. By explaining step by step how reporters go about their business, we have tried to take the mystery out of their transformations of two-month-long trials into two-column-long stories.

• The discussions are illustrated by hundreds of examples selected from scores of large and small newspapers around the country. We have tried to demonstrate our points, not just expound on them.

• The chapters are organized in what we believe is a logical order: building from the basics — words, sentences, paragraphs — to the complexities of writing and reporting longer stories.

• Our writing is based on thorough reporting. Rather than rely exclusively on our own experience, we've interviewed, and quoted, dozens of first-rate reporters. And we have tried to pass on not only their advice but a sense of the challenges, pressures and rewards of their jobs.

• Finally, this book, like a good news story, is designed to have some depth. The text emphasizes the basic stories and the traditional beats — such as police and city government — on which most reporters cut their teeth. But we've also devoted substantial chapters to specialized areas of coverage — business, science, education — that are increasingly making their presence felt on Page 1.

Journalism cannot be taught without a set of good assignments. The exercises in this book are intended both for beginning and somewhat more advanced reporters. Those who are just starting out might concentrate on the exercises in the first 26 chapters of the book and the initial exercises in the final four chapters. Those who have some experience in journalism might use the early chapters for review and concentrate on the later chapters.

We set four goals for ourselves in preparing the hundreds of assignments included here:

• First, we wanted the exercises to reflect our concern with introducing complex skills one step at a time. Readers will find plenty of fact sheets for writing leads (in Chapters 8 and 9) and stories (in Chapter 14 and all succeeding chapters). However, we have also included separate exercises on such skills as para-

v

graphing, using transitions and quotations, translating jargon, selecting information, supporting the lead, organizing the story, and using analogies and attribution. An additional advantage of such a wide variety of exercises is that readers are offered a wide choice of approaches to improving their skills.

• Second, we wanted the exercises to be as realistic as possible; there is no Mayor Jones from Hometown, U.S.A., here; there *are* speech transcripts, police reports, announcements, interviews, press releases, and masses of facts and quotes similar to those reporters must actually unscramble when the time comes to write a story. Our belief is that realistic exercises are both more meaningful and more fun.

• Third, we wanted the exercises to encourage readers to think like reporters. For example, rather than asking only that they write stories on city council meetings, we present readers sets of questions about local government that direct them to look through government records and find and talk to sources in government. It's important to know how to write up a city council meeting, but it's also important to begin to think about where and how information on the workings of government can be found.

• Finally, we wanted to offer readers exercises that do more than provide opportunities to practice journalism. We wanted, simultaneously, to offer them chances to think about words and how they are used, and we wanted to encourage visits to unfamiliar but important corners of the community—the board of adjustment, civil court, the local unemployment office, the research stacks of the local library. We hope our exercises are of some use in training better writers and better citizens, as well as better journalists.

We asked for help at many stages in the production of this book, and many people were kind enough to provide it. We are particularly grateful to all the thoughtful journalists who took the time to discuss their work with us. They include: Ted Rohrlich, Ron Harris and Kathryn Harris of the *Los Angeles Times;* Karen Arenson, William Serrin and James Reston of *The New York Times;* Tom French and Doreen Carvajal of the *St. Petersburg Times;* Joel Brinkley and Saundra Keyes of The (Louisville) *Courier-Journal;* Bob Greene and Stuart Diamond of *Newsday;* Dale Rice and Molly Ivins of the *Dallas Times Herald;* David Espo and Ken Herman of the Associated Press; Fred Barbash of *The Washington Post;* Paula LaRocque of *The Dallas Morning News;* Jim Detjen of *The Philadelphia Inquirer;* Louis Rose of the *St. Louis Post-Dispatch;* Don Melvin of *The Burlington Free Press;* Jim Flagg of The (Easton) *Express;* Leon Wynter of *The Wall Street Journal;* Michele Fuetsch of The (Bergen County, N.J.) *Record;* Walter Fee of *The Milwaukee Journal;* Jim Killackey of the *Daily Oklahoman;* Mike Cox of the (Austin) *American-Statesman;* Doug Rainey of the *La Crosse Tribune;* Bruce Maxwell of the *Rochester Post-Bulletin;* Tim Belnap of the *Detroit Free Press;* and Chris Welles, a free-lance writer. Special thanks, too, to Roy Peter Clark and the journalists and professors we each had a chance to meet, and learn from, at the Poynter Institute for Media Studies in St. Petersburg.

Many of the journalists we talked to have since moved on to other positions or other papers. Both Joel Brinkley and Stuart Diamond, for example, have joined *The New York Times.* But here and elsewhere in the book we have chosen to leave the people we interviewed at the jobs they held when they were interviewed.

Joshua Mills of *The New York Times* helped initiate this project and helped draft Chapters 10 and 27; Carey Lovelace and Hyman Bender helped with our research and some of the exercises. We appreciate the contributions they made.

Ted Rohrlich of the *Los Angeles Times;* David Rubin and Richard Cunningham of New York University; Stephen Solomon of *Inc.* magazine; and Arthur Engoron, an attorney, were kind enough to look over some of the chapters. Thanks, too, to another colleague, William Burrows, for his support, and to Shirley Biagi, of California State University, Sacramento, who shared her thoughts, along with galleys of her book on interviewing, with us.

We are also appreciative of the thoughtful reading and useful suggestions furnished at various stages in the development of our manuscript by Herbert Jackson of the William Paterson College of New Jersey, Junetta Davis of the University of Oklahoma, Mary Benedict of Indiana University, Cynthia Rawitch of California State University–Northridge, Alan Neckowitz of James Madison University, Robert Odom of St. Petersburg Junior College, Delbert McGuire of Colorado State University, Eleanor Lang of Southern Connecticut State College, Cecil Neth of Colorado State University, and Jo Ann Dickerson of the University of Texas at Arlington.

And, of course, we are grateful to our families for putting up with three years of often hectic, sometimes transatlantic, work on this book. Our wives—Esther Davidowitz and Kathy Lanson, one a reporter, the other an educator—read copy, saved us from errors and helped keep us smiling. The book is dedicated to them, with love.

Mitchell Stephens
Gerald Lanson

February 1986

List of Newspapers and Wire Services

The discussions in this book are illustrated by examples drawn from the stories and comments of the staff of the following newspapers (we have occasionally made minor changes in the printed examples so that they conform with the style used in the text):

Wire Services
Associated Press
Reuters
United Press International

Newspapers (by state)
Alabama
The Birmingham News

Arkansas
Arkansas Gazette

California
Los Angeles Times
Eastbay Today
The San Diego Union
San Francisco Chronicle

Colorado
Rocky Mountain News
The Denver Post

D.C.
The Washington Post

Florida
St. Petersburg Times
The Miami Herald

Georgia
The Atlanta Constitution

Illinois
Sun-Times
Chicago Tribune

Indiana
The Indianapolis Star

Iowa
The Des Moines Register

Kansas
The Hutchinson News

Kentucky
The Courier-Journal

Louisiana
The Times-Picayune

Massachusetts
The Boston Globe

Maryland
The Sun

Michigan
Detroit Free Press

Minnesota
Rochester Post-Bulletin
The Minneapolis Star and Tribune

Missouri
St. Louis Post-Dispatch

Nebraska
Omaha World-Herald

New Jersey
Asbury Park Press
The Record
The News
Trenton Times

New York
Adirondack Enterprise
Times Union
Newsday
Daily News
New York Post
Saratogian-Tri-County News
The New York Times
The Westsider
The Rockland Journal-News
The Wall Street Journal

Ohio
The Plain Dealer

Oklahoma
The Daily Oklahoman
Tulsa World

Oregon
The Oregonian

Pennsylvania
The Express
The Philadelphia Inquirer

Rhode Island
The Providence Bulletin
The Providence Journal

Tennessee
The Chattanooga Times
The Commercial Appeal

Texas
Austin American-Statesman
Dallas Times Herald
Houston Chronicle
Lufkin News
The Dallas Morning News

Vermont
The Burlington Free Press

Washington
The Seattle Times

West Virginia
Bluefield Daily Telegraph

Virginia
Richmond Times-Dispatch
Roanoke Times & World-News

Wisconsin
La Crosse Tribune
The Milwaukee Journal

National
USA Today

Contents

List of Exercises

Writing and Reporting the News

□ INTRODUCTION □

With county health insurance bills topping $5 million this year, the Bergen County freeholders say they can't afford to let Diane Belka, a widow with a 15-year-old daughter, work an extra hour a week to qualify for medical benefits.

Mrs. Belka, a part-time clerk from Lyndhurst, is among 22 county employees kept on a 19-hour work week, one short of the 20 needed for insurance coverage under state regulations.

Yet the freeholders provide health benefits to some of their political friends at public expense, even though these friends work fewer than 20 hours a week — if they work at all . . .

These paragraphs began a three-part series in *The (Bergen County, N.J.) Record* exposing a scam Republican county officials apparently used to reward political appointees.

The series, by reporter Michele Fuetsch, had some impact: Five political appointees were dropped from the county payroll; some changes were contemplated in the county's hiring policy; and the county prosecutor launched an investigation. But the fuss soon faded. The Democrats had unseated the Republican majority in an election just before the story ran. And as the prosecutor's investigation dragged on, the Democrats continued some of the same questionable practices. Fuetsch, who covers county government for *The Record,* found herself facing the chore of investigating the Democrats, too.

Fuetsch's series won second place in a state journalism contest. But she was offered no book contracts.

She made no television appearances. Hollywood never called. After all, first-rate reporters have been exposing similar scams almost as long as second-rate politicians have been devising them. Certainly, there was nothing glamorous about Fuetsch's reporting. She spent most of her time reading computer print-outs and talking with county workers. Her articles, in other words, were nothing more and nothing less than good, solid journalism — the type of journalism this book is seeking to encourage.

The first clue to Fuetsch's story emerged at a meeting in which she overheard the county personnel director mention that part-time workers were being kept on a 19-hour week because they would qualify for medical benefits if they worked 20 hours or more. Interesting.

Fuetsch went to interview the personnel director. He noted, off-handedly, that despite this policy of holding down the cost of benefits, some part-time political appointees *were* allowed to receive medical coverage. Very interesting.

Fuetsch contacted someone she knew and trusted in county government, one of her *sources.* He mentioned the name of a part-time political appointee who, sure enough, was getting medical benefits — benefits worth more than his salary.

"I felt like a detective who had found a body but who had absolutely no idea who the person was or how the person died," Fuetsch recalls. She believed she was onto a story, but getting the story and pinning it down would take hundreds of hours of work, done in the rare free moments she could find between covering meetings, speeches, fund-raising dinners and campaign appearances.

First, she waded through a four-inch-thick computer printout listing about 3,000 county employees. Fuetsch was looking for people with low salaries — part-time employees. There were hundreds of them. Then she had to find out whether these employees qualified as political appointees. Did they have any regular responsibilities? Did they even bother to show at some county office? Political appointees, she was learning, often did not. It took Fuetsch five weeks to get through all the names on the printout. Tracking down a single part-timer sometimes took dozens of phone calls. When she was finished, Fuetsch had a pile of blue index cards as thick as a healthy Sunday newspaper, with the name of a county employee on each.

The next question was what benefits, if any, the people on her cards were taking advantage of and how much they were costing the county. In order to calculate the value of medical benefits she needed the age of each of the employees plus details of their family situations. This required a search of county personnel records and many more dozens of phone calls. The blue cards were filling up.

Fuetsch interviewed all the suspect employees and the people who had hired them to give them a chance to comment on her findings. And she talked with numerous other people at all levels of government — from guards she had befriended at the county office building (many county workers were anxious to help expose this patronage scheme) to the state's pension director. She spent so much time at the county office building interviewing and digging through personnel records that one of the janitors assumed she worked there.

"By the end of my investigation," Fuetsch says, picking up the analogy to a detective on a murder case, "I had the entire life history of that murder victim, and I knew who murdered him."

Her blue cards were covered with facts, but molding those facts into a lively series of stories would take additional weeks. Fuetsch would have to guide readers through the intricacies of health plans. She would have to pare down the information she had worked so hard to gather so that it could be conveyed in three articles, each filled with about 2,000 well-chosen words. "Readability was uppermost in my mind," Fuetsch says. "Each impropriety had to be explained with concrete examples."

In working on this series, Michele Fuetsch demonstrated a number of the qualities that good reporters must have: curiosity, a healthy skepticism, attention to detail, and the ability to work with sources and use public records. She also showed the ability to write clearly and accurately about what she had found.

These are crucial qualities for anyone who gathers and communicates information for the public about the public's business, qualities that will be referred to many times in this book. But we choose this example primarily for another reason: because it shows how hard reporting is.

Often moving the news is exciting. Occasionally, reporters even have the satisfaction, as Michele Fuetsch did, of exposing one of the little tricks people in power play when the public's back is turned. But journalism, if it's being done well, is *always* difficult. It requires long hours tracking down sources, talking with people whose reputation you may be about to assault, reading through often tedious records, checking and rechecking facts. "You do your homework," is how columnist James Reston of *The New York Times* puts it.

"I've been able to reach the position I'm in simply by working harder than other reporters," asserts Stuart Diamond, an English major in college who became a well-respected environment writer for *Newsday* on Long Island, N.Y.

Good reporters study the fields they are covering. They spend whatever spare time they can muster reading relevant records, documents and journals. They are always looking for one more knowledgeable source. "You have to be willing to make the extra phone calls," advises David Espo, who has worked his way from the Associated Press's Cheyenne, Wyo., bureau to the AP's desk on Capitol Hill in Washington. "If you make a perfunctory effort, you're going to get a perfunctory story."

Good reporters also take great pains with the writing of their stories. They strain for slightly more exact, slightly more graceful wordings. They are brutal, unforgiving editors . . . of their own work. "I think the people who really make it in journalism are the ones who try to make every story special, who don't kiss off anything," says Joel Brinkley, who won a Pulitzer Prize for *The Courier-Journal* in Louisville, Ky., well before he turned 30.

To say that Michele Fuetsch, in uncovering that medical benefits scam, was both a good reporter and a hard-working reporter is redundant. Tenacity, thoroughness and tirelessness are a large part of what good reporting is all about.

An essay on the value of hard work might not seem the most inspiring introduction for a journalism textbook. Why not begin by recalling the glories of the press's investigation of Watergate or by quoting Thomas Jefferson on the importance of a free press? But then we believe there *is* something inspiring in the notion that in newspaper journalism industriousness pays off, that effort — more than wealth, looks, connections, maybe even more than talent — is the key to success.

This discussion of the difficulties of journalism should also be reassuring. If beginning reporters find themselves struggling, under deadline pressure, to pin down a fact or find the right word, it is not a sign that they aren't cut out for a career in journalism. Rather it is an indication that they have joined the struggle for precision in perception and expression that *is* the practice of journalism at its best. If the writing and reporting assignments in the chapters that follow seem too easy, *that* may be cause for worry.

Writing

■ PART ONE ■

Language

CHAPTER 1

Meanings

A *blackout* of undetermined origin cut off power last night . . . Lights *flickered* off throughout the city at 7:26.

The writer of these sentences, which appeared in *The Dallas Morning News,* wanted to inform readers that power had failed at 7:26, plunging the area into darkness. The words he chose to convey that, however, didn't work, as the paper's writing coach, Paula LaRocque, noted in her in-house newsletter. A *blackout* cannot cut off power; a *blackout* is what happens when power *is* cut off. What's more, power that is cut off precisely at 7:26 presumably does not *flicker*—blink on and off.

Just as the first thing a musician must worry about is hitting the right notes, the first thing a writer must worry about is choosing the right words. Reporters must choose words that are not only grammatically correct (See Chapter 3, Spelling and Grammar) but *semantically* precise—words should say what their authors mean. This is a more exacting challenge than it might seem to be, as that reporter for *The Dallas Morning News* learned.

The curse and the gift of the English language is the richness of its vocabulary. English offers us countless opportunities to err in our choice of words. But it also offers us, through its superabundance of words, the capability of describing the world with remarkable exactness. Consider, for example, all the different terms for situations in which someone has illegally taken someone else's property:

steal	extort	burglary
rob	blackmail	stickup
pilfer	lift	larceny
sack	swipe	ripoff
pinch	shoplift	holdup
mug	plunder	piracy
embezzle	filch	heist
swindle	knock off	second-story job
poach	purloin	theft

Faced with such a wealth of possibilities, the writer must choose well. It would be wrong, for example, to describe an incident in which a store has been robbed at gunpoint as a *theft.* Theft, by definition, does not involve the use or threat of violence. The right word here is *robbery.* Similarly, it would be wrong to report that someone has been stopped and *burglarized* on the way home. Burglaries are defined as acts of stealing after entering a building. The right words here would be *held up.*

Good writers possess two basic skills: They sense when they are using a word incorrectly and they know how to find an acceptable substitute. For many beginning reporters, mastering the first skill presents more problems than mastering the second. Some of us have been getting away with poorly chosen words all our lives; it may not have mattered much—our friends seem to have gotten the point. But newspaper readers won't be as tolerant.

Sometimes the use of an ambiguous wording simply causes an unintended chuckle . . . at the writer's expense. The following sentence appeared in the (Little Rock) *Arkansas Gazette:*

Four years ago, the 91 residents of McCaskill (Hempstead County) lived in fear of being *burned out* and faced rising insurance rates.

Burned out is an expression commonly used to describe a person who is exhausted from having worked too much on something. A better phrase here would have been *losing their homes to fire.*

Sometimes use of the wrong word will leave readers perplexed. How did readers of *The News* in Paterson, N.J., react to this sentence, which appeared on a Dec. 31?

While most people were preparing to ring out the old, someone rung out the new this week, depositing an infant in a cold parked car outside Riverside Hospital in Boonton Township.

Aside from the reporter's bad taste here in joking about an abandoned baby, the word *rung* is misused. *Rung* is the past participle of *ring;* there is, fortunately, no way to *ring out* a baby. The only way to save this sentence would be to cross it out and start again.

Some errors are more subtle. Is it correct to write, as one (New Orleans) *Times-Picayune* reporter did, that the conditions at the ceremony did not "dampen the jailhouse marriage" of a prisoner? No. *Spirits* can be dampened but not *marriages* (unless the couple spends time in the rain); and the story would be clearer if the reporter had used the more precise word *wedding* instead of *marriage.*

Sometimes use of the wrong word can cause legal trouble. You could be sued for libel for writing that a man has been *indicted* when he has only been *charged* (See Appendix D, Law).

If there is some doubt about the correct meaning of a word, look it up. Dictionaries are full of information about meanings, and they can answer many usage questions too, as can style books (See Appendix B, Style). It's also no sin to keep a usage book on your desk.

If reference books are unable to relieve your doubt about a word, leave it out, even if that requires recasting the entire sentence.

Reporters should be particularly wary in their choice of verbs of attribution (See Chapter 10, Attribution). It's quite easy to distort the news by mixing up these common verbs. This story, from the *San Francisco Chronicle,* misuses either the word *announced* or the word *emerged:*

The Interior Department *announced* yesterday that it was delaying its plans to lease sites off the Northern California coast for oil and gas drilling.

News of the postponement of the sale . . . *emerged* in testimony presented at a San Francisco congressional hearing . . .

Information that only *emerges* during a hearing has not been *announced.*

There are dozens of words like *announced* that can be used in specific circumstances to describe what someone said. Among the most common are:

told	maintained	suggested
stated	exclaimed	added
revealed	shouted	declared
indicated	recalled	charged
argued	noted	insisted
claimed	retorted	pointed out

All these words have narrower meanings than the blander—and thus more versatile—word *said.* They must be used with care. For example, the verb *indicate* tends to be vague. To say someone *claimed* something implies that there is reason to doubt it. *State* is for formal pronouncements, and something can be *pointed out* only if it's a fact.

Said, probably the most used verb in journalism, is still the best option in most cases. It solves the problem in that story from the *Chronicle:*

The Interior Department *said* yesterday that it was delaying its plan to lease sites off the Northern California coast for oil and gas drilling . . .

There is a place for alternatives to *said.* Reporters do not want to use the same word in every paragraph. But in a profession whose goal is accurate communication, the simple, familiar word is often the best choice.

Most errors of meaning are caused by reporters straining to use colorful words and expressions they are not quite able to control. Too many beginning reporters fancy themselves artists. They would be better off seeing themselves as artisans working with precision tools—the words of the English language.

Additional Reading

Do's, Don't's & Maybes of English Usage, Theodore Bernstein, Times Books, 1977.
Modern American Usage, Wilson Follett, Warner Books, 1977.
On Language, William Safire, Avon, 1981.
What's the Good Word?, William Safire, Times Books, 1982.
I Stand Corrected: More on Language, William Safire, Times Books, 1984.

▪ **A** ▪

Circle the word in parentheses that best completes each of the following sentences.

1. Two rooms had to be closed to the public after fire (destroyed/damaged) the art museum.

2. The governor said the results of the public opinion poll would have no (effect/affect) on his decision.

3. The mounted policewoman had a difficult time (reigning/reining) in her horse.

4. Our team has (less/fewer) tall players.

5. The mayor spoke first, (as/like) he always does.

6. (It is hoped/Hopefully) the mall will attract shoppers to the area.

7. She handed out (more than/over) 1,000 fliers announcing the meeting.

8. Her body will (lay/lie) in state in the Rotunda.

9. The councilman could not choose (among/between) the three proposals.

10. It was the first (annual/of what was to be an annual) dinner commemorating the victory.

11. The council will hold (its/it's) weekly meeting tonight.

12. The (principal/principle) of the school was to be the (principal/principle) speaker in favor of the (principal/principle) of equal educational opportunity.

13. The two men reached (a verbal/an oral) agreement. They believed it was unnecessary to write out a contract.

14. Lyndon Johnson's picture was (hung/hanged) next to one of his predecessor, John Kennedy.

15. Water flowed (continually/continuously) from the stream into the lake.

16. The (robber/thief) snuck in when we were all away.

17. Graduates of the two schools are different (from/than) each other.

18. She was (averse/adverse) to the idea.

19. He put his shoe (on/upon) his foot.

20. In his speech he (alluded/eluded) to the book.

▪ B ▪

Edit the following sentences to replace any incorrect wordings.

1. "I have no intention of voting for the bill," she charged.

2. He was drowned when he accidentally slipped into the pool.

3. The bride to be and her husband were inviting over 500 guests to the wedding.

4. The Saturday school program has been in affect for five years, she revealed. She claimed that her statistics were that more than 1,500 students had participated in it.

5. The vases were unique; there were very few others in the world like them.

6. The senator refuted the opponents of prayer in the schools.

7. Hargrove is an imminent attorney who includes many political leaders and movie stars among his cases.

8. Fellow workers surmised that he had a tendency to flout his aristocratic background and wealth on the job.

9. The suspect forced three customers to sprawl face down on the floor and then escaped with about $350 from the cash register, police noted.

10. The mayor reported that Donaldson was a disgrace to the city, adding that the parks had deteriorated severely under him. "I knew he was a bum when my predecessor appointed him," she stated.

▪ C ▪

Edit the following story to correct any errors in word choice.

It appears certain that the state legislature will adapt a proposal this session to curb drunken driving, but legislators are reticent to speculate on the provisions that will comprise the final bill.

Both Senate and Assembly committees have carried bills intended to make it easier to annul the licenses of drivers convicted of driving while intoxicated.

The principle feature of the Senate bill, which had been proposed continuously over the past five years by Sen. John Mackey, calls for the automatic revocation of a licensee within seven days following a conviction of drunken driving. Under the law presently in affect, a driver can drive for months while appealing the return of his license.

The Assembly's bill presents judges with the option of removing the license after a conviction. Beside this provision, the Assembly committee's law involves a plan intended to make it more facile for police officers to apprehend suspicious drivers and give them on-the-spot exams for drunkenness.

"Its too early to say what the final bill will look like," argued Sen. Mackey.

Mackey also declined questions on whether the bill might be combined with a plan requiring beer bottles to be returned to the store to protect the ecology from litter. "Your guess is as good as mine," he indicated.

CHAPTER 2

Plain English

In 1984, according to *The New York Times,* the U.S. Department of State removed the word "killing" from its reports on human rights violations in favor of the phrase "unlawful or arbitrary deprivation of human life."

This is an exaggerated example of the sort of language reporters must avoid. There's never an excuse in journalism for substituting an obscure, though presumably less upsetting, phrase for a blunt, direct word like "killing." Nor is there an excuse for using seven words where one would do: That's a waste of space and of reader's time.

Unlike some government officials, reporters are paid to tell it straight and tell it simply. Good writing is clear and concise.

Clarity

A newsroom is not the place for bad poets. The emphasis on style over content, on meaningful obscurity, found in some poetry and in some creative writing classes, has no place in journalism.

UNACCEPTABLE:
In a bloodbath of Homeric proportions, 289 of our brethren saw the hooded specter of death on the city's main thoroughfares last year.

Journalists tell news. They want to engage; they want to entertain; but their primary goal is always to communicate. Literary flourishes, obscure terms and jargon may impress; slang may amuse; but to communicate clearly journalists must rely on a vocabulary that is more easily understood.

ACCEPTABLE:
As of yesterday afternoon, 289 people had died on Dallas roads this year.

Dallas Times Herald

There are times when a writer can show a little style, particularly in feature stories, but style, too, can best be conveyed in simple, unvarnished language. Notice how simple the words are in this sentence from a war report by Ernest Hemingway, printed in *The New York Times* in 1937:

On the corner, twenty yards away, is a heap of rubble, smashed cement, and thrown up dirt, a single dead man, his torn clothes dusty, and a great hole in the sidewalk from which the gas from a broken main is rising, looking like a heat mirage in the cold morning air.*

Difficult Words and Slang

Those three-dollar words some people strain to fit in their sentences should be left in the dictionary. There is no sense in using a word that significant numbers of readers won't understand.

Ron Harris of the *Los Angeles Times* recalls being

---

* Louis L. Snyder and Richard B. Morris, editors, *A Treasury of Great Reporting,* second edition, 1962, Simon and Schuster, page 525.

criticized by an editor once for a sentence that used the word "indigent." "I wasn't thinking about the reader," Harris, now an editor himself, says. "You have to say, 'Wait a minute. Let's explain this.' What does indigent mean? It means poor."

UNACCEPTABLE:
A court edict has temporarily interdicted the dismissal of James Redburn, Brookhaven Town's environmental protection director, who has been the subject of considerable contention.

Slang, too, is out. Expressions that may be current on the street may still be unfamiliar in many of the homes in which a newspaper will be read. Slang also intrudes on the telling of the news; it forces the writer's personality on the reader in an unwanted way. And, adds Harris, it's just not "classy."

UNACCEPTABLE:
A court order has put the kibosh for now on the canning of James Redburn, Brookhaven Town's main man for environmental protection, who has been hassled a lot lately.

Journalists seek a more common language.

ACCEPTABLE:
A court order has temporarily blocked the firing of James Redburn, Brookhaven Town's embattled environmental protection director.*

(Long Island, N.Y.) *Newsday*

Here are more examples of potentially obscure words and clearer alternatives:

Difficult	*Slang*	*Common*
apprehend	bust	arrest
peevish	uptight	irritable
officer of the law	cop	policeman or policewoman
consequential	deep	significant
cannabis	pot	marijuana
extricate oneself	be history	leave

Jargon

Jargon is another enemy of clear writing. Many specialties have developed their own specialized languages. When writing about these jargon-infested professions and hobbies, the journalist must take responsibility for translating their specialized languages so they can be understood by a general audience. A failure to translate jargon will leave many readers confused.

Who but a sailing buff would be able to understand this sentence from *The New York Times:*

The 96-year-old square-rigger Wavertree is getting a new main deck to go with her new bowsprit . . .

* The name in this story has been changed.

If the reporter had been doing her job, the sentence might have read:

The 96-year-old Wavertree is getting a new main deck to go with her new "bowsprit"—the pole that projects from the front of the ship. Since its sails all face forward, the Wavertree is known as a "square-rigger."

One solution to the problem of jargon is to include both the unfamiliar term and its definition in the article.

UNACCEPTABLE:
The galaxy is more than 100 *light years* away.

ACCEPTABLE:
The galaxy is more than 100 light years away; in other words, it would take light more than 100 years to reach it.

But if the unfamiliar term is *not* important enough to force on the reader, it is wise to replace it completely with a translation.

UNACCEPTABLE:
Two years of declining *apartment occupancy rates* have hurt landlords.

ACCEPTABLE:
Landlords have been hurt by two years in which the percentage of apartments they have been able to rent has declined.

Beginning reporters will become entangled in thickets of jargon. Jargon is found in government —"the Iowa Civil Rights Commission *closed* (completed) a record 174 cases in September." It is found in legal proceedings—"the defense asked for a *change of venue* (a change in the site of the trial)." It is found in economics—"the drop in the *prime rate* (the interest rate at which favored customers can borrow) has increased the availability of mortgages." And it is found in science—"scientists did not agree on whether the chemical was a *teratogen* (causes birth defects)."

Even local undertakers have their own jargon: People don't die, they *pass away,* at which point they are referred to as "the loved one." These undertakers, like the Department of State with its "unlawful deprivation of human life," are trying to take the sting out of bad news. Such attempts to put a kinder face on events are called *euphemisms.* Euphemisms are also used to inflate: Garbage collectors become *sanitary engineers,* police become *law enforcement officers.* Though euphemisms are rampant in daily usage—there are no longer old people, just *senior citizens*—they have no place in clear writing. At best they confuse; at worst they distort reality.

Using simple language is not always easy, but it is not impossible, even on the most difficult stories. "If you really work at it," says *Philadelphia Inquirer* science writer Jim Detjen, "you can explain almost any scientific theory in words the average reader can understand."

Some jargon can be translated with the help of the dictionary. More often the solution is thorough reporting: asking a member of the commission to explain exactly what it means to "close a case," asking the court clerk to review the legal meaning of "changing the venue." Reporting is not complete until reporters understand every important term in their notes, and writing is not finished until writers have expressed every thought in their stories in plain English.

Conciseness

Every word in an article must not only be understood, it must have a purpose. A reader's time and a newspaper's space are too valuable to squander.

UNACCEPTABLE:
An agency of our federal government has stated its objection to the planned construction of a 15-story-high building designed to be used for offices, which would be located in the heart of Arlington. The agency said its primary concern was that the structure's penthouse roof "would mimic the Washington Monument."

ACCEPTABLE:
A federal agency has objected to construction of a 15-story office building in the heart of Arlington, arguing that the structure's penthouse roof "would mimic the Washington Monument."

The Washington Post

Redundancy

One way to waste words is to say things twice. A *15-story-high building* is the same size as a *15-story building.* Here is an example of redundancy that appeared in the *Los Angeles Times:*

. . . whenever the Redskins are ahead on points . . .

Is there any other way the Redskins, a football team, could be ahead? "Whenever the Redskins are ahead . . ." is sufficient.

One trick for smoking out redundant modifiers is to replace them with their opposites. If the resulting phrase makes no sense, then the original modifier may have been unnecessary. Since you cannot *partially* destroy something, it is redundant to say something has been *completely* destroyed.

Some other redundant or potentially redundant word combinations:

overexaggerate	two twins
future plans	quick second
controversial issue	very first

general consensus	true fact
sad frown	past history
personal feelings	assembled crowd
loud scream	dead corpse
little baby	definite proof
young freshman	an approximate estimate
close down	Jewish rabbi
new record	7 a.m. in the morning

Wasteful Phrases

Words also are wasted when a phrase is used where a single word would do. *Located in* can be replaced with no loss of meaning by *in*, for example. Here are some other potentially wasteful phrases:

Phrase	*Word*
at this point in time	now
as a result of	because
strike a tune	play
venture a suggestion	suggest
take action	act
with the exception of	except
was the recipient of	received
is of the opinion that	believes
in the event that	if
along the lines of	like
due to the fact that	because
with reference to	about
having to do with	about
in the near future	soon
at the present time	now
for the purpose of	to
in an effort to	to
in order to	to

Detour Words

Because of their vagueness, some words seem inevitably to lead to wordy sentences. *Involved* is perhaps the most common of these "detour words": The relationship it describes is too weak to be meaningful. Sentences frequently can be improved by substituting more specific words.

UNACCEPTABLE:
A 13-year-old student at Severn River Junior High School died yesterday after she was *involved* in an accident in the school's gymnasium.

ACCEPTABLE:
A 13-year-old student at Severn River Junior High School died yesterday after a freak accident in the school's gymnasium, where she was performing some basic maneuvers on the parallel bars.

The (Baltimore) *Sun*

UNACCEPTABLE:
Night and weekend service on the trolleys that use the tunnel routes will be *experiencing* interruptions.

ACCEPTABLE:
Night and weekend service on the trolleys that use the tunnel routes will be interrupted.

The Philadelphia Inquirer

One thing good journalists and *good* poets should have in common is an obsession with making each word they use count.

Additional Reading

On Writing Well: An Informal Guide to Writing Nonfiction, William Zinsser, Harper & Row, 1980.
A Civil Tongue, Edwin Newman, Warner Books, 1983.
Strictly Speaking, Edwin Newman, Warner Books, 1979.

▪ A ▪

Edit the following sentences where necessary so that they use clearer language.

1. He utilized the opportunity to endorse the president's prescription for economic recovery.

2. The folks there thought he was hot — one mean guitar player.

3. The governor's presence before the august legislature was meant to win over recalcitrant party members.

4. After the rumble he split for the hospital.

5. The long debate only served to obfuscate the issue.

6. He is a specialist in ichthyology, especially the classification of gobies.

7. He hit a rope over the ivy and into the centerfield bleachers to win the contest.

8. He had dated a veritable plethora of women.

9. They are still studying the problem of recidivism among former inmates of the large correctional facility.

10. Males and females are both admitted to the club, but they are required to dine in different rooms.

11. Brilliant beams of sunlight struggled to penetrate the surface of the water while the divers searched for the body.

12. More juveniles between the ages of 13 and 19 were arrested this year than last.

13. He clearly tended to anthropomorphize any sentient being.

14. Shortly thereafter they found a justice of the peace and tied the knot.

15. There were two octogenarians and seven septuagenarians participating in the teaching program.

▪ **B** ▪

Edit the following sentences where necessary to make them more concise.

1. He said that up to this point he had been unable to locate the small, two-week-old puppy anywhere.

2. The general consensus of all those who were assembled at the meeting was that the superintendent of schools had overexaggerated the effect budget cuts would have on extracurricular activities.

3. When she heard the loud scream, she burst into the room in a split second but the intruder who had been there already was gone.

4. The Coast Guard captain said he had been experiencing difficulty in removing oil from the hold of the leaking ship because the operation involved pulling a Coast Guard cutter up along next to the listing vessel in high seas.

5. Nearly 400 demonstrators ventured forth to a gathering at the Jackson County Jail yesterday to protest against conditions there.

6. One speaker, The Rev. James McVie, said he had definite proof that a fire that completely destroyed a section of the jail's eighth floor could have been prevented if the jail had a sprinkler system and sufficient guards.

7. The accident, which occurred at the corner of Waverly and Mercer streets, was not a direct or indirect result of the fact that it had been raining, the prosecutor said. He added that he would call witnesses in the near future to conclusively prove his contention.

8. She will move out of her soon to be vacant apartment after they are married in their wedding ceremony, which will be held at exactly 2 p.m. this afternoon.

9. The city's residents had experienced many dangerous tornados over the period of the last 15 years.

10. He is currently serving a life sentence.

11. The incumbent congresswoman pays a visit to her district once every week in an effort to remain close to the citizens who elected her.

12. He performed an autopsy to determine the cause of death.

13. The crash involved two cars that met head on.

14. It was a new first for the track team, a jump that set an all-time state record.

15. The company agreed to hold an annual meeting every year in a large major city.

16. He refused to engage in conversation with reference to the very last meeting.

17. The brand-new car that he had just bought represented an investment of $20,000.

18. She owns her own home.

19. If it were not for the unexpected surprise of the thunderstorm, the hot, burning fire might have caused a severe catastrophe.

20. The sideshow included little midgets, big giants and funny clowns.

■ **C** ■

Using research materials or interviews with experts, write explanations that could be used in a newspaper article for the following terms (the field in which the term is used is given in parentheses).

1. Consumer price index (economics)

2. Restraining order (law)

3. Middle C (music)

4. Crop rotation (agriculture)

5. Full-court press (sports)

6. Red shift (science)

7. Vehicular manslaughter (law)

8. Special education (education)

9. Multiple-family dwelling (government)

10. Behavior modification (psychology)

11. Kilowatt hour (energy)

12. Three-four defense (sports)

13. Second-degree burn (medicine)

14. Tornado warning (meteorology)

15. Iambic pentameter (literature)

▪ D ▪

Edit the following story so that it uses clearer language.

A vehicle, whose driver, police said, was intoxicated, smashed through the window of a downtown eating establishment, Paco's Tacos, yesterday, injuring two customers.

About 10 patrons were consuming their food and beverages at the establishment, at 63 Nicoli Ave., when the vehicle, a 1986 Toyota, crashed through the front window.

"At first I thought it was an earthquake, until I saw the front of the car next to my salad bar," said Ivan "Paco" Schwartz, the proprietor of the establishment.

Isabel Hannok, 32, of East Bedford, was seated at the table in closest proximity to the window when the car entered the establishment. Hannok suffered lacerations caused by the flying shards of glass, according to police.

Leland Beagle, 34, of Flushing, received abrasions and contusions when he dived under the salad bar, police said. Hannok and Beagle were both transported to Booth Hospital.

The alleged perpetrator was apprehended as he essayed an attempt to flee the edifice, according to Police Sgt. James Spoke. Sgt. Spoke identified him as Francis Jenkins, 24, of 13 Nicoli Ave.

"It was obvious that Jenkins had been drinking," Spoke said.

—
■ **E** ■
—

Edit the following story to make it more concise.

Incumbent Democratic Mayor Sheila Straus was reelected yesterday by an overwhelming landslide vote of New Brook City citizens.

Mayor Straus triumphantly defeated her one and only challenger and rival in the Election Day balloting, Republican Councilman Jose Ramirez, by a margin of 9,034 of the 53,496 votes that were cast. Straus was the recipient of 31,265 of the citizens' ballots while Ramirez was able to get only 22,231 losing votes.

"This is a victory for everyone who worked in my campaign," the mayor told her partisans and supporters in a brief two-sentence statement after her successful victory. "I want to thank you all very much."

Straus's vote total represented the very largest number of election votes ever obtained by a New Brook mayoral candidate for election in history. She received 27,443 votes when she was elected to her first four-year term in the mayor's office four years ago.

CHAPTER 3

Spelling and grammar

One major metropolitan newspaper reports accusations that a father and two sons sought "vengence" against two men they thought had attacked a younger son; another newspaper refers to a man accused of murder as a "defendent."

The correct spellings of the words "vengeance" and "defendant" are facts that can be checked in any English dictionary. When such simple and universal facts are wrong, it is difficult to trust the other information in the story. In journalism, spelling always counts.

Sloppy grammar poses a similar threat to a writer's credibility and perhaps a larger threat to a reader's understanding. What's wrong with the following sentence?

The councilman opposed the plan for the new sewage treatment plant, who had originally proposed the plant in the first place.

As written, this sentence makes it appear as if the treatment plant — made human — once proposed itself. The writer had meant to say that the *councilman,* who originally proposed a new sewage treatment plant, now opposed the plan to build one. But in trying to write that, the reporter allowed the modifying clause, the *who clause,* to get misplaced. The lesson: Keep modifiers next to what they are modifying.

Correct use of the language is vital in journalism because it aids clear communication and because it provides evidence of the care and the intelligence of the reporter. Journalists must pay strict attention not only to the facts in their stories (See Chapter 16, Facts) but also to the sentences, words and punctuation marks used to convey those facts. When journalists fail to do so, they can destroy their ability to communicate.

What was this reporter trying to tell us?

After stealing second base, the catcher threw the ball into centerfield and he raced to third.

Perhaps:

The baserunner stole second base and raced on to third when the catcher's throw went into centerfield.

Newspapers have copy editors to double-check spelling and grammar, among other things. But good reporters always seek to save themselves embarrassment by double-checking themselves. The fact that a story will be seen by a copy editor is no excuse for errors.

Many reporters seem to have been bad spellers from birth, but they still manage to turn in clean copy simply by consulting frequently with a dictionary. It usually takes less than 30 seconds to look up a word. If it's necessary to look up every word containing more than five letters, do so!

Proper names present a different problem. The best solution is to ask — twice if necessary — while reporting the story: "Was that Stephens with a *v* or with a *ph*?" (See Chapter 16, Facts).

Grammar can be harder to check; writers must develop an ear for it. Someone whose ear for words and their correct use proves unreliable can improve by studying. A good place to start is with *The Elements of Style* by William Strunk Jr. and E. B. White.

Here are a few of the errors that copy editors and writing coaches complain they see too often. (This discussion is not intended as a substitute for a good grammar book; several are listed in Additional Reading.)

Who, Which and That

So there was only one number *which* really counted in the debate, and that number was 1984.

The Dallas Morning News

"The worst and most common error I run into," says Paula LaRocque, writing coach for *The Morning News*, "is a misunderstanding of the words *that* and *which*." The above sentence, which LaRocque caught and displayed in her newsletter, *F.Y.I.*, uses *which* when it should use *that*. *Which* is used in non-essential clauses — should they be omitted, the sentence would still make sense. *That* is used in essential clauses.

UNACCEPTABLE:
The rock *which* he grabbed . . .

The *sign,* that had been hit many times before, stood at the entrance.

ACCEPTABLE:
The rock *that* he grabbed . . .

The sign, *which* had been hit many times before, . . .

Who refers to individuals only. Legislatures, field hockey teams and Cabbage Patch dolls are *whiches* or *thats,* depending on the circumstances. (*Who* is used as a subject in a sentence; *whom* replaces it as an object.)

UNACCEPTABLE:
The City Council, *who* had opposed tax increases in the past, voted unanimously for the measure.

ACCEPTABLE:
The City Council, *which* had opposed tax increases . . .

Verb Tense

The tense of the verbs in a story should be consistent. Writers should only switch from one tense to another when communicating a change in time.

UNACCEPTABLE:
The snow fell steadily for four hours. Then, suddenly, the wind picks up.

ACCEPTABLE:
The snow fell steadily for four hours. Then, suddenly, the wind picked up.

UNACCEPTABLE:
Oliver said he had no difficulty adjusting to Florida's long, hot summers. He lived there before.

ACCEPTABLE:
Oliver said he had no difficulty adjusting to Florida's long, hot summers. He had lived there before.

Agreement

Here's another *Dallas Morning News* sentence that was critiqued in LaRocque's *F.Y.I.*:

About all you can do to protect yourself is to thoroughly check out *the person* who is going to do the work before you hire *them.*

Singular nouns, such as *the person,* take singular verbs and singular pronouns, such as *him* or *her.* (Changing the sentence to read "the *people* who are going to do the work" would avoid the somewhat cumbersome *him* or *her.*)

Journalists violate the rule of agreement most frequently when dealing with collective nouns. These nouns — *group, team* and *council* are examples — take singular verbs and should be referred to by singular pronouns even though they refer to organizations of many.

UNACCEPTABLE:
The administration says *they* oppose the plan.

ACCEPTABLE:
The administration says *it* opposes the plan.

Misplaced Modifiers

Modifying clauses or phrases are comfortable in a sentence only when placed near whatever they are modifying. This sentence refers to an agent, Kalafatis, and the baseball player he represents, Honeycutt:

Once an excellent Class AAA hitter, Kalafatis says Honeycutt's record is deceptive . . .

The New York Times

Presumably it was Honeycutt, not Kalafatis, who was the excellent minor league hitter, but the clause seems to be referring to Kalafatis because it is placed next to his name.

Dangling participles — exaggerated versions of this problem — are phrases that seem to modify nothing.

UNACCEPTABLE:
After climbing into the space capsule, his instructions crackled over the radio.

ACCEPTABLE:
His instructions crackled over the radio after he had climbed into the space capsule.

Parallel Construction

Phrases used in a series must be constructed in similar fashion.

UNACCEPTABLE:
The United States Constitution guarantees all citizens the right to bear arms, vote and freedom of speech.

ACCEPTABLE:
The United States Constitution guarantees all citizens the right to bear arms, vote and speak freely.

LaRocque noted a similar problem in this sentence from the sports pages of *The Morning News:*

All week long, New York newspapers had reported that Martin would be fired for the *fifth* time in his volcanic career and *twice* as manager of the New York Yankees.

To be parallel with *fifth, twice* would have to be changed to *the second.*

Additional Reading

The Elements of Style, William Strunk Jr. and E. B. White, Macmillan, 1979.
When Words Collide: A Journalist's Guide to Grammar & Style, Laura Kessler and Duncan McDonald, Wadsworth, 1984.
Grammar for Journalists, E. L. Callihan, Chilton, 1979.

▪ A ▪

Correct any misspelled words in the following lists.

1. dicision	2. inferrence	3. batallion
refered	discreet	concensus
definate	imposter	barbecue
defensable	cemetary	supoena
parallel	drunkeness	liason
knowlege	questionaire	vacume
neccessary	leisure	miniscule
predecessor	rehersal	encyclapedia
circimstance	supercede	dietitian
suceed	performence	restaurateur
acheive	relevant	
dispensible	innoculate	
happenned	imminent	
wieght	fertalizer	
recommend	occurrence	
likeable	accidentally	
seperate	wierd	
occassionally	judgement	
cieling	compliment	
precede	embarrased	

▪ B ▪

Correct any grammatical errors in the following sentences.

1. The legislator that originally nominated her said nothing in her support.

2. These are a few among the many fine restaurants which France offers the gourmet.

3. Only the car in which he was riding was damaged.

4. He said he could quit the job, but only if he can be sure of getting another one quickly.

5. The series of home and away games are expected to attract the largest crowds of the year at either university.

6. The chief operating officer conceded that both his assistant and him received large bonuses.

7. The program is for workers who were employed in smokestack industries, are unclear how to fit into the 1980s and just lost their jobs.

8. Late for school four days in a row, the teacher forced the student to stay after school.

9. The county health department is searching for anyone whom, in the course of the day, may have seen the boy.

10. Each year the number of babies grow until soon there won't be enough food on the planet, he argued.

11. She throws the car into reverse and began to back out of the driveway.

12. The prime minister thanked the members of the crew of the plane that were so skillful in handling the sudden storm.

13. She finally saw a sculpture which interested her.

14. She was so attached to the dog who she had saved, that she mentioned it in her will.

15. The fire consumed four more houses on that block, quickly raging out of control.

16. He was one of eight men who is to be awarded a prize tonight.

17. Twice winner of the Blueberry Stakes, owner Sue Friedman decided to sell the horse for $500,000.

18. The council, who seemed tired after the long session, decided to adjourn.

19. The team decided they should return to fundamentals.

20. The stolen jewel was found by a local woman wrapped in a dirty rag.

▪ C ▪

Correct any spelling errors in the following article.

A former business coleague of Albert Spellman, the Delaware accountent accused of trying to swindel an elderly, wealthy woman, testafied yesterday that Spellman had recently been reciving alot of money from an anonamous source.

Philedelphia lawyer Fred Anderson says checks for hundreds of dollars arrived for Spellman in the mail. Anderson also said that Spellman, 46, who has been indited here on charges of fraud and conspirecy, had confieded a year ago that he, Spellman, was in "financially desparate straits," and was considering filing for bankrupcy.

Spellman alledgedly made thretening phone calls to Judy James, 76, a wealthy invalid. He then, it is charged, used his personal influence to convince her to pay him sizable "fees" to stop the calls, which James beleived came from mobsters.

At the end of an intence day of prosecution questioning, Anderson, a principle prosecution witness, conceeded, "In my judgement, it is not inconceivalbe that Spellman made those phone calls."

In seperate testimony on the preceeding day, Anderson — who had been supenaed by the court — said he had seen Spellman standing nervusly by a restaurant public telephone on June 4, around the same time one of the phone threats had been recieved by James.

If convicted, Spellman will face a sentance of up to 25 years.

▪ D ▪

Correct any grammatical errors in the following articles.

ONE

A driver, apparently intoxicated, dozed off momentarily at the wheel yesterday, causing an accident which critically injured he and his small son, according to police.

John Swados, 29, a Grand Lake auto mechanic, and son Mark, 10, was in critical condition at Lakeview Hospital, after Swados, returning home on Route 9W after an office party, apparently fell asleep at the wheel, causing him to lose control of the car, according to police.

Police say Swados's car leapt over a center divider, near Lake View Road, smashes through a rail fence, before it had crashed into a tree. Swados will be charged with speeding, negligence and under the influence of alcohol, police said.

Apparently dazed by the accident, highway patrol said they found Swados wandering several hundred yards away from where the car, a 1977 Volvo, who contained his son, lodged against a tree, who police freed from the wreckage. It occurred at 4 p.m.

TWO

The American Cancer Society has announced they will launch a massive, six-year study into the causes of cancer, a project involving nearly one million Americans.

The $2 billion study—similar in scope to an earlier American Medical Association cancer study—will examine a variety of factors, including lifestyle, how much you smoke, stress and environmental factors to determine which most contributes to the formation of the malignant disease, that yearly kills over 400,000 Americans.

(In 1967, after 13 years of research, the Cancer Society announced their findings definitively linking smoking to lung cancer.)

The project will begin Oct. 1. The American Cancer Society has selected 915,000 applicants, none of whom have a previous history of cancer after a nationwide search.

In October, each person participating in the study will fill out a detailed questionnaire outlining their lifestyle and what habits they have. Computers would be used to analyze all data. The experimental group is monitored during the next six years by the 85,000 ACS researchers, and subsequent information — including causes of death — are submitted to computer analysis.

All persons in the study, according to the ACS, are over 30 years old. A majority of them live in urban areas. A minority has families with a history of cancer.

□ CHAPTER 4 □

Sentence structure

Editors see the problem all too often: Reporters are so full of information about an event, so tuned in to its complexities, that they seem incapable of writing an account clear and straightforward enough for readers to understand. Their sentences appear hopelessly tangled.

If the fog fails to lift after a rewrite or two, veteran editors have been known to resort to this strategy: They simply ask reporters to *tell* them the story. "Forget what you wrote. Forget how complex it all is. Just *tell* me what it's all about." More often than not, after a moment's thought, frustrated reporters will recite a version of their story that is significantly simpler and more intelligible than anything they have been able to come up with at their keyboards. And instinctively, the sentence structure in the oral version will arrange itself in the most direct sequence: subject, verb, object—in that order.

There's a lesson here. The same basic, direct sentences that help keep things clear when we speak can also do the job when we write.

RICHMOND (AP)—A fire destroyed a block-square warehouse containing fertilizer yesterday.

Roanoke (Va.) *Times & World-News*

Subject: *fire;* verb: *destroyed;* object: *warehouse.*

Reporters who find their ideas disappearing in a tangle of adjectives, adverbs, interjections and clauses might step back and see whether they can find a few sharp and direct sentences to cut through the confusion. "It's nice to have things real simple," says Ron

Harris, assistant metropolitan editor of the *Los Angeles Times.*

Verbs

Editors or writing coaches, trying to diagnose a sentence's problems, frequently begin by examining its verb.

Action

The verb's job is to describe an action. Journalism is predominantly about actions, so its sentences generally work best when they are powered by strong verbs:

The United States *threatened* yesterday to *halt* payments to the United Nations and *withdraw* from the U.N. General Assembly if the assembly *voted* to expel Israel.

The (Bergen County, N.J.) *Record*

When adjectives and adverbs begin stealing the action, writing loses some of its power.

WEAK:
The United States said *threateningly* yesterday . . .

The *fast-moving* bullets went through the wall *quickly* . . .

BETTER:
The bullets *tore* through the wall.

Stories about dynamic events should have dynamic verbs:

Prime Minister Giovanni Spadolini yesterday *resurrected* his five-party coalition government that had fallen 17 days ago after the Socialists withdrew.

Reuters in The (Baltimore) Sun

WEAK:
. . . the camper in which they were riding was *involved* in an accident on a Staten Island highway.

(Long Island, N.Y.) Newsday

BETTER:
. . . the camper in which they were riding *flipped* on its side and *burst* into flames on a Staten Island highway.

One sign that the verbs are not carrying their load in sentences is overuse of forms of the verb *to be.*

WEAK:
The corner of 165th Street and Broadway *was* the most frequent destination on the route for passengers.

BETTER:
More passengers *took* the bus to 165th Street and Broadway than to any other stop.

To be, a relatively sedentary verb, is best used for states and conditions (it *was* cold) not actions — the water *froze.*

Active Voice

If verbs are to convey the action in a sentence, the subject should logically be the party doing the acting. Here the subject is Oklahoma Corporation Commissioner Jim Townsend; the action is grabbing a lead:

Oklahoma Corporation Commissioner Jim Townsend grabbed an early but substantial lead over challenger Charles Cleveland yesterday in the Democratic runoff for a two-year term on the utility rate-making panel.

Tulsa (Okla.) World

Too often, sentences are reversed so that the subject is what is being acted upon.

WEAK:
An early lead was grabbed by Oklahoma Corporation Commissioner Jim Townsend yesterday . . .

A sentence is in the *active voice* when the subject does the acting — the man shot the deer. It's in the *passive voice* when the subject is the recipient of the action — the deer was shot by the man. As a rule, sentences work best when cast in the active voice:

WEAK:
Support was expressed yesterday for a federal prosecutor by a group of black Richmond lawyers . . .

BETTER:
A group of black Richmond lawyers expressed support yesterday for a federal prosecutor . . .

Richmond (Va.) Times-Dispatch

Tense

Newspapers usually use the past tense, since most of the news they report happened at least hours before the paper reaches newsstands or doorsteps:

The U.S. Marines *returned* to Lebanon yesterday . . .

Los Angeles Times

The past tense protects a newspaper from looking foolish. An action could end in the hours after the paper was written but before it hits the street. If, for example, a teachers' strike were settled at 4 a.m., a story in that morning's newspaper about the previous night's negotiations would be merely dated in the past tense. In the present tense it would be wrong.

UNACCEPTABLE:
Representatives of Lakewood's 247 striking teachers and the Board of Education *are continuing* talks in an effort to end the 65-day walkout.

ACCEPTABLE:
Representatives of Lakewood's 247 striking teachers and the Board of Education *continued* round-the-clock negotiations last night in an effort to end the 65-day walkout.

There are occasions, however, when newspaper reporters slip into other tenses. If, for example, it seemed certain that an action that took place yesterday would still be taking place today, a reporter might use the present tense to give the story more immediacy:

Loyola College *is negotiating* to buy the 200-unit Wynnewood Towers apartment complex . . .

The (Baltimore) Sun

Negotiations like these are not likely to end at 4 a.m.

The striking National Football Players Association *is scrambling* to establish an all-star football league.

(Oakland, Ca.) Eastbay Today

The players, too, are not likely to give up by 4 a.m.

Sometimes, especially when news is several days old, reporters will substitute the present-perfect tense for the past tense in the lead paragraphs of their stories so that the story sounds fresher.

WEAK:
The First Reformed Church last week *converted* its basement into a dormitory for the homeless. . . .

BETTER:
The First Reformed Church *has converted* its basement into a dormitory for the homeless. . . .

One tense journalists should try to avoid is the future. We are not omniscient. We know what people say they will do, but we can't predict whether these actions will actually take place.

UNACCEPTABLE:
A plan that could save Northwest electric ratepayers $3 billion to $4 billion *will be presented* Monday. . . .

ACCEPTABLE:
A plan that could save Northwest electric ratepayers $3 billion to $4 billion *is scheduled to be presented* Monday . . .

Better to be cautious than wrong.

Clauses and Interjections

Were all the sentences in a section of a story to use the same structure, the writing would get too choppy.

WEAK:
The San Francisco Giants are the hottest team in baseball. *They were* suddenly discovered yesterday by the division's front-runners. *The Giants have* played the best baseball in the major leagues since June 27. *They have* come from near the bottom of their division to battle for first place with the Los Angeles Dodgers and the Atlanta Braves.

Clauses and interjections can help vary sentence structure and link related ideas.

BETTER:
The San Francisco Giants, *the hottest team in baseball,* were suddenly discovered yesterday by the division's front-runners. The Giants have played the best baseball in the major leagues since June 27, *coming from near the bottom of their division to battle for first place with the Los Angeles Dodgers and the Atlanta Braves.*

San Francisco Chronicle

But interruptions in the basic subject-verb-object flow of sentences can also get writers in trouble. The trouble usually starts when clauses and interjections grow too long, particularly when they are placed in the middle of a sentence, creating too much distance between subject and verb.

Roy Peter Clark, a former writing coach for the *St. Petersburg Times,* says there are two elements that he finds to be "the keys to clear, effective sentences." One is the use of active verbs. The other is the placement of the subject and verb. "If there are problems of jumbled syntax or focus, I'll usually look at where the subject and verb are," Clark explains. "If the subject and verb are separated, all sorts of confusion and complications start to set in."

UNACCEPTABLE:
The Elmwood Park Homeowners' Association, *which has strongly opposed the present rent ordinance and recently was denied by the council a chance to place a referendum abolishing rent control on the November ballot,* is unsatisfied by the proposed law.

The (Paterson, N.J.) News

The subject of this sentence is the *Elmwood Park Homeowners' Association;* the verb is *is unsatisfied.* The distance between them is 28 words. By the time the verb arrives in a sentence with such a long clause, readers may have forgotten the subject.

An 18-word prepositional phrase separated subject—*an ordinance*—and verb—*cleared*—in this poorly worded sentence, which began a front-page story in the (Chicago) *Sun-Times:*

An ordinance *to move 8,000 city workers under the blanket of civil service in the midst of Mayor Washington's firings* cleared a City Council committee yesterday.

Sometimes problems can be solved by reworking a sentence (and in this case improving the wording):

In an apparent response to Mayor Washington's attempts to cut the number of city employees, a City Council committee yesterday approved a plan to make an additional 8,000 city workers eligible for civil service protection.

More often, though, the solution is to split the sentence into two simpler sentences:

ACCEPTABLE:
The Elmwood Park Homeowners' Association, *which has strongly opposed the present rent ordinance,* is not satisfied with the proposed law. The council recently denied the association a chance to place a referendum abolishing rent control on the November ballot.

The first sentence in this rewrite uses a clause, but it is short enough not to interfere with readers' understanding of the sentence. Reporters do not have to shy away from using clauses and interjections. But they do have to be sure these interruptions do not grow unwieldy.

Points

Another way to sink sentences is to overload them with information.

UNACCEPTABLE:
The arrest of two men on murder charges and the discovery of a badly decomposed body yesterday afternoon ended a 10-day manhunt for an emotionally disturbed Massapequa Park man whose abandoned car was discovered on fire in a Suffolk park.

(Long Island, N.Y.) Newsday

It would be difficult for readers to follow this sentence the first time through. Indeed, the many points it tries to make are still a little confusing on second reading.

A sentence should not be asked to communicate more than a point or two. The fact that two men were arrested and charged with the murder is one point. The fact that the victim had been missing for 10 days is a second. When there are more points to make, more sentences should be used.

ACCEPTABLE:
Two men were arrested yesterday and charged with the murder of an emotionally disturbed Massapequa Park man for whom police had been searching for 10 days. Police said they believe a badly decomposed body discovered yesterday is that of the man, whose abandoned car was found on fire in a Suffolk park Aug. 13.

Sentence Length

How long should sentences be? Since there are so many different ways to write them, it is impossible to set any firm limits on their length. Nevertheless, there usually is an inverse relationship between sentence length and reader comprehension. The longer the sentence, the tougher it generally is to understand. It can't hurt, therefore, for beginning reporters to count words in their sentences. If they haven't typed a period by the time they reach 25, they should be looking for a place to put one. If the sentence includes 35 words or more, there's a good chance that it will be difficult for readers to understand.

UNACCEPTABLE:
Gaunt, glassy-eyed and possessionless, they crouch in the heat amid thousands of others, hungry and diseased, when they're not stooping over small, dry plots of rock-hard soil or waiting in tight lines for hours to get today's ration of food from international relief agencies: a bowl of rice gruel, two bananas, a bucket of brown drinking water.

Writing is clearest when the sentences are kept relatively short. But string together too many very short sentences, and writing will become choppy.

UNACCEPTABLE:
They look gaunt. Their eyes appear glassy. Their possessions were long ago left behind. They crouch in the heat. Around them are thousands of others like them. They are hungry and diseased. They stoop over small, dry plots. The soil is rock-hard. And they wait.
They wait in tight lines for hours. They want a ration of food from international relief agencies. It will include a bowl of rice, two bananas, a bucket of brown drinking water.
They wait for doctors to heal them.

Good writers mix simple short- and medium-length sentences to create a sort of "prose rhythm."

ACCEPTABLE:
Gaunt, glassy-eyed and possessionless, they crouch in the heat amid thousands of others, hungry and diseased. They stoop over small, dry plots of rock-hard soil. And they wait.
They wait in tight lines for hours to get today's ration of food from international relief agencies: a bowl of rice gruel, two bananas, a bucket of brown drinking water.
They wait for doctors to heal them.
The (Louisville, Ky.) *Courier-Journal* (See Chapter 26, Features)

■ **A** ■

Edit or rewrite the following sentences to improve their use of verbs.

1. The fire is still burning out of control.

2. The wildly moving car went from side to side down the street.

3. The ruling on the bill was made by a state appeals court judge.

4. The legislation was supported by the senator.

5. More than 200 Posdam residents left their homes yesterday when police told them a tanker truck had had an accident, turning over and letting toxic fumes escape into the neighborhood after a sudden large fire started in the chemicals.

6. Chambers said that the worst attack was the one which occurred on October 26 in which 33 Indians lost their lives in the barrage of bullets fired by government troops.

7. The pilot said the tensest moment of the trip was when he suddenly had to go around a passenger plane that he saw on his radar.

8. There was graffiti that was the work of two teenagers all over the walls and windows of the subway train.

9. The man lost his life when the building came down on top of him.

10. Firefighters from all over the county will arrive at the firehouse at 2 p.m. for a picnic, which will be followed, at 4 p.m., by a parade.

■ **B** ■

Rewrite the following sentences or passages to improve their sentence structure.

1. The car, which had been repaired by a team of mechanics flown in specially by its manufacturer at a cost of more than $30,000, finally started after four days of work.

2. Sloane returned from the store at 7 p.m. He found the front door open. The room was in a shambles. The television set was gone.

3. Instead of vetoing the $10 million tax cut, which he had attacked in a number of speeches, the governor in a speech today said he would refuse to sign the bill, a move that would have the same effect.

4. The teachers and the Board of Education representatives, who had been meeting for six weeks on and off but had been unable to forge an agreement, met twice—at 8 p.m. and 3 p.m.

5. Waving last month's crime statistics, which he had promised to find, over his head, Martin, who had said that crime would be the number one issue in his campaign for Missoula city councilman on the Republican ticket, said robberies had increased 12 percent in nine months.

6. Mahler called the accusation that he is a free spender a lie. He said he actually would cut city spending if elected. Mahler criticized his opponent, Ellen Haggerty, for "dirtying up the campaign." He said he wanted a campaign of "ideas, not name calling."

7. In an uncharacteristic move, the governor, who had said debate on the death penalty had already gotten too heated and created too much acrimony in the weeks since Hamilton had proposed the bill, said nothing on the subject.

8. In an effort to find support for the school budget, which faces a difficult test next week, the superintendent scheduled an open house.

9. Police arrested the suspect, who worked as a teller at the bank but had been on vacation the week of the robbery, after a two-week investigation, which they called the most detailed ever conducted for a bank robbery in the city.

10. The fire, which started in the basement and worked its way through the five-story building, was brought under control after a two-hour struggle by the Farmdale Fire Department, which received assistance from Woodlawn and Fairfield.

■ **C** ■

Edit the following story to improve its use of verbs.

A proposal through which there would be a large monument in the Lawnville town park in honor of fireman George Kemp, who lost his life last week, was approved last night by the Lawnville Borough Council.

Kemp's death came in a fire that left a house on Mulberry Avenue destroyed. He was hit by a falling beam, Fire Chief Al Ramone said.

The plan to build the monument was passed by a unanimous vote by the council after a speech in which Mayor Almonds said positive things about Kemp's contributions to the town.

Fire officials say they have not determined the cause of the Mulberry Avenue fire. They say they have not been able to contact the owners of the house in which Kemp was when he died.

The monument will be completed by early next year. The cost will be $13,000, Almonds said.

■ **D** ■

Edit the following story to improve its sentence structure.

A state judge ruled yesterday that Ardsley Utilities, which has embarked on a major effort to protect its high-voltage power lines from interference and damage during severe storms, **has the right to cut trees around those lines for that purpose.**

State Supreme Court Justice Albert Farrow, after lifting a 15-month injunction barring the utility from removing trees without permission from the property owners, threw out a suit brought with the support of the county Board of Supervisors on behalf of 430 Ardsley County residents whose property abuts the power lines.

The property owners had decided to file the suit after the company chopped down two oak trees in Garnersville. They hired Montalia attorney Vern Jounce. They claimed the contracts that had been signed with the company in the 1950s allowed the utility only to trim branches, not to remove entire trees.

In his ruling, which company lawyers said could affect up to 300 trees mostly in the southern half of the county, Judge Farrow said that the wording of the contracts is "clear and to the point" in granting the utility the right "to fell whole trees as and when it sees fit within the boundaries covered by the contracts."

CHAPTER 5

Analogies, metaphors and clichés

Drinking wine that has been stored in a metal drum or concrete tank is like spending a warm Sunday afternoon picnicking on plastic grass and sniffing paper flowers.

That, at least, is the opinion of Vincent Nemeth.

The Wall Street Journal

This sprightly opening to a feature story by William Burrows about a wine barrel maker does two things well: First, it leads with unusual verve into an explanation of how important a good, wood wine barrel is to Vincent Nemeth. Second, it engages readers through the cleverness of its images.

The emphasis on simplicity and precision in the previous chapters is not meant to scare reporters away from lively writing — especially in feature stories (See Chapter 26, Features). The words Burrows uses are simple, precise *and* lively.

This chapter promotes a device, used by Burrows, that can help reporters make their writing more vivid — the analogy. And it warns of two traps reporters often fall into while straining to enliven their writing — the mixed metaphor and the cliché.

Analogies

Malcolm Browne, a science writer for *The New York Times,* had to explain a new, extremely powerful "magnetic gun." Browne struggled to paint an understandable picture of the "current" that "creates an electromagnetic field" that drives "the projectile" in the gun forward. But the gun's power did not really come across until he interrupted these descriptions and definitions with this analogy:

It is like launching a bullet with a lightning bolt.

Analogies help reporters explain. By comparing relatively complex things to relatively familiar things — in this case a bullet and a lightning bolt — reporters can make difficult subjects comprehensible.

And well-chosen analogies can help enliven writing as well as help enlighten readers. This carefully constructed analogy helped brighten a piece on ocean life:

If anemones are the flowers of the sea and jellyfish the dancers, then bacteria are the janitors and recyclers.

The Providence (R.I.) *Journal*

A warning though: The use of analogy is not without its pitfalls, even in the hands of experienced reporters. The comparison must be apt. Many of the reporters covering the nuclear accident at Three Mile Island, for example, compared the radiation doses nearby residents were receiving to the radiation from dental or chest X-rays. But the radiation leaking from the crippled nuclear plant hit the whole body, including presumably more vulnerable areas, while medical X-rays are targeted to selected parts of the body. The analogy was misleading. (The levels of radiation escaping from the plant might more properly have been measured against the *whole body* radiation airline passengers or residents of Denver are exposed to because there is less atmosphere to block radiation from the sun at these higher elevations.)

Analogy can also tempt reporters into exaggeration, as in this sentence from the *Asbury Park* (N.J.) *Press:*

Area rail commuters may need the speed of a world class sprinter or the agility of a pro football player if the state's transit agency decides to go through with a plan to eliminate direct train service between the Jersey Shore and New York City.

The article that follows this rather dramatic sentence demonstrates only that the new plan would force area commuters to spend at least an additional eight minutes rushing through a crowded station. Being Tony Dorsett might help, but it hardly seems like a requirement for handling this problem.

If inaccuracy is the most serious error that can result from improper use of analogy, overwriting is the most common. Those journalists who fancy themselves fiction writers at heart cannot seem to resist inserting a "rosy-fingered dawn" or two at the first opportunity.

WEAK:
He looks, getting out of the limousine, like an inelegant giraffe struggling to shift its huge body into the parenthesis between two stately trees.

BETTER:
He is big enough so that he doesn't so much get out of the limousine as he unfolds.

The Washington Post

Mixed Metaphors

Many analogies employ metaphors—figures of speech in which something is spoken of as if it were something else. (Bacteria are not, in fact, janitors.) Metaphors create images. It is important to keep these images clear and consistent. The *New Yorker* magazine found this distasteful "mixed metaphor" in a column in the (Chicago) *Sun-Times:*

Reagan is using his tongue to paint himself into a corner . . .

The problem is that, after we have been presented with the image of Reagan *using his tongue,* it is hard to swallow the image of him *painting himself into a corner.* The metaphors clash.

For another example, *The* (Cleveland) *Plain Dealer* began a story with this impossible metaphor:

Cleveland Ukrainians know great strides are taken in little steps.

Strides *are* steps. You can't take big steps in little steps.

Try to work out the image in these sentences from *The* (Paterson, N.J.) *News:*

According to Bologna, divorce is like dying. It often puts a man on the brink of suicide.

Some mixed metaphors can have the same effect.

Clichés

When writing is full of *clichés*—tired expressions that have lost their originality through overuse—readers may begin to wonder whether the writer has anything fresh to say.

Here are some of the clichés found in one short *New York Times* opinion piece written by former President Richard Nixon:

the week that changed the world	bitter enemy
	over the long haul
hard-headed	height of folly
with open eyes	the bottom line

Expressions add liveliness to writing—if they are spontaneous. But when reporters grab the first expression that comes to mind, their writing is likely to make readers groan.

UNACCEPTABLE:
Boston School Committeeman John J. McDonough is thousands of dollars in debt and unprepared for the Nov. 3 election—but he's *feeling on top of the world.*

The Boston Globe

"Feeling on top of the world" is such an overused expression that any color in the picture it paints long ago faded. The reporter should have discarded this washed-out phrase and searched further. Perhaps the candidate could have been described as "smiling like a man with a few million dollars in his campaign treasury." (Grinning like a Cheshire cat would not do.) Sometimes it's safer simply to fall back on a more prosaic wording. "He says he is quite happy" would have summed up his mood effectively without evoking groans.

Some clichés are just moldy old proverbs:

A penny saved is a penny earned.
A stitch in time saves nine.
The grass is always greener on the other side.
He who pays the piper calls the tune.
Variety is the spice of life.

Some are metaphors that have been overused:

the cream of the crop	burning the midnight oil
a slap in the face	hitting the nail on the head
give the green light	a horse of a different color
no holds barred	came out smelling like a
dog tired	rose
raining cats and dogs	

Some clichés are just words—neither sayings nor metaphors—that have been used together so often that they seem inseparable:

a sigh of relief	in no uncertain terms
the rules of the game	breathless anticipation
ups and downs	sure thing
in the final analysis	finishing touches
goes without saying	loud and clear
remains to be seen	long holiday weekend
nestled in the valley	financial circles
needless to say	tension is high
powers that be	speculation was rampant
leave in a huff	fueling speculation
more of the same	fond farewell

When is a wording a cliché? Ask how readily it comes to mind. If the expression took no effort to find, it is often best to lose it again.

Instead of doing the expected with the language, good writers play with our expectations. Sports fans are used to reading about the "ceremonial throwing out of the first ball." George Vecsey, writing about two well-publicized gentlemen—George Steinbrenner and Yogi Berra—on the first day of baseball's spring training, decided to have some fun with that phrase:

. . . two dozen fans applauded as the two men ambled out for the ceremonial *first click of the camera.*

The New York Times

▪ A ▪

Write an analogy that could be used in a newspaper story to describe:

1. A car smashed in from the front and from behind

2. An avalanche having flattened three houses

3. A dachshund

4. A humid, 90-degree day in April

5. A frisbee

6. The Eiffel Tower

7. The Space Shuttle

8. Jimmy Carter's smile

9. Ronald Reagan's hairstyle

10. Walter Matthau's face

▪ **B** ▪

Rewrite the following sentences using analogies to make them clearer or livelier.

1. The stock market was up one day, down the next and then up again the day after that.

2. Fred Taylor was an extremely large man, who at 6 feet 5 inches and 260 pounds made his second-grade students look extremely small.

3. The baseball player had more success batting against that veteran pitcher than he had against any other pitcher in the league.

4. Since the drought began last year, getting a glass of water in a downtown restaurant has been almost impossible.

5. The computer terminal consists of a keyboard with all the letters of the alphabet, numbers and a few additional symbols laid out in rows, attached to a 12 inch by 9 inch screen on which words and pictures appear.

▪ C ▪

Edit the following sentences to remove any weak analogies, mixed metaphors or clichés.

1. The teenager was in critical condition, near death's door, her doctor said.

2. The sharp winds slapped against the oil rig like a fist.

3. The alderman's plan to nip the tax in the bud apparently fell on deaf ears as the council approved it by a 6–1 vote.

4. Only time will tell whether the rule will succeed in protecting the weaker sex from discrimination.

5. He ran the mile so fast that even a cheetah would have had trouble beating him.

6. Now that he is the one skating on thin ice, the shoe is on the other foot.

7. Signs that the economy is now on a firmer footing have the mayor's advisers thinking twice about the tax increase.

8. From time immemorial disaster has always seemed to loom on the horizon.

9. Without the state chairwoman's endorsement, his chances of winning the nomination were about as good as those of a tiny, wounded puppy trying to find a place in a world full of dog haters.

10. Mother Nature unleashed a hail storm of snow on the city, leaving the sanitation department with the Herculean task of cleaning up all the white stuff.

11. The fire licked at neighboring buildings like a huge yellow bulldozer.

12. The victim was at the ripe old age of 82.

13. Police said his attempt to beat a hasty retreat failed and he fell in a hail of bullets.

14. He said the new police cars, which are faster than a line drive hitting artificial turf, look like winners.

15. Exploding budget deficits could put a brake on the economy, clouding her chances.

16. Last but not least, Alfred Dobson threw his hat into the ring in the race for governor.

17. Demonstrating that it is never over until the last out, the team chalked up the victory with a three-run rally in the last half of the ninth inning.

18. Once the speaker warmed to her subject she minced few words.

19. He played with the idea like a cat playing with a ball of string.

20. Eating the potentially cancer-causing substance would be like swallowing a huge dose of cyanide.

■ **D** ■

Edit the following story to remove any weak analogies, mixed metaphors or clichés.

The crowd gathered at City Hall let out a roar of approval as one by one the members of New Milford High School's state championship football team stepped up to receive keys to the city from Mayor Frank Loge yesterday.

Lightning-fast running back Roger Guianos received the loudest ovation, but the approximately 200 proud-as-peacocks spectators put their hands together for each one of the 47 hard-working players and the team's three razor-sharp coaches.

When, last but not least, New Milford's tough-as-nails head coach Rod Dokawitz made it to the makeshift platform on the steps of the historic old building, the crowd stood as one to applaud the entire squad. New Milford's loyal fans made more noise than the A bomb at Hiroshima.

"If only you could have beaten Fairfield, then maybe we'd have something to celebrate," a grinning Mayor Loge quipped. New Milford suffered a heart-breaking defeat at the hands of Fairfield High School in the opening game of the season before chalking up 10 straight victories, including the wipe out of Lincoln Central in the state championship game Saturday.

CHAPTER 6

Objectivity

Opinions *are* voiced in newspapers. Editorial writers are allowed to take swings at politicians. Columnists are invited to sound off on pressing issues. Ann Landers is free to offer advice on dealing with a brooding spouse or an oppressive father-in-law. But almost all American newspapers strive to keep opinion out of their *news* columns and, therefore, out of the writing with which this book is concerned. The *Chicago Tribune* may endorse Ronald Reagan for president in its editorials, but it is expected to show no favor to Reagan or any other candidate in its news coverage of the campaign. That's *objectivity* as defined at most American newspapers.

This strict line between news and opinion was not always honored or even drawn. In the days when news organizations were small enough to reflect the personalities of individual printers and when there were enough papers to ensure that most points of view would be represented, newspapers were not shy about mixing their news and their politics.

Readers who bought Horace Greeley's *New York Tribune* in the 19th century knew they would get the news from a liberal, abolitionist perspective. If they wanted the news with a different tint, they could buy James Gordon Bennett's *New York Herald,* Henry Raymond's *New York Times* or any of the dozen or so papers being published in New York City at the time.

Today's news organizations have grown too large and too few to be personal vehicles. Few cities now have more than one or two newspapers, and there are few places to look to balance a slanted perspective on

the news. For whatever reasons, in the past century or so most American newspapers have, appropriately, decided to try to play it straight.

Objectivity is not a simple goal. It doesn't take a philosophy major to realize that there are innumerable possible perspectives on every event and that a choice of one of them represents a subjective decision of a sort. Three-thousand people enjoyed a concert. Is it fair in some ultimate sense to concentrate on the one person who was stabbed? Journalists have to accept the fact that they can never be free of this sort of philosophical bias. Subjective or not, they're going to write about the stabbing. But they must be on their guard against the danger of a cruder, more pernicious bias seeping into their stories.

Here are some of the guises in which opinion can sneak into news and feature writing.

Rooting

Journalists have feelings too. They like some of the people they write about. They dislike others. They agree with some of the statements they report. They are offended by others. They have their own political leanings.

Some people go into journalism to right wrongs. That's fine. Sometimes a fair and accurate marshaling of the facts can jolt the establishment, if not rearrange the world. The trick is to make sure the facts are doing the talking, not the reporter's own preconceived notions. It's fine to report malfeasance on the part of local Democrats, as long as the evidence is solid (See Chapter 16, Facts) and as long as the reporter would be as interested in similar misbehavior by Republicans.

Rupert Murdoch's *New York Post* is one newspaper that has consistently violated this rule and let its rooting interests color its news coverage. During the 1980 presidential election, for example, the *Post* buttressed its editorial support of Ronald Reagan with stories like: "Israel Fears Carter Victory" (the story contained no quotes from Israelis supporting this charge) or "Stars Want Ron to get the Part" (the *Post* found no stars supporting Carter). Such slanted coverage by a major newspaper is impossible to defend.

Ignoring

One candidate is loud and aggressive, another seeks out the press less frequently, a third seems likely to receive the smallest fraction of the vote. Do they deserve equal coverage?

Apportioning space in a story, or in stories, during a campaign is one of the trickiest tasks journalists face. Take the 1976 Democratic primary in New Hampshire. Jimmy Carter won 28 percent of the vote to Morris Udall's 24 percent, a victory most might consider comfortable but modest. *Time* and *Newsweek,* two of the country's most influential sources of news, saw it otherwise. According to David L. Paletz and Robert M. Entman, authors of *Media Power Politics,* the two magazines combined to give Carter *26 times* as much coverage as Udall in the issue that followed the primary. Carter was on the cover of both magazines. Is that fair? Is that reporting the political climate or creating the political climate?

Fairness requires a balancing act, but the balance will never please everyone. Aggressive candidates are going to claim more space than cautious candidates; major-party candidates are usually a bigger story than minor-party candidates. Still, reporters have to be sure cautious candidates and minor-party candidates are not ignored. Too much time spent tracking frontrunners and predicting their victories can make those predictions self-fulfilling.

Issues, even more than elections, are likely to have more than two sides. Fairness requires more than just some quotes from the "pros" and "cons." The "yeah, buts" and "maybes" may make blander copy but better sense. They deserve space, too. It's also better to bend a bit to make room for the views of so-called "extremists" and splinter groups than to condemn them to silence because their views seem extreme.

Agreeing

Sometimes it's the easy issues that cause trouble. Most of us probably agree that taxes are unpleasant, dictators objectionable and the Soviet Union's treatment of dissidents distasteful. It would be easy to write:

The city council did us a favor today, lowering the property tax by one percent.

In a long-overdue development, Attila the Hun has been ousted in a coup.

The Soviet Union took a well-deserved slap in the face today when a leading physicist spoke out in favor of human rights.

All these wordings, however, are unacceptable. Even widely shared opinion has no place in the news. The widely held opinions of one generation may later prove to be its bigotry.

During the 1950s, for example, *The New York Times* ran a story reporting hysterical charges that there were "sex perverts" (homosexuals) working in federal agencies. This story, which would offend many people today, apparently snuck by without notice because so many people then shared the belief that homosexuals were both perverted and dangerous. Each age tends to equate its most cherished beliefs with truth.

The work of good reporters can generally be read without embarrassment decades later precisely because they struggle to avoid confusing beliefs with truth.

Concluding

It is possible to add a touch of subjectivity to a story with just one, seemingly innocuous word:

The council voted to raise real estate taxes *only* 2 percent.

Yes, that 2 percent hike is less than the 6 percent increase that had been considered. But there are some who believe any tax increase is too high. The reporter's job is to present the facts and leave conclusions about those facts to readers.

This is not a call for know-nothing journalism. The reporter must communicate enough facts for the reader to understand the meaning of the story. Those needed to place developments in context must be included (See Chapter 15, Background and Context). Tell the reader the council had been considering a much higher tax increase. Include quotes from council members commenting on the reason for their decision. Compare the tax increase with that of past years and increases in comparable communities. But don't take that extra step of concluding that the tax went up *only* 2 percent.

UNACCEPTABLE:
The Society for Repentance and Flight from Sin,
the fanatical Muslim sect accused by the Egyptian
government in the assassination of Anwar Sadat . . .

Associated Press in the *Los Angeles Times*

There's a similar problem here. One person's "fanatical sect" is another person's orthodox congregation of committed believers. And the word "fanatical," while applied with some regularity to Islamic organizations, somehow rarely gets tagged onto Christian or Jewish groups. Even the designation "sect" seems loaded. The Methodists are never called a Christian "sect." It is sufficient, in this case, to note the charge the Egyptian government is making against this organization. Readers can decide for themselves what they find fanatical and what they find devout.

ACCEPTABLE:
The Society for Repentance and Flight From Sin, the Muslim group accused by the Egyptian government in the assassination of Anwar Sadat . . .

Similar difficulties arise when reporters label fighters who blow up bridges for a popular cause as "resistance fighters," while labeling fighters who blow up bridges for more questionable causes "terrorists." The solution again is simply to detail the damage done and avoid the name-calling entirely.

Writing objectively means writing so that your reader has a chance to agree or disagree with the action or comments of the newsmakers in the story, not with you.

Additional Reading

"Clout: Murdoch's Political *Post,*" Mitchell Stephens, *Columbia Journalism Review,* July/August 1982.

▪ A ▪

Edit the following sentences to remove any potentially subjective wordings.

1. Fortunately, he was able to remove the Communist menace from his union.

2. The big-spending Democrats have dominated the City Council for 20 years.

3. The black militants blocked the auditorium's entranceway, making it impossible for the South African envoy to address the audience.

4. The convicted child-molester got what he deserved: a nine-year sentence.

5. The Nicaraguan freedom fighters set up base in Honduras and promised to overthrow the leftist government within a year.

6. With luck, the drought will end on Wednesday when heavy rains are expected.

7. The union had received a whopping 9-percent salary increase two years ago.

8. The heroic teen-ager jumped into the pool but sadly was unable to reach the baby.

9. She was able to destroy that argument by pointing out that abortion is a form of murder.

10. The protesters shouted obscenities at police.

11. With their usual insensitivity to the problems of the poor, the Republicans voted to cut taxes and spending.

12. He rashly accused his opponent of lying and cheating.

13. The governor and her staff struggled heroically to keep the budget under $600 million.

14. Government troops liberated a southern town that had been seized by extremist rebels last week.

15. The economy has been helped by the fiscally sound policies used by business to keep down wages.

16. Only Alderman Harry Kanes was willing to come forward and call the decision to raise the council's own salary "a ripoff."

17. Welfare freeloaders receive $97 million each year.

18. The radical troublemakers advocated civil disobedience as a means of bringing the troops home from Central America.

19. He refused to be interviewed about the accounting mess that had put his agency $100,000 over budget.

20. On the reviewing stand were Republican candidate Stella Shapiro, who smiled and waved to the marchers; Democratic candidate Janice Jerome, who seemed filled with pride at the performances of the city's high school students; and Citizens Party candidate George Ikels.

Edit the following story to remove any potentially subjective wordings.

The state Assembly, after wasting eight hours debating what obviously would be the proper procedure to employ, voted last night to expel Assemblywoman Alice Tallyrand of North Amboy, who has been arrested for viciously abusing and neglecting her 5-year-old son.

The Assembly voted 136 – 1 in favor of the toughly worded motion by Assemblyman Theodore Wolinski of Saddle Brook that removed Tallyrand from her seat immediately for "inhuman behavior." The only negative note was cast by Assemblyman Mark Adler of New Falls, a bleeding-heart liberal from New Falls who not coincidentally shared an office with Tallyrand. Predictably, the left-leaning Democrat said that the Assembly should not act until Tallyrand "has had her day in court."

Tallyrand was finally arrested Friday night on charges of child abuse. Police said they had received reports over a number of months from Tallyrand's neighbors accusing her of actually forcing her son, William, to stand at attention for hours at a time in their backyard.

Tallyrand, who won custody of the boy in a bitter divorce trial two years ago, still claims she is innocent of the charges. She, of course, refused to present a defense or give an opinion about the Assembly's decision last night.

The Assembly's debate on how to handle the awful charges against one of its members began at noon and stretched on into the evening as one nervous Democrat after another expressed concern about the propriety of acting on a case that has not yet come to trial.

Three weak Democratic-supported motions that would have merely expressed the Assembly's "concern" about the charges were defeated with the honor-bound Republican majority standing firm behind efforts to invoke sterner punishment.

When it appeared certain that no watered-down action would sneak through, all the Democrats except the eccentric Adler voted with the Republicans in support of expulsion. Said one: "We don't want to be accused of condoning child abuse." Hardly a heroic stance for an elected official to take.

PART TWO

Leads

CHAPTER 7

News judgment

Ted Rohrlich of the *Los Angeles Times* was looking through a file of search warrants when something caught his eye: the name Los Angeles Dodgers. The warrant, he discovered, had been issued to search for evidence of a scheme to sell phony tickets to Dodger games.

Rohrlich knew he had found news. He would have an exclusive.

The ability to recognize news is the one indispensable skill at all levels of journalism. Editors need this skill to decide which of the flood of press releases and tips they get every day are worth pursuing, and which stories in each day's paper deserve the most prominence. Reporters like Ted Rohrlich need it to help find stories and to determine which aspects of these stories they should focus on. Writers need it to decide which of the facts they have collected they should *lead* with — use in their first paragraph.

Most journalists take their *news sense* for granted. Many maintain news judgment comes only through experience. We disagree. We believe there are two things beginning reporters can do to improve their sense of what's news.

First, reporters can study the news. A familiarity with the news is necessary to understand its habits and special preferences. Anyone considering a job in journalism should read, and read critically, at least one newspaper every day. As often as possible, that paper should be one of the country's best such as *The New York Times, The Washington Post,* the *Los Angeles Times, The Philadelphia Inquirer* or *The Wall Street Journal.* It's also necessary to follow national and local broadcast newscasts and to read at least one of the weekly news magazines.

A second technique for learning news judgment is to analyze in detail the qualities that make something newsworthy. That is what this chapter does. It breaks down that abstract attribute — newsworthiness — into ten somewhat less mystical qualities: impact, weight, controversy, emotion, uniqueness, prominence, proximity, timeliness, currency and educational value.

Impact

On a routine day, the Milwaukee Common Council's decision to approve the sale of an old junior high school for conversion to a shelter for the homeless might have begun, or *led,* a local reporter's story. But at the same meeting, the council also approved a plan to change winter parking rules throughout the city. The parking change affected more readers' lives. It had greater *impact* on the community. And it is the news the reporter began with:

The Milwaukee Common Council has approved permanent one-side-only parking for much of the city from Dec. 1 to March 1.

The Milwaukee Journal

The school sale was mentioned, but lower in the story.

Reporters are constantly measuring what effect

events have on their readers. A tiny fly can be more newsworthy than a space shuttle landing if that fly and its offspring have a taste for fruit and you are writing for a newspaper in a fruit-producing region.

Political and economic stories receive so much attention because they frequently have a profound impact on our lives. A vote on Social Security benefits can swell or shrink the monthly check received by many readers. A slight fluctuation in the prime lending rate may ultimately make it more difficult for readers to buy a home or find a job.

All other things being equal—and they rarely are—facts and events with the greatest impact on the most readers have the greatest news value.

Weight

Fourteen persons in Nassau County, N.Y., were charged with welfare fraud. But two of them, a husband and wife, were accused of defrauding the county out of more money than the other 12 combined. Their alleged crime had more weight; it deserved more emphasis than the charges against the other suspects.

> A Freeport husband and wife who Nassau County officials say cheated the county out of more than $133,000 in welfare payments over an 11-year period were among 14 persons charged yesterday with welfare fraud.
>
> *(Long Island, N.Y.) Newsday*

Loss of life has more weight than injury, and injuries generally are more newsworthy than loss of property:

> A taxi driver was shot and wounded during a holdup early yesterday morning in North Philadelphia.
>
> *The Philadelphia Inquirer*

The taxi driver in this story was robbed of $30, a fact that is clearly outweighed by his injury. (Without the injury, this story would not have made the newspaper.)

A murder has more weight than a robbery; a robbery more weight than a burglary. The weight required for a story to make the newspaper will vary depending on the size of the city or town in which that paper circulates. *Austin American-Statesman* reporter Mike Cox notes that murders are definitely news in Austin, Texas. But Cox remembers a Houston reporter joking that there were so many homicides in his city that "if it doesn't have to do with voodoo, I'm not interested."

Some stories are newsworthy because they have historical weight. The gradual erosion of the Parthenon in Athens because of air pollution has little di-

rect impact on American readers. But it has historical significance and many papers have printed reports about it.

Controversy

Candidates will state their views on dozens of issues during a political campaign. The press will choose to focus not only on those that have impact, but on those that are controversial.

When two candidates for governor of Maryland took opposite sides on the issue of providing tax breaks for the parents of children in private schools, *The Washington Post* covered their dispute on the front of its Metropolitan Section:

> Maryland's Republican gubernatorial candidate, Robert A. Pascal, told a convention of educators yesterday that he favors tuition tax credits, and Democratic Gov. Harry Hughes, who drew louder applause, said he opposes the plan.
>
> *The Washington Post*

The news loves arguments, debates, charges, countercharges and all-out fights. Newspapers rarely pay much attention to the pace at which governmental organizations spend their money, but if a congresswoman attacks that pace, it becomes controversial; it becomes news.

> The Cuyahoga Metropolitan Housing Authority has been awarded $1.7 million in federal grants to upgrade properties, but it isn't spending the money fast enough to suit one critic.
>
> *The (Cleveland) Plain Dealer*

Emotion

Some news appeals directly to our emotions. Deaths of young children are treated as especially newsworthy because they are especially moving. A New Jersey fire in which five people died might not ordinarily have made the front page of the second section of *The New York Times*. But it became a bigger story because all five victims were children:

> Five children, including a 4-month-old boy lost when his mother stumbled during a desperate escape attempt, were killed in a house fire early today.
>
> *Associated Press in The New York Times*

Heroic exploits—a passerby capturing an alleged mugger or balloonists crossing the Pacific—also touch our emotions. And, while no major American daily will print smut, stories with a hint of sex have their appeal, too. A divorce trial in Florida was covered regularly by *The Washington Post* in part, no doubt, because it was steamy:

> A gardener testified today he saw socialite Paula Ross embracing and kissing two of her alleged lovers at the Ross mansion.*
>
> United Press International in *The Washington Post*

Readers are not always concerned only with what is most important. Reporters must take into account these human interests.

Uniqueness

The Russians putting three more astronauts into orbit is no longer of much news value. But when one of them is a woman, the story increases in importance:

> Svetlana Saviskaya, a 34-year-old champion pilot and parachutist, became the second woman in space yesterday, joining two men aboard the Soviet capsule Soyuz T-7.
>
> *The Atlanta Constitution*

Firsts, largests and leasts make news: the first derailment in the 30-year history of a passenger railroad line, the highest highway death toll ever on a Labor Day weekend, the least rain ever to fall here in April.

Uniqueness is also the standard behind that old journalism cliché, "When a dog bites a man, it's not news. But when a man bites a dog, it is news."

This example appeared in the *San Francisco Chronicle,* a newspaper with a special taste for the bizarre and unlikely:

> Members of the Blond family were quietly watching the film "Cat and Mouse" on television Sunday night when they were attacked—by their own cat.

Prominence

The news is not democratic. No matter what a journalist's attitude toward human life, it should be apparent that the death of Nancy Reagan's stepfather is bigger news than the death of another, equally successful neurosurgeon in Arizona would have been. That is why plans for his funeral made the front page of papers as far away as the *Adirondack Enterprise* in New York.

Events in the lives of particularly well-known people are given particular attention by the press. Newspapers in the United States would have no interest in the story of a man in London who snuck into the bedroom of an ordinary woman and chatted for ten minutes. But when that woman is the Queen of En-

gland, the story becomes front-page news in major newspapers around the world.

Relatively minor arrests don't make Page 6 of a big city newspaper unless the person arrested is prominent:

> White Sox outfielder Biff Henderson was arrested yesterday at his North Side apartment on narcotics and weapons violations charges.**
>
> (Chicago) *Sun-Times*

And allegations of ticket scams are a lot bigger news when they involve an organization as prominent and popular as the Los Angeles Dodgers.

Proximity

The Nuclear Regulatory Commission had released a list of nuclear plants with a special problem and had ranked them in order of the seriousness of the problem. The problem was most severe, the NRC said, at a plant in Hartsville, S.C. But when a New York newspaper reported the story, it concentrated instead on the 7th and 15th plants on that list:

> The reactor walls of some nuclear power plants—including Indian Point 3 in Westchester and the Ginna plant near Rochester—are becoming dangerously brittle and may rupture unless "modifications" are made, the Nuclear Regulatory Commission staff warned in a report yesterday.
>
> (New York) *Daily News*

Why Westchester and Rochester rather than Hartsville? They are in New York State. The problems of plants there are of more local interest than the potentially more serious troubles of a reactor in Hartsville, S.C.

Readers are interested in the problems, people and places they know. All other things being equal, the closer the news is, the bigger it is.

The defeat of a councilman in San Francisco warrants a significant story in local papers, but it may not be mentioned in the *Los Angeles Times*. One death in the newspaper's readership area often will command more attention than half-a-dozen deaths in another state. And the closing of one small soda plant in town may be more newsworthy than the closing of a major automotive plant in Detroit.

Timeliness

The news is impatient. Yesterday's headlines fade fast. Monday's dramatic murder may not even be

---

* The name in this story has been changed.

** The name in this story has been changed.

newsworthy enough to mention in the paper again Thursday.

Most news that appears in daily newspapers happened either yesterday or today. Even in major stories, such as a sensational trial or a plane crash, the news each succeeding day must emphasize what is new; the reporter must search for a fresh, more timely aspect of the story—a *second-day angle.*

Notice how the articles that appeared on the second and third days on which this plane crash was covered each found new angles of the story to emphasize:

> An Eastern Airlines Boeing 727 jetliner carrying at least 115 passengers and a crew of eight on a nonstop flight from New Orleans to New York crashed in flames *yesterday* at the edge of Kennedy International Airport while attempting to land during an electrical storm.
>
> *The New York Times* (Wednesday)

> The pilots of at least two other airlines headed for Kennedy International Airport just ahead of the Eastern Airlines jet that crashed Tuesday, killing 110 persons, reported vicious shifts in air currents that created severe hazards during the landing approach.
>
> *The New York Times* (Thursday)

> Strong sentiment appeared to be mounting among government and airline officials *yesterday* for improved storm-warning systems and other measures to protect planes from the hazards of thunderstorms and other violent weather.
>
> *The New York Times* (Friday)

The news must be kept fresh.

Currency

The news must also take into account what's on people's minds. When Thanksgiving is approaching, a story about a new technique for breeding turkeys becomes more newsworthy. As April 15 gets nearer, we're a bit more likely to hear about proposals to change the tax laws.

The New York *Daily News* might have found room on another day for a story on a man from Colorado who became seriously ill after swallowing three apparently contaminated headache tablets. But the story made Page 3 because five people had recently died from contaminated Tylenol capsules:

> A Denver-area man who took three Extra Strength Excedrin capsules apparently contaminated with toxic mercuric chloride was in critical condition today in a Denver-area hospital.

Readers were worried about contaminated medicines. Therefore, the importance of anything relating to that subject was magnified.

Reporters and editors sometimes look for a current event or trend that will enable them to investigate ordinarily less newsworthy subjects. The Tylenol deaths, for example, provided such a *news peg* for discussions of the problems of packaging over-the-counter drugs in such a way that they cannot be tampered with. Similarly, the death from starvation of an elderly man might provide a news peg for a discussion of the problem of poverty among the elderly.

Educational Value

As journalists attempt to reflect on, as well as react to, an often puzzling world, more and more stories are being written that are designed to make us more knowledgeable rather than merely better informed.

"You want to make some sense out of the things that are in the news," is how *Philadelphia Inquirer* science writer Jim Detjen puts it. "If the weather is all screwed up, I might do a piece on El Niño and other ocean currents, and consider what effect they might have on the weather."

In part because of this concern with educating readers, special sections are proliferating that include articles that explain, as well as report on, science and business. The better newspapers today aren't merely telling readers that a space shuttle has been launched; they are discussing how it works. They aren't waiting for war to break out before providing behind-the-scenes glimpses of the workings of governments thousands of miles away. And they increasingly are offering readers guidance about personal decisions, from mortgaging a home to selecting a psychiatrist.

Perhaps newspapers are becoming less hesitant about telling us what they think we should know rather than just what they think we want to know. Or perhaps we as readers are demanding to be told more. Whichever is the case, newspapers have gone into the business of educating:

> LUANDA, Angola—For those who view Africa as a chessboard of opposed forces, Angola is a critical piece.
>
> It is not, perhaps, the dominant piece in the region—in economic and military terms, that would be South Africa—but it is certainly a principal warrior in black Africa's campaign in South Africa . . .

This piece, which devoted some 30 paragraphs to discussing Angola's place in Africa, appeared in *The New York Times* at a time in which there was no compelling reason for writing about Angola. The country was relatively peaceful; no event had thrust it into the news. Yet the paper considered it a good time to reflect on the balance of power in that part of the world.

An understanding of these ten qualities will not answer all questions of news judgment. It is unlikely that you could program them into a computer and get the computer to select the correct angle for a story. For one thing, these qualities will often have to be weighed against one another.

A legislature may have voted to provide a scholarship fund for the children of a policeman killed on duty (that has emotional appeal) on the same day that it approved a new welfare office in your town (prox-imity) and voted to raise the sales tax by a percentage point statewide (impact). Which angle should be emphasized in a story about the legislature's actions? It takes common sense to balance these different considerations. Here common sense says lead with the sales tax increase. Its widespread impact on the price of most purchases in the state outweighs the emotional appeal and local interest of the other two actions. (The welfare office might warrant its own, smaller, story.)

■ A ■

Check the item with greater news value, all other things being equal, in each of the following pairs.

1 _____ City Council met from 8 to 10 p.m. tonight.

_____ City Council increases fine for illegal parking $10.

2 _____ Hurricane headed toward this city.

_____ Two die as hurricane hits Caribbean island.

3 _____ New flyweight boxing champion.

_____ New heavyweight boxing champion.

4 _____ Drug store robbed, $10,000 stolen.

_____ Shoe store robbed, $50 stolen, owner killed.

5 _____ "Decent business people are the backbone of this town's economy," said president of local Chamber of Commerce.

_____ "Greedy business people are ruining this town's economy," said president of local Chamber of Commerce.

6 _____ Car kills woman hurrying home for Christmas dinner.

_____ Car kills woman hurrying to dentist's appointment.

7 _____ Police still investigating death of two infants two days ago.

_____ Teen-ager dies today, police to investigate.

8 _____ Mayor's limousine sideswipes woman's car causing $100 in damages.

_____ Two cars collide downtown causing $2,000 in damages.

9 _____ Fifteen-year-old boy criticizes governor's politics.

_____ Governor criticizes 15-year-old boy's politics.

10 _____ Five cases of malaria reported here, no deaths.

_____ Five die from malaria in India.

11 _____ Halley's Comet can be seen in town tonight.

_____ New movie can be seen in town tonight.

12 _____ Two people found starved to death on Dec. 1.

_____ Two people found starved to death on Dec. 25.

13 _____ Seventy-eight-year-old woman raped.

_____ Twenty-eight-year-old woman raped.

14 _____ Eight-year-old found dead in collapsed building.

_____ Uncle of 8-year-old found dead in collapsed building.

15 _____ New progress on cancer treatment.

_____ New progress on flu treatment.

16 _____ Legislature passes new tax.

_____ Legislature designates Monday "Housewives Day."

17 _____ Policewoman sues for sex discrimination.

_____ Policeman sues for sex discrimination.

18 _____ Mayor fires fire commissioner.

_____ Mayor hires new fire commissioner.

19 _____ Federal Reserve says it will lower interest rates.

_____ Dow Jones Index up seven points.

20 _____ City's baseball team wins fourth straight.

_____ State college basketball team makes final round of national basketball playoffs — "the final four."

21 _____ Long lines at unemployment office the day stock market suffers record losses.

_____ Long lines at unemployment office the day after local team loses the World Series.

22 _____ Local professor comes up with new explanation for formation of the solar system.

_____ Local teen-ager wins award for magazine sales.

23 _____ City Council votes to increase judges' salaries.

_____ City Council votes to increase its members own salaries.

24 _____ Widely used painkiller found ineffective.

_____ Experimental glaucoma treatment found ineffective.

25 _____ Alleged robber shot by policeman.

_____ Policeman shot by alleged robber.

▪ B ▪

Indicate by writing an *M* which item in each of these sets has the most news value; indicate by writing an *L* which has the least news value. (Again assume that all other considerations are equal.)

1 _____ Jury selection.

_____ Testimony of key witness.

_____ Verdict.

2 _____ Local football team's coach fired.

_____ Local football team wins preseason game.

_____ Local football team wins regular season game.

_____ Local football team wins Super Bowl.

3 _____ "We made a mistake," mayor says.

_____ "We were right," mayor says.

_____ "They made a mistake," mayor says.

4 At a board of education meeting:

_____ Disciplinary action taken against a principal.

_____ Disciplinary action taken against a teacher.

_____ Disciplinary action taken against a student.

5 In raid on allegedly illegal gambling club:

_____ Minister arrested.

_____ Teacher arrested.

_____ Businessman arrested.

CHAPTER 8

Hard leads

It is the rare news event that commands our attention regardless of the way it's presented. Masses of information tease our senses daily; much of it we let pass by. We pay attention to what we recognize — quickly — to be of interest.

Good newspaper reporters know this. They know few readers scan, let alone read, everything in the paper. So reporters use a simple trick: They try to hook readers by placing their most intriguing information at the top of the story — where the readers will be sure to spot it.

The top of the story, generally its first paragraph, is called the *lead*. In a story about three men, including a judge, who have been arrested for disorderly conduct, the judge's arrest will dominate the lead paragraph. The other two men are less newsworthy.

In a story about a press conference in which the mayor announces that she's promoting a police sergeant to lieutenant, ordering the pruning of oak trees on Main Street and firing the housing commissioner, the housing commissioner's dismissal will lead the story. The other two announcements probably won't even get in print.

In a feature story, reporters might best catch a reader's eye with an unusual description, an alluring little tale or a clever twist of a phrase — those are called *soft leads* (See Chapter 9, Soft Leads). But stories about significant breaking events don't need to get fancy to attract attention to themselves. Most news stories begin with *hard leads* — short summaries

of the most newsworthy information in the story, the hard facts.

Here is a concise presentation of the most newsworthy information in a story — a hard lead:

President Reagan yesterday rejected quotas or tariffs for the import-plagued American footwear industry.

The Boston Globe

The choice of what to lead with and the wording of the lead are two crucial decisions in the writing of any story. "The lead helps the reader and writer find focus," says Roy Peter Clark, the former *St. Petersburg Times* writing coach, now with the Poynter Institute for Media Studies in St. Petersburg, Fla.

Length

Hard leads must be tight. A flabby, overstuffed first paragraph is no way to seduce readers.

UNACCEPTABLE:
In 1977 nurses at North Shore University Hospital in Manhasset voted that they wanted to be represented by the state nurses union. The hospital refused to recognize the union as bargaining agent for the nurses. Now the nurses have won the right to be represented by the union.

Hard leads are rarely more than one sentence long and almost never longer than two sentences. The first paragraph is the last place a reporter would want a wasted word or a redundancy.

ACCEPTABLE:
Nurses at North Shore University Hospital in Manhasset have won the right to be represented by the state nurses union after five years of resistance by hospital officials.

(Long Island, N.Y.) *Newsday*

Leads usually should be less than 35 words long (though there are exceptions). Often the shortest leads are the most powerful. Consider this lead from *The New York Times* on July 2, 1969:

Men have landed and walked on the moon.

Eight words can capture history.

Choosing the Lead

A reporter for *The Record* in Bergen County, N.J., received the following information from the Englewood Police Department:

"An alarm notified us at 12:36 this afternoon that there had been a robbery at the First State Bank at 1 State St. A car was sent and was unable to locate the suspect. Teller Andrea Dormis told us that she was working at a drive-in window at 12:31 when she was asked to turn over money. She gave the robber a paper bag filled with $5,500 in unmarked bills. She said the robber was a white male, wearing a black leather jacket, a scarf and riding a black motorcycle. She said he pulled up to the window, pulled out a gun and handed her a paper bag and a note reading, 'Fill this bag with money.' She did not know the make of the motorcycle and said she saw no license plate. She said the motorcycle left, heading east on Palisade Avenue. We are investigating."*

Choosing what information to include in the lead is an exercise in news judgment (See Chapter 7, News Judgment).

UNACCEPTABLE:
An alarm notified police yesterday that there had been a robbery at the First State Bank in Englewood.

The use of the alarm itself is not particularly weighty or unique. It should not be mentioned in the lead.

UNACCEPTABLE:
Police are investigating a robbery at the First State Bank in Englewood yesterday.

Police would be expected to investigate any crime. The fact that they are investigating this one is not very newsworthy.

UNACCEPTABLE:
The First State Bank was robbed of $5,500 yesterday, according to police.

The amount of money taken is important, but a $5,500 robbery hardly has much weight. What makes this story interesting is the unique method employed by the robber. That must be included in the lead.

ACCEPTABLE:
A man on a motorcycle rode up to the drive-in window of the First State Bank in Englewood yesterday, pulled a gun on the teller and rode off with $5,500, according to police.

The lead must include the most newsworthy elements in the story. When covering a big story, the problem often is which of a number of weighty facts to leave out of the lead. On lesser stories, the problem may be deciding which fact is appealing enough to get the reader's attention. There are plenty of close calls; two reporters covering the same story may come up with two different leads. But there still are right leads and wrong leads on any story.

Here is the wrong lead:

Two people were killed when a truck collided with a car yesterday in Mill County.

The right lead is:

A 10-month-old girl and her mother were killed yesterday when the car in which they were driving was hit by a truck in Mill County.

And another wrong lead:

Mayor Alfred Ellison announced today that Jim Barber has been appointed city attorney.

The right lead for this story is:

Mayor Alfred Ellison today fired City Attorney Roland Maston, who has been accused of conflict of interest in the Red River Dam case.

The Five Ws

Journalists used to have a simple formula for writing a lead: Just answer the "five Ws" — *who? what? when? where?* and *why?* This lead does:

D.C. Mayor Marion Barry, forced by the Reagan Administration to cut city borrowing from the U.S. Treasury, yesterday proposed a municipal construction program for 1983 that has no new costly buildings or other big-ticket projects.

The Washington Post

Who — Mayor Barry; what — the construction program; when — yesterday; where — D.C.; and why — because he was forced to cut city borrowing.

---

* The names of the people and the name and address of the bank in this story have been changed.

Modern reporters, however, frequently will omit one or two of the five Ws to keep their leads from getting too cluttered. This lead from the same issue of *The Washington Post,* for example, does not say when or why:

Pentagon officials have thought up a new way to persuade the military services to shut down excess bases: Let commanders keep control of the money saved.

Still, even if they are not all answered, it is helpful to consider the five Ws when writing a lead. These are questions readers will have on their minds. The "when" — usually yesterday or, on some newspapers, the day of the week — is particularly hard to ignore. It must be included in any lead worded in the past tense.

UNACCEPTABLE:
Three young sisters and their father, who had rushed back into their burning house when he heard screams for help, died in a fire in Northwest Baltimore.

ACCEPTABLE:
Three young sisters and their father, who had rushed back into their burning house when he heard screams for help, died *yesterday morning* in a fire in Northwest Baltimore.

The (Baltimore) *Sun*

And while it is inadvisable to strain to squeeze the answers to all the other five Ws into the lead, they will all have to be included somewhere in the body of the story (See Chapter 13, Information Selection).

Details

The news is full of names, times, addresses and ages. Most of those details will be included in the story. Which should be included in the lead? Certainly, the fewer the better. The lead's job is to catch the reader's attention, and unfamiliar names or insignificant facts are not exactly grabbers.

As a rule, leave a proper name out of the lead unless it belongs to someone well known.

WEAK:
U.S. District Court Judge Harold H. Greene yesterday refused to dismiss the federal antitrust suit against American Telephone & Telegraph Co. . . .

BETTER:
A *federal judge* yesterday refused to dismiss the federal antitrust suit against American Telephone & Telegraph Co. . . .

The Washington Post

ACCEPTABLE:
British Prime Minister Margaret Thatcher aligned herself firmly with the United States yesterday in its

campaign to pressure New Zealand into permitting nuclear-powered warships into its ports.

USA Today

The British prime minister's name is simply more newsworthy than the name of a federal judge.

A newspaper in a small town, where everybody is relatively well known, will include more names in its leads than a newspaper in a large city.

Times, addresses and ages only deserve mention in the lead if there is something interesting about them. The peace treaty ending World War I was signed on November (the eleventh month) 11 at 11 a.m. The exact time might have made it into the lead on that story because of its historic nature — and because of the coincidence of the numbers.

Exact addresses are difficult to justify in any lead. Usually mention of the neighborhood or city is sufficient. Occasionally it might be necessary to mention the street or the intersection in the lead if, for example, there might be some confusion about which branch of the bank in a neighborhood was robbed.

This lead from a short item in *The Washington Post* violates three of these rules:

Anthony Brady, 18, of no fixed address, was arrested yesterday and charged with armed robbery of the Safeway store at 3830 Georgia Ave., NW, D.C., police reported.*

Only friends of Anthony Brady, people fascinated by the behavior of 18-year-olds, and patrons of that Safeway store would be likely to read on. In a city as large as Washington, that is not a large percentage of the paper's audience.

Context

News does not occur in a vacuum. Yesterday's news may be related to last week's or last year's (See Chapter 15, Background and Context). In some cases that tie-in is noteworthy enough to include in the lead. It provides the *context* without which the story cannot be properly understood.

A masked man yesterday robbed a Pleasant Grove 7-Eleven of $4,500 in cash and fired a shot at the store manager before fleeing, police said. *It was the fifth robbery of a Dallas 7-Eleven this week.*

Dallas Times Herald

Sometimes the context is the most newsworthy element of a story:

At a time when some employees soon may be required to take time off without pay to help ease Los Angeles County's budget problems, the Board of

* The name in this story has been changed.

Supervisors is considering giving salary bonuses to selected department heads.

Los Angeles Times

On many stories the context or background is not newsworthy enough to earn a place in the lead.

UNACCEPTABLE:

A man on a motorcycle rode up to the drive-in window of the First State Bank in Englewood yesterday, pulled a gun on the teller and rode off with $5,500, according to police. *The First State Bank was last robbed two years ago.*

But on stories that *do* have a significant history, context and background may be needed in the lead to help those readers who have not kept a scrapbook on the story.

UNACCEPTABLE:

A Baltimore widow has died of cancer.

ACCEPTABLE:

A Baltimore widow *who won an out-of-court settlement of an estimated $500,000 from an asbestos manufacturer* has died of cancer *she contended was caused by her exposure to the substance.*

The Associated Press in *The Washington Post*

The Lead's Lead

The way in which a reporter starts a lead often indicates what element of the lead that reporter considers most newsworthy. It is frequently useful for reporters to ask themselves which of the five Ws is most newsworthy in the story and then to begin the lead with that fact.

In many leads, the "what" is most important . . . and comes first:

LOS ANGELES (AP)—*Festivities honoring the Los Angeles Lakers for winning the National Basketball Association championship* were cut short yesterday because of the heat and the crush of a crowd of about 6,000 at a City Hall ceremony.

The New York Times

Many stories are news only because of the important people in them. The predictions on the economy from this UPI story in *The Miami Herald* are of interest only because of the importance of the person making them. The lead begins with the "who":

Budget Director David Stockman said yesterday that high interest rates, high unemployment and large federal deficits are only temporary—part of the "cure, not the problem" of the ailing economy.

An increasing number of stories consider the reason for an action—its "why"—significant enough to emphasize in the lead. The "why" rarely will be explained in the very first couple of words of the lead—

that position is almost always reserved for the "what" and "who." But leads can be formulated to get the "why" right near the top:

President Reagan, *attempting to stem what he called a "hemorrhage of leaks of classified information,"* warned government employees yesterday that he would investigate any further disclosures by "all legal methods."

The Philadelphia Inquirer

The remaining two Ws, "when" and "where," rarely dominate the lead. Of course, there are exceptions, as in that favorite "when" lead on April 15:

Midnight tonight is the deadline for filing federal income tax returns.

In most newspaper stories, when is yesterday. That fact is not newsworthy enough to begin a lead with.

UNACCEPTABLE:

Yesterday, the Pearl River School Board ratified a new two-year contract with the union representing about 40 teaching assistants.

ACCEPTABLE:

The Pearl River School Board *yesterday* ratified a new two-year contract with the union representing about 40 teaching assistants.

The Rockland Journal-News

Points

Some leads make one point:

The chemical disaster in Bhopal, India, has prompted the Environmental Protection Agency to examine the adequacy of its air quality programs, new EPA Administrator Lee Thomas said yesterday.

USA Today

Some leads include two independent but related points, as does this lead on two aspects of the president's thinking on war and peace:

President Reagan said today that "nuclear war cannot be won and must never be fought" but that peace depended on public support for a continuing American military buildup.

The New York Times

And some leads summarize a series of related points—here, the effects of a rainstorm:

Rescue workers in northern California yesterday dug through tons of mud loosed by a violent rainstorm that killed about 25 people, forced the Golden Gate Bridge to close for almost 20 hours and caused an estimated $100 million damage.

Houston Chronicle

How many points should a lead include? The rule, as usual, is the simpler the better . . . the fewer points the better. A lead that makes one point will read better than a lead that makes two. But if more than one element of the story is newsworthy enough, it will be necessary to write a lead that introduces two or more primary themes in a story (see Chapter 14, Organization). Both points the president made on military policy were newsworthy; they both belonged in the lead. The deaths, the closing of that famous bridge and the property damage were also all quite newsworthy and, therefore, all belonged in the lead.

But multiple theme leads should be used only if the extra points are equally newsworthy:

WEAK:
     The Environmental Protection Agency will make reauthorization of the Clean Water Act a priority, and the chemical disaster in Bhopal, India, has prompted the EPA to examine the adequacy of its air quality programs, new EPA Administrator Lee Thomas said yesterday.

A desire to keep the Clean Water Act in effect is newsworthy but not as newsworthy as an evaluation of the adequacy of air quality programs in the wake of the nightmarish disaster at Bhopal.

Label Leads

Too often beginning reporters, fearful of selecting the wrong information for their leads, fall back on a lead that includes no important information at all. Instead of reporting whatever significant actions were taken at a meeting, they begin by merely informing readers that the meeting took place. The leads they produce are called *label leads*. They label an event instead of reporting on it.

UNACCEPTABLE:
     The Los Angeles County Board of Supervisors met yesterday in regular session in the County Building.

The fact that the board met yesterday is not news. The news is what happened at the meeting.

ACCEPTABLE:
     The Los Angeles Board of Supervisors yesterday authorized reopening the Hall of Justice jail to house weekend prisoners.

Los Angeles Times

UNACCEPTABLE:
     John Frankenheimer, the out-of-work Iowa father whose suicide threat created an outpouring of sympathy across the nation, appeared yesterday in U.S. District Court in Minneapolis.

The news is not that this man appeared in court. The news is what happened to him there.

ACCEPTABLE:
     John Frankenheimer, the out-of-work Iowa father whose suicide threat created an outpouring of sympathy across the nation, was indicted yesterday in U.S. District Court in Minneapolis on 18 counts of food stamp fraud.*

The Des Moines Register

The Angle

The decision all reporters must make on what points to include in their leads has an importance that extends beyond the initial paragraph — the story that follows will have to emphasize the same points that are emphasized in the lead. In other words, the lead must be written with the rest of the story in mind; it establishes the story's *angle*.

If the lead talks about an arrest for drunken driving, the story cannot switch and concentrate on the sentencing of the person who was arrested. If the story is going to focus on the sentencing, then the lead must focus on the sentencing.

Reporters sitting down to write a lead must ask themselves: What is the most weighty, emotional or unique aspect of this story? What will readers want to know about it? The lead will establish this angle; the rest of the story will have to follow in the same direction — it will *support* the points made in the lead (See Chapter 14, Organization).

* The name in this story has been changed.

▪ **A** ▪

Rewrite the following leads to make them more effective.

1. Yesterday the City Planning Commission met to consider the fate of Redwood Corp.'s plan to build a new Pathmark supermarket on a site at 345 Jones Road in Albertson. The plan was approved by a vote of 5–2.

2. The wind storms yesterday knocked over power lines causing blackouts in Rosemont, broke branches off trees throughout the area, toppled an oak tree in Fairmont and knocked over some garbage cans. Power was off in Rosemont for six hours before the Rosemont Electric Company was able to restore service to the about 800 affected homes.

3. Maria Ramero, 23, of 154 East Lansing Blvd. in Riverdale, and her daughter, Jessica Ramero, 4, of the same address, were killed when their car collided with a milk truck at 4:13 p.m. at the corner of Wayne and First streets in Riverdale yesterday.

4. Hancock High School met Caldwell High School for the state women's basketball championship yesterday at Caldwell, and Caldwell won in double overtime by a score of 52–50.

5. Mayor Eliot Runsfeld announced yesterday that Highway Commissioner Judith Sand will remain one of his good friends and an important and trusted adviser to his administration, but that she will resign her position in the city government. City Attorney Melvin Battel had announced last week that he is investigating charges that Sand accepted bribes from contractors.

6. Jury Foreman Henry Norton announced yesterday that Lawrence Addison, 28, was guilty of first-degree murder in the shooting deaths last fall of Frieda Krump, 16, Jon Hayworth, 17, and Linda Robbins, 16, all of Berkeley.

7. Gov. William Davis announced yesterday that he will not seek reelection to a second term as governor next year. Davis said he made his decision after discussions with his wife and "long and hard soul searching." "This is a 24-hour-a-day job and it leaves no time for family," the governor said. "I am simply not willing to give up my family life for another four years."

8. About 100 policemen from the state police barracks in nearby Canton under the direction of State Police Capt. Roger Thomas used machine guns and tear gas to regain control of the Danbury State Penitentiary at 3 p.m. yesterday from a group of rioting prisoners who had been demanding improvements in prison conditions.

9. The Nantucket Board of Aldermen voted last night to spend $100 on this year's July 4th children's party, to cancel its next weekly meeting because of the three-day weekend and to fire Police Chief Paul Eddings because of his refusal to enforce the city's ban on topless bathing.

10. Three people were killed in an auto accident yesterday. Their car hit a utility pole at the corner of Dwayne and Broderick roads. The three people were all seniors at Southside High School. They were driving home from a high school football game at Southside.

▪ B ▪

Write hard news leads based on each of the following collections of information. In each case you are writing for a newspaper dated tomorrow and read in the town in which the events occurred.

ONE

1. Santa Barbara County Board of Supervisors met tonight at City Hall, 8 p.m.

2. A memorial minute was read for the late William Hussel, former city attorney, who passed away this week.

3. After discussion, the supervisors voted 5 – 0 to lengthen the hours of operation of all county parks by 15 minutes.

4. Parks will now be open from 7 a.m. to 9:15 p.m.

5. Beach parks, however, will remain on their old hours.

6. County Agricultural Commissioner Graydon Hall made a special report.

7. Hall reported that the gypsy moth had recently been detected in sections of the county.

8. Hall says research he has done suggests the moth could damage, by eating the leaves and ruining their health, thousands of trees in the county.

9. Hall warned that spread of the gypsy moth could threaten the county's million-dollar citrus industry.

10. Hall said only five of the pests had been seen in the county, but that he was afraid they would multiply.

11. This, Hall reported, was the first time the gypsy moth had been seen in this area.

12. Hall said he would investigate aerial spraying alternatives but that nothing had been decided on what to do.

13. This was the first announcement of the sighting of gypsy moths in the county.

TWO

Talked to Newton Fire Chief Thomas Hanlon. He told me: Fire today at Beekman Plaza Hotel, corner of Best and Spring Sts.; detected at 2:05 p.m., under control by 10:15 p.m.; hotel burned to ground; nearly 120 residents forced to evacuate hotel; none of residents dead, 22 residents injured, 12 injuries serious; one fireman killed when hit by falling beam, 3 other firemen injured, two of them seriously; fire started in kitchen; damage estimated at $5 million; Beekman Plaza is town's oldest hotel — built in 1887; dead fireman — George Honan, 43, of 23 Elm St., Newton, father of three, married.

THREE

1. Upton Mayor Jane Rosenquist held news conference today at 3 p.m.

2. Announced she will run for governor.

3. "I am convinced that I can best help the people of this city by working to solve problems on the state level," she said.

4. Quote from Rosenquist exactly three weeks ago: "It would be foolish for me to leave the people of this city behind and run for higher office. I will finish out my term. You have my pledge."

5. Rosenquist asked about her pledge: "I don't want to discuss that. I believe I have explained why I have decided to run."

6. Rosenquist, a Republican, said she will enter Republican primary for governor . . . primary held in June.

FOUR

Sgt. Howard Black of Worchester police provided all info: Robbery and assault; victim Sean O'Casey; location — in front of Fairview Housing Project in Southside section of Worchester; time — app. 9:45 p.m. this evening; all info. on assault Black says is from his own interview with O'Casey; says O'Casey not available to talk to reporters (check at hospital confirms this); O'Casey attacked by four youths as he was exiting house of parishioner; hit in face with chunk of ice thrown by one kid; forced to ground; hit, kicked and scratched by four youths; left bleeding on ground; youths fled with O'Casey's wallet, including credit cards and $38 in cash; O'Casey, a Catholic priest, St. Paul's Church in Southside; was wearing clerical garb; no suspects; Black says he is investigating; third attack this month on member of clergy in Southside (check of newspaper records confirms this); Black refused to discuss why clergy were targets.

FIVE

From a statement released today by the ownership of the Pavillion Restaurant, considered one of the better and more expensive restaurants in Jackson:

"The Pavillion Restaurant, the city's finest eating establishment, has always been known for its fierce commitment to the best quality and freshest ingredients in its food. We want to state today that this commitment remains. We will use nothing but the best in our cooking. We also want to announce, in accordance with our policy of the utmost in concern for our customers, that after receiving a few reports of stomachaches following meals eaten at the Pavillion last Saturday, we investigated and found a batch of garden peas that was rotten. They apparently caused some mild cases of food poisoning. These peas pose no serious health hazard. But in accordance with a request of the city's Department of Public Health, we are making public the problem for the first time today and inviting any customers who experienced discomfort following a meal on Saturday to return for another meal *gratis*."

SIX

1. Construction work has been ongoing at the new Railway Hotel, at the corner of French Street and Conduit Avenue in Ralston for six months.
2. A 200-ft.-tall crane has been used in the construction.
3. The crane toppled over and fell to the pavement on Conduit Avenue at 7 a.m. today.
4. Damage: Serious damage to sidewalk and pavement of Conduit Avenue; two parked cars smashed and seriously damaged; two windows on shops on Conduit Avenue smashed by asphalt loosened by the crane.
5. No people injured, though crane landed within three feet of a group of four construction workers.
6. No explanation yet for what went wrong.
7. Driver of crane uninjured.
8. Crane owned and operated by Axel Construction Company.

SEVEN

According to Dave Humal, owner of the Flicks Theater:

1. The movie "Please Don't" is a romantic comedy.
2. As of today it has now been playing at the Flicks movie theater downtown for 49 consecutive weeks.
3. In the 24 years the Flicks movie theater has been in existence, the longest playing movie had been "Rambo," which played at the theater for 48 consecutive weeks in 1985 and early 1986.
4. That makes "Please Don't" the new record holder at the Flicks.

EIGHT

From a speech today by George Jeffers, a local businessman, running in the Republican primary for Galveston City Council president against incumbent June Ratner: "Councilwoman Ratner is clearly a nice woman. We all like her. But it is just as clear that she has been a poor city council president. I have done some research in the council meeting minutes and I have found that Ratner speaks very little at the meetings, that she plays no leadership role and that she rarely succeeds in convincing other council members to follow her views."

NINE

From an announcement by Bismark Police Chief Andrew Haney today: "As you all know, the city's financial troubles have forced a 15 percent cutback in our uniformed force in the past year. Today I want to announce three measures designed to make better use of our police officers: First, we are going to end the practice of sending one officer each year to the FBI's special training school. Second, we are going to try to shift the burden for filling out the paper work on arrests increasingly to our non-uniformed clerical personnel. And finally, we are going to reduce the number of officers in the department's patrol cars at any one time from two to one. We will now use one-person patrols exclusively, instead of our former two-person patrols. I want to emphasize that none of the changes will affect the number of police patrol cars patroling the city at any one time and, therefore, that they will not affect the safety of our citizens."

TEN

In excavation work for the foundation of the new Twenty-First Century Tower office building at 4th and Sugarmill streets in Park Slope, four unusual items were found, Tara Jenkins, spokeswoman for the Continental Construction Corporation, said in an announcement today. The items were:

1. An Indian Head penny, dated 1896.
2. Three Indian arrowheads, of indeterminate date.
3. A Brooklyn Dodgers baseball memento, from 1951.
4. Five fossils of dinosaur bones.

Jenkins says: "The penny, the arrowheads and the baseball memento have been donated by Continental to the Sugarmill elementary school for use in their historical discussions. The bones have been taken to the American Museum of Natural History in New York City. Steven Studwell, an assistant curator at the Museum, has been here. All the items were found by construction workers within the past two weeks."

Steven Studwell in a telephone interview says: "Yes, I was there yesterday, and we're sure they are dinosaur bones—the first ever found in Ty County. They would be about one million years old. But more exact dating and identification will have to await our tests."

Carol Locazio, of the Coin and Stamp store on 4th Street, in an interview says: "Yes, that coin, an 1896 Indian Head, is probably worth about 25 cents today, depending on what shape it is in."

ELEVEN

Information from Eugene Police Sgt. Jerome Calley:

1. Automobile accident on east bound lane of Fremont Expressway, 200 yards from the Montville Road exit, at 10:32 p.m. this evening.
2. Green Chevrolet pickup truck, driven by Susan Harvey, 53, of 6 South Greenwood Avenue here, apparently spun around and smashed into red Ford Escort driven by Jim Hardwood, 29, of 3 Mill Valley Road here; both vehicles had been heading east on the expressway.
3. Also in Escort was: Hardwood's wife, Alison Hardwood, 26, of same address. Mrs. Hardwood was in her sixth month of pregnancy.
4. Both occupants of Escort were killed in accident. Occupant of pickup injured and taken to Beth Israel Hospital.
5. It had been raining for three hours previous to the accident and we believe

pickup hydro-planed on wet road surface. Both cars going, we estimate, about 60 mph.

Information from Susan George at Beth Israel Hospital:

1. Susan Harvey is in fair condition with a broken shoulder and serious facial cuts.

TWELVE

1. Roberta and Alan Fine of 66 Hotchkins Drive in Harworth reported their son Jerome, 12, missing to police two days ago after he failed to return home from school in the afternoon.
2. Betty and Arthur Angelo of 89 Hotchkins Drive in Harworth had reported their son Sandy, 12—a good friend of Jerome Fine—missing at the same time.
3. Harworth Police Officer Ellen Saunders: "We had the whole force looking for those boys. I guess you could call it a full-scale search."
4. Jerome Fine and Sandy Angelo returned to their homes on their own today— they had been officially missing for two days.
5. Jerome Fine: "We decided we would go camping in the woods. I guess we didn't think about our folks. The camping? It was great, but boy I feel awful."
6. Sandy Angelo: "It was just a little camping trip, that was all. But I guess I see now we should have told somebody."

THIRTEEN

From a statement by East Brook School Board President Walter Schapp: "The science lab and computer facilities at the East Brook High School are simply inadequate for training young men and women who will have to deal with the scientific problems of the 21st century. We simply do not have enough money in our already-overburdened operating budget to upgrade these facilities and, therefore, I am announcing tonight that the School Board at its meeting tonight has voted 5–0 to ask the voters to okay next month a $2.5 million bond issue to fund a total revamping of the High School's science facilities. The money will enable us to build three new science labs, four thoroughly equipped new science classrooms and a state-of-the-art instructional computer center."

FOURTEEN

1. The Shelterbrook town library held its annual Book Fair today.
2. More than 200 people from all over the state attended, including Gov. Doris Elliott.
3. People had a chance to buy the library's excess books and to see a number of special exhibits mounted by the library's staff and educators throughout Shelterbrook.
4. This was the 150th annual Shelterbrook Book Fair.
5. Shelterbrook's is the oldest continuing book fair in the United States.
6. Special exhibits and a birthday cake were there in honor of the big birthday.

FIFTEEN

At a meeting of the Redding Friends of the Parks tonight, the following actions were taken (wording from official transcript):

1. To appoint Stanley Howard acting secretary tonight to take the minutes.
2. To change next month's meeting to an informal coffee-cake session on Sunday morning.
3. To write a letter expressing the RFOTP's extreme concern and dismay on the subject of Redding Mayor E. W. Getty's plan to close Riverside Park.

4. To write a letter praising the Redding Police Department for its "Keep Our Parks Safe" campaign.

5. To raise $150 to restore the softball backstop at East Franklin Field.

SIXTEEN

Firecrackers are a continuing problem in Ardsley . . . According to Harold Marman, police chief, three boys—Alex Hurt, 18, Freddy Dorset, 18, and Samuel Block Jr., 19—were arrested this evening and charged with illegal possession of firecrackers. Marman said: "One of our cars responded to a report that two boys had been injured by firecrackers in front of Flashy's Video Arcade, on South Road. When they arrived they found Hurt suffering a hand injury and Block with injuries to the hand and face. Hurt had burns on the palm and three fingers of his right hand—second degree burns, the hospital said. Block had second degree burns on his right hand and on his right cheek. According to the two boys, a large firecracker, called an 'Ashcan,' they were playing with went off prematurely. Our officers found additional firecrackers on Block, Hurt and on another boy, Dorset. They all are being charged with possessing those firecrackers. Block and Hurt were taken to the hospital. Dorset was booked, then released." According to Susan Alphonse, of St. James Hospital, Hurt and Block are in good condition. Alphonse confirms Marman's description of their burns.

SEVENTEEN

From statement today by Sharon Mayor David Bernard: "We've all been reading these stories in the paper that Fire Commissioner Carl Dean, one of the finest public servants it has been my pleasure to know, slipped up somewhere on his handling of his personal finances, that Carl somehow ended up receiving a consultant's fee from a company that sold equipment to the Fire Department. Now I think those charges are false. I think Carl Dean is innocent. But I know the county prosecutor is looking into the charges. We all read that in the paper yesterday. And just to avoid even the hint of any impropriety while she investigates, I'm going, and Carl agrees with me on this, to suspend Commissioner Dean, without pay, until the investigation into this by the county prosecutor is complete. Assistant Commissioner Jill Davis will run the Fire Department until Carl returns."

EIGHTEEN

1. Fontana Windows President Sylvia Sidney held a press conference today in Shreveport at 11 a.m.

2. "Business has not been good in the past three years," she said.

3. "Fontana has lost a total of $1.8 million in three years," she said.

4. "Clearly we have to cut back somewhere, and I am afraid our cutback is going to have to be here in Shreveport," she said.

5. "As of Monday we will be permanently closing our Shreveport factory," she said.

6. "This will enable us to keep open our two other factories—in Belldown and Green River," she said.

7. "Obviously Shreveport workers will receive full severance benefits in line with their contract," she said.

8. Fontana's factory here in Shreveport employs 108 men and women.

NINETEEN

District Attorney Jake Milborne announced today: "As part of my office's continuing investigation of governmental ethics I have to report that we have found two minor technical violations of the state ethics code here. Mayoral Assistant Gail House failed to disclose a $3,500 loan she received from Reliance State Bank on her financial disclosure form. And city Recreation and Arts Director Doyle Victor failed to disclose earnings of $4,670 in interest and dividends on two investments on his financial disclosure form. We have found no evidence of conflict of interest in either case. We do not intend to prosecute, and both officials have refiled correct forms. But we have made these problems known to Mayor Hildy Brooks, and we are, as is our policy, making them public now."

TWENTY

Wow, was it ever a cold one today! Temps fell to minus four at 4:00 a.m. this a.m. The National Weather Service says that's the third coldest temp ever recorded for this date here . . . temp only hit 8 degrees for a high this afternoon . . . and the city certainly suffered, that's for sure: Parents and children alike suffered from red faces and running noses; kids had to be sent home before lunch from the Hill Street Elementary School and Westside Junior High when heating systems at the schools proved unable to get the places warm enough; and didn't we all have trouble getting those cars and vehicles started? The local AAA reported that today it received more calls for assistance from motorists here than ever before in its history. Yes, cold may be good for polar bears and igloos, but it certainly takes its price on our town!

CHAPTER 9

Soft leads

Justice is, after all, supposed to be blind. On Long Island, however, it has been charged that justice just couldn't keep its eyes open.

It all happened in a Mineola courtroom at a divorce trial. Eyewitnesses say Supreme Court Justice George Krauss fell asleep and snored loudly.*

(New York) *Daily News*

This lead has little in common with the hard news leads discussed in the previous chapter; it teases readers and withholds the most newsworthy facts until the second paragraph. But this lead is undeniably effective. The way it introduces the story of a judge who apparently took a snooze on the bench will certainly catch readers' attention. Written in the more traditional style, the lead would still be interesting but less compelling:

A Supreme Court justice fell asleep and snored loudly during a divorce trial in Mineola yesterday, eyewitnesses reported.

Not all stories begin by hammering home the hard facts. Some reporters rely on a well-turned phrase or ironic twist—a *zinger,* as in that example from the *Daily News*—to hook their readers. Others lure readers into the story with a little tale—an *anecdote*—intended to introduce the story's main theme through an example illustrating that theme. Still others begin by *setting the scene* of the story. And, on those rare occasions when an interview subject says something so striking and to the point that no paraphrase could communicate what the story is about so clearly, reporters may lead with a *quotation.*

All four of these types of leads—the *zinger,* the *anecdote,* the *scene setter* and the *quote*—are *soft leads.* Rather than weighing in immediately with the hard news, soft leads delay, for as little as a sentence or as much as several paragraphs, the delivery of the story's basic facts.

This lighter, more subtle approach to the news is used at the top of many, if not most, timeless stories, or features (See Chapter 26, Features). Some soft leads, particularly zingers, are also used atop news accounts of timely but offbeat events in an effort to make the news livelier.

Hard leads are just one paragraph long. Soft leads may be longer, as much as four or five paragraphs in all. In such cases, soft leads generally end with a paragraph that clarifies what the story is about—that specifies how the turn of phrase, anecdote or description at the top of the piece relates to the general themes of the article. This paragraph is called the *nut graf.* In the two-paragraph soft lead that opened this chapter, the nut graf is the second paragraph—it outlines the basic facts.

Zingers

Some leads grab readers with a snappy or clever phrase, often a play on words:

Charles Williams is going to leave the driving to others. New Year's Eve marked the last day of his

---

* The name in this story has been changed.

25-year, 2.5-million mile, accident-free career as a bus driver with Greyhound lines.

The Indianapolis Star

This line led a news feature on the dearth of blacks in the Mafia:

The Mafia is not an equal opportunity employer.

The Wall Street Journal

Zingers are particularly effective in highlighting the unlikely or seemingly absurd:

The U.S. Postal Service has added something to the snow, rain, sleet and gloom of night that it says will not stay its couriers from their appointed rounds.

It is called nuclear war.

. . . Postal planners went before a House Post Office subcommittee yesterday to outline a 400-page plan for delivering the mail after a holocaust.

The Washington Post News Service

To be effective, these punchy introductions must be kept short.

UNACCEPTABLE:

The U.S. Postal Service has added something to that familiar list of trials and obstacles — snow, rain, sleet and gloom of night — that it says will not stay its hardy and tireless couriers from what are commonly known as their appointed rounds.

In an effort to make the deterrent threat credible, it has introduced a plan for delivering the mail in the event of the unthinkable — nuclear war.

And a zinger must in fact zing, not plop.

UNACCEPTABLE:

The old saying that the grass is always greener on the other side of the fence isn't necessarily true when it comes to utility rates.

The (Portland) *Oregonian*

This is no place for tired or unclear writing.

Anecdotes

Sometimes reporters try to interest readers in an issue by telling the story of one or more people whose experience makes the subject vivid. This dramatic lead to a story on avalanche science conveys just how dangerous avalanches can be:

On a sunny morning in April 1967, Ron Perla found himself on ski patrol perched atop a block of snow, many hundreds of yards wide, that was itself perched above a long, slick ski run.

Suddenly, the snow gave way under his weight touching off an avalanche. Beneath thick blankets of powder, Perla was carried half a mile down the Utah mountain at about 100 miles an hour. He fell unconscious. Rescuers later told Perla they had dug him out of an icy tomb — the fingers of his left hand were all that had shown above the snow piled at the bottom of the slope.

In the years since the spill, Perla has retained a respect for avalanches that borders on awe . . . "The power that soft, white snow can have during an avalanche is just astounding," he said, recalling why he chose to join the small band of men and women who have devoted their careers to avalanche science.

The New York Times

The dictionary defines an anecdote as a short, entertaining account of an event. When these leads get long or dull they are in trouble.

Scene Setters

Good writing communicates the feel of an event. Some leads, called scene setters or descriptive leads, draw readers into a story by painting a picture of where it takes place. This visual image, like the tale in the anecdotal lead, introduces the flavor, if not the substance, of the story that follows:

A red and white sign stands between the parking lot and the main bathing beach at Gateway National Recreation Area on Sandy Hook. Its message, "unprotected beach," is meant as a warning that the sands are unpatrolled. It could just as well be lamenting the beach's plight.

Only a few giant steps are needed to span the distance between the sign and the high-tide mark. Along the narrow beach, tangles of utility cables and uprooted poison ivy, beach plum and bayberry are all that remain of last summer's dunes.

A decade ago the water line was 300 yards away.

The beach at Sandy Hook — along with many others along New Jersey's 137-mile coastline — is vanishing.

The (Bergen County, N.J.) *Record*

These leads may provide an opportunity for creative, colorful writing: "Along the narrow beach, tangles of utility cables and uprooted poison ivy, beach plum and bayberry are all that remain of last summer's dunes." But they shouldn't be used as opportunities for verbosity and affectation. Sometimes leads that set the scene read like parodies:

Emma and Alfred Mitchell are surrounded by broken beer bottles, crumbling cigarette packages and other rubbish. But even when trespassers start grass fires, the couple never complains.

They can't. The Mitchells are buried in Mount Prospect Cemetery, Neptune Township.

Asbury Park (N.J.) *Press*

Quotations

Quotes should only be used as leads when they are short and to the point, and they should only be used in those *rare* instances when the newsmaker has said something that introduces the story better than the reporter can:

> "Real jobs," said Gerald Detoia, with a touch of awe and hope. "They say that they have real jobs in there."
>
> The 20-year-old Detoia has had quite enough in recent months of combing the classifieds, pounding the pavement and trying to track down people said to know people who think a job might open up somewhere. Finally he stood at a door with "real jobs" behind it.
>
> Unfortunately he stood along with hundreds, then thousands of others as word spread fast that Marriott Hotels Inc. was hiring a complete staff for a new hotel next to the Nassau Coliseum.
>
> *The New York Times* News Service in *The Milwaukee Journal*

Too often reporters resort to quote leads when they just can't seem to come up with a lead on their own.

UNACCEPTABLE:

> "Their major concern was whether he had had extensive X-rays or radiation of that type," said an Arizona woman whose husband died of leukemia and who testified yesterday that her community was never warned that fallout from atomic tests in Nevada might create a health hazard.

This is a fine quote. It will be used high in the story (See Chapter 11, Quotations), but it does not get to the essence of the news; it does not belong in the lead.

ACCEPTABLE:

> An Arizona woman whose husband died of leukemia testified yesterday that her community was never warned that fallout from atomic tests in Nevada might create a health hazard.
>
> *Associated Press*

The Angle

Soft leads are not just writing exercises. They have a job to do—the same task performed by a hard news lead. A soft lead, too, must engage readers by highlighting the most newsworthy element, or elements, of a story, and a soft lead must also establish the angle that the story will follow.

If the story is about a daring rescue performed by a man in a wheelchair, it won't do to start with some largely irrelevant reference to why the man happened to be there in the first place.

UNACCEPTABLE:

> Joseph Santos can't say why he decided to go in his wheelchair to the public dock at Bellmore Creek yesterday.
>
> *Newsday* Service in *The Milwaukee Journal*

ACCEPTABLE:

> Joseph Santos was sitting in his wheelchair on the public dock at Bellmore Creek yesterday when he saw 5-year-old Kim Burke topple into the water.

The following anecdotal lead appears to be introducing a story about an interesting arrest.

UNACCEPTABLE:

> A Hull police officer spotted the car at 5:12 p.m., on December 29.
>
> The automobile was heading north on Shore Drive in Hull, travelling at an approximate speed of 10 miles per hour and weaving back and forth across the lanes of the road.
>
> A breathalyzer test showed that the driver's blood-alcohol level was .26. Under Massachusetts law, a driver with a .10 blood-alcohol level is legally drunk. That's about three drinks in an hour's time.
>
> *The Boston Globe*

The story, however, turned out to be about a local judge who, after announcing a crackdown on drunken driving, sentenced the car's driver to a year in jail. The lead here obscures rather than highlights the news.

A reporter's job is to communicate the news. No matter how clever or well written a soft lead is, it is of no value unless it leads the reader directly to that news.

Appropriateness

Soft leads can be used to discuss serious subjects:

> Beginning next month, there's one thing that poor people in El Paso will be able to afford: a divorce.
>
> . . . the El Paso bar will become what is believed to be the first lawyers' group in the nation to require its members to perform community service legal work—specifically, to handle two divorce cases for poor people each year, and to do it for free, officials said.
>
> *Dallas Times Herald*

These leads can also be effective when the news is timely, but of interest more because of its uniqueness or emotion than its impact or weight. The lead that opened this chapter began such a story.

But most editors agree that on fast-breaking and important news stories a soft lead only gets in the way. Florida readers, for example, might have wondered why they were asked to wade through this zinger before getting to the pressing news that a frost was threatening their state's citrus crop and tourist industry:

> The paunchy old men of the L. Street Brownies bath club won't need to test their stamina any more by dipping their toes in the wintry waters of Boston Harbor.
>
> After today, they might as well mug for the camera in Miami.
>
> *The Miami Herald*

There is another consideration in deciding where to use a soft lead: These leads—especially zingers—often employ humor, and there are some stories in which humor simply doesn't fit.

UNACCEPTABLE:
> Students aren't the only ones taking a holiday break this year.
>
> *Omaha World-Herald*

That hardly seems an appropriate way to begin a story about 5,600 temporarily laid-off workers.

Dilly-Dallying

An opening anecdote or description is intended to draw the reader into the story, not to be the story. Too many soft leads meander, testing the patience of readers.

One morning the *Los Angeles Times* kicked off its daily "column one" news feature with six paragraphs crammed with descriptions and details about a suit involving 27 Japanese appliance firms. A reader had to plow through to paragraph seven to confirm that this was a story about the difficulties of providing a jury trial in certain civil cases.

"I don't want to lay down a flat rule, but if you have to drift seven or eight grafs down the page, you begin saying, 'Why am I reading about this?'" concedes *Los Angeles Times* Executive Editor William F. Thomas.

Most editors agree that the nut graf—which pins down exactly what the story is about—should appear by the fourth or fifth paragraph, if not sooner. Anecdotes and descriptions at the top of a story shouldn't be allowed to wander indefinitely.

Control

Some of the constraints of hard news writing are pushed aside when reporters choose a less direct approach to their stories. Soft leads not only allow but demand greater freedom of style. It is this very freedom, however, that makes the writing of soft leads so difficult for many reporters.

Too many writers strain, in the words of William Zinsser, author of *On Writing Well,* "to commit an act of literature." They fuss and fool around and use words and phrases they do not know how to control. The results can be woeful, as in the sentence from *The (Paterson, N.J.) News* that was first discussed in Chapter 1, Meanings. It was used to lead a story about a baby abandoned a week before the New Year:

> While most people were preparing to ring out the old, someone rang out the new this week . . .

The solution, as usual, is simplicity. Many of the examples of acceptable soft leads quoted in this chapter are colorful and creative, but none employ great poetry or spectacular prose. These leads are clear and simple. They use words the writer could control and they are dedicated to the news, not to literature.

Additional Readings

"Jell-O Journalism: Reporters Are Going Soft in Their Leads," Gerald Lanson and Mitchell Stephens, *Washington Journalism Review,* April 1982.

"Plotting the First Graph: Why Hard-Boiled Leads Aren't Necessarily Good Leads," Roy Peter Clark, *Washington Journalism Review,* October 1982.

▪ A ▪

Rewrite the following soft leads to make them more effective.

ONE

"Boy, I just really can't believe this day is reality," said Charles Riggins. "I feel really lucky about having this chance."

A brisk breeze nipped at the sails of the S.S. Pinafore as Riggins and his son, Arthur, hauled up the anchor. She was a fine boat, 37 feet in length with a full-scale cabin sleeping eight below. There even was the most modern of kitchens, complete with food grinder, and a gas toilet to eliminate unpleasant odors that could cut appetite. Built in 1957 and reoutfitted last year, she showed none of the wear of her years at sea — a lucky thing, since the Riggins had 3,000 miles of ocean before them before reaching land again.

As a child, the older Riggins, 61, had begun to form his dream of following the route the Pilgrims took to this country more than 350 years ago. Now, after four months of preparation and 36 years as a pharmacist, he and his son were ready to begin.

TWO

No sunlight leaked into the room. The curtains were drawn and a dark green material covered the walls. Alex Victor was dressed in a maroon pullover sweater, as he sat alone at the square wooden table. The soft light left half his face in shadow. Victor opened the match by sliding a finely detailed white Queen pawn two spaces forward on the black and white checkered board. The clock was pushed, giving his opponent, Hans Astor, one hour to move.

Astor, a tall man with thinning hair, never moved. He wasn't there. Astor had refused to play the game, for the state championship, unless he were paid an additional $2,000 for expenses. He wasn't.

When the big hand on the timing clock returned to the twelve, the game was declared over, and Victor had won his first state championship. No state championship match had ever been so short — one move.

THREE

Hospital food. How he hated hospital food. But the nurse brought another tray and Jim Peller, a 9-year-old cancer patient at Elmwood Hospital, ate some of it all the same.

Yes, the food at the hospital is hardly great, but today Peller had something to look forward to. A group of performers from the Midwest Circus was scheduled to give a performance in his room.

And, sure enough, at 2 p.m., right on time, the show started. A clown with orange hair, a huge purple nose and baggy red pants was the first to arrive in Peller's room. He was juggling four pink balls as he strolled in and stood at the foot of Peller's bed.

Two more clowns came into the room soon, along with a magician who made three tongue depressors and a thermometer disappear. Finally an animal trainer with three trained poodles came in, and the poodles walked on their hind legs all around Peller's yellow hospital room — number 253 in Elmwood.

The benefit performance — which lasted an hour and a half — was arranged by Davorah McNelly, manager of the circus, after she heard from hospital administrators that Peller was a circus fan and felt badly that he couldn't attend the show.

FOUR

First, sometime in December, the shiny, lightweight aluminum pots began to come out of the dishwasher with a faint, bluish-like film on them. That, recalls Irene Berg, thinking back to where it all started, was the first sign of the troubles that went on to plague her day in and day out ever since.

For the Bergs, a family of four who had lived 12 years at 43 Selmon Way, things would only get worse. Next, a sweet odor, not unlike the ether that used to be used as an anesthetic in hospitals, emanated from their water pipes, wrinkling their noses.

The health inspector would not sample the water until he had been badgered by the Bergs for weeks. Then he sampled only for bacteria. The tests came back negative. Still, things didn't seem right. By March, Irene was finding herself the victim of searing, pounding headaches several days a week. Her younger daughter, Alissa, 12, a seventh-grader at Armonk High School, complained of dizziness and missed 12 days of school. Her husband, Robert, lost his appetite, she says, looking back.

Now, Irene Berg knows why. She feels vindicated but is scared. The city released the results of more far-reaching tests yesterday and the news wasn't good. The Bergs found their well contains the highest level of industrial solvent ever found in the state in drinking water.

FIVE

When Oscar Martin turned 5, his parents bought the beat-up, rickety and un-painted piano that still sits on the porch of their house on Sickles Lane. Oscar took to it immediately, crying when his mother told him it was time for bed. Within 24 hours, the tow-headed little boy, still in kindergarten, had picked out the melody of "Yankee Doodle," his favorite song.

As the years went by, Oscar began to study formally with Olivia Bartow, the music teacher at the grammar school. But if Beethoven, Bach and Brahms filled his lessons, beebop and boogie-woogie filled his spare time.

Even so, Oscar went off to college to study medicine. He lasted six months before the lure of his band, the "Martinettes," a six-member jazz ensemble, pulled him back. Within five years he'd progressed from the bars of Lincoln, Nebraska, to the Queens Court in Buckingham Palace.

"I guess Oscar had a bug for music from the age he was in diapers," recalls his father, Handley Martin. "Even his crying was musical."

Oscar Martin returned to the two-story white house with blue trim on Sickles Lane yesterday for his first visit in five years. Later, as 400 neighbors gathered around the bandstand in Van Dyke Park, he gave a benefit concert for the hospital auxiliary. And no one could miss the symbolism of the opening number of the now 32-year-old internationally renowned jazz musician. It was an old favorite with a new twist — Impressionistic Arrangement of Yankee Doodle in E Flat.

▪ **B** ▪

Write soft leads for stories based on the following collections of information. In each case you are writing for a newspaper dated tomorrow and read in the town where the events occurred.

ONE

1. Emilia Staunton Grant celebrated her 95th birthday today at the Elmira Gardens, a nursing home at 397 Orient Ave., in Mansfield.

2. She was joined by six children, two of whom had come from out of state, 13 of her 15 grandchildren and six great-grandchildren.

3. Among her gifts was a cake, three feet in diameter with 95 candles. She blew them out with the help of an 86-year-old friend.

4. "If someone had told me I'd live to be 95 about 50 years ago, I'd have thought it was the Devil talking," she said. "Then I'd learned to take it one day at a time. Maybe that's why I'm still around."

5. Fifty-one years ago, Mrs. Grant was told she had a rare form of liver cancer. Doctors operated but still told her she would be lucky to live two years. Six months later, without explanation, the disease went into remission.

6. Mrs. Grant's first husband, Alexander Grant, died in 1961 of a heart attack. She remarried at the age of 73 but separated from her second husband, Peter Randle, a year later on the grounds of incompatibility.

7. "Emilia Grant takes life in her own hands," said Gerald Poldin, a nurse at the home. "She is one spunky lady."

8. Mrs. Grant served as president of the school board from 1948 to 1960. She taught high school English for 28 years after her youngest child entered school.

TWO

1. Dominic Zaretti drives a taxi for the Golden Medallion Co. in Hamilton.

2. Every Friday afternoon before he gets off work, he stops for coffee at Sam & Louis's luncheonette and buys a $1 state lottery ticket on the way out, Zaretti said.

3. The state lottery helps raise money for education. Eighty percent of the weekly take goes to whomever picks the correct six numbers between 1 and 40. The other 20 percent goes to the state. If more than one person chooses the right combination of six numbers, the prize is split.

4. Last Friday when Zaretti bought his lottery ticket, no one had bought the right number in three weeks. The state lottery pool had risen to $8 million.

5. Zaretti said he was sitting at the counter filling out his lottery card when the waitress came up. Her name is Patricia Augusta, and Zaretti said he has known her for six years but only by her first name, "Pat." Sometimes he said he's shared his dreams with her of starting a restaurant if he wins the lottery.

6. Last Friday was Pat's birthday, Zaretti said. She told him to put down the month and day of her birthday as two of the numbers on his card and the four numbers on his cab license as the other four.

7. Today Zaretti became the largest lottery winner in state history. He will receive $400,000 a year for the next 20 years or $8 million.

8. "Without Pat, I'd still be hawking fares," he said. "The first thing I plan to do is quit. The second is to open a restaurant and the third will be to make Pat manager. Oh yes, I'm giving her a $10,000 tip next time I stop by for coffee. That's the least I could do."

9. Zaretti is 46, divorced, and lives in a one-bedroom apartment in a two-family house in town.

THREE

1. Many Americans associate the fashion of nude and topless bathing with the stylish beaches of southern France.
2. Nude bathing isn't prohibited on French beaches.
3. Louis Hammond conducted a poll among 1,235 French adults over age 18 to get their views on nude bathing. The poll was conducted last month between the 13th and 19th of the month.
4. The poll was a random sample with a 5 percent margin of error, fairly typical for a poll.
5. In answer to the question, "Have you or would you ever bathe nude on a public beach?" 83 percent said "no," 12 percent "yes" and 5 percent, "don't know."
6. In answer to the question, "Would you be offended if others bathed nude on a public beach?" the answers were "no," 27 percent, "yes," 64 percent, and "don't know," 9 percent.

FOUR

1. This afternoon, Parker Bros., the manufacturer of the popular board game Monopoly, sponsored the first Monopoly Tournament ever in Vineland.
2. Contest took place at the Holiday Inn on West End Avenue.
3. Match began at 10 a.m. and lasted until 5 p.m. There were four 90-minute games in which players were eliminated.
4. Winner is Nancy Rafferty, a graphic designer. Her brother, Paul, also played. Nancy is 27; Paul 29. Paul is a pilot with Eastern Airlines.
5. At the end of the final game, Nancy had $24,000 in Monopoly money stacked in front of her and owned most hotel chains on the board.
6. "I wish I could use some of this to pay my real rent," she says. "Or I'd use it to buy a ticket to Paris and eat on the banks of the Seine. Or maybe I'd just buy the Playboy Club in Atlantic City and turn it into the Playgirl Club. Complete with guys walking around in hotpants and muscle T-shirts."
7. "I suspect there's some kind of graft going on here," said Paul, joking. "Nancy has never won a family Monopoly game in her life. We've been playing since we were 10 and she always loses. Who loaded the dice?"
8. Twenty-five contestants began the tournament. Nancy is now eligible to enter the state Monopoly contest next month at the capitol. The grand prize? A week's paid vacation to Atlantic City.
9. The object of Monopoly, of course, is to become the wealthiest player by accumulating property. Nancy said she latched onto Park Place and Boardwalk early in the game and had the good luck of building hotels on both just before three people landed on them. Boardwalk and Park Place are the most expensive properties on the board.
10. "I've always had expensive tastes," said Miss Rafferty, who wore blue jeans and a Monopoly T-shirt to the tournament.

FIVE

1. Temperatures have been in the 90s in Louisville all week. Today they are supposed to break 100. It will be seven straight days of temperatures over 90, a record.
2. Sun rose at 6:03 a.m. today. At that time, temperature was 82 degrees.
3. Air thick and moist on 8:15 a.m. bus downtown. The air conditioner is broken and the bus, a No. 9 bus going from Elton Plaza to Main Street is standing room only.

4. Ella Lewis is a passenger. She's a heavyset woman in her 50s. Sweat drips from her forehead. She pulls out a large red handkerchief and mops her brow. Her cotton blouse sticks to her stomach and is soaked under the arms. "I've always liked saunas," she says. "But they're always followed by a cold shower and a cool drink. I'm about ready to take my clothes off and run through town screaming." She declines to give her address or age.

5. Gene Patrick, 28, of 147 Ferguson Boulevard, also on that bus: "They always say there's two sure things, death and taxes. There's really a third. That's that the bus won't have air-conditioning on the hottest day of the year." Patrick is wearing yellow shorts, a blue polo shirt and sandals. He's carrying a leather briefcase and says he is a lawyer. He's also licking a raspberry popsicle. "It's like guerrilla war; you've got to adjust. I began eating these instead of cereal on Tuesday. At least your mouth stays cool. I'm not sure my partners are thrilled with my dress but my clients haven't exactly been wearing wool suits either."
He works for Kassen, Bartley and Miller.

SIX

Two months ago. Call came in to the Shippenberg police station. Baby abandoned on steps of St. Mary's Church, Franklin Street. Police sent Officer Michael Shipmann, 36, to investigate.

"I couldn't believe anyone would just abandon a child like that," he says today. "But there she was, just perched on the step."

Baby girl, two weeks old, taken to Holy Name Hospital. Treated for exposure. Released to an adoption agency.

Shipmann and wife, Helen, 34, had no children. Filed to take in child as foster child along with 15 couples who read of incident in the paper. Agency, the Gladwin Home for Parents and Children, chose the Shipmanns.

No one ever claims the child. Today, the agency called the Shipmanns and tells them they can adopt the child, who they've named Martha. "This is the greatest day in my life," Shipmann says. "We had talked about adoption before but couldn't face the agencies, the waiting, the uncertainty. With Martha, the last two months have been wonderful and scary. Wonderful because we love her. Scary because there was always that fear someone would come back. Now that can't happen."

Talking in the living room of their home at 6 Parker Circle. Martha, 13 pounds, sits on knee in yellow footie pajamas. Coos from time to time. "I've never been a very religious person," Helen says. "But some things seem like providence. It's hard to remember all the free time we had and hard to imagine how we could have filled it."

Shipmanns given permission to adopt today. Tomorrow will go to Surrogate Court to file preliminary papers.

SEVEN

Bruce Ridley, 26, and his wife Kim, 27, moved into their new home at 66 Barkley Way, Hillcrest. Moved today. Interview with Mr. Ridley: "It was incredible. I went to the attic to check the roof and there on the beam I could just make out that someone had carved the name Hiram J. Ridley. I called the local Historical Society and sure enough my father's grandfather had built this house in 1889."

EIGHT

Tornado ripped up three trailers at Hunt's Corner this morning. Empty except for one. Alice Korn was baking bread in her kitchen. Miss Korn is 24 and works nights as a nurse at Hopkins Medical Center. That's where she woke up at 3 p.m. but she was in a hospital bed. You interview her at the hospital.

"It's a miracle really. Right out of Wizard of Oz. That's all I could think of, that and that I wondered how I would die. It was about 9:30 in the morning. The sky got black, absolutely black. The clouds were enormous and low and black. And then this funnel starts coming down, couldn't have been five miles away. It was monstrous, maybe a half mile wide. I ran out of the trailer and I was headed toward the gulley when I just was swept off my feet. Then I was in the cloud with everything swirling by and the ground passing below like in an airplane. A mattress went by and I just wanted to lay on it and go to sleep. Next thing I knew I woke up here. They told me a farmer found me lying in a cow pasture. Amazingly I didn't break anything. I sure feel like I went 15 rounds in a heavyweight fight though. I can't describe it really. I lost my home. I lost everything I own. I'm bruised and black and blue, but I feel real calm. I feel like I've gotten a second chance when I really shouldn't be here at all."

At Hunt's Corner everything is devastated. Miss Korn's trailer, which she'd been in minutes before the tornado hit, is bent around a tree in the shape of a V 50 yards from its foundation. The field Miss Korn landed in is 225 yards to the northeast. She apparently was thrown out of the funnel as it bounced off a hill.

NINE

From interview with Green River Mayor Kenneth Denton today: "How many years have I been on this job now? Two. Well, I'll tell you something. I don't like it. I've had a lot of jobs in my life . . . been working for 36 years now . . . but I've never had a job as bad as this. There's tension and pressure from the moment I wake up in the morning to, you know, the moment I finally — and believe me it takes a while these days — fall asleep. I got to worry about whether taxes will go up, who should be fired, who hired, whether the police are doing their job, why that old lady was mugged downtown, whether the schools need more money, whether, you know, the Memorial Day parade should be on Sunday or Monday this year, whether the homeless need another shelter. On and on the worries go, and what do I get for doing, well, my level best to untangle all these problems? I get grief, that's what I get. I get grief from my fellow Republicans and grief from the Democrats, and grief from officials and grief from ordinary citizens. You know, I hear more complaints and nastiness in one day nowadays than I heard in a year in my other jobs. I walk down the street, and people must say to themselves, 'Hey, there's the mayor; let's toss him some grief.' Great job, huh? I hate it!"

TEN

1. Police officers Darrel Hanson and Jill Platt arrived on scene at 3:46 p.m.

2. Hanson: "A crowd of, oh, I'd say 12 people had gathered around the tree. They were all looking up, so when we arrived we looked up, too. It was the damnedest sight. A white dog with black spots. I'm something of a dog lover myself. Looked to me like part fox terrier, part cocker spaniel. Got no idea how it got there."

3. Platt: "We were called by a Susan Hersh; the tree was in front of her house. That's 1613 Willowbridge Road in Rosewood. She said she's never seen the dog before. It wasn't wearing a tag. So we had no way of identifying it. It was perched about a third of the way out on a thick branch about ten feet off the ground. Darrel was able to start climbing up the tree. He began calling to the dog. Called it 'Checker.' He tried to calm it and get a reading on whether it would bite. He let Checker sniff his hand, then gently grabbed the dog. Lowered it down to me."

4. Hanson: "None of the people there had any idea what the dog was doing up in the tree. I can't believe it could have climbed up by itself. Maybe some kids put it up there as a prank. The dog is going to the pound. Nice dog. Could use a good home."

PART THREE

Stories

CHAPTER 10

Attribution

A 27-year-old man was arrested on Christmas Eve in South Carolina *on charges of* fatally shooting a Port Authority police officer Monday.

The suspect, George Redoux, of Elizabeth, N.J., was arrested at his brother-in-law's apartment in a housing project in Simpsonville, 10 miles from Greenville, *according to Detective Steven Harris of the Greenville Police Department.*

Detective Harris said Redoux, who *was described* as "armed and dangerous" in a multi-state alarm, surrendered without resistance as police cars converged on the housing project at 7 p.m. Authorities had been alerted to Redoux's presence by an anonymous caller, *the detectives said* . . .

The Hudson County Prosecutor, Fred Zimmer, said that several witnesses had viewed a photograph of Redoux in New Jersey and had "positively identified" him as the gunman.*

The New York Times

A few days after this story appeared, George Redoux was released and all charges against him were dropped. The police admitted that they had arrested the wrong man. Yet *The New York Times* reporter who wrote the story could look back on it without embarrassment.

The story never says that Redoux had fatally shot the police officer, only that he was arrested on charges of fatally shooting him . . . which was true. The story does not say that Redoux was armed and dangerous, only that he was described in an alarm as being "armed and dangerous" . . . which was true. The story never says that witnesses had positively identified Redoux, only that a prosecutor said Redoux had been "positively identified" . . . and the prosecutor did say that.

This story was carefully written. All potentially questionable or controversial information was properly *attributed*—the source of the information was identified. The circumstances of the arrest were *attributed* to a detective who participated in the arrest. The evidence allegedly implicating Redoux was *attributed* to the county prosecutor. (*The Times,* of course, did publicize the fact that all charges against Redoux were dropped.)

Here are some additional examples of attribution:

Jimmy Daniels, a 7th grader at Sadler Junior High School, was dead at the scene with a bullet wound to the head, *said Detective Robert Medley.***

Tulsa (Okla.) World

The Reagan Administration's decision this week to withdraw proposed new federal bilingual education rules may have symbolic importance but is not expected to have much immediate effect, *according to experts in the field.*

Los Angeles Times

Press Secretary Beverly Hubble said Grassley is to be treated for a tightening of muscles in his lower esophagus that interferes with the passage of food.

The Des Moines (Iowa) Register

---

* The names in this story have been changed.

** The names in this story have been changed.

When to Attribute

In any story all the facts have a source. Some come from officials or witnesses, some come from records or documents, some come from reference sources. It would be possible to place attribution in every sentence in a story. But attributing every fact in a story would make the story almost unreadable.

UNACCEPTABLE:
The 1912 sinking of the Titanic took 1,517 lives, *according to an encyclopedia.*

The number of deaths on the Titanic, mentioned in a story on the death of more than 800 people on an Indonesian ship, is independently verifiable. There is no question or controversy about that number. The attribution adds nothing to the story.

ACCEPTABLE:
The 1912 sinking of the Titanic took 1,517 lives.
                                    Associated Press

More often than not, however, information does have to be attributed. Here's why and when:

Opinion

Two people watching a basketball game would undoubtedly agree on which team had won. The final score, since it is independently verifiable, would not have to be attributed to the official scorer or the press information officer for one of the teams. But two people watching a presidential debate might very well reach different conclusions about who had won. Those conclusions would be subjective — opinions; they would require attribution. A reporter, guarding a reputation as an unbiased observer (See Chapter 6, Objectivity), must attribute any opinions, any subjective comments, that appear in a news story.

UNACCEPTABLE:
The city should not ask for a federal license to build the dam and all studies should be stopped at once.

ACCEPTABLE:
The city should not ask for a federal license to build the dam and all studies should be stopped at once, *the utility said.*
                                    The Seattle Times

UNACCEPTABLE:
Brzezinski expressed concern over the nostalgic desire of some Republicans for military superiority.

ACCEPTABLE:
Brzezinski expressed concern over *what he described as* the nostalgic desire of some Republicans for military superiority.
                                    The New York Times

Informing Readers

All of us trust some people more than others. Thorough identification of the sources of potentially controversial information in a story allows the reader to judge whether that information is believable.

UNACCEPTABLE:
President Carter was lying throughout the Great Debate last night.

Says who? For readers to judge the credibility of this charge they need to know who said it; they need attribution. The story appeared in the *New York Post,* and this sentence was attributed to "an expert on detecting lies." Later in the story readers learn that that expert is "vice president of the International School of Polygraph Science." That information certainly helps. Now we are in a position to begin judging the value of this statement about the debate.

However, the *Post* neglected to include an additional piece of information in its attribution that would have helped readers even more: This expert was also a Republican candidate for the state assembly and, therefore, no friend of Jimmy Carter. Readers deserve complete identification of the sources to whom potentially controversial information is attributed.

Attribution also informs readers of the scope of the reporting that has been done to produce the story. If a reporter covering a rent strike by tenants has talked only with the landlord and the building's employees, that will show in the attribution, and the story will be revealed as potentially biased and underreported.

Protecting Newsmakers

People in the news are subject to countless charges and attacks. Politicians are denounced. Judges are accused of bias. Coaches have their intelligence questioned. Suspects are formally charged with crimes. Reporters should never just spread nasty rumors or pick up charges repeated on the street (See Appendix D, Law). But some charges should be reported — particularly formal criminal charges. When any such controversial statement appears in the newspaper, it must be carefully attributed.

UNACCEPTABLE:
President Abolhassan Bani-Sadr backs counter-revolutionary groups and is out of touch with Iranian society.

ACCEPTABLE:
The Islamic Republican Party accused President Abolhassan Bani-Sadr of backing counter-revolutionary groups and of being out of touch with Iranian society.
                                    Reuters

The need to use attribution to protect newsmakers becomes crucial when they are charged with crimes. Until the judicial system has had its say, there are no criminals, just suspects. No one can be identified as having committed a crime; only allegations of someone's potentially criminal behavior can be reported.

UNACCEPTABLE:
Andrew Fell was arrested after he slashed a shopkeeper with his pocket knife in a dispute over egg prices.

ACCEPTABLE:
Andrew Fell was arrested, *police said,* after he slashed a shopkeeper with his pocket knife in a dispute over egg prices.

Should the caveat "innocent until proven guilty" slip your mind, remember George Redoux . . . accused of a crime he did not commit.

UNACCEPTABLE:
A 27-year-old man was arrested on Christmas Eve in South Carolina for fatally shooting a Port Authority police officer Monday.

To protect Redoux's rights here it is necessary to make clear that he is merely *being charged* with this crime. Technically this is not attribution — no source is indicated — but it does the same job.

ACCEPTABLE:
A 27-year-old man was arrested on Christmas Eve in South Carolina *on charges of* fatally shooting a Port Authority police officer Monday.

The New York Times

Protecting the Writer

Reporters are responsible for their decisions on whom to quote in a story (See Chapter 11, Quotations). But if a reporter has selected credible sources, that reporter certainly is not expected to stand behind every point those sources make. One purpose of attribution is to make clear that this is the newsmaker's point of view, not the reporter's. If the reporter has attributed a snide comment on the ethics of suburbanites to the mayor, the angry letters can go to the mayor, not the reporter.

UNACCEPTABLE:
The evening socializing is beginning to take its toll. Some legislators are less efficient this year because they aren't getting enough sleep.

ACCEPTABLE:
The evening socializing is beginning to take its toll, *according to state Rep. Walter Conlon.* Some legislators are less efficient this year, *he said,* because they aren't getting enough sleep.

The Des Moines (Iowa) *Register*

The writer of this story in the *San Francisco Chronicle* has chosen to stand behind a rather strong claim made by a dentist:

A Beverly Hills dentist described in San Francisco yesterday his *vastly improved* version of invisible dental braces — attached not to the front but to the back of the teeth.

It is prudent to leave such claims to the newsmakers:

. . . *what he called* his vastly improved version . . .

Adding Credibility

Reporters borrow expertise on the subjects they are covering from their sources. Attribution assures readers that these experts stand behind the information presented in the news.

WEAK:
The neutron warheads are designed to destroy attacking Soviet tanks by sickening and killing their crews with shafts of intense radiation.

BETTER:
The neutron warheads, *according to military specialists,* are designed to destroy attacking Soviet tanks by sickening and killing their crews with shafts of intense radiation.

St. Louis Post-Dispatch

A reporter's credibility is always suspect when announcing someone else's state of mind. So statements about a newsmaker's thoughts, hopes or emotions should be attributed.

UNACCEPTABLE:
Thompson hoped to deliver his message later today.

ACCEPTABLE:
Thompson said he hoped to deliver his message later today.

St. Louis Post-Dispatch

Guidelines

The use of attribution often seems to confuse beginning reporters. Perhaps this is because the rules of attribution are applied more strictly in journalism than in most other forms of communication.

Here are some additional guidelines intended to take the confusion out of this subject:

Overattribution

While too little attribution can leave a story vague and subjective, too much attribution can make it seem sluggish and amateurish. As mentioned above, facts that are not subject to interpretation and that can be verified independently should not be attributed. For example, it is not necessary to attribute the fact that Chicago is on Lake Michigan to an atlas.

While information connecting a suspect to a crime must be verified, some facts about that potential crime can be established and do not require attribution.

UNACCEPTABLE:
The victim allegedly died.

A person's death is independently verifiable. Facts that can be verified independently can be reported without attribution, if the reporter has done the verification.

Similarly, if the reporter was there to witness the event, attribution would rarely be necessary.

UNACCEPTABLE:
According to witnesses including this reporter, the former hostages and members of their families in the audience applauded his remarks.

ACCEPTABLE:
The former hostages and members of their families in the audience applauded his remarks.

The Seattle Times

The amount of verification reporters demand for a fact before they will use it without attribution should depend on the degree of controversy involved. Applause is not generally a matter of controversy. But in discussing a crime committed in that audience, reporters would not want to rely on their casual observations of what happened.

ACCEPTABLE:
Police said two persons were wounded by shots fired in the audience.

For matters of record—such as criminal charges—reporters will rely on officials they trust. Information on specific criminal charges will appear, without attribution, based on the report of a trusted police official:

He was charged with armed robbery.

A cautionary note, however: Some facts that seem non-controversial and independently verifiable may be less solid than they appear. For example, the official who tells a reporter how many people were killed in a train wreck two hours ago may not have the final figures. Death counts have a way of changing. In the story the figure should be carefully attributed to that official. A week later in a follow-up article, after all the wreckage has been searched and the seriously ill treated, it will be safe to print the number dead in that crash without attributing it to an official. By then that statistic will be part of the verifiable public record.

All questionable or controversial facts in a story need attribution. But one attribution per fact is sufficient.

UNACCEPTABLE:
Sgt. Murphy said Walker *allegedly* ran away from the scene.

ACCEPTABLE:
Sgt. Murphy said Walker ran away from the scene.

UNACCEPTABLE:
Reagan announced he is *reportedly* abolishing the council on wage and price stability.

ACCEPTABLE:
Reagan announced he is abolishing the council on wage and price stability.

The Chattanooga (Tenn.) *Times*

Indirect Attribution

Rather than continually repeating phrases such as *according to . . .* or *. . . police said,* reporters occasionally use shorthand expression to indicate attribution.

The victim *was identified* as Burton Feroe.

Was identified here is shorthand for *was identified by police* or other officials. This *indirect attribution* saves words, yet still makes clear the fact that the identification was not simply made by the reporter. The identification of a body is not independently verifiable, but it is generally not controversial. It is safe to use indirect attribution here.

Many forms of indirect attribution use the passive voice (See Chapter 4, Sentence Structure): *was reported, was scheduled, was listed in satisfactory condition.* Because they do not clearly identify the source of the information, these wordings should be reserved for noncontroversial information for which the source can be inferred.

Perhaps the most common examples of indirect attribution are adverbs such as *allegedly, reportedly* or *apparently.* These words do not do the job that standard forms of attribution do because they do not identify the source of the allegation or report. "He *allegedly* shot him," does not protect the suspect as effectively as: "*Police said* he shot him."

WEAK:
Gompertz *allegedly* walked off with the money.

BETTER:
According to police, Gompertz walked off with the money.

Allegedly should be used in a sentence in place of attribution only if previous sentences make clear exactly who is responsible for the allegation:

According to police, Gompertz robbed the store. He then *allegedly* walked off with the money.

Reportedly and *apparently* are even weaker words and are the least effective forms of attribution. They should not be used in discussion of something as controversial as potentially criminal behavior.

UNACCEPTABLE:
According to police, Gompertz robbed the store. He then *reportedly* walked off with the money.

One final note on al*leg*edly: The word derives from the same Latin root as *leg*al. It should be reserved for potentially criminal matters and not used for more frivolous charges.

UNACCEPTABLE:
He *allegedly* does not like chocolate.

Placement of Attribution

Attribution can be placed at the beginning of a sentence:

According to police, he was in the building at the time of the murder.

In the middle:

He was in the building, *according to police,* at the time of the murder.

Or at the end:

He was in the building at the time of the murder, *according to police.*

Attribution carries the most weight at the beginning of a sentence because the reader then knows who is responsible for the information before reading the information. So when the source is as important as the information itself, the attribution should come first.

WEAK:
Not all crimes require police to shoot a fleeing suspect, *according to Police Chief Joseph G. McAtee.*

BETTER:
Police Chief Joseph G. McAtee said yesterday that not all crimes require police to shoot a fleeing suspect.

The Indianapolis Star

Attribution is also placed at the beginning of a sentence to alert readers when the reporter is switching sources (See Chapter 11, Quotations). Attribution is held until the end of the sentence in the *lead,* unless, again, the source is as important as the information. Otherwise placement of attribution is just a matter of style. It's wise to vary it to keep a story from sounding stilted.

■ A ■

Edit the following sentences where necessary to improve their use of attribution.

1. He was arrested for shooting her.

2. Police said they were told he was allegedly seen leaving the building.

3. Cole attacked his opponent, Mary Simmons, in a speech before the Chamber of Commerce. Simmons is a free-spender. She has no concept of the value of the taxpayers' money.

4. The police arrived and determined that Grimes had been drinking.

5. Officials of the state Agriculture Department discussed the threat posed by the fruit fly with reporters. That tiny bug could cripple the entire state's produce industry.

6. Anthea Jones died, according to Mercy Hospital Spokesman Pete Kaplan.

7. The candidate then outlined plans for the most effective campaign this city has ever seen.

8. Police said Montoya left the store 20 minutes later. He apparently was carrying some stolen purses and wallets.

9. The state's economy will improve sharply next year, according to the governor.

10. The victim, Randall Peters, allegedly had stab wounds all over his body.

11. Police had no suspects.

12. Increasing labor costs are a serious problem in this area. The Coalition for a Stronger Economy presented a plan yesterday that, if approved by local governments, would help alleviate that problem.

13. According to the council secretary Robert Paxton, the council approved the park plan by a vote of 9–1.

14. Police said Menkin hit the other car after running a red light. Menkin then ran south on Orchard Street with police in pursuit.

15. The victim was identified as Michael Brewer of 13 Old Mill Lane.

16. The worst accident in the United States involving a commercial airliner occurred in 1972 when 357 people were killed in a midair crash, according to FAA records.

17. The mayor said his opponent had a history of waffling on the issues. He alleged that Olson had changed his position on a tax increase three times.

18. The three burn victims were listed in critical condition, according to a hospital spokesman.

19. The president said he supported covert aid to the Nicaraguan rebels because the country has fallen into the hands of leftists who intend to spread their revolutionary ideals elsewhere.

20. Zevin met with the press at midnight and discussed the tremendous impact on the campaign his opponent's arrest for drunken driving will have.

▪ **B** ▪

No attribution is included in the following stories, but the source for the information in each paragraph is listed to the left of the paragraph. Edit the stories, rewriting where necessary, so that they include proper attribution.

ONE

1. Police Officer Jane Shaw and arrest record

A 72-year-old man has been arrested and charged with robbing a shoe store in East Milford.

2. Officer Shaw

Eliot Anderson, a retired construction worker, entered the store, Jake's Shoes at 42 Milford Ave., at 2 p.m. yesterday, pulled out a knife and demanded that the store's owner, Jake O'Brien, hand over all the money in the cash register.

3. Jake O'Brien

"He looked like a nice old man, but then I saw the knife." O'Brien gave the man approximately $550, and then the robber hurried out of the store.

4. Officer Shaw

O'Brien quickly called police and gave them a description of the robber. Officer Jane Shaw spotted Anderson, who fit O'Brien's description, walking south on Milford Avenue. He was carrying a four-inch knife and had $550 in his pocket.

5. Officer Shaw and arrest record

Anderson, who lives at 28 Forest St. in East Milford, was charged with robbery and released after posting $2,000 bail.

TWO

1. Report of local Environmental Commission released yesterday

The city is allowing too much development of low-lying areas, a practice that could lead to serious flooding.

2. The report

In the past year, nearly 70 acres of swampy land along Conshohocken Brook have been developed, raising the water table.

3. Articles in your paper two weeks ago

Two weeks ago, residents of Holly Court, which is about a half mile downstream from the newly completed Shady Grove condominiums, complained that the construction had flooded their basements and yards.

4. The report

Further construction in low-lying areas, such as the land near Conshohocken Brook, could raise water tables even more. If water tables go up, there will be more flooding, serious flooding.

5. Commission Chairwoman Gladys Sternhell

"The Planning Board has approved a half dozen applications for new construction without even setting stringent drainage requirements. We urge the council to review these applications more carefully."

6. Planning Board Chairman Johannes Pizetsner, in response

"Every town has its do gooders and I guess they have their place. But this town needs more taxable property. It has one of the highest tax bases in the county."

7. Report on city finances provided two months ago by the City Council when it passed the budget

A homeowner currently pays $2,750 in city and school taxes on a home valued at $95,000, the average for the community.

8. City planning maps

Nearly 300 acres of city land remains undeveloped because of drainage problems. Most of it is along Conshohocken Brook.

THREE

1. Report of the state Assembly Appropriations Committee released today

The housing inspection program run by the state cannot insure the safety of tenants.

2. The report

The current system of spot inspections of rental properties leaves most apartments "uninspected and unprotected."

3. Five committee members from both parties and a copy of Engoron's speech

The report was written by the Assembly Appropriations Committee after a speech by Assemblywoman Annie Engoron expressed concern over state housing inspection policy.

4. Statement by Engoron, who is on the committee, yesterday

"The state Housing Department is pro-landlord and is not really concerned with protecting tenants."

5. Statement by Dick Fried, spokesman for the department, yesterday

The Housing Department is still studying the committee's report, and will have no comment on it at this time. "But the charge that the department is pro-landlord is absurd."

6. Old newspaper stories in the paper's library

When the Housing Department's budget was cut by $150,000 last year, the department was forced to lay off 35 of its 124 inspectors and to switch from regular periodic inspections of apartments to irregular spot inspections.

7. The report

There are not enough inspectors in the field to maintain contact with all the state's rental properties. Landlords know they are no longer being watched that closely.

8. Transcripts printed in the report

The committee heard testimony from a number of tenants who complained their landlords seemed much less concerned with upholding standards in their buildings. Some complained of days without heat and hot water.

9. Transcript printed in the report

State Housing Commissioner Jake Wolf denied the tenants' charges in testimony before the committee. He told the committee that through more efficient procedures his reduced staff of inspectors is able to monitor housing at least as well as in the past.

10. Statement by Engoron confirmed by committee secretary

Assemblywoman Engoron has introduced a bill to increase funding for the Housing Department by $200,000 next year and to require yearly inspections of all rental property in the state.

▪ C ▪

Edit the following story to improve its use of attribution.

Brian McAuliffe, a chief inspector for the state's Industrial Control Board, said yesterday that the board has fined Serpico Chemical Co. $5,000 for failing to maintain air pollution-control equipment and for installing other equipment without permit.

McAuliffe said yesterday that his inspectors allegedly found during a visit to the chemical plant last September that some pollution-control devices "had just literally rusted away." The inspectors, McAuliffe said, also found that the firm, located on State Highway 7 and Tuckerton Road, according to town maps, had installed or moved more than 40 pieces of equipment without obtaining state permits required for a change in operation.

Serpico President Allen Turner would not comment on the fine, which, lawyers for the state and company said, was negotiated by the attorney-general's office and company lawyers.

Deputy Attorney General John Gregson said that under an order signed by the company, the state would return 80 percent of the fine if Serpico installs new pollution equipment by March 1.

Anthony Armani, a senior environmental specialist with the Industrial Control Board, said that the company already has applied for permits for some new equipment.

McAuliffe and Armani said they did not know which of Serpico Chemical Co.'s processes had been operating without pollution-control equipment.

According to President Turner, the Industrial Control Board and records filed with the federal Environmental Protection Agency, Serpico manufactures about two dozen chemicals used in plastics. Nearby residents have complained for years about a sickeningly sweet odor that emanates from the plant on some days, old newspaper articles show. McAuliffe said the firm would be installing additional odor-control equipment.

CHAPTER 11

Quotations

"It's kind of sad to think of Pluto as a Teamster."

That was the reaction of a visitor to Walt Disney World when she was asked about a vote by the park's employees, some of whom portray cartoon characters, to join a union. The Associated Press reporter who had sought the visitor's opinion must have known he had gotten a good quote. It expressed a personal viewpoint, and it did so colorfully. It helped bring the story to life.

Thousands of miles away another AP reporter got this quote from a businessman worried about "undesirables" in town. "If we could get rid of the dirtbags and dopers, we'd be okay," the businessman said. Again, this comment, nakedly subjective, helped bring the emotions behind the news to life.

Much of the news is about the actions, ideas, achievements, travails and emotions of people. Often the best way of conveying people's thoughts and experiences is through their exact words. Quotes usually provide the spice and sometimes some of the substance of the news. Reporters listen as keenly for the original, vivid or funny remark—the "good quote" —as students listen for hints about what's going to be on a final exam.

Direct Quotes

Direct quotes—quotes at least a sentence long— should be used when many of a speaker's exact words

bear repeating. Sentences tend to be quotable when they fit into one of the following categories:

Colorful Statements

A colonial officer, William Prescott, ordered his troops at Bunker Hill during the Revolutionary War to withhold their gunfire until the British troops could be seen clearly. Paraphrased, that is not a particularly interesting command. But the power of Prescott's language, in this direct quote, has kept his command alive for centuries:

"Don't fire until you see the whites of their eyes."

A more recent United Press International story included the remarks a British explorer made upon returning from a 14-month trip around the poles and seeing his wife. Here the wry humor of his simple language made a direct quotation worthwhile:

"How do you do? Are you my wife?"

Nothing the reporter could have composed could have captured the scene better.

Subjective Comments

Restrained by the rules of objectivity (See Chapter 6, Objectivity), reporters must leave the expression of opinions to those they are interviewing. Those opinions, and the passions behind them, are communicated best in those people's own words.

This direct quote was from a mother who was ejected from a restaurant for breast-feeding her baby in public:

"You wouldn't want to eat your dinner in the restroom. Why should my baby have to?"

Associated Press in the (New York) *Daily News*

And this statement was made by a 71-year-old artist who journeyed from Florida to Washington, D.C., to protest the president's budget cuts:

"Our Social Security is down to $420 a month. Our food stamps were cut to $13 a month. I decided I was going to Washington on my broomstick to tell that man off."

The Washington Post

There is no more powerful way of presenting this woman's case or of explaining her motivation.

The quote at the beginning of this chapter that it was "kind of sad to think of Pluto as a Teamster" obviously represented an opinion. Teamster members and supporters might find it "kind of nice."

Eyewitness Reports

Eyewitnesses were there the moment it happened. You weren't. Readers will want the drama of their eyewitness recollections to enliven your more composed reconstructions.

Here, a policeman injured in a gun battle is talking:

"I was in the doorway. We were firing directly at each other. There wasn't time to think about being nervous. He was trying to kill us."

(Chicago) *Sun-Times*

Expert Knowledge

If someone knows more about a subject than the reporter does, it's often most convincing to let them talk directly to the reader for a sentence or two. Tennis star Tracy Austin has more credibility than the reporter would have in explaining why she had difficulty defeating another player, Kelly Henry:

"Kelly doesn't hit the ball hard. She's a retriever. I should have cut the ball off her lobs and been more aggressive."

The Philadelphia Inquirer

Important Statements

The views of some people—the president, the mayor, the House majority leader, the head of a striking union—are so important that readers deserve to know exactly what they have to say about some of the issues that come before them. Government leaders in the United States and the Soviet Union shaped their statements with great care immediately following the death of Leonid Brezhnev. Their words deserved airing rather than characterization or summary:

"It is in this spirit of seriousness and hope that we have come to Moscow," [Vice President] Bush said. "We have come to declare to the Soviet leaders, to the Soviet people and to the world that the United States is devoted to the pursuit of peace and a reduction of global tensions."

The New York Times

Partial Quotes

When reporters choose to quote just a word, a phrase or a fragment of a newsmaker's sentence, they are using a *partial quote:*

The surgeon general of the United States, C. Everett Koop, said today that there was *"very solid"* evidence that non-smokers had suffered lung disease from exposure to cigarette smoke.

The New York Times

There are three situations in which these partial quotes make sense:

Weak Sentences

Newsmakers cannot always be counted on to come up with a useable sentence. Sometimes only part of a sentence is worth quoting.

UNACCEPTABLE:
"It's a little something else, I guess I'd say, to have so much cheap politicking in so many expensive commercials."

In a case like this, the best option is to select only the compelling words, if there are any, to use as a partial quote.

ACCEPTABLE:
The candidate complained of what he called "so much cheap politicking in so many expensive commercials."

Key Words

Readers don't need to read the exact wording of an investigator's detailed description of the circumstances of a robbery. The reporter can paraphrase those circumstances, with attribution, more effectively. But the potentially controversial charge that the crime was committed by someone working at the place that was robbed is worth expressing in the investigator's own words:

In what investigators termed *"an inside job,"* two men, one posing as a maintenance man, entered the cashier's office in the building . . . taped the mouth, arms and feet of part-time cashier Barbara Summers and took the money from an open safe, police said.

The Philadelphia Inquirer

When a few key words deserve highlighting, a partial quote is called for.

Leads

In a news lead, there rarely is room for a direct quote. If the newsmaker's own words are newsworthy enough for the top of the story (See Chapter 8, Hard Leads), it is generally necessary to pull out just the most important phrase or two.

LONDON — President Reagan, addressing members of the British Parliament in London's majestic Westminster Palace, yesterday proposed that the United States and other democracies pursue a plan of countering Soviet principles that he said he hopes would *"leave Marxism-Leninism in the ash-heap of history."*

Los Angeles Times

Partial quotes should never be used to cover sloppy note taking. It won't do to substitute a sentence spotted with partial quotes for the direct quote the reporter didn't quite get. Except in the lead, a good direct quote is usually more effective than a paraphrase sprinkled with partial quotes.

WEAK:
Jim Clark's ability to "recognize defeat" is in question, Sen. Thomas V. "Mike" Miller Jr. said. He charged that Miller "can't count votes."

BETTER:
"Jim Clark doesn't have the ability to recognize defeat," said Sen. Thomas V. "Mike" Miller Jr. "He can't count votes."

The (Baltimore) Sun

Paraphrasing

Quotes, despite their effectiveness, can't be allowed to take over a story. Most of the story can be better conveyed by paraphrasing, by communicating the newsmaker's ideas through the reporter's own more succinct, more direct sentences. Journalists are paid in large part because of their ability to write. Is it surprising that they can often write better than the people who interest them can talk?

UNACCEPTABLE:
"We followed the perpetrator to the building which he lived in and began a stake out of the premises," explained Sgt. Rudolph Gomez. "After a four-hour wait he came out again and we apprehended him and brought him back to the station house."

There's nothing compelling in Gomez's words here. The reporter should paraphrase.

ACCEPTABLE:
The suspect was arrested after a four-hour stakeout of his home, Sgt. Rudolph Gomez said.

Paraphrasing should be used anytime the reporter can say it better than the newsmaker. Flat, dull quotes are worse than no quotes at all.

UNACCEPTABLE:
"I think it's a good idea," said Councilman Steve Robertson. "I'm voting for it."

ACCEPTABLE:
Councilman Steve Robertson said he would vote for the proposal.

Complex explanations are, generally, also best paraphrased:

For the first time in 12 years, the enrollment in the Milwaukee Public Schools went up this month, Lee R. McMurrin, superintendent of schools, said yesterday.

McMurrin said the enrollment on Sept. 17, the day the official enrollment is taken statewide, was 87,402, about 1,400 more than had been expected and about 100 more than last year.

The Milwaukee Journal

But if the quote is vivid or poignant, forget the paraphrase. Let the speaker talk:

UNACCEPTABLE:
White said there were many noisy and bold drug dealers and she could watch them hide their drugs in nearby bushes and trees.

ACCEPTABLE:
"It was a jungle, a three-ring circus," White declared. "They were so bold and so noisy. We'd watch them hide their dope in our bushes and trees, and they'd look at you to let you know they saw you."

Los Angeles Times

Form

In the body of a story, quotes generally are more effective when they lead off a paragraph, with the attribution *after* the first sentence of the quote. The quote is livelier than the attribution; it deserves to go first. This quote is from an Iowa crop duster who walked away from the crash of his light aircraft:

WEAK:
He said: "This is a heckuva way to start a day. I must be getting better, must be doing something right because the last time I tangled with a power line in 1976 I broke my hip and my arm . . ."

BETTER:

"This is a heckuva way to start a day," he said. "I must be getting better, must be doing something right because the last time I tangled with a power line in 1976 I broke my hip and my arm . . ."

The Des Moines (Iowa) *Register*

The attribution should come *before* the quote when the person speaking is more important than what the person is saying and when some fact about the speaker must be explained at the start:

The mayor refused to answer the charge directly, but he did have this comment: "Somehow this issue always seems to rise to the surface during an election year."

Attribution also should come first when it is necessary to show that another person is now speaking.

UNACCEPTABLE:

"We certainly don't want all the parents sending their kids to school in fear," said William Hayes, who was running the meeting in the absence of the board president.

"And we don't want to send our kids to school out of the district either," said Lemmo.

(New York) *Saratogian-Tri-County News*

This wording could confuse readers. It reads, at first, as if the second quote is also from Hayes.

ACCEPTABLE:

"We certainly don't want all the parents sending their kids to school in fear," said William Hayes, who was running the meeting in the absence of the board president.

Added Lemmo: "And we don't want to send our kids to school out of the district either."

In a quotation more than a sentence long, attribution is needed only once in each paragraph and is usually found at the end of the first sentence.

UNACCEPTABLE:

"I'll be frank with you," he told the lawyers. "I don't think that's going to happen," he continued.

ACCEPTABLE:

"I'll be frank with you," he told the lawyers. "I don't think that's going to happen."

In many but not all cases, additional paragraphs in a long running quote are reattributed to the speaker. Each distinct time a person is quoted in a story, the quote requires its own attribution.

A note on capitalization: The first word of any *direct quote* should be capitalized, whether it comes *before* the attribution:

"*A* live power line is an emergency," he said. "A dead power line is not. A live power line dances and sparks. It's easy to detect the difference."

St. Petersburg (Fla.) *Times*

Or *after* the attribution:

He said, "*A* live power line is an emergency . . ."

The first word of a *partial quote* in the middle of a sentence (unless it's a proper noun), however, is lower case:

Former Gov. Edwin W. Edwards charged that he had made "sweetheart deals" with two campaign supporters for state contracts.

The (New Orleans) *Times-Picayune*

Length

WEAK:

"We could have gone anywhere in the United States but we chose to come to Bluefield," Gary Harrison, vice president of Flowers Industries, . . . said yesterday. "We could have gone to Bristol [Va.], Ashland [Ky.] or to Charleston, but we decided to come to Bluefield. There were two or three different reasons we did so. The trade area is good. We have an opportunity to sell baked goods here. And the manpower is here."

Bluefield (W. Va.) *Daily Telegraph*

This reporter seemed not to know where to start or end the quote. Quotes should rarely run more than a few sentences. The writer's job is to select the sentences that make the point most effectively. In this case, four sentences from Harrison could have done the job.

BETTER:

"We could have gone anywhere in the United States but we chose to come to Bluefield," Gary Harrison, vice president of Flowers Industries, said yesterday. "The trade area is good. We have an opportunity to sell baked goods here. And the manpower is here."

Choruses

A quote should never be attributed to more than one person — unless the people interviewed managed to answer in unison like a Greek chorus.

UNACCEPTABLE:
"The time has come for the government to stop ignoring the elderly," the protesters argued.

ACCEPTABLE:
"The time has come for the government to stop ignoring the problems of the elderly," one protester argued. Many of her fellow demonstrators said they agreed.

Dishonest Quotes

When readers see words in quotation marks they have a right to expect that they are reading the exact words of the person to whom the quote is attributed — not a paraphrase, an approximation or a fabrication.

Quotes should never be invented, or *piped.* Always avoid the temptation to create a fictitious and anonymous taxi driver to say what you think someone should have said about an event. Such dissembling poses a profound threat to the credibility of journalism.

If a reporter fails to catch the exact words of a quote, it is also dishonest to try to recreate what the reporter recalls the newsmaker was saying. Readers deserve quotes, not guesses.

Movie ads occasionally have been known to quote the lone positive comment from a review while ignoring the mass of slaps and digs that surround it. Such practices certainly have no place in news reporting. Reporters must always be sure that quotes not only were taken verbatim, but that they are true to the overall meaning and context of the speaker's remarks.

If a member of the planning commission said this: "The new highway would simply create too many environmental problems for the city, though we see the highway's economic value," it would be unfair to quote only: "We see the highway's economic value."

Reporters should apply the highest standards of honesty and fairness in reporting others' words.

Editing Quotes

Most editors would agree, however, that reporters can make some minor changes in the quotes they use, *as long as the meaning and tone of the quote remain true to that used by the speaker.*

It is acceptable to correct a minor grammatical error in a quote. "The commission has to do *their* job" can become "The commission has to do *its* job." But more significant changes in wording must be placed in brackets within the quotation to indicate that those were *not* the speaker's words:

"I think the nursing care [at LaRabida] was more than reasonable," said Jacobsen.

Chicago Tribune

It is also acceptable, even advisable, to remove, without notice, the meaningless throwaway phrases with which some of us punctuate our conversations: "*Well,* it was, *you know,* one of the most frightening and sickening experiences I ever had." More significant deletions from a sentence used as a direct quote should be indicated by using three dots: "It was one of the most frightening . . . experiences I ever had."

Minor editing of quotes must be practiced evenhandedly, or not at all. The reporter who corrects the minor grammatical errors in the quotes of one candidate but leaves the embarrassing little fluffs in those of his opponent is practicing a type of bias.

Responsibility for Quotes

It is your article. You must remain in control of it no matter who else is being quoted.

Reporters are not responsible for the opinions expressed in the quotes they choose, but they are responsible for the decision on which opinions to present. Their selection must be informative and fair (See Chapter 6, Objectivity).

Similarly, reporters — though they won't be totally satisfied with the wording of all the quotes they use — must be responsible for their clarity and relevance.

"But that's exactly what she said!" is not an acceptable explanation for why a confusing or misleading quote was used. She may have said it, but it was the reporter who decided to use it. Quotes either must be used in such a way that they make sense or not used at all.

The use of quotation marks is no excuse for sloppy journalism.

▪ **A** ▪

Rewrite each of the following passages to make them more effective. Use either a paraphrase, a partial quote or a direct quote. The sentences would each be part of longer stories.

1. The governor's press secretary, Shana Haloran: "The governor will not be commenting on the prison strike until 2 p.m. tomorrow, when he will have something to say on it."

2. Mayor John Ahern: "Well, c'mon now. You know, it's been 14 years since we've had a tax revaluation. I've thought it over enough; that's for damn sure. I decided we had waited long enough, okay?"

3. Police Officer Sheila Aurora: "We have picked up one suspect in the case — a white, 23-year-old male by the name of Conrad O'Leary, who was seen leaving the building. He has been booked and charged with homicide in the case."

4. Principal Gregory James: "Ah, students, students. Yeah, a flagpole sitter. No, no. No decision has been made on disciplining him yet, but very, very scary watching. I can tell you that."

5. Joanne Page, president of striking Sewers Union Local 45: "I just hope those bosses in there have got the message by now because I can't tell how tired I am of repeating it. I mean, we've stuck by our guns from the beginning of this thing, right? I'd say our reluctance to go back is a mile deep and a mile wide."

6. Coach Red Bernard: "Well, I'll sketch it out a little for you if you'd like. You see we had the other end, Gene Bronowski, running a fly pattern, and we thought the quarterback he could get the ball to him deep. But he saw Miller open in the flat. Do you see how surprised I was?"

7. Truck driver Amos Enders: "Yeah, I was right behind them when they crashed. I've never seen anything like it. Frightening? When I saw them hit my heart skipped two beats; I'll tell you. No, I don't know what caused it. I'm not gonna guess for you. I can't believe anyone got out of those cars alive."

8. Fire Chief Elma Sanborn: "Our trucks arrived on the scene at 11 p.m. We had the fire under control by 1 a.m. But those were a tough two hours."

9. Dancer Al Hawkins: "Look, they can arrest me every day. They can come and stop my show every day, and twice on Sunday. They can walk right in here anytime they want. But I'm going to get on that stage. I'm going to take my clothes off. I'll do my act in jail if necessary."

10. Meat Packers Association President Janet Glazer: "Yes, looking for a convention site, our organization is. Yes, we've been around a lot in the search; all over, really. Yes, your town's Show of Shows Center, too! Yes, that's the snazziest one I've seen, all right."

▪ B ▪

Rewrite the information in each of the inserts in the following stories so that it can be used effectively at that place in the story. Use direct quotes, partial quotes or paraphrases.

ONE

The Rev. James Wilcox was appointed to fill an interim seat on the Lampley Town Council yesterday, making him the first black to serve on the council in the town's 147-year history.

The appointment, made by Mayor Hodding V. Martin, filled a seat left vacant by Councilman Rafer Anderson, who resigned two weeks ago for family reasons. Wilcox's term will run until November, when he will be eligible to seek reelection.

Insert:

Gerald Havermale, 45, Town Council member for 12 years, owns Havermale's Hardware Store at 656 Market Square. "I was real pleased about Wilcox's appointment. Reverend Wilcox is a close personal friend. I've known the guy for many years, ever since he became minister of our church. We've served on several committees together. He's, well, a very intelligent man, and there aren't many who have his knowledge of Lampley matters. I think he'll have no problem at all getting reelected in November. He'll add an active, knowledgeable voice to the Lampley Town Council. Frankly, I have problems working with some of those guys, but I'm sure Wilcox and I will get along just fine."

Wilcox, 47, is the senior pastor of the First Congregational Church at 91 DePew Terrace. He has chaired the town's Task Force for Education and has served on many civic committees. He is married and has two sons, 13 and 11.

TWO

A two-ton crane lifting girders on top of a downtown bank building crashed onto the roof of the building yesterday afternoon, knocking loose pieces of brick and granite that then plummeted five stories onto South Avenue, battering cars, smashing store windows and snarling traffic.

The shower of stones caused an estimated $70,000 in damage. Nine cars were hit by the falling bricks and stones, and three store windows were shattered. A half-dozen pedestrians suffered minor injuries, police said.

The 140-foot crane hit the roof of the Midland Bank on 45 Cooper St. at about 3 p.m. Pieces of the wall around the roof, where the crane hit and came to a rest, fell to the street, sending pedestrians scurrying for cover and backing up traffic on downtown streets for several hours.

Insert:

Glenna Fox, 26, clerk in the city government building across the street: "I was on my way back from my lunch hour. Suddenly I heard a loud crash and everybody began running every which way. It was incredible. I said to myself, 'Oh, boy. I'm Chicken Little come alive.' The sky may not have actually been falling but an awful lot was coming out of it."

Emergency workers treated five people at the scene for cuts caused by flying glass. One man sprained his ankle while rushing for cover, police said.

Insert:

Anna Zirps, 56, owns and runs Joey's delicatessen two doors down from Haynes Bank. She was cut by glass from the shattered front window of the deli. "I was just standing here, you know, serving customers and what not and then all of a sudden there's people screaming outside and stones bouncin' off cars. Then I heard a crash and my right shoulder felt like it had run into a cactus tree. I'm okay really, but the salami and fruit salad are a mess. Can you imagine? What a strange afternoon."

The cause of the accident is being investigated, according to a spokesman for Martel Industries, the firm supervising construction of a workroom on the roof of the five-story building. The crane had passed a safety inspection only two weeks ago, the spokesman said.

Insert:

Hugh Evans, 46, of 16 Baylor St., a burly redhead who stands 6 feet 2 inches tall and weighs 210 pounds, was part of the four-man construction crew working on the roof. "I don't know what caused it. Beats me. We were just loading a bunch of girders, something we do every day, and, all of a sudden, the crane tilted and started to wobble. Then it fell. The operator jumped out just in time."

THREE

More than 300 Newport State College students crowded into the waiting area at McNee County Airport last night to cheer the return of sprinter Evonne Simpson after her record-breaking performance at the National College Games.

Earlier in the day Ms. Simpson had run the 100-meter dash in 10.24 seconds, the fastest time ever by a woman collegiate athlete, at the meet in Philadelphia.

Insert:

Crowd of students, dressed mostly in blue jeans and button-down shirts, waved banners and yelled as Ms. Simpson and her coach, Hilda Baum, walked through the door into the waiting room from the runway. Crowd yelled in unison: "We want Evonne! We want Evonne."

Insert:

Ms. Simpson, 20-years-old, a sophomore at Newport State. She is 5-foot-8, weighs 118 pounds, has brown eyes, and is wearing a red and white Newport State sweatsuit. She enters the waiting room and raises her right hand, curled into a fist, into the air, and shouts, "All right! All right!" She hugs several apparent friends in the crowd. While in the waiting room she says: "I am just so thankful for all the support and encouragement that all the students at Newport State have given me. This isn't just my record, it's their record, too, in a sense. It's funny to think back, but I almost didn't come to school here. I originally was interested in going to a bigger school, but the scholarship here just was too good. I certainly don't have any regrets now. I'll tell you something else: I thought I'd never be as happy again as I was after I ran that race, but the way I feel after this welcome here comes pretty close."

The race began at 1:30 p.m. at Franklin Field in calm, clear weather. Ms. Simpson broke first from the starting blocks and led throughout, beating her nearest challenger, Bernice Duvall of UCLA, by nearly two meters. Ms. Simpson's time broke the former record, held by Betsy Meghan of the University of Kentucky, by five-hundredths of a second.

Insert:

Coach Hilda Baum, 31-years-old, a graduate of Newport in 1978 and former state champion in the 100- and 200-meter dashes, says after arriving in the waiting room: "Wonderful! Wonderful! Just wonderful to see such a crowd of fans and supporters gathered here at the airport. You know, it's been a real boost to Evonne throughout her career here to have so much interest in track and field on campus. You know, I've thought this over carefully; Evonne is the most gifted athlete we've ever had at this school, and what is more amazing, you know, is that she works far harder than athletes with far less talent. This is no fluke; it was just a matter of time before she got the record."

A ragged motorcade of students' cars escorted Ms. Simpson from the airport to the campus, honking their horns along the way.

She was greeted at the main gate of the campus by still more students and Newport State President Lauren Sethkins.

Insert:

Dr. Sethkins, 43-years-old, in her fifth year as president, says: "I watched the race on television and it was great, incredible. I must admit I'm quite a sports fan, and particularly a fan of Simpson's. I don't know if you're aware that she's not only a great runner, but a great young woman. And what a turnout we've had to welcome her. Well, in my five years here I've never seen this campus more spirited. I mean, this will be remembered as one of Newport State's finest days."

CHAPTER 12

Mechanics

A look through any newsroom in the hours before deadline time will inevitably turn up a few reporters with eyes upturned, as if searching for inspiration in the ceiling. No one who attempts to turn events into words can completely escape these moments of perplexity. This book is dedicated to reducing, at least, the number of questions it is necessary to ask the ceiling.

The basic mechanics for constructing a news story, for example, should not have to be reinvented each time a reporter faces an empty piece of paper or computer screen. This chapter presents some guidelines for two important elements of those mechanics — paragraphing and the use of transitions.

Paragraphs

The paragraphs used in newspaper journalism are shorter than those used in most other types of writing. Often newspaper paragraphs are just a sentence long; rarely do they go on for more than a few sentences.

Each paragraph, or *graf,* usually should contain only one idea: A new thought, a new person talking, and it is time to start a new graf.

Notice how the paragraphs are divided at the beginning of this historic story:

WASHINGTON, D.C. — Richard Milhous Nixon, the 37th president of the United States, announced last night that he had given up his long and arduous fight to remain in office and would resign, effective at noon today.

Gerald Rudolph Ford, whom Nixon nominated for vice president last Oct. 12, will be sworn in tomorrow at the same hour as the 38th president, to serve out the 895 days remaining in Nixon's second term.

Less than two years after his landslide re-election victory, Nixon, in a conciliatory address on national television, said that he was leaving not with a sense of bitterness but with a hope that his departure would start a "process of healing that is so desperately needed in America."

The New York Times

Newspaper paragraphs are kept so short for three reasons: Short grafs make it easier for busy readers to follow what's happening; they make it easier for editors to add, delete and rearrange information; and they help break up the mass of "gray" print crammed in the narrow columns used by many papers.

But paragraphs can certainly be too short. Every sentence does not deserve a graf of its own.

WEAK:
Shortly after noon, Ronald L. Ziegler, the president's confidant and press secretary, his face saddened and weary, appeared in the crowded White House press room and announced that the president would go on national television tonight to address the American people.

As with most previous such announcements, he did not say what the president would talk about.

Two sentences on the same thought, such as these two, should be combined into one graf. But any change in idea, occasion, outlook or person commands a change of paragraph.

UNACCEPTABLE:

At 11 a.m. today, as crowds for the third day gathered along Pennsylvania Avenue outside the White House, President Nixon summoned Ford to his Oval Office and officially informed him that he would submit his resignation tomorrow to the secretary of state, as provided by federal law, and that Ford would become president. Shortly after noon, Ronald L. Ziegler, the president's confidant and press secretary, his face saddened and weary, appeared in the crowded White House press room and announced that the president would go on national radio and television tonight to address the American people. As with most previous announcements, he did not say what the president would talk about.

ACCEPTABLE:

At 11 a.m. today, as crowds for the third day gathered along Pennsylvania Avenue outside the White House, President Nixon summoned Ford to his Oval Office and officially informed him that he would submit his resignation tomorrow to the secretary of state, as provided by federal law, and that Ford would become president.

Shortly after noon, Ronald L. Ziegler, the president's confidant and press secretary, his face saddened and weary, appeared in the crowded White House press room and announced that the president would go on national radio and television tonight to address the American people. As with most previous announcements, he did not say what the president would talk about.

The New York Times

Paragraphing should not be difficult once beginning reporters learn to accept the idea that a graf can end after a sentence or two.

Transitions

Here are two consecutive paragraphs from a *Los Angeles Times* story:

Continuing his attacks on gang graffiti, City Attorney Ira Reiner yesterday announced a plan for Los Angeles business leaders to pay for paint and other materials to clean up messages left by street gang members.

The Los Angeles County Board of Supervisors voted to continue funding for a separate anti-gang program, the $1.3-million Community Youth Gang Services Project.

These two paragraphs, making two separate points, seem to fit together poorly. There is no flow. The solution? The *Times* reporters who wrote the story solved the problem by adding one word: *meanwhile.* That word, placed at the start of the second paragraph eased the switch from thought to thought.

Meanwhile is an example of a transitional word. Without such words, which serve to ease sometimes abrupt shifts from idea to idea, many stories would be choppy and confusing. The *Los Angeles Times* re-

porters used three other transitional words at the beginning of paragraphs in that story — *while, although* and *but.* These words, and others like them, help stories flow.

Logical Connections

All transitional words work by emphasizing a relationship between thoughts. Some underline a logical connection between ideas, as does this introduction to a paragraph in *The Philadelphia Inquirer* that followed a discussion of a complex strike:

As a result of the labor differences . . .

These transitions also call attention to such direct connections:

therefore	so
consequently	because

Time Connections

Some transitions point to a relationship in time. Here are three examples from a different *Los Angeles Times* article:

At the time, the government announced that Israeli forces had been ordered in . . .

Meanwhile, Zev Schiff, the military correspondent of the newspaper Haaretz, reported . . .

Before the government's earlier decision . . .

And some other time transitions:

while	over the years
at the same time	since
concurrently	following
then	later
the previous day	afterward

Place Connections

Other transitions point to relationships in location. It may be a direct relationship:

in the same building	nearby
also in Washington	across the street

Or the transitional word may simply indicate to the reader that the location has switched by mentioning the new location:

on Capitol Hill
in Beirut

Contrasts

Among the most commonly used transitions are those that indicate contrast between ideas:

Administration officials said yesterday that U.S. Marines will leave Lebanon when the Lebanese government decides it has the situation well in hand . . .

But the administration was sending conflicting signals about the length of the mission.

The (Baltimore) *Sun*

Other such words include:

however	in contrast
nevertheless	on the other hand
nonetheless	still
notwithstanding	despite

Additions

A final group of transitional words indicates that the reader is about to get more:

The grand jury . . . was scheduled to adjourn this week . . .

Another grand jury will be sworn in next week . . .

The Washington Post

Other examples are:

also	in another development
in addition	besides
and	moreover

Natural Connections

Some transitions work smoothly without transitional words because the wording refers back to something mentioned in the previous paragraph:

Rockefeller . . . discussed the organization's programs at a luncheon *meeting* of the Women's Forum . . .

The meeting was the fourth of a series of "Newsleader" luncheons held by the Women's Forum . . .

The New York Times

No transitional words are needed when paragraphs can be made to fit this snugly.

UNACCEPTABLE:

Rockefeller . . . discussed the organization's programs at a luncheon meeting of the Women's Forum . . .

The meeting, *in addition,* was the fourth of a series of "Newsleader" luncheons held by the Women's Forum.

Pitfalls

Transitional words have their own special meanings and must be used with the same care as any other tools in the language.

UNACCEPTABLE:

While he was tired, he still finished the task in three hours.

ACCEPTABLE:

Although he was tired, he finished the task in three hours.

UNACCEPTABLE:

She received the award for the fourth time. *However,* three other winners were named.

ACCEPTABLE:

She received the award for the fourth time. Three other winners were named *as well.*

It would be easy to overuse transitions. A story that had a transitional word in front of every paragraph would sputter like a car with a flooded gas line. But beginning reporters generally use too few rather than too many transitional words. They often fail to take advantage of this simple trick for keeping paragraphs from grinding against one another.

▪ A ▪

Indicate where new paragraphs should begin in each of the following stories.

ONE

As soon as Mayor Kennely left the city yesterday for three weeks at his vacation home in Raleigh, workmen moved into his office in City Hall to begin installing a new wooden floor. The floor, being installed by Freemont Floor and Ceiling at a cost of $1,250, will replace the vinyl flooring placed in the office at the beginning of Mayor Kennely's first term, six years ago. The mayor's office had had a wooden floor since City Hall was first built in 1905 but Kennely's predecessor, Angie Lairmont, an avid golfer, had left many cleat marks on the floor of the office, where she often practiced her putting, according to Mayor Kennely. Kennely said he had decided to install the vinyl, at a cost of $460, to cover the cleat marks. "Now we finally have money in the budget to restore this beautiful room, owned by the people, to its original condition," the mayor said, before leaving for his summer home. The construction work is expected to take all of the three weeks Kennely will be away.

TWO

Royal Plumbing Supplies Co. is expected to report a record $100,000 profit this year, Blake Securities Co. said in a forecast released yesterday. Blake's report said Royal's total sales should reach a company record of $900,000 by the end of the year. It predicted that Royal will sell more than $200,000 in supplies out-of-state this year. Royal made a profit of $55,000 last year. Earlier this year the company's president, Elena Hargrove, had predicted that Royal would do substantially better this year.

THREE

An East Waldwick woman, Helene Beegle, yesterday became the first $2 million winner in the state's Get Rich Instant Lottery. Beegle scraped the lottery ticket she bought at 1 p.m. yesterday at Sam's Stationery Shop, on Rickles Road, and saw the numbers "2,000,000." "I almost fainted," Beegle recalled at state lottery head-quarters. "I hugged Martin Silver, who owns the store, and then I ran to the phone to call my husband." Beegle, 37, of 23 Hayloft Lane, is manager of the 7-Eleven store on Rickles Road. Her husband, Woodrow, is assistant manager of the store. The money, the largest prize in the history of the state lottery, is to be paid out in $100,000 installments every year for 20 years. "We haven't yet decided what we'll do with the money," Beegle said. "But we sure won't be selling any more coffee at 7-Eleven."

FOUR

Elizabeth Burma, who was convicted of murdering a policeman, was sentenced today to life in prison. In sentencing Burma, Judge Robert Hendricks called her crime "heinous," but said the fact that she is a mother convinced him not to give her the death penalty. Burma, 31, who has a 9-year-old son, was found guilty Friday of shooting to death Patrolman James Ganey last March after Ganey tried to arrest her for child abuse. Burma's son, Joseph, has been living in a foster home since the incident. Ganey's widow, Maryann, attended every day of the two-month trial. "I think it's a farce," she said after the sentencing. "Burma should be killed." In an interview with reporters after he handed down the sentence, Hendricks defended his decision. "I simply cannot condemn any child, no matter what his mother has done, to be an orphan," the judge said. "I hope he never lives with his mother again, but at least he'll know she is alive." Burma will be eligible for parole in 25 years.

FIVE

The City Council yesterday approved a plan to sell the Hightop Elementary School building to the county to be used as an arts center. Under the plan, the county's Artistic Development Agency, which will pay $214,000 for the building, will rent studios in the building at below market rates to artists, musicians, craftspeople and writers. "We think this is a great thing the county is doing," said Council President Sarah Levine after the vote. "And we hope it will help make Andersonville a center for arts in the state." The council approved the plan unanimously. Mayor Robert Scortino, a supporter of the arts center, is expected to sign the bill within the week. Athena Harris, director of the county agency, told the council that the county is ready to buy the school immediately. The arts center could begin operations early next year, Harris said. The Board of Education closed the Hightop School two years ago because of declining elementary school enrollment in the area. Levine told the council that the board envisioned no future need for the building. Levine said the council still must decide how to allocate the $214,000. An amendment to the bill, proposed by Councilwoman Sheila McGee, under which the money would have been used to purchase new uniforms and training equipment for all the city's high school sports teams, was defeated by a vote of 4–1.

■ **B** ■

Add transitions where necessary in the following sets of paragraphs.

ONE

"The new transit plan will cut traffic and save gasoline throughout the state," Gov. Pressman said.

Mayor Hugh McCarthy argued, in a press conference following the governor's announcement, that the proposal would hurt rather than help transit in the city. "Our taxes will go up, and our buses will remain just as slow," McCarthy said.

The mayor said he will fight the plan.

TWO

Police said Runnion entered the store at 1 a.m. He pulled a gun and demanded all the money in the cash register, they said.

Runnion left on foot and was arrested two hours later, according to police.

THREE

Nole's Hardware owner Jim Nole reported that Christmas business has declined 40 percent compared to last year. He said he was not sure he could afford to stay open.

Art Blaine, of Blaine's Shoes, said that he has seen some positive signs that the shopping center could recover from its Christmas-season slump this year. Blaine said that he was sure he will keep his store in the center.

FOUR

"I am going to end this slump and put the people of the county back to work," Fredericks told the cheering crowd.

He promised to cut crime throughout the county.

FIVE

The top floor of the building was destroyed, fire officials said. There was serious smoke and water damage in every room on the ground floor, they said.

Classes are unlikely to resume in the building this year, according to Superintendent Smith.

SIX

The damage in Redding included five willow trees overturned, three windows smashed and two cars dented by falling branches, according to the Redding Fire Department.

Redding police reported that traffic was blocked on the Freemont Expressway for 45 minutes by some large branches that had fallen onto the roadway.

An undetermined number of trees fell and one house, at 6 Pine Road, suffered structural damage in Hastings, according to the Hastings police.

SEVEN

For Jennifer Sandusky, 8, of 127-63 E. Motor Ave., the snow meant a day off from school and a chance to perfect her snowball throwing technique. "I wish it snowed like this everyday," she told a reporter.

Her father, William Sandusky, 45, looked like he was not having much fun as he attempted to remove the mounds of snow from his driveway.

EIGHT

Howard's Hardware store, at 34 Ridge Road, was the first store the robbers visited, police said. According to police, the three men pulled a gun on the owner, Axel Howard, and made off with $340 from his cash register.

They moved on to the Safeway supermarket, at 60 Ridge Road, where five customers were robbed of a total of $705, and $3,300 was taken from the store's safe and cash registers.

The owner of the Downtown Lunch Place, Pat Singleton, was robbed of $450 before the three men escaped from the area.

NINE

The labor leader called on the city to pay more attention to the problem of unemployment and less attention to the problems of golfers and tennis players.

His speech was the first sign that local union heads are willing to criticize the Democratic mayor.

TEN

The comet may be visible from parts of the state on the nights of May 3 and 4 this year, according to the astronomer.

Halley's Comet, which is due to make one of its periodic visits to our section of the solar system, may be visible this year.

■ **C** ■

Add transitions where necessary in the following story.

Newport Schools Superintendent John Alvers has reported that he has received two death threats following Newport High's first losing football season since World War II.

Alvers said yesterday that both threats were made in calls to his office. Both callers, he said, threatened his life if he did not fire football coach Red Molman, whom Alvers hired last year.

Alvers maintained that he is perfectly satisfied with the job Molman has done with the team. Newport High had a 3 and 5 record in football this year. The team won 7 games and lost 1 last year, under coach Blandon Phillips. It was 7 and 1 the previous year.

Sgt. Harry Elms said Alvers's report is being investigated. There is little likelihood of tracing the source of the calls, Elms said.

Security has been increased in his offices, Alvers reports. He said he does not believe he is in any real danger.

The Newport High Alumni Association has called for Alvers to fire Molman. The Boosters Association voted in a meeting last week to advise Alvers to give Molman a chance.

CHAPTER 13

Information selection

Any news event is surrounded by a mass of facts. There are the broader points that can be made—the story's primary focus (established in the lead) supporting information and secondary themes. And then there are the fine points—details such as times, ages, addresses, names and descriptions.

Decisions on what to emphasize in a story require news judgment (See Chapter 7, News Judgment). But reporters also must balance the need to answer readers' questions thoroughly against the need to communicate clearly in a limited space. Readers should neither be beaten down by a barrage of unimportant details nor left wondering about a point in the story that was raised but not explained.

Selectivity

Two Dallas men were killed yesterday when their single-engine airplane crashed in southwest Collin County shortly after takeoff from Addison Airport.

Dallas Times Herald

There are any number of points that might be made in a story about the crash of a small plane. The reporter might have considered the circumstances that brought each of the victims to the plane that day. The story might have touched on the safety history of the plane, the personal backgrounds of the victims and the actions of emergency crews.

But the story written for the *Times Herald*—just eight paragraphs long—mentioned none of these points. It confined itself to what the reporter considered the essential details about the crash and its victims. The story also noted that both victims were experienced pilots, that the area in which the crash occurred was well known as a place where pilots attempt aerobatic stunts, and that the Federal Aviation Administration would investigate.

The other points—optional information, which might have been included in a longer story—had to be scrapped. (Obviously, had the victims survived, the actions of emergency rescue crews would no longer have been optional.)

Journalism, it has been said, is the process of elimination. Any event significant or interesting enough to be labeled news trails behind it an almost endless train of circumstances and ramifications. What murder does not profoundly rattle a few dozen people? What governmental policy does not alter relationships in our society in some way? Reporters put hours into pursuing causes and effects. But though it can be painful to realize, many of these hard-won points simply won't fit in the story.

Although space limitations take most of the blame, journalists have another reason for restricting the number of points they allow in their stories—clarity. A story that tries to explain too much usually winds up explaining almost nothing.

Here is how the beginning of the story on that airplane crash might have read if the reporter had tried to squeeze everything in.

UNACCEPTABLE:

Two Dallas men, who left that city about 8 a.m. yesterday to drive 47 miles to Addison Airport for a day's flying, were killed when their 8-year-old, gray, two-seater, single-engine plane crashed in southwest Collin County shortly after taking off in clear but slightly breezy weather.

Collin County Justice of the Peace Andy Howard, 45, who knew some of the pilots at the airport and occasionally flew his own plane there as well, identified the victims as Gene Thomas, 37, about 6-foot-2 and 190 pounds, of 45121 King Lane, and Robert Clayburn, 46, about 5-foot-8 and 175 pounds, of 778 Seminole St. Collin County Sheriff's Deputy Joe Gergen, 31, who has participated in a state training program in emergency rescue, said Thomas was the pilot.

Gergen said both victims, one of whom had two grown children, the other of whom was single, were experienced pilots. He said Thomas, a math professor at Southern State University, who, colleagues said, had taught two courses that morning, had an airline transport pilot's license. Clayburn, who had had the day off before accepting an invitation to join Thomas on the flight, according to a friend, had a commercial pilot's license.

The plane, a two-seat Vitrol Skybird — a small plane with a strong safety record, according to its manufacturer — crashed about 7 p.m. It was the second crash of a small plane in the Dallas area this year.*

Good reporters have learned to avoid the temptation to say too much. They use their news judgment to rank the points that might be made about a story, and then, often ruthlessly, they slash off most of the lesser points. Although news stories will be full of facts, these facts will rarely be used to support more than a few points.

ACCEPTABLE:

Two Dallas men were killed yesterday when their single-engine airplane crashed in southwest Collin County shortly after takeoff from Addison Airport.

Collin County Justice of the Peace Andy Howard identified the victims as Gene Thomas, 37, of 45121 King Lane, and Robert Clayburn, 46, of 778 Seminole St. Collin County Sheriff's Deputy Joe Gergen said Thomas was the pilot.

Gergen said both men were experienced pilots. He said Thomas, a math professor at Southern State University, had an airline transport pilot's license, and Clayburn had a commercial pilot's license.

The plane, a two-seat Vitrol Skybird, crashed about 7 p.m. . . .**

Dallas Times Herald

Thoroughness

Reporters must be selective, but they also must be thorough. The information that a reporter *does* de-

* Names and other facts have been changed in this story, and some entirely fictitious information has been added in UNACCEPTABLE examples.
** This story has been reprinted with permission of the *Dallas Times Herald*.

cide to include in a story must be fully explained. Those points that are made must be made clear. The basic questions readers might have about them must be anticipated and, where possible, answered. A story's *lead* might not answer all the five Ws — who? what? when? where? and why? — but the complete *story* must try to answer them all.

Not all readers will be interested in the details — names, addresses, ages, times. That's why they are usually held out of the lead. However, if these details contribute to an understanding of the story, they should be included in the story for those readers who are interested.

Who

The identity of the protagonists in a news story can be pinned down in a number of ways, the first being the most obvious:

Names

Names usually will not be mentioned in a story's lead — the names of the two victims were not included in the lead of that *Times Herald* story on the airplane crash — but the full names of all the significant characters in a story must be given the first time each is mentioned in the body of the story. Full names are essential information.

The *Times Herald* story names the victims, the justice of the peace who identified the victims and the sheriff who told the reporter who piloted the ill-fated plane. There were, according to that sheriff, no witnesses, but if there had been witnesses to quote, they would have been named, too.

There are only three situations in which names might be withheld:

- If the person's role in the story is so insignificant as to make exact identification unnecessary: Police reporting routine crimes they didn't personally investigate needn't be named.
- If the reporter has agreed in advance with a source to withhold a name (See Chapter 19, Sources).
- If identifying the person would, in the paper's view, be an unwarranted invasion of privacy. Most papers, for example, do not print the names of rape victims or of juveniles charged with minor crimes. And police may ask that the names of people who have died be withheld for a short time until police can get in touch with their relatives:

The victims' identities were being withheld until relatives could be notified, Lt. Christiansen said.

Associated Press

Titles and professions

Titles should be included whenever they are relevant, whenever a person is appearing in the story in a professional role. *Collin County Justice of the Peace* Andy Howard was on the job when he released the names of the two victims of the crash. His title is relevant. However, had *Assistant Store Manager* Fred Strauss seen the plane go down, his title would not have been included. His being a witness would have had nothing to do with his exact professional position. The story might, however, have included some less specific information on this hypothetical witness's profession — Fred Strauss, *who works at a nearby grocery store* — to give the reader an idea of where he fit in. The professions, though not necessarily the full titles, of the two victims of the plane crash *are* essential information in a story about their deaths so that readers have some indication of who these two men — central to the story — were.

Ages

Ages are newsworthy when they are surprising — an 83-year-old marathoner, for example — and when they help establish a profile of a major figure in a story. Readers should be told the ages of the victims of the plane crash — not only to satisfy curiosity about the tragedy but because their ages further establish the victims' exact identities. However, the age of the justice of the peace is irrelevant.

Readers want to know — and should be told — the age of a woman suspected of robbing a bank; they won't require the age of the councilwoman who introduced a bill.

When former Secretary of State Henry A. Kissinger was hospitalized for coronary bypass surgery, *The New York Times* erred in not giving his age. Clearly age is essential in a story about a patient with a health problem.

Addresses

Addresses establish a person's exact identification. It is necessary that important characters in a story — victims and suspects, for example — be identified by age and address so they won't be confused with others who have similar names.

Gene Thomas of *45121 King Lane* died in that plane crash. Any readers who know another Gene Thomas can rest assured. Justice of the Peace Andy Howard's address is not necessary, however. His title helps keep him from being mistaken for someone else. But more importantly, the consequences of any mistaken identify in his case would be small.

Race and religion

The NAACP struggled a few decades ago to keep news organizations from routinely mentioning the race of black people arrested for crimes. When a suspect was white, of course, the fact was never mentioned. The race or religion of a person should be mentioned only in the rare case when that information is relevant to the story or when it would be useful in helping to arrest a suspect in a crime. When an Arab leader meets with leaders of local Jewish organizations, religious identification becomes important. When police issue a bulletin for a suspected robber described as "a tall white man with a blond beard and a large scar on his forehead," the description should be printed. But if the best the police can do is to say the man was "white, about 6 feet tall and of average weight," leave it out.

This description of a suspect in a car theft, which appeared in a newspaper printed on Tuesday about a crime that occurred Sunday, should not have been printed:

Police are looking for a black male about 6-foot-3, 190 pounds, and wearing dark clothes and a black ski cap.

The (Bergen County, N.J.) *Record*

Presumably, the suspect had changed his "dark clothes and ski cap" after two days. Even if he hadn't, a few dozen people a day might fit his description on an average city street.

What

Readers will always want to know exactly what happened:

The plane, a two-seat Vitrol Skybird, crashed about 7 p.m. . . . in a maize field.

Dallas Times Herald

The "what" is often the most obvious question to answer in a story. But like most questions, it can have more than one answer. Beginning reporters occasionally make do with the most superficial answer and miss the story (See Chapter 8, Hard Leads).

UNACCEPTABLE:
The City Council met for three hours yesterday at City Hall to discuss the municipal budget.

ACCEPTABLE:
Trash collection is scheduled to be cut from three to two days a week in an effort to reduce a deficit in the city's budget, the City Council decided yesterday.

When

Every news story needs a "when" of some sort. Sometimes "yesterday," "last night" or the day of the week will do. But in stories describing sudden and dramatic events, exact times should be given. In the plane crash story, it is of some interest to note, as the reporter did, that the plane crashed at about 7 p.m. and that the victims were pronounced dead at about 7:45 p.m.

Where

It's not necessary to repeat the address of city hall in every story. But readers normally should be told *exactly* where a fire broke out, where traffic is being detoured or where a plane crashed. In this case, the plane crashed "in a maize field 120 feet from Baccus Road and about 1 and a half miles west of Preston Road."

On less dramatic stories, such as a speech, the "where" should be included, but a *detailed* address is not necessary:

"The cost of medical care is increasing at an astounding rate," Stein told a convention of the American Medical Association at the Sheraton Plaza Hotel on Route 17.

Why

This is often the hardest question to answer for readers, but reporters must try. The reporter who wrote the *Times Herald* story was unable to get much information on why the plane crashed, but readers were told what the reporter did find out: that the area where the plane crashed was considered a good spot in which to attempt aerobatic tricks, that both men were experienced pilots and that the plane in which they were flying was capable of performing such tricks.

"Why" must always be asked, and when the answer is "we don't know," it should appear prominently nonetheless:

The spokeswoman refused to discuss why the product was withdrawn.

▪ A ▪

If a story were to be written based on the following sets of facts, which facts definitely should be included? Which might be included, depending on how much space was available for the story? And which should not be included? Write "yes" next to the facts that would be essential; "maybe" next to those that would be optional — depending on length; and "no" next to those that should be ignored.

ONE

_____ 1. A silver-and-gold chalice was stolen from a church on the west side.

_____ 2. The gold-lined cup has a cross at the base. Several large diamonds adorn the outside.

_____ 3. The church is 87 years old.

_____ 4. The chalice was stolen only minutes after it was used during Mass.

_____ 5. The church's name is St. Catherine's.

_____ 6. Police say they have no suspects in the case.

_____ 7. The church has three similar chalices.

_____ 8. The chalice was valued at $2,500.

_____ 9. The church last reported a theft four years ago.

_____ 10. The church is located in a neighborhood that has been hard hit by unemployment.

_____ 11. About 150 people attended the mass.

_____ 12. Chalice believed stolen at about 11:30 a.m.

_____ 13. Address of church is 295 Hunter Street.

_____ 14. Church is a beautiful granite building.

_____ 15. Chalice noticed missing by an altar boy, John Gibbons.

_____ 16. Information came from police.

TWO

_____ 1. Rome Councilwoman Sheila Albers announces that she will run in the Democratic primary to seek the nomination for lieutenant governor.

_____ 2. Albers is best known for her support of the gay rights bill in the Rome Council. She says she will work for a similar bill if elected to state office.

_____ 3. Rome Mayor John Raymond also has declared his candidacy for the Democratic nomination for lieutenant governor.

_____ 4. Albers attended Antioch College. Raymond attended George Washington University.

_____ 5. Albers is 38, Raymond is 49.

_____ 6. Albers ran unsuccessfully against Raymond for mayor last year.

_____ 7. Albers says she supports the president's foreign policy.

_____ 8. Albers has served for six years on the council. Before that she managed a record store in Rome.

_____ 9. Albers says that the state needs to increase its aid to local school districts.

_____ 10. Albers says she is concerned about the plight of Soviet dissidents.

_____ 11. Thus far no other candidates have declared for the primary.

_____ 12. Raymond declared two weeks ago.

_____ 13. Raymond is a lawyer.

_____ 14. Raymond served on the council 12 years before winning mayor's election.

_____ 15. Raymond has been a bitter opponent of Albers in city meetings.

THREE

_____ 1. Information provided by police.

_____ 2. Officer spoken to was Joseph Altobelli.

_____ 3. He is 29 years old.

_____ 4. A gas station was broken into over the weekend.

_____ 5. It was closed at the time.

_____ 6. Station on Greenwood Turnpike in Kanesville.

_____ 7. Police have no suspects.

_____ 8. Police said they will investigate.

_____ 9. Burglar entered by forcing the lock.

_____ 10. Station had a soda and candy machine. Nothing taken from them.

_____ 11. Burglar did break into a safe with a hammer and chisel.

_____ 12. $679 in cash stolen.

_____ 13. Most of the money was in $5 and $10 bills.

FOUR

_____ 1. Allen Rodgers sued the town of Valley Stream yesterday.

_____ 2. Rodgers is 13 years old.

_____ 3. Rodgers lives on 19 Myrtle Ave.

_____ 4. Rodgers' hobby is stamp collecting.

_____ 5. Rodgers is black.

_____ 6. On April 9, Rodgers and his friends were playing baseball in Memorial Park.

_____ 7. Rodgers plays on that field frequently.

_____ 8. Running between first and second base he tripped and shattered his kneecap on a rock protruding from the dirt.

_____ 9. It was a Tuesday afternoon.

_____ 10. Part of his kneecap was removed.

———— **11.** He was on crutches for six months.

———— **12.** It was raining the day he was hurt. The field was muddy.

———— **13.** Rodgers was wearing baseball spikes.

———— **14.** The field is owned and maintained by the Town of Valley Stream.

———— **15.** Suit contends town was negligent in not removing the rock from the basepaths.

———— **16.** Rodgers' father, Noel Rodgers, is a lawyer.

———— **17.** Noel Rodgers is 43 years old.

———— **18.** The town says no one has ever been injured on the field before.

———— **19.** His doctor says Rodgers will walk with a limp for the rest of his life.

———— **20.** Suit asks for $2 million in damages.

FIVE

———— **1.** State legislature approved plan to impose a 1 percent state sales tax yesterday.

———— **2.** Bill had been proposed by Assemblyman James Jones of Murdoch (the city in which your paper is published).

———— **3.** Jones's age—41.

———— **4.** Jones's address—15 Amber Road.

———— **5.** Governor must still sign the bill.

———— **6.** Governor's name—Bill Freeman.

———— **7.** Governor's age—53.

———— **8.** If approved tax would go into effect May 1.

———— **9.** Tax would cover all products except food.

———— **10.** Vote on tax—48–44.

———— **11.** Bill had been opposed by Assemblywoman Ellen Glassman of Murdoch.

———— **12.** Glassman's age—45.

———— **13.** Glassman's address—12–67 Robin Court.

———— **14.** Glassman said tax would be paid by the poor.

———— **15.** Jones said tax needed to maintain city services.

———— **16.** Jones a Republican.

———— **17.** Glassman a Democrat.

———— **18.** Freeman a Democrat.

———— **19.** Governor has not announced his position on the bill.

———— **20.** Bill approved by legislature at 3:45 p.m.

———— **21.** Legislature meets in state capitol, at One State Street.

———— **22.** After approving the tax, the legislature approved a motion to adjourn for the day.

SIX

_____ 1. An apparently crazed cat wreaked havoc on an apartment building in Freeport yesterday.

_____ 2. Information from officer at 3rd Precinct.

_____ 3. Officer's name — Sgt. Nick Pollard.

_____ 4. Cat entered first apartment at 4:30 p.m.

_____ 5. Apartment belonged to Sally Real.

_____ 6. Cat tore down curtains.

_____ 7. Cat scratched Real's two children.

_____ 8. Children's names — Aaron and Emilia.

_____ 9. Children's ages — 4 (Aaron) and 6 (Emilia).

_____ 10. Sally Real's age — 32.

_____ 11. Real is divorced.

_____ 12. Cat entered second apartment at 4:55 p.m.

_____ 13. Apartment belonged to Joe and Mary Sipser.

_____ 14. Joe Sipser — 52, Mary Sipser — 54.

_____ 15. Sipsers have no children.

_____ 16. Cat bit and scratched Mary Sipser.

_____ 17. Cat jumped onto Joe Sipser but did not hurt him.

_____ 18. Cat escaped into hallway and into street.

_____ 19. Cat was black Siamese.

_____ 20. Owner's name George Grover.

_____ 21. Grover's age — 83.

_____ 22. Grover says cat had never misbehaved before.

_____ 23. Cat's name — Tabby.

_____ 24. Cat's age — 3.

_____ 25. ASPCA searching for cat.

_____ 26. Building's address — 68 Front Street.

_____ 27. Building six stories tall.

_____ 28. Real lives on second floor.

_____ 29. Sipser lives on first floor.

_____ 30. Grover lives on first floor.

_____ 31. Real children not seriously injured, not hospitalized.

_____ 32. Mary Sipser treated at Booth Hospital for severe cut, then released.

_____ 33. Booth Hospital's address — 1 Booth Street.

SEVEN

       1. Car crashes into telephone pole yesterday.

       2. Man killed in car.

       3. Victim's name — Arthur Fredericks.

       4. Victim's address — 60 Redfern Road, East Albens.

       5. Victim's age — 24.

       6. Victim's race — black.

       7. Victim's profession — plumbing supplies salesman.

       8. No other passengers in car.

       9. Police officer on scene — Dean Rich.

       10. Officer's address — 4 Palace Court, East Albens.

       11. Officer's age — 35.

       12. Officer's race — black.

       13. Rich says car skidded for 30 yards on wet pavement before hitting pole.

       14. Rich says victim was dead when he arrived at Lincoln Hospital.

       15. Rich says no sign of foul play and no sign victim had been drinking.

       16. Rich says victim had stopped for gas at service station four miles from scene of accident.

       17. Scene of accident in front of house at 33 Blackburn St., East Albens.

       18. Allen and Sarah Fredericks live next door, 31 Blackburn St. They were victim's parents.

       19. Time of accident — 6:30 p.m.

       20. Had been raining steadily for six hours before the accident.

       21. Victim has no criminal record.

CHAPTER 14

Organization

"Too many reporters fail to think about their readers," says Ron Harris, assistant metropolitan editor of the *Los Angeles Times*. This chapter will look at a number of strategies for organizing stories so that they are easy for readers to follow.

The Inverted Pyramid

On most news stories, reporters do busy readers a favor: They present the most newsworthy information first and relegate less crucial facts to the bottom of the story. An essay works toward a conclusion; a work of fiction builds to a climax; but a news story usually winds down to facts of less and less importance.

This special technique for organizing stories—in which information is presented in descending order of newsworthiness—is called the *inverted pyramid*. An inverted pyramid is big at the top and gets smaller and smaller toward the bottom. Most news stories have the big news at the top (See Chapter 8, Hard Leads) and facts of decreasing importance as the stories continue toward their end.

This concept, taught to journalists for so long that it has become something of a cliché, can be oversimplified. But the inverted pyramid should be kept in mind when it comes time to organize facts into a news story. Reporters usually will informally rank the information they have by its news value and then proceed in approximately that order.

This Associated Press story, which appeared in *The Boston Globe,* provides a useful example of how the inverted pyramid and other organizing principles operate:

(1) BANGKOK, Thailand—Eleven children are to fly out of Vietnam today for reunions with American fathers they have not seen for most of their lives, U.S. officials said yesterday.

(2) Four boys and seven girls, aged 7 to 15, will fly from Ho Chi Minh City—formerly Saigon—to Bangkok for a stopover of several days before continuing on to new homes in the United States, said Donald Colin, a U.S. embassy officer.

(3) Vietnamese officials gave permission for the 11 children to leave. They are among 88 Amerasians in Vietnam documented as American citizens.

(4) Private agencies estimate the total number of Amerasians in Vietnam at between 25,000 and 50,000—many the children of American civilians or servicemen stationed there during the Vietnam war.

(5) The embassy says it has files on 3,740 Amerasian children who "have a burning desire to leave Vietnam now" and estimates a total of 8,000 "unassimilated" ones may want to leave.

(6) Colin said one American father, Fred Arthur of Portland, Oregon, will be aboard an Air France flight with representatives of seven private U.S. agencies when the plane lands in Ho Chi Minh City.

(7) Arthur's daughter Susan, whom he has not seen in 14 years, will be waiting. But all other reunions will take place in the United States, Colin said.

(8) Many of the Amerasian children live in or around Ho Chi Minh City. Some live in orphanages, but

others roam the streets selling peanuts, candy and movie tickets.

(9) The Vietnamese government says there is no official discrimination against these children. But racism and discrimination are common and many of the youngsters are barred from schools and job opportunities, according to mothers of the children.

(10) "They suffer the emotional and psychological consequences of being Amerasians," Colin said.

(11) "Letting out these kids is more than a gesture by the Vietnamese," Pearl S. Buck Foundation Director John A. Shade Jr. said yesterday. "It's a signal. I pray to God it's a new beginning."

(12) There is legislation pending in Congress to make it easier for Amerasian children to come to the United States.*

The most newsworthy point in this story is at the top—the timely news that 11 children with American fathers are to leave Vietnam today. The situation of other, similar children in Vietnam is of less news value; the specific story of a father and daughter, while certainly interesting, perhaps of less news value still; and the background details on the treatment of Amerasian children in Vietnam is the least newsworthy element of the story.

The arrangement of information in descending order of news value helps editors as well as those readers who have no time to read from beginning to end. Editors forced to cut a story's length could, if rushed, simply start chopping from the bottom up without fear that vital information would be sacrificed.

Had *Globe* editors needed to, they could easily have shortened the story of the Amerasian children without stopping to rearrange the information in it. In fact, this piece could have been ended after any paragraph with the possible exception of the second and the sixth. It still would have been a sound, self-contained story.

Supporting the Lead

The lead represents a decision on what is most newsworthy in a story (See Chapter 8, Hard Leads). It can be seen as a promise to readers of what is to come. The paragraphs that immediately follow the lead must deliver on that promise—they must *support* the lead.

If the lead is about a drug arrest, the next few paragraphs can't wander off into a discussion of the problem of drugs in schools. If the lead is about the school board's decision to eliminate courses in Spanish, much of the rest of the story will have to be about that

decision, not about wage negotiations with the teachers' union.

Support paragraphs fill out the information provided in the first graf. They bolster the lead's credibility and fill in some of the details.

Look, for example, at the first two paragraphs of the story about the Amerasian children. The lead tells us that 11 children will leave Vietnam for reunions with their American fathers. The information is attributed to unnamed "U.S. officials." Any further details would clutter the lead, obscuring the news.

By the second paragraph, though, it's time to begin providing these details. Here we learn the ages of the children and how many are girls and boys. This helps answer the question raised by the lead: Who is involved? We also learn specifically where they will fly from and how long it will take them to arrive. (The actual day they were to leave Vietnam would have been included here had it been available.) Finally, the paragraph adds credibility, a kind of proof, to the information by attributing it to a specific U.S. embassy officer.

Stories that fail to support their leads promptly can frustrate and confuse readers. This story from the *Houston Chronicle* takes much too long—until grafs 6 and 7—to support its lead by explaining *what* happened:

BALTIMORE (UPI)—Three maximum-security inmates and five guards were shot in an attempted breakout at the Maryland Penitentiary, officials said. Four of the guards were shot by other guards.

No escapes or serious injuries were reported in yesterday's incident, police said.

"It was horrifying, terrible," said Ken Neal, who was visiting his brother. "We saw guards running about with shotguns. My brother figured it was an escape."

Earlier, officials [had] recommended the dismissal of 14 guards at an adjacent prisoner reception unit. The guards had staged a sickout last week to protest staffing at the main penitentiary.

Corrections Commissioner Jon P. Galley said, "Any report, whether done by union or management, will prove that staffing is one of the major causes for escapes and inmate uprisings."

The shooting began at about 1:30 p.m. when the inmates—two convicted killers and an armed robber—took a female guard hostage in the prison yard and commandeered a shotgun and a revolver, said prison spokeswoman Beverly Marable.

*The inmates shot guard George Bellows, who returned fire, hitting the inmates in the legs and the female guard in the foot, [Marable said.] . . .***

For a more dramatic example, *The Washington Post,* during the second year of Ronald Reagan's pres-

---

* The names and the address of the father and daughter in this story have been changed. The story has been reprinted with the permission of the Associated Press.

** The names of the prisoner's brother and the guard in this story have been changed.

idency, led a story about his national security adviser with this information:

> . . . William P. Clark has dampened the internal power struggles and policy disagreements that marred much of Reagan administration policy during its first year.

The Post story that followed included *no* facts supporting this claim — not in the next few grafs or anywhere else.

Supporting the lead should be the first priority when beginning the body of a news story. Here is a simple story that does the job thoroughly:

> Weekend service on the trolleys that use the subway-surface tunnel routes will be interrupted for the next two weeks, SEPTA officials said yesterday.
>
> Service on Route 10, 11, 13 and 36 trolleys will be interrupted between Juniper and 40th streets from 10 p.m. Friday to 5 a.m. Monday because of Center City Commuter Tunnel construction, officials said.
>
> Passengers can take the Market-Frankford line to 40th Street and transfer there to the trolleys.
>
> *The Philadelphia Inquirer*

Elaborating

Once the lead has been supported — its main points solidly grounded — the reporter can begin broadening the basis of the story. Additional information can be supplied; less pressing questions can be answered.

In *The Boston Globe* story about the Amerasian children, grafs 3 to 5 help to elaborate on the significance of the children leaving by saying how many remain — these three grafs provide context (See Chapter 15, Background and Context). Paragraphs 6 and 7 also provide additional details by focusing on one particular American father and his Amerasian daughter. None of these paragraphs is needed to support the lead, but they add significantly to the meaning and impact of the story.

Not all stories or all main points made within a story will benefit from elaboration. It may not be worth the space. Lead support is required. Elaboration — the addition of extra details and explanation — is an option.

Secondary Themes

If the story is long enough, after supporting the lead and elaborating on the main themes, reporters can begin introducing secondary themes.

Paragraphs 8 through 10 of the Amerasian story develop a new theme that would probably not be missed if it were left out. These paragraphs look at how the children are treated in Vietnam. The final paragraph touches on another secondary theme — efforts in this country to help more Amerasians immigrate.

As discussed in Chapter 13, Information Selection, the number of points that can be made in a newspaper story is limited. If there is room for secondary points, they should be covered one at a time, and only after the main themes of the story have been dealt with.

So a simple story should be organized along these lines:

1. Lead
2. Support
3. Elaboration (if any)
4. Secondary themes (if any)

Like Ideas Together

Good stories start with a design. Experienced reporters may not take the trouble to write out an outline in advance, but they certainly keep one in their heads. They decide what ideas they plan to cover, and they organize these ideas so that they are developed one at a time.

Nothing breaks the flow of a story more effectively than the jumbling of ideas.

UNACCEPTABLE:

> Private agencies estimate the total number of Amerasians in Vietnam at between 25,000 and 50,000 — many the children of American civilians or servicemen stationed there during the Vietnam war.
>
> Colin said one American father, Fred Arthur of Portland, Ore., will be aboard an Air France flight with representatives of seven private U.S. agencies when the plane lands in Ho Chi Minh City.
>
> There is legislation pending in Congress to make it easier for Amerasian children to come to the United States.
>
> Arthur's daughter, Susan, whom he has not seen in 14 years, will be waiting. But all other reunions will take place in the United States, Colin said.
>
> The embassy says it has files on 3,740 Amerasian children who "have a burning desire to leave Vietnam now" and estimates a total of 8,000 "unassimilated" ones may want to leave.

Related ideas were kept together in this story as it appeared in *The Boston Globe*. For example, the three paragraphs discussing how many children of American heritage are in Vietnam come one after another. So do the paragraphs about the American father and his daughter and the paragraphs about the condition of these children in Vietnam.

It makes no sense to ignore the natural connections between ideas when organizing a story. It is difficult enough to make a story read smoothly when it does proceed logically from idea to related idea (See Chapter 12, Mechanics).

Two or More Primary Themes

The stories discussed so far in this chapter make one basic point in their leads. A story must be organized somewhat differently when it raises two or more points of such equal, or nearly equal, importance that they all are introduced at the top of the story.

These additional main elements may be incorporated in the lead (See Chapter 8, Hard Leads):

> Teachers struck at all three schools in Waldwick, N.J., yesterday, while striking teachers in the Deer Park Union Free School District on Long Island suspended their walkout, which began last Friday.
>
> *The New York Times*

Or they may be introduced in the second graf:

Theme A
> NEW YORK (UPI)—A stickup man dressed as a police officer stole antique jewelry valued at $1 million from a Manhattan antique store yesterday, police said.

Theme B
> In another heist reported by police yesterday, a Park Avenue firm was broken into over the weekend and art objects valued at nearly $2 million were stolen.
>
> (Long Island, N.Y.) *Newsday*

Each of these elements must then be supported, and possibly elaborated on, in the story. All the primary themes introduced in the lead should be developed before secondary themes are introduced. And —following the *like ideas together* rule—each should be developed completely before the next is considered.

Here is how the reporter proceeded after the first two grafs in that *Newsday* story:

Support Theme A
> In the jewelry theft, Lt. Frederick Stein of the East 67th Street station house said, the "police officer" arrived at Ares Antiques, 961 Madison Ave., at the store's 10 a.m. opening time.
>
> Stein said the store was still locked, but the clerk on duty opened the door and admitted the stickup man without question when he saw the uniform. The robber pulled a handgun, handcuffed the clerk and ordered him to lie on the floor, according to Lt. Stein.
>
> The robber and an accomplice then scooped up antique jewelry valued at $1 million, mostly crowns and necklaces, from two opened safes and fled, Lt. Stein said.

Support Theme B
> In the art theft, officials of the William B. O'Boyle Co. at 99 Park Ave. reported $1.8 million worth of art objects, along with 10 Krugerrands and $2,000 in cash had been taken. The art objects included 37 pieces of preColombian art.

A basic dual-element story, then, will be ordered like this:

1. Introduction of theme A and theme B in first graf or two.
2. Support for theme A.
3. Elaboration on theme A (if necessary).
4. Support for theme B.
5. Elaboration on theme B (if necessary).
6. Secondary themes (if any).

A story with three main elements will follow a similar pattern:

1. Introduction of themes A, B and C in first graf or two.
2. Support for theme A.
3. Elaboration on theme A (if necessary).
4. Support for theme B.
5. Elaboration on theme B (if necessary).
6. Support for theme C.
7. Elaboration on theme C (if necessary).
8. Secondary themes (if any).

Chronology

Purely chronological stories begin at the beginning of an event and end at the end—a rarity in journalism. They are most commonly found in features (See Chapter 26, Features). But occasionally, news stories also flow chronologically:

> GRAND MARAIS, Minn. (AP)—Drawn by messages from "some higher power," Mitchell Irving and Esther Sklaire drove last month from St. Paul to the frozen wilderness of northeastern Minnesota to wait for a flying saucer, authorities say.
>
> For more than four weeks they waited in their car, apparently eating vitamins and drinking water from nearby Loon Lake.
>
> On Monday, a motorist found Irving, 38, an electrician from West St. Paul, semiconscious on Gunflint Trail, 41 miles northwest of here. Rescue squad members found Sklaire, 48, dead in the front seat of the car a few hundred yards off the main road.
>
> An autopsy determined she died from a combination of hypothermia, dehydration and starvation . . .*
>
> (New York) *Daily News*

More frequently chronological accounts are mixed with non-chronological sections of news stories. After the basics of the story are laid out in the lead and in one or more support paragraphs, a writer may switch to a narrative, chronological recounting of the event. This technique is particularly effective in police, fire and disaster stories and in any other account in which

---

* The names in this story have been changed.

the narrative itself is compelling enough to hold the reader's interest.

Here's an example:

> A Long Island mother was critically burned yesterday when she raced through the flames in her home in an attempt to rescue her two children who had already been taken out a first-floor window by a neighbor, police said.
>
> The children's father, who suffered minor burns, was prevented from reentering the house by firemen who found his wife — overcome by smoke — lying under a bed in her daughter's room, according to Nassau County police.
>
> *Chronology begins*   A neighbor noticed smoke coming from the windows of the home of Bert and June Beaumont on Anderson Avenue in Roslyn about 8:30 a.m.
>
> The neighbor, Robert Stanton, 34, told his wife to call the Fire Department, then vaulted a four-foot fence separating the two houses.
>
> Police said Stanton, who operates a hardware store in Manhasset, reached up and grabbed the Beaumont children, Andrea, 10, and Bert Jr., 7, as they leaned out a window, gasping for air.
>
> Beaumont, 38, leaped out of a first-floor window on the other side of the house and ran to the children's bedroom window, police said. When he realized the children were safe but his wife was still inside, he tried to reenter the house . . .*
>
> (New York) *Daily News*

Chronological accounts can be effective in organizing complex events into a coherent story. Readers may find a confusing series of occurrences easier to follow if they are presented in the order in which they happened. A reporter may choose to tell most of the story chronologically, or simply two or three grafs. It is perfectly acceptable to mix these accounts into a story that otherwise follows the inverted pyramid.

Bullets

Just as lists help us organize our lives, they can help reporters organize stories. In order to make lists clear in newspaper stories — and to set them off from the rest of the story — each point will be indented and preceded by a small, dark circle (indicated by an asterisk on the typewriter or keyboard).

These little circles are called *bullets*. They give reporters a means of organizing and setting apart a series of similar points. Here is an example from a

* The names and addresses in this story have been changed.

story on a United Nations vote against a Cuban proposal to debate the status of Puerto Rico:

> Friday's vote was attributed by diplomats to three factors:
>
> • Forceful lobbying by the United States. Ambassador Jeane Kirkpatrick informed her colleagues in a memorandum that a debate on Puerto Rico would be a violation of U.S. sovereignty.
> • Legal tradition. The Cuban proposal asked delegates to reverse a 1953 General Assembly decision that Puerto Rico is a self-governing territory.
> • Inept Cuban diplomacy. As chairman of the so-called non-aligned group of nearly 100 countries, Cuba has aroused resentment by zealously pushing Soviet policies and by dictatorial conduct toward other members of the group.
>
> *Dallas Times Herald*

Bullets should be used selectively. Points should only be arranged as bullets if they can be made in a sentence or two. Each bulleted item also should employ a similar sentence structure. Finally, bullets should be used only when three or more points need to be made.

UNACCEPTABLE:
In other action last night, the council:

> • Voted 5–3 to close Memorial Park each night at 10 p.m. The council's action followed reports that teen-agers have been terrorizing residents living next to the park by breaking their windows and shooting holes in their garbage cans. Councilman John Rose called the actions "disgraceful," but said some means should be made to keep the park open for "decent kids."
> • In an action that angered some and delighted others, lifted an ordinance forbidding video-game parlors in the borough.

The solution here is to forget the bullets and return to normal paragraphs and prose.

After Soft Leads

Stories that begin with zingers, anecdotes, descriptions or quotes (See Chapter 9, Soft Leads) must still obey most of the rules outlined in this chapter: The story must follow and support the angle established — no matter how cleverly — by the lead; themes must be elaborated on . . . one at a time; like ideas should be kept together.

Nevertheless, most features found in newspapers (See Chapter 26, Features) differ from a news story in one crucial way: Such stories rarely follow the inverted pyramid. Instead of petering out, they may build to a climax or conclusion. In this way, they may be more similar in form to an essay or a work of fiction. This means that a feature story may introduce some important themes far down in the story. (The lead, though, must still indicate the overriding theme of the story—See Chapter 9, Soft Leads.)

There are a number of strategies for organizing feature stories. Some features, as mentioned above, begin at the beginning and end at the end. They are chronological. Others use spatial relationships to lend order. A piece about the changes in a neighborhood over time, for example, might move the reader from north to south or from east to west. Still others move from the statement of a problem to consideration of its solutions.

A well-crafted feature also may return at the end to the incident introduced in its lead. In this way, the final paragraphs help tie together the story. These final grafs—sometimes called the *snapper* or *kicker* —are often viewed as second in importance only to the lead.

Here are the first four paragraphs of a substantial *New York Times* feature about home sharing by the elderly:

MONTICELLO, N.Y.—When 74-year-old Joan Howitt broke a hip last winter, the fear of not knowing where she would live when she left the hospital almost broke her spirit.

Mary Beaman, 72, said the stillness of her rambling house, near Sackett Lake, where she has lived for 50 years, began to grate on her last January. Now the two women are living together, sharing Mrs. Beaman's house, thanks to a match made by a Sullivan County project for the elderly.

Having a companion, Mrs. Beaman said, "gave new life to the old house."

Like Mrs. Howitt and Mrs. Beaman, a growing number of elderly people in the New York metropolitan area and nationwide are sharing homes—to save money, stave off loneliness and avoid going to a nursing home, according to social workers and other authorities on problems of the aging . . .

And here are the last three grafs of that story. Notice how the writer manages to wind back to where she began:

. . . "Sometimes it just doesn't work," said Enrico DeGironimo, assistant coordinator of the Community Outreach Program for Senior Adults . . . in Piscataway, N.J.

"Older people have set habits. Sometimes finances force them to consider shared housing, but then they feel like someone has moved into their territory. Or from the home-seeker's view, they may feel displaced."

Mrs. Howitt said, however, that even though she could hardly see, the corners and turns of Mrs. Beaman's house had become familiar to her. "It's become my home," she said. "And Mary has become my family."

▪ A ▪

Number the grafs (not written in final form) in the order in which they should appear in each of the following news stories.

ONE

_____ Jordan was charged with second-degree murder, auto theft and motor vehicle violations.

_____ The bus, which was empty, was stolen from its depot on Broadway at 8:30 a.m. Suspect is Leon Jordan, 32, of Ellington Avenue, police said.

_____ After a 20 minute chase, police said, Jordan finally forced to curb on Belair Street and Broadway.

_____ A man who apparently was drunk stole a city bus yesterday morning and drove it wildly down Broadway, killing a pedestrian and injuring three other people, police said.

_____ Dead identified as Juliana Franck, 76, of 8205 Broadway. She was struck while crossing Broadway a block from her house.

_____ Franck declared dead on arrival at Lady of Mercy Hospital.

_____ Three persons slightly injured when the bus hit a taxi cab 10 minutes later at Broadway and Hudson Street.

TWO

_____ Police said Ramirez was helping his sister, Angelita, 26, the owner, close up the store at 10 p.m. when the three armed men approached.

_____ Ramirez lived with his relatives uptown.

_____ Police said that "for no apparent reason" the gunman assigned to guard Ramirez and his sister shot Ramirez through the head.

_____ One of the robbers, all of whom wore ski masks, forced the brother and sister to lie face down in the store's aisle, police said.

_____ A grocery clerk who arrived here from Mexico six weeks ago and went to work in his sister's store was shot to death yesterday. He was shot by one of three robbers who escaped with $500, police said yesterday.

_____ The robbers escaped on foot.

_____ Miguel Ramirez, 24, was pronounced dead on arrival at the Jonas Salk Medical Center after he was shot in the head at Angelita's Grocery on 252 Sycamore Boulevard.

_____ The robbers drew guns and demanded money, police said.

_____ Miss Ramirez told them there was a bag with $500 behind the register. Two gunmen went to look while the third watched the brother and sister.

THREE

_____ Lewis Browning, 35, of 29 W. 9th St., and Thomas Browning, of 261 Pontiac Court, were charged with conspiring to force Anatoli Povorsky, 72, from her two-bedroom apartment in the building they own at 16 Dyer St.

———————   The indictment alleges that the damage was done March 16 when Miss Povorsky was on vacation. It says the brothers entered the apartment with plumbing tools in order to jimmy the kitchen sink, causing it to run constantly. They also destroyed the vegetable drawer and rack in the refrigerator and clogged up the toilet, the indictment charges.

———————   The indictment, handed up in Superior Court, charged the brothers with drawing up a false lease and with breaking the sink, refrigerator and toilet in the apartment in an effort to show Miss Povorsky did not take care of the premises.

———————   Miss Povorsky, who is protected under city rent control statutes, pays $175 a month for the apartment. She has lived there 45 years. Equivalent apartments in the building not protected by rent control statutes are being let for $845 a month.

———————   Two brothers indicted yesterday; charged with illegally attempting to force out elderly tenant in building they own.

———————   The Brownings also own four other buildings on Dyer Street, including Dyer Tower, one of the most expensive and fashionable apartment buildings in city.

FOUR

———————   In Denver, Colo., residents were digging out from a record-breaking 38 inches of snow that fell in just 22 hours.

———————   The National Weather Service is predicting continued wet weather and below normal temperatures over all parts of the country other than the Northeast in the next 30 days.

———————   In Sapulpa, Okla., hailstones the size of baseballs cracked car and shop windows and sent a dozen people to the hospital, where they were treated for cuts and bruises.

———————   Strange spring weather continued to plague the Mountain and Plain states yesterday with snow in Denver, hail in Oklahoma and near hurricane-force winds in New Mexico.

———————   The storm in Denver, officially a blizzard, left motorists stranded in cars for up to 13 hours, closed Interstate 40 and obliterated the first signs of spring. Three people were believed to be missing.

———————   A wind storm, with gusts up to 72 miles an hour, buffeted Alamogordo, N.M., tearing down trees and power lines and leaving sections of the town without electricity for more than eight hours.

FIVE

———————   Downtown, only the tops of parking meters were visible and shop owners could be seen rowing down Main Street, trying to salvage what they could.

———————   It was believed to be the worst flood in Sheridan's history.

———————   A family of three whose one-story bungalow at 4 Elm St. was less than a block from the river was reported missing and believed drowned. They were identified as Allie Ng, 36; his wife, Sue, 34, and their son, Ted, 4. By morning water covered all but the roof of their home.

——————— The water swirled into the homes of hundreds of residents as they slept at about 3 a.m. when the river suddenly poured over embankments at First Street and at Main Street.

——————— "The damage just on Main Street could well run into the hundreds of thousands of dollars," said Mayor Robert Ridley. "I have asked the governor to declare Sheridan a disaster area."

——————— The Beaverhead River, swollen from a week of constant rain, overflowed its banks early this morning and flooded downtown Sheridan, leaving at least two dead and three missing.

——————— The Beaverhead has not overflowed its banks since 1918 when only 400 people lived in Sheridan.

——————— Nellis Chandler, 24, of 815 Aubrey Road, and his cousin, Dana Chandler, 28, of 34 Carson St., had been attempting to reinforce the First Street embankment when they were caught in the turbulent water and drowned.

▪ B ▪

The leads are already written for the following stories. Complete each of the stories using the facts listed after the lead.

ONE

A truck loaded with live chickens overturned on the Ventura Freeway here yesterday, filling the freeway with chickens and causing rush-hour traffic delays of up to one hour.

1. Truck and chickens owned by Acme Farms of Ventura; driver was Anthony Devaldi, 36, of Ventura.

2. From interview with Police Sgt. Fred Gompers on scene: "The truck was driving north when Devaldi seems to have lost control. It skidded for about 50 yards before overturning a quarter mile south of the Freemont Street exit. This was at 4:05 p.m. Devaldi was unhurt. No other vehicles involved."

3. More from Gompers: "Many of the chickens were killed in the crash, but about 60 chickens escaped onto the road. We have no word on exactly how many chickens were on the truck. My partner and I immediately called for help. Three other squad cars arrived, and two officers directed traffic and supervised the removal of the truck while four of us chased chickens. You had to sort of fall on top of them and give them a good hug. Then we stuffed them back into cages from the truck. Most seemed sort of dazed, so they weren't that hard to catch."

4. More from Gompers: "For a while the freeway there looked like a chicken farm. But we had it cleared of chickens and the truck towed away by 5:15 p.m. The truck and chickens had completely blocked northbound traffic for at least 45 minutes, and southbound traffic was partially obstructed by the chickens for about that long. Some drivers were delayed up to one hour. Nothing longer than that."

5. Gompers says no criminal charges will be filed.

6. Devaldi and representatives of Acme say they don't want to talk about the accident at this point with the media.

7. From interview with Sally Burrows, of East Harrington, a driver in northbound lane of freeway who says she was delayed 45 minutes by accident: "You had to see it. I have never seen anything like that: four police officers chasing these dozens of chickens around the Ventura Freeway. Yeah, I'll be late getting home, but, you know, it was worth it for the entertainment."

TWO

The Bullock Pipe factory and the Hardwood Lumber Products factory here say they'll be expanding their workforce this month to meet increased demand.

1. Bullock is located on Greene Street. It now employs 104 people here in Bloomsbury. Hardwood Lumber employs 88 here. It is on George Avenue.

2. From a statement by Bullock Vice President James Robertson: "Our sales increased 28 percent last month over the same period last year. People are buying more and more of our pipe. We are going to need 25 new workers here by the end of the month to keep up with demand. The positions will all be on the assembly line. They will be full time and they will pay a starting wage of $15 an hour."

3. From an interview with Joan Nedelka, president of Hardwood Lumber Company: "Yes, what you heard is true. Hardwood is having a solid year, a very solid year. Our new chestnut coffee tables are leading the way but our line of traditional furniture is selling better than ever also. Sales for the last quarter were up 17 percent over the same time last year. Yes, that's the quarter that

ended on the first of last month. So we plan to add 15 workers. Eight openings will be for experienced carpenters and seven will be on our production lines. Salaries commensurate with experience."

4. From the interview with Robertson: "Things are looking good for our company, and we think that that means things are also going to be looking up for this town's economy. We hope to hire additional workers in the coming months if sales continue to rise."

THREE

The crowd of about forty people cheered wildly as he crossed the finish line on Howard Road and collapsed into the arms of his mother.

The runner then waved feebly to acknowledge the cheers, sat down on the pavement and took off one of his legs.

Julian Nance, 19, who lost his right leg in an automobile accident three years ago, ran the 14 miles between Hartford and Westbrook alone yesterday in an effort to raise money to improve Westbrook's facilities for the disabled.

1. Nance ran using an artificial leg; run took 2 hours 10 minutes.

2. Nance visited local business people before run. He got pledges for total of $6,500, if he finished run.

3. Alice Woodward, owner of Woodward Hardware, who pledged $300 in an interview after run: "How could you not respect a boy like this? He fought so hard to come back from what happened to him. I wanted to help out his cause."

4. Nance in interview after run: "Well, I guess I did it. I never had run more than 8 miles in training. But those people cheering sure made it easier. I'll tell you though, that fake leg got to feeling a little sore. But right now I feel great."

5. More from Nance interview: "You know, I haven't decided exactly what I'm going to do with the money. But there surely are enough things in this town that need to be done. We need a social center for the disabled. We need a transportation vehicle to enable people in wheelchairs to get around. We need more ramps on our sidewalks and in our buildings for these people. I'm lucky. I can still walk and run. Some people are stuck in wheelchairs."

6. Friends of Nance, some in wheelchairs, along route. They cheered him on before finish line and gave him cups of water.

7. From interview with Maureen Nance, 43, his mother: "Proud? I think this is the happiest day of my life. To see that boy come back from what he's been through and do something like this for what he believes in, I am just thrilled by it. Until that accident, I didn't know he had it in him. Now, I see that he won't let anything stop him from doing what he believes in."

8. Crowd starts to move to cars and leave; Nance's mother helps by picking up artificial leg; she hands Nance crutches; he takes two wooden crutches and starts walking, using them, to car; mother gets behind wheel; they leave.

9. Facts on Nance: Sophomore at Westbrook Junior College; political science major; lost father when he was 12; lost leg at age 16 when bike he was riding hit by a car; in hospital then for eight months; founder of Westbrook Disabled Person's Rights Association—has 28 members; never ran or jogged before his accident.

▪ C ▪

Write stories based on each of the following collections of information. In each case you are writing for a newspaper dated tomorrow and read in the town or county where the event occurred.

ONE

From interview with Chief Andrew Phegley of East Meadowbrook Fire Department: "Men were called at 10 this morning to answer at 4 West 10th Street, downtown here . . . When we arrived we saw flames coming from window on second floor of two-story frame house . . . Were able to control fire in 20 minutes . . . When we went inside we found severe damage to most of the top floor of the house . . . then we found the body . . . He was 18 months old, name: Sam Robbins. My guess is smoke inhalation killed him. An autopsy will be done. No adults were home when we arrived . . . neighbor turned in alarm . . . Mother, Rebecca Robbins, 28. She arrived minutes after we did. She was crying wildly and we had to restrain her from running into the flames. Managed to tell us she'd put Sam down for a nap at 9:30 and gone shopping for some groceries . . . Father she said is Eric Robbins, 29. He works at King's Shoes . . . Mother says the family had a wood-burning stove on. We're investigating whether it could have caused the fire . . . Let me tell you, seeing that body was one of my worst experiences in 35 years of firefighting."

TWO

All information supplied by Sgt. Whit Russell of the Paoli police department: "There was a bad accident at the Paoli train station today. 22-year-old kid, a senior at Havermore College here, was killed trying to be a Good Samaritan. Seems as if he was waiting for the Eastbound commuter train to come in, the 8:23, when he noticed this guy lying on the tracks. He jumped down on the tracks to help him and found out the guy was just soused. At 8:15 in the morning. Guy had an empty bottle of Jim Beam in his hand. Just then people on the platform heard the train whistle — it's a local-only stop, and the train was an express — and started yelling to the kid to get off the track. He picked up the drunk and threw him to the side. I guess he figured he had time to jump after him, but the train just ran over him. The local would have been slowing down and he would have had time. But the express must have been going through at 30 or 40 miles an hour. Victim's name was Danny McGruder. Like I said, he was 22, a senior at Havermore College majoring in Economics. Lived on campus. Nice kid, played soccer, served on the student council. His family lives in 427 Chestnut St. in Philadelphia. No, the drunk wasn't hurt at all. We're still not sure of his identity but no question McGruder saved his life. I guess you could say he was a hero, but life isn't always that kind to heroes, you know."

THREE

This is for a Rockland County newspaper. The source is county Police Officer Judith Bergman.

1. Quite a wind storm hit the southeast corner of the county this morning. Real freaky. Was quite calm when winds began howling about 8:45 a.m. Clocked at between 45 and 63 mph. Gusty.

2. Kids had a hard time walking to school. Some had to chase hats that blew off.

3. Winds broke off some power lines. 5,000 customers of Orange Electrical Co. had their power interrupted from about 9 until 4:02 p.m. All the customers were homes and businesses in towns of Nyack, Piermont and Sparkill in the southeastern corner of the county.

4. Rush hour also was messed up. Big tree branches broke off along Route 9W and Route 59.

5. "It certainly wasn't a day to go for a drive. I got in my car, you know, to check for speeders on 59 before it hit and before I knew it I was out there directing traffic. When the power went out so did the traffic lights, and with the tree limbs down all over everything pretty much came to a standstill for an hour. It was the kind of rush hour when you wished you owned a horse."

6. Tree house came down in James Smith's back yard. He lives at 343 Wellington Place, Nyack.

7. "Some people were lucky and didn't lose power, but most of the electricity in those three towns was out all day."

FOUR

Transcript of a speech by Democratic Mayor Harrison Fredericks of Jonesville at 11 a.m. this morning at City Hall: "I have an important announcement to make to you today. As you all know, the drug problem in River Park, or as it's sometimes called, Needle Park, downtown has gotten totally out of control in recent years. Our police staff, under the fine leadership of Commissioner Jane Lovejoy, has done its best, but has still been unable to prevent the open exchange of drugs in what should be a place for city residents to enjoy themselves and escape some of the pressures of city life. I think I speak for most of the decent people of this city when I say that I have had enough. Starting tomorrow I am going to order Commissioner Lovejoy to triple police patrols in the area. I am going to ask Governor Richard Ramos to increase the penalties for drug use and drug sales in this state. And right now, I am warning those people who persist in using illegal drugs that this city will no longer tolerate their immoral and irreligious behavior. We have had enough. Thank you. Any questions?"

The mayor is asked where the additional police patrols will come from. He replies: "Sure, we are not in a position, without raising taxes, to increase the size of the police force, but I am confident Commissioner Lovejoy will be able to find the additional officers for the park without weakening protection in other parts of the city. As to the exact number of police who will be assigned, I'm not at liberty to say that."

Commissioner Lovejoy is contacted. Lovejoy says she welcomes the mayor's plan and, of course, will follow his orders. She says there is now one officer in the park at most hours of the day. She says she is not sure where she will find the additional men on her 68 person force.

Republican City Council President Frank Shapiro is contacted about the mayor's plan: "Is that what he said? It sounds like another publicity stunt to me . . . Robbing Peter to pay Paul. To fight crime in this city we need more police officers, not just a reshuffling of the ones we have."

FIVE

The following on the telephone from Grover Brandon, director of press relations for Howell County Airport near here: "Did you hear? Here's what happened: A Midwest Airlines 727 jet (the plane was carrying 73 people plus 5 crew members from Chicago) had some trouble here today. No, nobody seriously hurt. I'll tell you what happened. The plane is coming in for a landing — perfect weather, sunny, no clouds or fog — but it comes in much too late on the runway — was using our main runway — number two. It landed maybe 150 yards further down the runway than it's supposed to land. The problem is that it just ran out of runway at the end. The plane, of course, wasn't able to slow down in time. So, it kept going past our runway . . . right onto the soy field — owned by John McPherson — that abuts the airport. We estimated that it ran 75 yards through the soy fields before stopping. Hey, this is why you want — they encourage it in fact — to have flat land near airports, in case something like this should occur. So, we had no damage to the plane. After the boys from the FAA take a look, we'll just get a little tractor and move her to the terminal, no problem. Five people on the plane say they were hurt a little — soy fields are a little bumpier than airport runways, you know — but only one was taken to the hospital. Wait, I think I have her name here — it's Helen Bennett; she lives at 51 First Drive here in Howell.

Final

So, as I said, the Federal Aviation Administration will want to look this over — they said they'll have some people down here tomorrow. We don't know what went wrong."

A visit to the scene, and the Boeing 727, painted orange and black, can be seen, after long tire marks, sitting in the soy field. One passenger, Jack Frankel, 58, from Chicago, still at airport. Frankel in interview: "We didn't know what happened. We were landing okay and then suddenly everything started to get incredibly bumpy. A few people screamed, but soon we came to a stop."

Midwest airline official says pilot's name was George Hancock, refuses to comment further, says Hancock is not available for an interview, says no crew members are available, says it was flight 505 from O'Hare airport, says incident occurred at 1:35 p.m.

A call to Howell Hospital, spokeswoman Hilda Ringel says passenger, Helen Bennett, 38, had a broken wrist bone set, has since been sent home.

No answer at Bennett's house.

SIX

Meeting of Millsburg Recreation Committee this evening at which following action is taken:

1. By a 5–0 vote additional $35 given to swing fund for Oak Street Playground at the corner of Kings Row and Presidents Street.
2. Committee member Steve Fairmont: "That is one of the most used playgrounds in the city. Let's make sure the kids who use it have decent, safe swings."
3. By a vote of 4–1 city's annual Memorial Day parade is canceled this year.
4. Committee member Jill Peters (supported proposal): "It was just a disaster last year. We had one band, a few firefighters and no more than 50 spectators watching the parade. I love parades, but if the people of this town would prefer to stay home and watch baseball on TV, why should we spend $500 preparing for a parade?"
5. Committee member Willa Creel (supported proposal): "I agree with Jill. It's not our job to force things down people's throats. If they don't want to come watch the parade, why go to all the trouble? Many of us put in long hours on the parade last year, for what?"
6. Committee member Alona Irving (opposed proposal): "I don't like this one bit. What are we doing here? That parade has been held in this city for 58 years. Okay, we had one bad year. I wish we would try to publicize it better and maybe make it more attractive — maybe include some rock bands for the younger people — rather than just give up on it."

Some research in the newspaper clips confirms the committee member's statements about the age of the parade, the cost of last year's parade (500 dollars) and the number of spectators there.

A call to Mayor David Jones gets the following: "It's the committee's job to decide things like this. I don't want to comment on it."

A call to Alan Greenwood, president of local chapter of Veterans of Foreign Wars, gets the following: "Yeah, I heard they were going to cancel the parade. What can I say? The sad thing is that they couldn't get enough people to show up at the parade last year. I guess people don't much care about Memorial Day around here anymore."

7. Meeting was at City Hall at Municipal Plaza. It began at 8 p.m. and lasted until 10:25 p.m.

SEVEN

1. Sherri Hall is an active citizen of Sterling.
2. She is 37, grew up in town, lives at 7 Garber Hill Road, husband is Vernon Hall, sales manager at Scott's Chrysler-Plymouth in Sterling.

3. Sherri and Vernon have three kids: Tom — 8; Suzanne — 10; and Shelly — 11. Sherri is a housewife.

4. Six months ago Sherri Hall was ejected by a guard from a Sterling Town Council meeting for refusing to sit down and stop talking during a council discussion of the budget for the town's parks.

5. The council voted to cut expenditures on the parks by 12 percent. Town has four parks totaling 65 acres for its 13,000 citizens.

6. Sherri was an opponent of the cut.

7. "Parks are the heart of any town," she had told a reporter after the meeting. "Our parks need more, not less money. I can't just sit by and watch them fall apart further."

8. After that meeting Sherri formed Citizens for a Green Sterling. This organization has picketed Town Hall twice for more support for parks.

9. Text of speech this afternoon by Sherri Hall in front of crowd of 16, including supporters, passersby and reporters on steps of Town Hall: "Hello. How are you all? I think you all know something about the history of my involvement in Sterling's politics. For 36 years I was just another ordinary citizen. I don't think I had attended more than two Town Council meetings in my life. Then suddenly I was on the front page of the local paper and the radio station wanted an interview. I have always cared about this town. I had assumed our politicians cared as much as I did. But when I heard about that plan to actually cut the parks budget six months ago, I decided I better see for myself what they were up to. Well, I saw. And as you all know I was so outraged by what I saw that I couldn't hold still. Later with the help of some of you I formed the CGS. Well, we've accomplished a lot. But it soon became clear to me that there's plenty more to be done. They approved that 12 percent cut as you know. The parks are in awful shape. The schools and libraries and buses and benches of this town aren't in such good shape either. Something has to be done. We need government leaders in this town who care about this town. We need officials who aren't just interested in dollars and cents and all that politician talk. We need officials who care about schools and libraries and buses and benches . . . and about the heart of Sterling — it's parks. So that's why I'm announcing today that I've decided to run for Mayor of Sterling. I'm going to run against Mayor Jerome Barrett — who supported that cut in parks — in the Democratic primary on the 11th of next month. If I win I'm going to make sure this town spends more money on parks and things used by its people. They threw me out of Town Hall once. But I'm going to be coming back."

10. Reporter asks Sherri where she plans to find the money to spend on the improvements she detailed. Sherri's reply: "We are studying that and we will release a detailed plan soon."

11. Barrett in telephone interview after Sherri's announcement: "I welcome her into the race. I think it's good for the town to have as many as possible of its citizens involved in politics. I don't think she understands municipal finance at all, but the voters will have plenty of time to educate her about that."

12. In Sterling, Mayor chairs Town Council meetings.

EIGHT

1. Burglary at 103 Gedney St. in Howorth: Happened sometime between 10 a.m. Saturday and 6 p.m. today.

2. Owner away on vacation at Grand Lake, Colo.

3. House a two-story colonial on a half-acre at the end of Gedney. Borders River View Country Club.

4. Owner, Richard Phelps, 62, returned with wife, Patricia, 59, at 6 p.m. Saw nothing amiss.

5. At 7 p.m. Phelps went to office in house and noticed small safe ajar. Personal papers and stock certificates untouched. TV, radio, cash in bedroom drawer also untouched.

6. Taken from safe: gold jewelry valued at $4,300 and a collection of early English and American coins valued at $15,500. Figures come from appraisal done for Phelps by Deemer, Stein & Goltz, Inc.

7. All above information from Detective Hugo Kolk, who investigated. Kolk said that one or more burglars entered house by kicking in a basement window in northeast corner facing golf course of country club.

8. "This looks like a professional job to me from all the evidence I have so far anyway. Used a window away from neighbors, selective pickup, no fingerprints, you name it. Right now we are at square one. You gotta believe the person knew about that coin collection though. There was no dilly dallying here." — Kolk.

9. Phelps: "What can I say? A hell of a way to end a vacation. I've been collecting those coins for 35 years. They mean more than money to me."

10. Phelps is attorney for the city of Howorth, a part-time position. He also has his own law firm.

NINE

1. Meeting of Albertson Village Council: Held at Village Hall, 1 Van Dyke Drive.

2. Began at 7:35 p.m. Ended 10:19.

3. Minutes of last meeting approved.

4. Council votes 5–0 to send letter of thanks to Jennifer Rowe for donating new American flag for pole in Conners Park.

5. Douglas Marsico, 36, of 19 Oak Brook Road, read the council a petition signed by 14 residents on Oak Brook Road. Five of his neighbors were among the audience of 12 people.

6. Petition: "Dear Mayor and Council: Last September the village agreed to construct a curb along Oak Brook Road between Hill Street and the cul-de-sac. We who live on the block had requested the curb to prevent erosion of our lawns and to keep parishioners of St. Ann's Church from accidentally parking on our lawns. Some of us now wish we had not sought the curbing. With all due respect, it was not installed properly. It is now extremely difficult to enter any driveway on the street with any car without scraping a muffler or tailpipe. We've discussed this with the Department of Public Works and they've hemmed and hawed. It's time to do more. We ask that the curb be lowered by whatever amount necessary so that we can once again use our driveways without ruining our cars."

7. Mayor DeLong suggests that Department of Public Works Director Andrew Cobb be asked to investigate and report in 14 days. Other members of council agree.

8. After meeting. Interview with Mayor Ralph DeLong. "This, frankly, is the first I've heard of the problem on Oak Brook. As you heard, we've instructed Andy Cobb of the Department of Public Works to look into the matter and report back to us in two weeks. Who did the work? I really don't remember. You should check with Mr. Cobb."

9. Andy Cobb: "Yeh, it was O & D Construction Company. They won the contract on bid. They were the low bidder for paving and curbs for the area. I've got it here. They bid $35,500 on the job. This was just a small part of it. Some people just aren't satisfied no matter what you do for them."

10. Marsico: "Did he say that? People should only have enemies like he is our

friend. Here's the facts. I've started parking on the street because the curb knocks the stuffings out of my muffler every time I pull into the driveway."

TEN

Study of the National Teachers Association released today:

1. Average income of public school teachers in U.S.: $18,927, five years ago.

2. Average salary this year, $22,530.

3. Damon Josephson, president of the NTA, an organization representing some 275,000 teachers nationwide: "These figures don't say much for public confidence in education. During these five years inflation was a total of 22 percent. Teachers' salaries rose 19 percent. How can the public ask for quality education when it isn't willing to pay for quality teachers? I'll tell you how I think public education can begin to change for the better in this country. When teachers get a decent wage."

4. You check with state NTA. Average salary in your state is $22,860 this year, slightly above national average, says Gertrude Beer, President of the state NTA.

5. Figures for local teachers here in Green River, provided by Supt. Jane Bidlack. Average salary for 152 teachers in district is $21,275 this year. "Yes, we are below the national and state average but the figure is misleading." Bidlack: "This is one of the few areas in state where enrollment is growing. Lots of our teachers are young and vital. They have little experience so they are less expensive. We hired them because they are good though, not because they are cheap."

6. Bidlack: "Average starting salary in district is $17,350 this year."

7. NTA study: Average starting salary nationwide is $16,425.

8. Survey based on responses from local NTA chapters in 17,032 districts. Represents 93 percent of all districts in the country.

CHAPTER 15

Background and context

Most news stories center on a set of facts that emerge the day the story is written. Yet few stories are complete when they stand on those facts alone. News must be placed in perspective. It must be weighed against what has happened already, what will happen next, and what of a comparable nature is also happening currently.

When such explanatory information gives depth to a story but is not essential to its meaning, it is known as *background*. Background facts usually are placed near the bottom of a story; they can be cut if space is tight (See Chapter 14, Organization). For example, the following paragraphs from a story about an 11-month-old girl who received a new liver and a new lease on life are valuable but not *required* to understand the story. They are the 25th and 26th paragraphs of a 26-paragraph story. They provide background:

Two children are waiting for livers at the Minnesota hospital. Forty-nine adults and children are waiting at the University of Pittsburgh.

"Since our liver program began in 1981," a Pittsburgh spokesman said, "32 adults and 16 children have died waiting."

The Washington Post

Sometimes background information is essential; it is needed to place the breaking events in *context*. This contextual material provides a framework necessary for understanding the news. Context usually appears at the top of the story—sometimes in the lead (See Chapter 8, Hard Leads).

When, for example, the Environmental Protection Agency proposed new standards for levels of lead in gasoline, newspapers around the country noted prominently in their stories that the decision had been reached reluctantly. They were taking note of the *context* of the decision. A reporter who had merely noted the decision without this context would have missed a major portion of the news.

UNACCEPTABLE:
The Reagan administration yesterday proposed more stringent rules governing lead levels in gasoline.

ACCEPTABLE:
The Reagan administration, *bowing to environmentalists' concerns about the danger of lead poisoning among children,* yesterday proposed more stringent rules governing lead levels in gasoline.

The proposal ended months of behind-the-scenes struggle and represented a dramatic reversal from the administration's position when it placed the present standards on a regulatory "hit list" last year.

Associated Press in *The* (Baltimore) *Sun*

The Past

Many stories stretch on for days and even months. Each time the subject is revisited, reporters must remind readers, who cannot be expected to have read and remembered each previous installment, of the basic facts of the story. One of the most important

171

uses of background is to provide this quick briefing for readers on ongoing events.

This story is about a place — the Love Canal — that has been in the news for years:

Attorney General Robert Abrams yesterday urged New York State to delay plans to resell homes near the Love Canal toxic waste dump in Niagara Falls, N.Y.

The background, included relatively high up, was in the fourth graf:

The Love Canal, a filled in trench containing 21,800 tons of dangerous chemicals, became a symbol for many people of toxic waste disaster after chemicals were discovered leaking from the site in 1978.

The New York Times

The secret is always to provide this little history lesson thoroughly enough so that a reader who has read nothing else on the subject will be able to understand the story, but briefly enough so that those who have been keeping up will not be bored. It wouldn't do to devote a significant portion of each new story on the Love Canal to a review of its history. Generally, the relevant past history of a much reported event can be summed up in one to three paragraphs. Less familiar stories may require more background.

The past can also be used to provide more newsworthy facts — context. Such looks back come in particularly handy when covering politics.

Politicians are pragmatic people. Their views have been known to change from year to year, if not month to month. Their often self-serving visions of the future are not always realized. Part of a reporter's job is to keep politicians and other newsmakers honest. One way of doing that is to compare statements and predictions made by newsmakers with their past pronouncements . . . as recorded in old newspaper stories and in their own literature (See Chapter 18, Research).

When, for example, President Reagan claimed in June 1982 that "all of last year we were talking about a sluggish economy," the reporter for *The New York Times* was prepared to set that statement in context:

Actually, Reagan had predicted early last year that enactment of his economic program would generate economic growth before the end of 1981.

Comparison

The weight of an event (See Chapter 7, News Judgment) is often best indicated through comparison. It is incumbent on the reporter to tell readers if a race was run in the *fastest* time ever, the tax increase was *twice*

as large as last year's or the plane crash was the *worst* ever in the state.

Here the comparison *is* the news, so it was placed in the lead:

Domestic new-car sales continue to sputter, with the five major automakers yesterday reporting *their lowest daily selling rate for mid-October in 24 years.*

The (Bergen County, N.J.) Record

The comparison may be less newsworthy when the drama in an event is self-evident. In this story about the collapse of a scaffolding from which 51 workers fell 170 feet to their deaths, the comparison, which set the context, appeared lower in the story than usual. It was in the third graf:

Eleven members of a family were among the victims of the accident, which Gov. John D. Rockefeller 4th termed *the worst non-mining industrial accident in the state's history.*

The New York Times

Comparisons are of little value, however, if they are not specific.

WEAK:
An unusual number of primary contests have emerged in Nassau County this year, election officials said yesterday.

(Long Island, N.Y.) Newsday

For readers to gain a clear understanding of the primary situation, the reporter would have had to compare the number of contests this year with the number in previous years. "Unusual" tells us little.

Patterns

The news tends to be repetitious. Sometimes, however, that repetition seems to be more than a matter of chance. If five buildings burn down on the same block within two months, a pattern has emerged whether police have established a connection among the fires or not. Reporters should let readers know something unusual is going on, and they should let them know prominently in the story:

An abandoned warehouse on Gatlin Road burned to the ground early yesterday morning in a fire police described as being of suspicious origin.

It was the fifth fire in a four-square-block area in the past two months. A mother and her two children were killed Sept. 24 when a fire raced through their second-floor apartment two blocks from yesterday's blaze at the Cherney Co. warehouse on 235 Gatlin Road.

Fire officials said yesterday that they do not know whether any of the five fires are connected. They said, however, that all appeared to be the work of arsonists.

Future

Our legislative and judicial systems are as much process as product. A verdict may be overturned on appeal; an amendment passed by an assembly committee may lose in the assembly only to be approved in the state senate, approved when resubmitted to the assembly, and then vetoed along with the rest of the bill by the governor. For stories to be meaningful, this process—or at least the next steps in it—must be explained within the first several paragraphs of a story:

With Halloween six days away and the Tylenol poisonings on their minds, legislators in both houses yesterday approved measures setting a six-month mandatory sentence for anyone caught giving out poisoned candy or other deadly treats.

The measure will now . . . go to Governor Kean. W. Cary Edwards, Kean's chief counsel, said the administration would have to study the bill to see if it adds anything useful to mandatory minimums already on the books.

The (Bergen County, N.J.) Record

The future, in other words, can also place events in context.

▪ A ▪

Which of the background facts listed below definitely should be included in stories on the following subjects? Which might be included, depending on how much space was available for the story? And which should not be included? Write "yes" next to the facts that would be essential; "maybe" next to those that would be optional — depending on length; and "no" next to those that should be ignored.

ONE

Police Commissioner Steven Leary orders officers not to fire their guns unless first fired upon.

_____ 1. Leary appointed to job when predecessor resigned to run unsuccessfully for mayor.

_____ 2. Leary's nomination as commissioner had been opposed by some community groups because they considered him too much of a "hard liner," too much of a "law and order man."

_____ 3. Leary had served as assistant commissioner in Columbus, Ohio, before accepting this job.

_____ 4. One week ago a teen-ager was killed by a policeman who said he thought the youth was about to pull a gun on him. No gun was found on the teen-ager.

_____ 5. The mayor has said he will review Leary's handling of this situation.

TWO

Local high school senior Mark Egan runs the mile in 4:04 to win the mile race at the state high school championships.

_____ 1. Egan transferred here from an out-of-state school two years ago.

_____ 2. Egan's time would have set a record for high school students in his old state.

_____ 3. This was the fastest he has ever run the mile.

_____ 4. His time tied the record for the fastest mile ever run by a high school student in this state.

_____ 5. Jack Renaldo, of Oakdale High, ran a 4:04 in a meet in this state three years ago.

_____ 6. Egan plans to run in the national high school championships in June.

_____ 7. The third fastest mile ever run in the state was run by Steven Wild, also of Oakdale, two years ago.

THREE

Two people were killed when the car in which they were riding slammed into a wall next to a curve on the Shoreline Highway.

_____ 1. There had been two other fatal accidents at that curve in the past three years.

_____ 2. The state had been scheduled to widen the curve, beginning next week.

_____ 3. Anti-nuclear demonstrators had marched on that section of Shoreline Parkway last week.

_____   **4.** Money for widening the curve had been approved by the state Highway Department six months ago.

FOUR

The scores of city high school juniors on a standardized national test drop 1 percent from previous year's scores.

_____   **1.** Scores on test nationwide were the same as in previous year.

_____   **2.** Scores in the city had dropped an average of 1 percent in each of previous four years.

_____   **3.** New reading and math programs were introduced here this year to stop declining scores.

_____   **4.** School Supt. Sue Jamison, just before scores were announced, called this test "not perfect, but certainly not something we can ignore."

_____   **5.** Scores in a neighboring city increased 1 percent this year.

FIVE

President of local bank dies of heart attack while getting out of his limousine in business district.

_____   **1.** Two other local bank presidents have died of heart attacks within past decade.

_____   **2.** Bank had recently announced profit for year of $130,000.

_____   **3.** Bank president had a history of heart trouble.

_____   **4.** Bank president had recently instituted an employee physical fitness program, citing lessons he had learned from his own condition.

▪ B ▪

Additional contextual or background information is listed after each of the following stories. Add the information, if needed, at the appropriate spots in the stories.

ONE

A 43-year-old priest waiting for a bus on upper Green Street was robbed at knife-point last night by two teen-agers, police said.

The priest, Rev. Peter Santangello of St. Mary's Church on East 87th Street and Parker Boulevard, was dressed in clerical garb when he was held up at 11:45 p.m. at the deserted bus stop near the corner of Centre Avenue, according to Sgt. Raoul Valenzuela.

Santangello was not injured, Sgt. Valenzuela said.

Valenzuela said two youths, both about 16 years old, approached Santangello and demanded a bag he was carrying. When the priest refused, one of them pulled a knife, while the other grabbed the bag, Valenzuela said.

Police said they have no suspects.

Additional Information:

1. This was the fourth robbery of a priest in the city this month.
2. Rev. Ambrose McIntyre and Rev. Joseph Santos were held up while working late at St. Francis's Church in the suburb of Cherry Woods, five miles from the site of last night's robbery. Rev. Stephen Riley was robbed while walking home from St. Paul's a mile further south on Centre Avenue three weeks ago. None of the priests was injured.
3. Police say they have no evidence of a connection among the robberies.

TWO

Police investigators will be interviewing hundreds of residents of the Point Pleasant area today in an effort to find someone who saw 8-year-old Cindy Wolf before she disappeared Thursday afternoon.

According to Lt. James Flaske, investigators will concentrate on an eight-block area around the child's home at 324 West Meadow Road. They will be looking for someone who may have seen the thin, blonde-haired girl after she got off her school bus at 3:20 p.m. Thursday on West Meadow Road, Flaske said. Cindy was wearing an orange slicker and had her hair in braids.

Lt. Flaske said that police have no leads in the case.

Additional Information:
1. Cindy Wolf's parents, Henry and Alma Wolf, reported her missing Thursday evening when she failed to return from school.
2. She was last seen by school bus driver Richmond Avery, getting off the bus.
3. Henry Wolf was the prosecutor responsible for sending five reputed members of an organized-crime family to jail last summer, but police have no information linking his daughter's disappearance to that case.

THREE

Mayor Ellen Goodman has endorsed Sam Streeter in the runoff election for the Democratic nomination for city controller.

Streeter, a local businessman, is running against former Councilman George Harris for the right to face incumbent Arthur Greener in the November election.

"Streeter's business experience makes him the best person for the job," Goodman said in a press conference at City Hall today.

Streeter welcomed the mayor's endorsement. "I think it gives my campaign a big boost in these crucial final days," he said. The runoff election will be held next Tuesday.

However, Harris discounted the significance of the mayor's move. "Voters in this city are going to make up their own minds," he said.

Additional Information:

1. Streeter received 34 percent of the vote in the Democratic primary two weeks ago; Harris received 22 percent; the rest of the vote was split among three other candidates.
2. The mayor had declined to endorse any of the candidates in the primary.

FOUR

The City Council voted last night to impose a 3 percent sales tax on all retail sales in the city.

The council approved the new tax by a vote of 4–3.

Councilwoman Greta Almalfi, who gave no indication of how she would vote during the debate, cast the deciding vote in favor of the new tax.

Councilman William Ruckham, the most vocal proponent of the sales tax, which would take effect on January 1, estimated that it would raise $350,000 in its first year.

"This tax will finally give the city the money it needs to keep its schools and roads in decent repair," Ruckham said during last night's debate.

Opponents of the tax argued that it would hurt business in the city and place an unfair burden on the poor. "If we need a tax, and I'm not sure we do, let it be a graduated income tax," said Michele Flurenski, head of the council's Finance Committee. "A graduated income tax would spare those who cannot afford to pay and would protect the retail businesses that are so important to this town."

However, Al Freedberg, another supporter of the sales tax on the council, defended it as "the simplest, least painful way for the city to pay its bills."

Almalfi refused to discuss her vote after the meeting.

Additional Information:

1. The city has never before had a sales tax.
2. The council defeated similar proposals twice in the last six months, by votes of 4–3, with Almalfi voting against them both times.
3. The tax bill must still be signed by Mayor Hedrick Armstrong, a long-time supporter of a sales tax.
4. The tax bill must also be approved by the state legislature, which rarely has interfered with local tax plans in the past.

FIVE

The rock group The Rage announced yesterday that it will play a concert here on May 26 to benefit Municipal Hospital.

According to lead singer, Owl Saul, the concert, at the Music Factory, could raise as much as $50,000 for the hospital. All receipts from the show will go to the hospital.

"We care about the people of this town," Saul said. "We recognize that we have a debt to them. This is our way of expressing that care and repaying some of that debt."

Municipal Hospital Director Alison Burt said she was pleased to hear of the benefit concert. "We are working to upgrade our facilities, and this money will be a big help in that effort," Burt said.

Additional Information:

1. The Rage had the best-selling record album in the United States last month.
2. Last Aug. 16 two people were injured in a stampede to the stage at a Rage concert at the Music Factory; one — 19-year-old Seymour Hamilton, who lived on West Street — later died.
3. Both the people injured at the concert were treated at Municipal Hospital.

Reporting

▪ PART FOUR ▪

Techniques

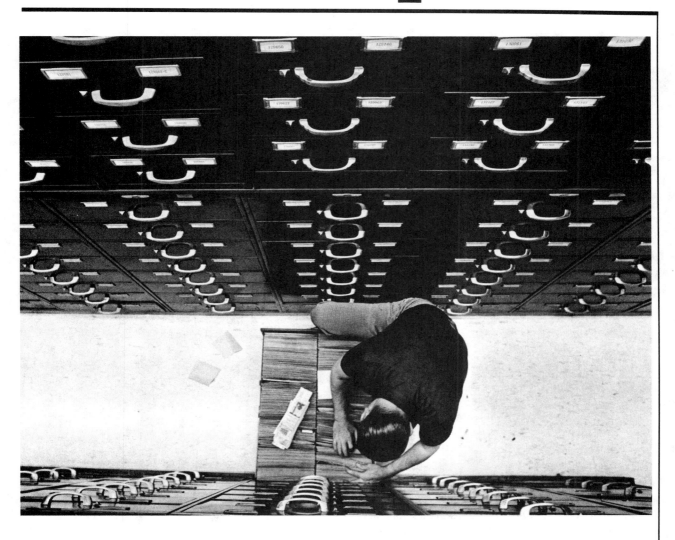

CHAPTER 16

Facts

Jimmy is 8 years old and a third-generation heroin addict, a precocious little boy with sandy hair, velvety brown eyes and needle marks freckling the baby-smooth skin of his thin brown arms.

So began *The Washington Post* story that in 1982 was awarded one of journalism's most respected prizes, a Pulitzer. It was a powerful story, but it was not true. Jimmy did not exist. The prize was withdrawn; the paper's pride shaken.

Journalism is about things that are true. Not the elemental truths of artists and philosophers — the police stations, city halls and business offices where reporters pick up their information do not generally deal in eternal *verités*. A journalist's truths are tentative, clapboard structures banged together out of stripped-down, unvarnished facts. It is a fact that the suspects were arrested and charged with murder. Six months from now the fact may be that they were found innocent of that charge. Similarly, it is a fact that the governor said she would veto the proposal. It is a fact that the fire was at the corner of Miller Avenue and 43rd Street. It is *not* a fact that that *Washington Post* reporter found an 8-year-old heroin addict.

Reporters should be suspicious of any story that can't be tied to solid fact. They should be uncomfortable with predictions, speculation and attempts at mind reading. The best reporters continually struggle to cut through the evasions and the distortions of newsmakers, but they do so by piecing together patterns of facts, not by voicing an opinion.

Checking

Joseph Pulitzer, the renowned turn-of-the-century editor and publisher, used to say there were three things he demanded of his reporters: "Accuracy, accuracy and accuracy." As Pulitzer undoubtedly realized, those are not simple demands. Facts are notoriously slippery. They can get lost while being transmitted from someone's memory to someone's mouth and from that mouth to another person's ear. They can wander off somewhere before hitting a note pad. That's why reporters handle facts with so much care.

Many a reporter has jumped out of bed at 3 a.m., grabbed a telephone book and checked for the third time to make sure that a name was spelled right. Facts make reporters paranoid . . . and they should. The reporter who made up that story about the young addict was fired. Reporters who can't get addresses right don't last long either.

For a start, reporters must check the spelling of the name of every unfamiliar person they meet on a story. Many interviews begin with the request, "Before we get started, could you just go over the spelling of your name?" And many interviews end with, "May I just make sure I spelled your name right?" Reporters will ask a police officer for the spelling of the name of a victim or suspect, then double-check with the arrest record (facts seem a little more reliable when they are written down). If the victim was hurt or killed, the hospital or coroner also may be consulted.

And names are just a start. The address, the age, the name of the place where someone works, the time, the cause of death, the name of the hospital, the attribution, the explanation—stories are masses of facts, and each one must be worried over:

> A Chicago fireman was killed yesterday by a flash of fire when he rushed into an empty burning home on the Far South Side after neighbors reportedly told firemen that three children were trapped inside.
>
> Sidney Brown, 32, of 7915 S. Peoria St., assigned to Engine Co. 75, was pronounced dead at 4:20 p.m. of burns and smoke inhalation in Roseland Community Hospital.
>
> *Chicago Tribune*

Getting the facts right does not depend exclusively on asking and reasking, checking and rechecking. It may take some thought: "Hey, the police are saying it happened at Shady Knoll Road and Strawberry Lane in Southbrook, but those two roads intersect in West Orange!" Then it's back to asking and reasking, checking and rechecking.

Reporters soon realize that no matter how great the quotes they've obtained, how solid their understanding, how engaging their writing, if one digit in a number, one letter in a street name, is wrong, somebody is going to spot it. There may be a letter; a correction may have to be run. A reporter's credibility rests on every fact.

Proof

Not all facts are as straightforward as a name, an address or an age. Where people's reputations are at stake, information requires corroboration as well as attribution, no matter how carefully it's reported.

Charges against people, unless they are made during trials or other official proceedings (See Chapter 25, Courts) don't just have to be double-checked to make sure they have been transcribed properly. They have to be, in some sense, proven.

During their celebrated Watergate investigation, Bob Woodward and Carl Bernstein of *The Washington Post* refused to report any charges until they had been confirmed by two sources—two reliable sources. That should be taken as a minimum standard for any reporter who has been handed some ready-to-fling mud. Documented proof—records—are even better when available. One source saying that the state attorney general is a hidden partner in a race track invites further investigation, not a story. Some trustworthy form of confirmation, and an interview with the accused person, will be needed before the charge can appear in print—carefully attributed, of course.

Much more than the reporter's credibility rests on the confirmation of such a "fact."

Interpretation

Newspaper readers will not always be satisfied with simple accounts of who said what to whom when. They often have seen the newsmakers themselves talking on television the previous evening. When their newspaper comes out the next morning, they may want a little more: Why did they say that? What did it mean? Newspaper reporters increasingly are asked to *interpret* the news.

There are dangers here. Interpretation too often leads to guesswork and subjectivity. For example, one *New York Times* reporter, writing on a visit by President Reagan to Great Britain, said that, "In style, Mr. Reagan pleased and almost charmed Britain" with his "genial and relaxed manner." Three days later, another *New York Times* reporter wrote that British newspapers, in assessing the same visit, "commented on the lack of spontaneity or common touch to his [Reagan's] appearances."

Where are the facts there? Where are the facts when the *Los Angeles Times* concludes that a speech by Reagan before the British Parliament was "generally well-received," while *The New York Times* reports a day later that the same speech "stunned many Britons, including a number of leading conservatives."

Too frequently, reporters take their orders to explain causes and effects as license to take leave of the facts. They certainly do their readers no service with unsupported and possibly unfounded speculation that a speech was "generally well-received."

As usual in journalism, the solution is to include more facts. Facts do not just fill all the little holes in a story; they anchor it and keep it from wandering too far from observable reality. Instead of indulging in guesswork, R. W. Apple of *The New York Times* managed to say something about reaction to that speech Reagan gave by noting the generally overlooked fact that "only about 30 of the 225 members of the Labour Party" chose to show up in Parliament to hear Reagan.

It is more difficult to find a fact illustrating reaction to a speech than simply to take a stab at summing up that reaction yourself. But good reporters always are ready to make the extra effort. The order to interpret, to analyze, to explain the news should be seen as an order to find more, not fewer, facts—to conduct that extra interview in search of a quote that might explain why, to read that extra document in search of a crucial explanation, to observe the scene more closely in search of a telling detail.

Reporters are people who watch, read, ask and listen, with notebook out and pen in hand. They should also be interested in nuances, concepts and ideas, but they should be looking to translate these subtler thoughts into what is essentially the language of journalism — the language of facts.

Additional Reading

"Trust Me Journalism: The Hidden Dangers of Increasing Analysis and Interpretation in the Daily Press," Gerald Lanson and Mitchell Stephens, *Washington Journalism Review,* November 1982.

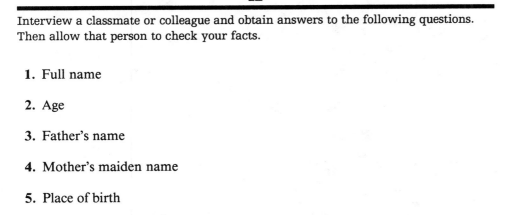

Interview a classmate or colleague and obtain answers to the following questions. Then allow that person to check your facts.

1. Full name

2. Age

3. Father's name

4. Mother's maiden name

5. Place of birth

6. Date of birth

7. Names, ages and occupations of any brothers and sisters

8. Schools attended

9. Employment history

10. Address

11. Religion

12. Hobbies

13. Major in college

14. Minor in college

15. Career goals

▪ B ▪

Using a dictionary, almanac, encyclopedia, atlas or other reference materials, correct any factual errors in the following information.

1. Iceland is located just north of Greenland.

2. Raphael, an Italian painter, lived from 1493 to 1520.

3. The New York Mets were in the World Series in 1969 and 1970.

4. Richard Nixon was Dwight Eisenhower's vice president.

5. The sitar is a Moroccan stringed instrument.

6. Texas has the largest land area of any state in the United States.

7. Ronald Reagan had no children by his second marriage.

8. West Germany has the largest army of any West European country.

9. The United States purchased Alaska from Russia.

10. The highest judicial position in the United States is chief justice of the Supreme Court.

▪ C ▪

ONE

Note what is wrong with the facts in this description of a robbery provided by a witness:

"Yeah, sure. I remember the exact moment it occurred. I was the only customer in the store. It had just opened. I was standing in front of the supermarket—by the milk—and it was exactly 8:22 . . . I know because I was looking at my watch . . . when these two Hispanic guys dressed in purple pushed through the doors and ran up to one of the checkout girls. One pulled out a pistol from beneath what looked like an army overcoat, aimed it at the nylons of the checkout lady and shouted something like "Vite! Vite! Or you'll never walk again." The manager jumped down from his booth and the second guy pulled a rifle, I believe it was a Colt, so he couldn't get near her, while the first guy was covering all the rest of us who had stopped shopping and had run over to see what all the banging was about. Anyway, the checkout woman looked at the gun on her and started clearing out everything in her drawer . . . lots of loose bills and checks and food stamps . . . and all these coupons and even the money from her pants pockets. It was right out of Hill Street Blues, you know, that show with James Garner . . . The manager was there reaching into the drawer too and stuffing things into these white A & P bags yelling, "Don't shoot!" as the robber just sits there smoking a cigarette . . . And then they were gone . . . these two tough guys . . . you could see their muscles . . . and they drive away in a 1985 Toyota Accord with green California plates . . . sorry, I just couldn't see the number."

TWO

The desk sergeant for the state police gives you this story. Note what's wrong with his facts.

"Yeah, we arrested a woman for driving while intoxicated on state Route 45 in Ainsley. Weird story. Do you know the highway? It's straight as an arrow for miles, two lanes and a shoulder on each side and a grassy area dividing the north- and southbound lanes. It's 3:22 a.m. and the highway is deserted. Well, Officer Keith Bart was driving southbound, all by himself, when he looks out the driver's window and sees this green car driving right toward all the traffic on the northbound lane. Officer Keith didn't waste any time. He crossed the grassy median and put his car sideways so this green car couldn't get around him . . . Luckily no one else was on the road although they probably would have spotted him because it was getting light. Keith jumps out and just in time. The blue car smashed right into the side by the door. It pushed the police car about 20 feet, slamming it into Keith's partner, Leslie Locke. She sprained her knee. The woman driving the car seemed dazed. We found some marijuana in the glove compartment and it was clear she was stoned out of her mind. Her name was Elizabeth Aramor. She's 42 and lives in Stanton in the High Tor apartments. She's already been convicted at police headquarters."

▪ **D** ▪

Write a story based on the following information. You are writing for a newspaper dated tomorrow and read in the town where the event occurred.

1. Basketball game tonight between Hawthorne State College (located here in Hawthorne) and Raintree College (located in Raintree County in this state).

2. Before the game Hawthorne one game behind Raintree in Central Conference. Raintree in first; Hawthorne in second. Before game, four games to play before end of season for each team. Conference winner automatically in national college championship tournament this year.

3. Last night final score: Raintree 72, Hawthorne 75.

4. Half-time score: Raintree 52, Hawthorne 37.

5. Raintree ahead until 2:38 left in second half.

6. Raintree high scorers: Al Kosman — 14, James Gutworth — 10.

7. Hawthorne high scorers: John Coleman — 28, Ralph Stokes — 10.

8. From interview after game with Kosman: "Okay, I'll talk with you, but only for a minute. I hated it, okay. It was awful. It felt like someone put a lid over our basket in the second half. Nothing we put up would go in."

9. From interview after the game with Coleman: "Hey, I'm still in shock, or something. I just wanted the ball, if you understand what I'm saying. You know, I've had big nights before, but to do it against Raintree was really something special. Hey, we're number one."

10. After game Hawthorne's record: in conference 10–2, overall 17–6; Raintree's record: in conference 10–2, overall 19–5.

CHAPTER 17

Story origination

Good reporters don't wait for the news to come to them; they search for it.

Editors do assign many stories, of course. But reporters have to learn to develop their own stories, too, both out of those assignments and in areas that their editors may know nothing about. An editor may assign a reporter to cover a press conference, but it's up to the reporter to determine what the news is there and whether the news might be part of a larger trend or pattern worth pursuing the next day.

And reporters who are assigned a *beat* — a specific area of coverage such as police, the courts, city government or a whole town — will be responsible not only for knowing when press conferences and meetings are going to be held, but also, where possible, for breaking a story beforehand.

Plenty of news is never announced. Stories about the trends, the squabbles, the dirt and the subtler movements and fluctuations that lie behind events are uncovered by reporters who know whom to listen to and how and where to look.

"[*Philadelphia Inquirer* Editor] Gene Roberts used to say that really important things seep and creep," recalls Molly Ivins, a *Dallas Times Herald* columnist who once worked with Roberts at *The New York Times.* "No one ever held a press conference to announce that there was an enormous migration of blacks from South to North."

This chapter will talk about ways of finding the news. Some are conventional: These are strategies for winnowing the news from the thickets of often self-serving information that sprout or are planted under the light cast by any news organization. Some are unconventional: The biggest stories sometimes go to reporters who can spot the news that grows, untended and overlooked, in the shade.

Press Releases

In our society of sellers, promoters and campaigners, almost everyone seems to have a message to transmit and almost everyone seems conscious of the media's ability to amplify those messages. Hundreds of messages find their way into newsrooms each day in the form of press releases. They announce a rock star's new manager, the findings of a government study or the date of the elementary school's next PTA meeting. Many are written by public relations professionals — people whose job it is to spread news of their clients.

Many press releases are designed to appear as complete news stories from the dateline at the top to the *30* at the bottom (see Appendix A, Format). They are intended to slip unedited into a hole in a lazy journalist's newspaper. The vast majority are more likely to end up in the newsroom's garbage bin.

Press releases are always worth reading, however; they just might plant the seed of a good story. But they should be read with the understanding that long or short, frivolous or serious, from the government or from a company, all press releases have two limitations: First, they are unlikely to tell the complete story; you are not going to learn from the press release that that rock star has already fired four different managers. Second, press releases don't merely pass on information; they pass it on in a way that reflects favorably on the person or organization that sent them, or, in the case of potentially negative or alarming news, they downplay its impact. The press release's description of that star as "the best songwriter since Bob Dylan" should not necessarily be swallowed whole. Nor should a company's insistence that it decided to file for reorganization under bankruptcy laws so that it could "emerge even stronger."

Gerald Lanson, one of the authors of this book, was covering the environment for *The Record,* in Bergen County, N.J., when a press release, excerpted here, arrived from the state Department of Environmental Protection.

TRENTON—The Department of Environmental Protection (DEP) today released the initial results of a major statewide groundwater testing project which is examining 500 wells for selected toxic and cancer-causing chemicals.

Environmental Protection Commissioner Rocco D. Ricci said results from the first 250 wells tested in 12 counties show that water quality, in most cases, was found to be far better than federal drinking water standards. No wells were found to pose an immediate danger to human health, Ricci emphasized.

Ricci said 20 violations of the federal standards were found and DEP is now conducting follow-up testing at these sites to identify the sources of pollution. None of the contaminated wells are sources of potable water supplies, Ricci said . . .

Press releases like this should be viewed as potential starting points for stories, not as anything approaching finished products. First, reporters glance through them to see if there is any news. Sometimes, the news may not be what the release's author chooses to highlight.

In this case, the reporter knew enough about the subject to see beyond the cheery statements in the release's second paragraph. He knew that meeting federal standards was not that impressive because for most of the chemicals no federal standards existed. And he knew that the presence of any amount of these chemicals in drinking water was cause for some concern.

The intriguing news in the release was that "almost all of the wells tested contained traces of some of the chemicals under investigation," a fact the release did not get around to mentioning until its fifth paragraph.

If a release leads to a trail worth following, the next step for reporters is to find someone who can guide them in the right direction. Every release designates someone as a press contact and gives that person's phone number. Reporters should either call the press contact or someone else they know to be more knowledgeable. A call, if nothing else, verifies that the release is authentic. It also starts the real reporting.

When Lanson received the release from the New Jersey environmental agency, he chose to call Dr. Peter Preuss, who had supervised the testing program, instead of either Commissioner Ricci or the agency's spokesman. In an interview with Preuss, Lanson tried to determine what wells had been tested, particularly in his area of the state; what levels of contaminants had been found and how great a danger they posed.

Here is how his story began:

TRENTON—A sampling of the state's underground water supplies has revealed that they are widely contaminated with low levels of potentially cancer-causing chemicals.

State-sponsored tests of 250 public and private wells for 50 toxic and potentially cancer-causing chemicals have shown that almost all contained at least traces of some of the chemicals, according to a report released yesterday by the Department of Environmental Protection (DEP).

Eight of the wells sampled are in Bergen County, and 11 are in Passaic County. The report said none of the 250 wells presented an immediate threat to public health.

But Dr. Peter Preuss, head of the DEP's cancer program, said the presence of even trace quantities of potentially cancer-causing substances raised the possibility of long-term effects on health.

"I think [the test results] are a cause for concern and that it will require a fair amount of effort to determine the boundaries for that concern," he said. "If you have a large population exposed to low levels [of potentially cancer-causing chemicals] over a long period of time, then there will be some added risk of cancer. We don't know what that risk will be."

The (Bergen County, N.J.) *Record*

Most press releases are more straightforward: Someone has been hired, fired or honored; something has been scheduled or accomplished; something has changed. But all press releases should be examined and, when newsworthy, reported with a critical eye.

Tips

All good reporters have troops of sources they rely on to alert them regularly to potential news (See Chapter 19, Sources). Veteran police reporter Mike Cox of the *Austin American-Statesman* was at home when a former prisoner who had filed a widely reported suit that led to prison reform in Texas was arrested again and charged with armed robbery. One of Cox's sources in the police department quickly gave him a call, and the next morning Cox had a front-page story.

Cox expects such tips from his sources ("I'll get angry if I don't get a call," he says), and he knows to what extent he can trust the information he gets from the sources on whom he relies.

Sometimes tips come from a relative stranger. One morning in Lufkin, Texas, a local builder walked into the newsroom of the *Lufkin News* and started telling a story about his nephew who he claimed died while training with the Marines in San Diego. Ken Herman was the only reporter on duty, and he was called in to listen.

"It's not unusual for someone to walk into the newsroom unmolested on a small newspaper," Herman explains. "Some you can't help. Some you don't believe. This was one where we were able to pursue it and we got some answers." The *Lufkin News* pursued this tip on questionable Marine training tactics well enough and found enough answers to win a Pulitzer Prize.

People who think they have a story try to corral reporters in person, they try to reach them on the phone and they try to contact them by mail. Doreen Carvajal, who covers the police for the *St. Petersburg Times,* once received a letter maintaining that a veteran police sergeant had resigned after being arrested a second time for indecent exposure. Few reporters will ignore such tips — this is one route to scoops — but all good reporters will check them out thoroughly and obtain solid corroborating evidence before allowing a tip from any source to get into print (See Chapter 16, Facts). "Sometimes tips check out, sometimes they don't," says Carvajal. "This time it checked out."

Records

When Bruce Maxwell was hired as an investigative reporter for the *Rochester* (Minn.) *Post-Bulletin,* he had a hunch that he could find his first story before ever setting foot in the state.

Maxwell, who was completing a graduate reporting program in Washington, D.C., visited the Nuclear Regulatory Commission's public documents room and asked for the *reportable occurrences* file for the Prairie Island nuclear power plant located near his new newspaper. In the file, which contains documents related to any problems at a plant, a single sentence caught his attention: It said a used radioactive fuel assembly had come apart nearly two years before while being moved underwater in a storage tank.

That single sentence in a NRC report led three months later to a four-part series that began like this:

Nearly two years ago, a nuclear fuel assembly containing highly radioactive fuel elements broke in two while it was being moved at the Prairie Island nuclear power plant.

No one knows what caused the failure, even though several investigations have been conducted during the last 20 months . . .

The weight of scientific opinion says that mishaps like that at Prairie Island do not threaten public safety.

Instead, the significance of the Prairie Island incident lies in the fact that it serves as a microcosm of problems plaguing the U.S. nuclear industry.

Reporters can find somewhat less difficult stories by, for example, spotting a well-known name or an unusual crime in police or court records, an unusually large number hidden in a business's otherwise ordinary quarterly report, or an exceptionally high expense account filed by the city manager.

Localizing

When federal, state or county governments pass laws, enact regulations and appropriate funds, their actions eventually affect the lives of people. Too often, though, newspapers dutifully print blow-by-blow accounts from the wire services of legislative battles only to lose interest when the impact of the change begins to be felt at home.

There are exceptions: When the National Commission on Excellence in Education issued a report decrying the state of public education, many newspapers reacted by looking at problems and solutions in their own schools. "When a national commission puts out a report talking about a rising tide of mediocrity in the schools, it suggests local stories you almost have to do," says Saundra Keyes, education writer for *The Courier-Journal* in Louisville, Ky. "One suggestion was that students waste their electives. So you go to your own schools and see what's happening. Another issue was merit pay for teachers, which raises the issue of how local teachers are paid and evaluated."

The effects of recession, inflation and unemployment are just a few other national stories that reporters can localize, and humanize, by looking at how people are coping in their readership area.

Such localizing can be overdone. Reporters can grow so consumed with uncovering local manifestations of national trends that they lose sight of the idiosyncrasies that make their area distinctive. But as long as reporters use national trends as tools to understand better what is happening locally — instead of trying to force a national perspective on local events — these national and regional stories can be useful sources of local story ideas.

Regionalizing

In the era of suburban sprawl, the regional newspaper, serving several dozen or more independent communities, is fast taking the place of the urban newspaper that serves a single, cohesive metropolitan area. Papers like *The Record* in New Jersey and *Newsday* on Long Island serve no single dominant community. And major, metropolitan papers such as *The Washington Post,* the *Los Angeles Times* and *The Philadelphia Inquirer* have sections tailored to meet the tastes of their expanding suburban audiences.

It becomes virtually impossible to provide thorough municipal coverage for dozens of small towns whose residents read the same paper; newspapers aren't thick enough for that. It also isn't good business. Residents in Carle Place, Long Island, don't much care about a run-of-the-mill school budget fight in Hicksville, Long Island.

Faced with the challenge of building a cohesive readership out of an audience with disparate municipal loyalties, most regional newspapers encourage their reporters to look for *trend stories* — reports on issues that cut across the borders separating suburban towns. In other words, reporters on these papers are asked to *regionalize* their stories. If they come upon a dispute in the town they cover about the difficulty the elderly are having finding affordable housing, reporters might examine the problem of housing for the elderly in other towns in the region as well. And if they hear a complaint at a city council meeting about shopping centers hurting local downtown shops, reporters might look into whether other main-street shop owners in the region are facing hard times.

Story ideas, then, travel in both directions in journalism: Local stories grow out of events and decisions at a national, state and regional level, and regional stories evolve from what starts as a local issue.

Unannounced Stories

Some reporters just seem lucky. When Tom French, a court reporter for the *St. Petersburg Times,* took out his checkbook to pay for a record one day, the man who ran the record store saw his name, figured out he was a reporter and immediately began telling him about a strange incident in which the store owner was involved. French ended up with an off-beat piece on how the record store was sued for $1.74 — it cost the plaintiff $40 just to file the suit.

There is a certain amount of luck in reporting. But because good reporters do things to increase their chances of getting lucky, good luck often seems to follow them around. And while some of the stories they stumble onto are merely cute — a $1.74 lawsuit

—many will be refreshingly original precisely because they are unexpected and are not derived from conventional news sources.

Here are some ways to improve your "luck":

Staying Alert

"If you keep your eyes and ears open, if you ask about things, you'll come up with good stories," says Doug Rainey, city hall reporter for the *La Crosse* (Wis.) *Tribune.*

Rainey recalls a reporter's alertness paying off one snowy night years ago when Rainey was an editor on *The Hutchinson News* in central Kansas. While driving home, that reporter noticed a city plow clearing the public golf course, although plenty of people were still trapped in their homes by the snow and no one was exactly lining up at the first tee.

"It was a totally useless activity, and at the same time people were calling and complaining that streets weren't being cleared," recalls Rainey. The paper ran the story. Well before the following winter, Hutchinson had a new director of public works.

Routine meetings needn't be covered routinely either. A reporter for *The Record* in New Jersey took note when a lawyer in the audience at a town government meeting strayed from the agenda to complain that new maps designating certain areas of the town a "flood plain" might keep his client, a shopping center, from expanding. The comment took all of five minutes but it piqued the reporter's curiosity. He did some research and the result, months later, was an award-winning series on how state and federal flood control programs were placing restrictions on land use that could devalue millions of acres of developed and undeveloped land around the country.

This story was perhaps too subtle to have been heralded by press conferences and demonstrations. It was one of those stories that, in Gene Roberts's words, "seep and creep."

Brainstorming

Sometimes a reporter's brain, a reporter's creativity, requires a little nudging. In a memo to reporters at *The Boston Globe,* Don Murray, who has served as the paper's writing coach, suggested, among other things, that reporters could find story ideas by sitting down and working up a quick list of topics that might interest local readers — crime, commuting, property taxes, public schools, shopping, perhaps.* They then could pick one topic and do some free associating, getting as specific as possible.

* Murray's ideas are spelled out in his book *Writing for Your Readers* (See Additional Reading).

It might work like this:

Public education.
For gifted children?
Special programs?
More or fewer than a decade ago?
Are they more or less conventional?
Do these students get bored in school?
Do they leave a year early to attend college?
How do they do in college academically if they enroll early?
What about emotionally?
Has anyone ever traced what happens to students who enter college before age 16?
Can I find students who left area high schools early and enrolled in college?

While few reporters may actually play this particular game, most find some time to think about readers' interests and to let their minds wander over those interests looking for fresh angles.

Wandering

Sometimes, Murray advises, story ideas can be found by letting your body as well as your mind wander. Take some free time and visit a videogame parlor, an old-age home, a bowling alley. If you usually drive to work, walk or take a bus. Drive through an area you haven't been to before. A few more ideas, suggested in Murray's memo: "Shop in a supermarket where people on welfare shop. Stand in line at an unemployment office and listen to what people are saying. Sit in a waiting room at a clinic. Watch a ballgame from the bleachers."

A story idea is just a fresh perspective on some aspect of life. Sometimes all it takes is a break in the routine to obtain that new perspective.

Reading

There are thousands of magazines in the United States, and they cater to a wide variety of interests. Occasionally reporters can find a fresh slant on a story just by looking through a magazine they wouldn't normally read — perhaps one read by bird watchers, hang-glide enthusiasts or health-food lovers. Murray suggests buying a different magazine every week.

And don't forget the ads. One freelancer developed a story on computerized voice boxes after she saw an ad for one in *Discover* magazine.

Questioning

Just walking down the street with a good reporter can be enlightening. Like three-year-old children, many reporters seem to question everything: What are they building over there? Who owns the new office building next to it? Is this new development putting a strain on the roads? Where do all the people who work there park? Where do they eat lunch?

Most questions will lead to simple, unsurprising answers, but some might lead to a story. For example, after talking to people in that new office complex, a reporter may find they *are* having trouble parking, getting on and off the highway, and getting a bite to eat. The new construction may have left services seriously overburdened. An important story, but no one was going to send out a press release about it; no one was going to stage a demonstration.

Alert reporters tend to get "lucky."

Additional Reading

Writing for Your Readers: Notes on the Writer's Craft from The Boston Globe, Donald Murray, Globe Pequot, 1983.

▪ A ▪

In a sentence or two, identify the most newsworthy information from a local perspective in the following local press release, record, and national story. List the people you would contact and the questions you would ask to develop these stories.

ONE

ALLIED BUS CORPORATION

Press contact: Judy Ringold
Phone: 403-3423

The Board of Directors of the Allied Bus Corporation, the leader in public school transport in this area, proudly announced today that it has selected a new president, James T. McLintock.

Mr. McLintock served as vice president of Allied for the past five years. Before that he was the company's treasurer.

Mr. McLintock joined Allied in 1976 after ten years with the Reynolds Trucking Company here. He is 44 years old and a graduate of Pennsylvania State University.

"I am proud to be offered this wonderful opportunity to serve the company and to work closely with the Board of Directors," Mr. McLintock said. "I am also honored to be following in the footsteps of Bill Howard. He is a fine man and but for all this foolishness would still be in this job. Now it's time to look ahead."

The Board of Directors also announced today that it had accepted "with extreme regret" the resignation of President William Howard. Mr. Howard submitted his resignation today so that he can devote all his energies to discrediting what he called the district attorney's "systematic campaign of leaks and innuendo" intended to raise questions about the propriety of Howard's dealings with the Remington Board of Education. In submitting his resignation, Mr. Howard reiterated that he had offered no bribes and made no promises in negotiating a contract with Remington school officials.

The news?

People to contact?

Questions to ask?

TWO

Agenda for Potter City Council meeting this evening:

1. Adoption of minutes from last week's meeting.
2. Moment of silence for Patricia Real of Hillbrook Elementary School who passed away on Sunday.
3. Approval of Zoning Commission's waiver of regulations to allow completion of Westview water tower.
4. Police and Fire Committee Reports on Marine Fitness tests conducted among all uniformed men and women.
5. Housing Committee report on full occupancy of the Seally Project.
6. Salary Committee report on proposal to raise council salaries 15 percent.
7. Environment Committee report on plans for Earth Day planting of a tree.
8. New business.
9. Adjournment.

The news?

People to contact?

Questions to ask?

THREE

WASHINGTON, D.C. — The nation's taverns and bars are experiencing their worst year in a half century, according to a report issued today by the Retail Alcoholic Beverage Council.

The RABC said up to 12 percent of the taverns and bars will face bankruptcy this year unless the public starts drinking more in public again. The number of these establishments has declined 9 percent in the last five years.

The report attributed the decline to the increasing tendency of Americans to stay home in the evening and watch television. It said, "the era of the neighborhood bar may have passed . . ."

The news?

People to contact?

Questions to ask?

▪ B. Story Ideas ▪

1. Walk through an unfamiliar neighborhood and talk to people who live and work there. Compile a list of four story ideas about life there or about how things have changed in the last decade.

2. List two stories you might write on each of these topics in your area.

   a. College dating patterns

   b. Commuting

   c. College enrollment and recruitment

   d. Health awareness in diet

   e. The use of food stamps

   f. Changing tastes in popular music

   g. Discount stores

   h. The women's movement

   i. The Boy Scouts

   j. Unemployment

▪ C ▪

Write a story based on the following collection of facts. Assume you are writing for a newspaper dated tomorrow and read in the city of Culver.

The following press release was received yesterday in the newsroom:

The Office of Mayor Robert Gold
Contact:
Roberta Feinstein, press secretary
Phone: 456-9898

Mayor Robert Gold announced today that he has succeeded in arranging for the United Filmmakers Company to use Culver for 12 days of on-location shooting for their new film, "Terror Downtown."

Mayor Gold said he estimates that United Filmmakers will bring $900,000 worth of business into the city while they are filming.

"This is another major step in our economic recovery," Mayor Gold exclaimed. "I want this to be the city film companies turn to when they are looking for a scenic downtown area."

The agreement comes after four days of intense negotiations between the mayor and his special cultural adviser, Susan James, and "Terror Downtown's" executive producer, Hilda Mae Brown. "Terror Downtown" will be directed by Jonas Sawyer. The cast has not been announced.

Filming will begin July 23. Three full blocks of Main Street between First and Fourth Avenues will be shut to all pedestrian and automobile traffic seven days a week from 9 a.m. to 4 p.m. during the filming, so that the filmmakers can shoot "a realistic version of what would happen if a very small nuclear device exploded in an American city." The filming will end Aug. 3.

"We realize that there will be some inconvenience associated with the filming, but we will try to make sure that all workers in the small affected area use back exits and arrive at work before the filming begins," the mayor said. "We have received every assurance from the filmmakers that there will be absolutely no danger to the public in making this important movie.

"United Filmmakers has agreed to compensate all merchants along Main Street in accordance with what we believe to be a very fair formula," the mayor added.

From interview with Gold: "Now, you tell me, isn't this just the sort of thing our town needs? Do you realize how much business these folks are going to bring us? Do you think there's a chance in the world any mayor would say 'no' to such an offer? Yes, the name of the movie is a little disconcerting, but from our point of view it's all about business, money downtown, not terror downtown. Maybe some of those workers will be a little upset, but I have to think of all our citizens, right? I'm thinking about $900,000, not about a few people having to use back exits. No, I can't disclose the compensation formula; Susan's still working on that."

From interview with Brown: "I want to emphasize that this is a very serious film, about a serious subject — nuclear war. We were looking for a plain, average, routine if you will, American city. We found it. Viewers will see what would happen to such a city if the unthinkable happened. No, no, there's no danger. This is a movie. We could end the world on a soundstage; we certainly can fake nuclear war in a small city. Still, you have to realize that any film is quite a production, and this one will certainly make its presence felt in the city. We're bringing in a lot of people, and we're trying to show something that isn't pretty. What will it look like? Not at all pleasant. Just this side of obliteration. No, we haven't finalized the compensation agreement yet, but our lawyers know what's fair. Now I can't go into exactly how we will transform your downtown, or exactly what our logistics will be like. Jonas will be working on that, now."

From interview with Fred H. Lane, head of the Main Street Merchants' Association: "Yes, Bob and Susan have told us about this. I can't say we're excited. Apprehensive is more like it. I told Susan to be very careful on what she said 'yes' to. We all hope she was. We've scheduled a meeting for a week from Friday to sit down and talk with Susan and Bob, the mayor, about all this. There are certainly some questions we're going to want answered. How much is the film company going to pay each of us? What is it going to do to our business, for those of us in retail? (Lane owns Lane's Shoes at 78 Main.) Will there be any damage? Will we be able to get to work?"

□ CHAPTER 18 □

Research

When a judge from the St. Louis area, William H. Webster, was first said to be under consideration as the new head of the FBI, Louis J. Rose of the *St. Louis Post-Dispatch* was asked to write an article about him based on interviews with people who knew the judge and his work. "Everyone said he was a straight-laced, honest guy," Rose recalls. Writing under deadline pressure, Rose simply reported what they said.

But were all these people right about Webster? When the judge was formally nominated for the FBI job, Rose, an investigative reporter, was given time to do a thorough check on this local man who was about to be given the nation's number one law enforcement position. Was Webster as clean as people seemed to think?

With the exception of some calls to sources in Las Vegas to see if the judge had a gambling problem, Rose based his investigation exclusively on records, almost exclusively on public records.

At the county "recorder of deeds office," Rose found *real estate records* that enabled him to track down "every piece of property Webster's family or his wife's family had owned over the last 20 years." (Real estate and real estate tax records are always public in the United States, though the name of the office where they can be found will vary from state to state.)

He went through records of *probate court* decisions on the wills and estates left by members of Webster's family who had died. (These are always public, too.) Through probate records, Rose was able to determine what stocks and bonds the judge and his wife had

inherited. Rose then compared that list of investments with the list of the hundreds of cases that Webster had heard as a judge. Was there any conflict of interest?

In Missouri's *uniform commercial code records,* Rose came upon a William H. Webster who owed more than $1,000 on some appliance. (Loans for appliances or equipment are listed in these records.) It turned out to be another William H. Webster.

Rose found Webster's *marriage license records,* his *driving license records* (not generally public), his *voting records* (where he voted, not whom he voted for). He checked through the files in criminal court. Had Webster or a member of his family ever been arrested? Rose even tracked down Webster's high school yearbook. "I don't think there was a public record that I left untouched," he says. The whole process, Rose estimates, took three and a half to four weeks.

The result: "Webster came out clean," Rose says. "I wrote a story saying that we went into his finances and that the image presented by those who knew him was pretty much what the public record showed."

Not every investigation will uncover dirt. This was not as hot a story, to be sure, as it would have been had Rose in fact found some corruption, but it was news nevertheless. The picture of Webster's finances Rose was able to present in his story was so complete that it included an estimate of the judge's wealth that turned out to vary by only about $4,000 from that Webster himself later provided.

Most successful investigative reporting is based on

exhaustive research efforts similar, in direction if not in scope, to the one Rose used to check out Webster. But research is not just something that investigative reporters do. It is something all reporters do on virtually every story. More often than not reporters will measure the time they have to spend on a story in hours, not weeks. They won't be poring over probate records every day. Still, hardly a day will go by without at least a few looks through the newspaper's files, the phone book, a government directory, a reference book or some public record.

The Clips

"The *first* thing you do is start reading your own publication," Leon Wynter of *The Wall Street Journal* advises new reporters. The competition should be read (or watched or listened to), too. A thorough daily reading of the paper will instruct reporters on the types of stories editors, and presumably readers, seem to fancy. It can also save a reporter from the embarrassment of having to admit, "No, I didn't see the front-page story Sunday about the Briar Ridge group home. If I had, I wouldn't have proposed the story."

Of course, even the most conscientious reader of the newspaper won't remember every story over a period of weeks and months. That's why reporters turn so frequently to the clips.

The *clip files* hold the memory of a newspaper. Stories are clipped as they appear in the paper and are filed in the paper's library, or *morgue*. On small newspapers with inadequate libraries, good reporters will immediately start their own clip files. In good libraries, clips typically are cross-referenced by subject, by company or organization and by individual. A single clip might be filed in four or five different places. For example, a story about a train accident in which chlorine gas leaked from a tanker might be filed under TRAIN ACCIDENTS, CHLORINE, the name of the railroad company and the name of the town in which the accident occurred. A story on the YMCA director's appointment to the local Planning Board might be filed under PLANNING BOARD: APPOINTMENTS, the director's name and YMCA. (Newspapers are beginning to place their morgues on computer, allowing for a more extensive cross-referencing system.)

Reporters must know what news is old to figure out what's new. If they neglect to check the clips, they risk repeating last year's or even last week's story. What has been written about the morale problem among teachers at the local high school? They also risk leaving out important background and contextual information (See Chapter 15, Background and Context). Were last year's salary negotiations particularly bitter? Have this many teachers ever resigned in a single year before? Have similar morale problems plagued other schools? The clips may tell.

References

Though good clip files are a critical foundation for good reporting, they are by no means the only research tools used by reporters. Hundreds of other collections of information can aid reporters in gathering facts and help add depth to their writing. Some, like the phone book, are used daily. Others are used more selectively. Here is a list of basic references reporters consult:

The Phone Book

Most people, including many well-known people and public officials, list their phone numbers. So if a key source won't give out a home number, try the white pages; the phone book may be more forthcoming. And that number will be nice to know should an emergency—a jail break, a toxic spill, an earthquake—make it necessary to suspend normal rules of etiquette and seek information at an odd hour.

Phone books provide more than numbers. They are a good place to double-check the address or the spelling of a source's name. Phone books have rescued more than one reporter returning to the newsroom late at night after a heated municipal meeting at which a half-dozen unfamiliar people spoke. (Names of public officials can be checked in the *city directories* distributed by municipalities.)

Newspapers also will buy special *reverse directories,* in which listings are arranged by address in geographical order, rather than by name in alphabetical order. If there's been a fire, reverse directories can quickly provide the names and phone numbers of the people—possible witnesses—who live next door. And if the state has decided to turn Anderson Avenue into Anderson Freeway, this is one way of tracking down—in a hurry—the names and numbers of the people who will be most directly affected.

A Dictionary

Any one of a number will do. *The Oxford English Dictionary* is the most comprehensive, but it's also 13 volumes. *The American Heritage Dictionary of English Language* is useful because it includes proper names and the votes of a distinguished review board of writers impaneled to consider which modern usages are "acceptable" in good writing. Most newsrooms will have an unabridged dictionary on hand, often *Webster's New International,* which the

Associated Press recommends. Keep a pocket dictionary on your desk anyway in case you need to know what a jacaranda is five minutes before deadline. (It's a tropical tree.)

An Almanac

They've decided to name a high school in town after Jimmy Carter. Was he the 40th president of the United States? The candidate is making a stop in Redwood Falls, Minn. How many people live there? Almanacs are chock full of such facts (Carter was the 39th; Redwood Falls boasts 5,210 residents, according to the 1980 census). *The World Almanac,* one of the most widely used, survived the death of the newspaper that began it—Joseph Pulitzer's *New York World.*

Biographical Sketches

The *Who's Who* collection still leads the field. Biographical material used in the brief profiles these books contain was submitted by those being profiled. This is the place to turn for basic facts—wedding date, degrees—not for dirt.

Periodical Indexes

These provide the best way of finding out what has been written nationally about a subject and where it's been published. Generally indexes are arranged by topic and subtopic—*Employees, Training,* for example. Articles about each subtopic from a variety of publications are listed beneath the heading in descending chronological order. The best-known index is *Reader's Guide to Periodical Literature,* which lists articles from nearly 200 popular magazines. Another major general index is the *Magazine Index,* available only on microfilm, which lists articles in nearly 400 magazines. Dozens of other specialty indexes exist, from the *Art Index* to *Psychological Abstracts.* Most good newspaper, college and public libraries will have some periodical indexes.

Newspaper Indexes

For a story about local water problems, it might be useful to see what *The New York Times* has written about water shortages in the Southwest. *The Times Index* catalogs each article run in the daily paper by category and date. It can be found in most major libraries in the United States. The *Christian Science Monitor, Chicago Tribune, Los Angeles Times, The Washington Post* and *The Wall Street Journal* also publish indexes.

Federal, State, County and City Directories

At the federal level, the *Congressional Directory* tells who is in Congress, who works for our congressmen and women, and who serves on what committee. It includes lots more, such as phone numbers, biographical sketches of elected representatives and listings of high-level employees in the Judicial and Executive branches. Another key federal reference is the *United States Government Manual.* It lists all federal offices down to the regional level and gives the phone numbers, addresses and responsibilities of the people who hold them. This is the basic primer for sorting through the federal bureaucracy.

Similar directories exist at all levels of government. They can be used to find anyone from the local dog catcher to the sanitary engineer, and are indispensable references for a reporter's desk.

Federal and State Registers

These documents hold valuable information for both originating and backgrounding stories. They contain all proposed and final federal or state regulations. (The federal version can be penetrated by using the *Federal Register Index.*) These are the places to look to find out the exact wording of those regulations on funeral homes.

The Encyclopedia of Associations

If you are looking for an association representing virtually any field, you'll find it here. Among the more than 17,000 entries are the National Education Association, the American Association of Aardvark Aficionados and the Musical Box Society. Addresses, phone numbers and the names of key personnel—potential sources—are included. A second volume breaks down the same entries alphabetically by state, city and top official.

Atlases

In addition to the international variety, several mapmakers, including *Hammond,* publish comprehensive street maps of most towns and cities in the country. They can be invaluable when trying to trace the exact route of the proposed Anderson Freeway or when driving through a snowstorm late at night to visit some outraged citizen whose house is about to become a median divider.

Familiar Quotations by Bartlett

For a story on divorce you need to know who proclaimed that "marriages are made in heaven." You'll find out herein. Bartlett's is one of several places to check if you are feeling literary (*Oxford Dictionary of Quotations* is a good alternative), but don't overdo it. (The answer, by the way, is Alfred Lord Tennyson.)

Computer Databanks

Faster to use, more comprehensive, but still somewhat more expensive, computer *databanks*—indexed collections of information—are just beginning to challenge reference books as a source of information. And newspapers are beginning to see how valuable all this easily accessed *data* can be for their reporters. Even with a modest home computer terminal, a reporter can tap into well over a thousand databanks, costing anywhere from a few dollars to upwards of $300 an hour to use. Type the proper codes and then the word "jacaranda" into the terminal, and you can get a listing of magazine and journal articles that have discussed the jacaranda.

It is possible that all the other items on this list of reference materials will be replaced before the end of this century with improved versions of the final item. In the meantime, the ultimate print reference for figuring out where to begin looking for advice on anything from fishing to forensic medicine is *The Directory of Directories*—which, as you might guess, contains information about 7,000 *other* directories.

Records

The frontlines in reporters' endless battles to keep those who hold power honest are not in the televised press conferences or the dramatic personal confrontations, but in the dusty back rooms where the files are kept. Most of the actions of government, and many of the actions of business, must be recorded on paper. The "dead bodies" buried by officials can often be exhumed only by a search of these papers.

"Some beginning reporters think they can hang out a shingle reading 'investigative reporter' and then sit back and wait for Deep Throat to walk in the door," notes Bruce Maxwell, an investigative reporter for the *Rochester* (Minn.) *Post-Bulletin.* "It simply doesn't work that way."

No matter how carefully you phrase the question, you are unlikely to get the mayor to admit that he owns some of the land at a site he's pushing for a new shopping center. But proof might exist in the county records of deeds and mortgages. No one will put out a press release announcing inequities in the town's reassessment of all the homes in its boundaries, but a search through the records of the local tax assessor might show the homes of certain city officials assessed at below the value of comparable properties. The hospital may deny any knowledge of drugs being diverted by its staff, but the forms the hospital must file with the Drug Enforcement Administration may show theft of drugs to be a major problem there. Did the congressman rely heavily on the contributions of oil companies in his reelection campaign? Federal Election Commission reports will tell. Is it true that the mayor opposed the convention center while a councilman? Check the minutes of the council meetings.

"Often reporters don't realize what a gold mine of information there is in public records," says Louis Rose.

Good reporters, like Rose, know where records are and know how to use them. Some of the written information available to reporters is discussed in the Coverage and Specialized Coverage sections. For additional information on records and their uses in investigations, we suggest membership in the Investigative Reporters and Editors (IRE) association, located in Columbia, Mo. A $20-a-year membership includes a subscription to *The IRE Journal,* which regularly features articles on where and how to look for potentially newsworthy information.

Statistics

If public records are a gold mine, *statistics* provide some of the biggest nuggets. Reading records often means keeping an eye on the numbers in them—the statistics that hold the key to such stories as overpriced military supplies (revelations of a $640 toilet seat caused the military some indigestion in early 1985) and underenforced laws (why did the fire department conduct half as many safety inspections as it did last year?). Numbers also provide the basis for stories about changes in housing prices, grocery bills and student performance on standardized tests, not to mention stories about tax bills, train fares and wage increases.

Perhaps no newspaper relies as heavily on statistics as *USA Today,* the Gannett newspaper chain's attempt to start a truly national newspaper. Each day on its front page, *USA Today* publishes a graph that it calls "USA Snapshots: A look at statistics that shape the nation." Many of the four- and five-paragraph news items that dominate the paper also rely on statistical reports:

We're spending less on food overall, even though we eat out more, says a new report today by The Conference Board.

The private business research group says:

- Food expenditures now are 17 percent of our income, down from 19 percent in 1970.
- 32 percent of our food dollars are spent in restaurants, up from 28 percent in the 1970s and 17 percent in the 1960s . . .

USA Today

As does virtually any statistical story, this piece concentrated on those few numbers considered of greatest interest to readers. Just as reporters covering a meeting pick two or three morsels of news from a page-long menu of topics (See Chapter 22, Meetings, Speeches and Press Conferences), reporters culling through a report look only for those numbers most likely to satisfy readers' hunger. Typically, these compare something this month or year or decade with something last month or last year or last decade. (Reporters must be careful that such comparisons are valid. It wouldn't do to compare last year's crime rate in the city with this year's if in the interim the city annexed three suburban counties.)

No matter how choice the raw numbers, they rarely make the lead. When readers are left with too much raw data to unravel themselves, they are likely to turn the page. This wouldn't work as a lead:

UNACCEPTABLE:
In 1984, there were 538,051 reported felonies in New York City. Of these, 1,422 were murders, 3,833 were rapes and 78,816 were robberies. During the same year, 9 people were murdered in the subways, 21 were raped there and 5,999 were robbed.

Percentages might work in a lead, but often it's best to lead simply with words—words that tell readers what the numbers mean:

ACCEPTABLE:
There is an image of New York City's subway system, derived in part from the appearance of the trains and stations, as a lurid underground kingdom ruled by murderers, rapists and muggers where a subway rider's life sometimes has less value than a token. But the crime statistics belie at least part of that image. The subways are not the cleanest transportation system in town, but they are often the fastest and, by any measure, the safest.

The New York Times

The numbers that supported this somewhat unconventional lead were included in the story that followed. Although even there they were kept from crowding each other; they were carefully explained . . . with words.

Statistics are also valuable as a truth test. A statement by the mayor maintaining that his administration has been more successful in reducing violent crime than that of any mayor in the city's history should immediately send reporters scurrying to the files at city hall, the police department, or their news-

paper's morgues. The story reporting the mayor's claim will certainly want to mention the fact that violent crime has increased 5 percent during the mayor's term and that it decreased 8 percent during the term of a mayor in the 1940s.

Statistics themselves also can be used to fudge, misrepresent or lie. To support his claim, the mayor might come up with statistics that conveniently omit the World War II years, that fail to consider rape a violent crime or—and it happens—that get the arithmetic wrong. The numbers newsmakers present reporters should be evaluated with as critical an eye as any other information they release.

As our society collects more and more numbers, more and more sophisticated techniques are being employed to evaluate them. It helps if reporters have some familiarity with advanced statistical methods, but on most stories simple high school math will do. There were 1,240 violent crimes (including rape) in the city the year before the mayor took office; 1,302 last year; an increase of (1,302 minus 1,240) 62 or (62 is to 1,240 as x is to 100) 5 percent.

Reporters' Files

It must have been a disconcerting experience to watch I. F. Stone read a newspaper. Stone, who covered Washington with great skill for many years for his own newsletter, didn't so much read a paper as rip it. The stories he tore out—and he seemed to pull as many as he left—were destined for a place somewhere in his personal files.

Any reporters who want to develop areas of expertise—and that should mean *all* reporters—should keep files. Reporters simply can't allow all the potentially useful information that passes through the hands of well-read people to pass out of their hands again. It makes no sense to be assigned a story on the safety of a local bridge and then to have to sit around searching your brain to remember where you read that article about a bridge somewhere that collapsed killing 18 people. File systems, to borrow Marshall McLuhan's concept, are a necessary "extension" of a reporter's memory.

Additional Reading

Finding Facts Fast, Alden Todd, Ten Speed Press, 1979.
The Basic Guide to Research Sources, Ed. Robert O'Brien and Joanne Soderman, New American Library, 1975.
The Reporter's Handbook: An Investigator's Guide to Documents and Techniques, Ed. John Ullman and Steve Honeyman, St. Martin's Press, 1983.
How to Investigate Your Friends and Enemies, Louis J. Rose, Albion Press, 1981.

▪ A ▪

Try to locate the following reference books in a local public or college library, and then answer these questions for each of the books:

What general information does it contain?
How is the material organized and cross-referenced (by author, subject, title, etc.)?
What are two specific examples of information available in the source?

1. Dunn & Bradstreet Million Dollar Directory

2. Research Centers Directory

3. Dictionary of Music and Musicians

4. Black's Law Dictionary

5. Jane's All The World's Aircraft

6. Stedman's Medical Dictionary

7. Famous First Facts

8. Editor & Publisher Yearbook

9. Columbia Lippincott Gazetteer of the World

10. Statistical Abstract of the United States

11. Current Contents

12. The Encyclopedia of American Facts and Dates

13. The Washington Information Directory

14. Congressional Quarterly Weekly

15. Facts on File

Answer the following questions using references available at the library. Indicate what source you used to answer the question and what page the answer appeared on.

1. How many murders were reported in Houston, Texas, last year?

2. What is the longest river in the world and how long is it?

3. When and where was Rudolph Nureyev born?

4. How many pounds of potatoes were grown in Idaho last year?

5. Who is the president of Peru?

6. Who is the governor of Hawaii? What party does he belong to?

7. What is the population of Aix-en-Provence, France? What "department" (or province) in France is it a part of?

8. Who said, "There is no substitute for hard work?"

9. What is the state tree of Florida?

10. How many cars did Japan export two years ago? What company exported the most cars?

11. What is the population of Cleveland, Ohio?

12. Who won the Academy Award for best actor in 1985?

13. What baseball team was in first place in the Eastern Division of the American League on July 4, 1985?

14. What are the ages of the president of the United States and the secretary general of the Communist Party of the Soviet Union?

15. Who won the gold and silver medals in the slalom at the 1984 Winter Olympics? What was the time of the winner?

▪ C ▪

Write a story based on the following report, released today, and interviews. Assume you are writing for a newspaper in the town of Worley.

The United Teachers Association has compiled a report comparing the starting teachers' salaries at 198 school districts in your state. Listed below are starting salaries in all the districts in Boone County and their ranking compared with other districts in the state. The statewide average and the high and low for the state are included.

School District	This Year Starting Salary	State Rank	1982 Starting Salary	State Rank
Boonton	$17,145	99	$13,280	78
Compton	$17,890	63	$14,100	61
Crosby	$19,430	9	$15,690	12
Evergreen	$20,050	1	$15,600	13
Fulton	$18,045	54	$14,995	34
Monroe	$19,170	18	$16,200	5
Narberth	$17,675	78	$13,775	66
Norwood	$18,900	27	$15,100	24
Ringtree	$19,660	7 (tie)	$15,500	15
Salem	$18,675	38	$14,395	56
Westminster	$19,800	3	$16,500	1
Worley	$17,250	96	$12,300	112
State average	$17,100		$12,750	
State high	$20,050		$16,500	
State low	$15,400		$10,970	

Worley Supt. of Schools Michael Morrisey:

"I think the report shows we are ready to compete for quality teachers. In 1982 we ranked 112 of 198 schools in the state and were below the state average. Now we rank 96th in the state. In both percentages and in pure dollars we've increased salaries more than any other district in the county during that period. You do the math and you'll see that I'm right."

Vera Brookes, president of the Worley Teachers Association:

"I didn't know being mediocre was something to be proud of. The only reason we've come as far as we have is that we threatened to strike in 1982 after five years of 2.5 percent wage increases. Let's face it. This is one of the wealthier school districts in the wealthiest county in the state and we still rank — if I'm right — almost dead last in the county. Sure the board has made improvements but I think this demonstrates it has no right to rest on its laurels."

▪ D ▪

Using records available at a local city hall or municipal building, answer the following questions about the mayor or the elected head of the town government.

1. Did the mayor support or oppose the municipal budget last year?

2. What is the mayor's salary?

3. How much is the mayor's house assessed for? How much are his neighbor's houses assessed for?

4. Does the mayor or his family own any other property in town?

5. Does the mayor receive an expense account? How much did he or she spend in expenses last year?

■ **E** ■

1. If a local public or college library has on file the reports of the General Accounting Office, an investigative arm of Congress, select one of the reports and, acting as though the report were released today, write a news story for tomorrow's paper on its findings. At the end of the story list five followup questions you would want to ask and list whom you would contact to answer them.

2. If a local public or college library has on file the *Uniform Crime Report for the United States,* compare the most recent report with that of the previous year. Write a news story about how crime patterns have or have not changed either in your state or the nearest large city. At the end of the story list five followup questions you would want to ask and list whom you would contact to answer them.

CHAPTER 19

Sources

Bob Greene's break came under the letter V. Vizzini. Salvatore Vizzini.

When Greene spotted the name in his well-worn source book, it brought back memories of "a pretty fair evening" of eating, drinking and talking more than a decade earlier. Greene was an investigative reporter; Vizzini had been a federal narcotics agent who kept tabs on the international drug trade. At the time, Greene had had no interest in writing about Vizzini's work. But Vizzini's name had still found its way into Greene's thick collection of names, telephone numbers and addresses. They had exchanged Christmas cards, Vizzini's arriving from around the world.

Now Bob Greene was trying to trace the international heroin trail for a series of articles in *Newsday.* He contacted Salvatore Vizzini, and it turned out that Vizzini would supply the road map. He opened doors to people familiar with the Turkish underworld; he opened doors to undercover police in France. He helped Greene win a Pulitzer Prize.

It was no accident. Bob Greene knows what sources mean. Each year "eight or nine" people in Jersey City, N.J., get Christmas cards from him, though he last saw some of them 35 years ago when he reported there. Now an assistant managing editor with *Newsday,* Greene says he has "trimmed down" his Christmas list to about 1,800 people. Many get personal notes along with the card.

All reporters need tips; they need quotes; they need people to be their eyes and ears in the places they aren't. They need sources.

"If you tell students one thing, tell them how incredibly important sources are," says Tim Belnap, a court reporter for the *Detroit Free Press.* "You have to develop them—take them to lunch, call them—even when you aren't working on a story."

This chapter is about how to find sources, how to train them and how to deal with them. The Coverage chapters will discuss in more detail the types of sources available on different beats.

Who

Journalism is detective work. Simply figuring out whom to contact about that plan to turn the downtown shopping district into a mall can take the industriousness and astuteness of a sleuth.

Reporters might start with the officials for and against the plan at city hall and, perhaps, at the Chamber of Commerce. Then they might stroll around the area interviewing store owners, residents and shoppers. That's easy enough, but good reporters will want to find out more.

A good way of deciding whom to ask is to figure out what questions need to be answered. Will the mall affect traffic? People in the planning office or the police traffic division may have opinions. They also may know where to uncover studies on the impact a mall might have on the area. Will the mall push up rents? Landlords and tenant groups might have something to say about that; housing officials, too. Will the mall help revitalize the business district? An expert on urban redevelopment could offer an educated guess based on the experiences of similar cities. Who stands to make money? Local realtors might know; so, obviously, will the owners of the property the mall will be built on (city tax records can be used as a first step in finding out who they are).

With such questions in mind, reporters will make a list of the types of people they will want to talk to on a story. The next job is finding actual names. A reporter looking for an expert on urban redevelopment, for example, might start with a call to the sociology or urban planning department at the nearest university or to the federal department of Housing and Urban Development in Washington. It can take ten calls just to track down a source whose comments may be boiled down to a single quote in the article. This could be a hundred-call story. Many are. Good sources are hard to find.

Reporters should spread a wide net. A story on that mall that quotes only boosters of the project will, assuming the project does have some critics, be flawed. Sources should be chosen to represent various hues on the political spectrum, various interest groups, officials and nonofficials.

It's hard work to start every story from scratch. That's why reporters—especially those assigned to cover a regular *beat* such as police, the courts or local politics—fill their phonebooks with the names of people who can provide regular guidance and tips. These people—faithful, reliable sources—are accumulated over time. Reporters start by pumping their predecessors on the beat for names—at *Newsday,* on Long Island, N.Y., a list of sources and their phone numbers is kept for each beat and passed on from reporter to reporter. But reporters might not share their best sources, and it's better in some ways to find your own: Personal chemistry has something to do with who helps whom.

Good sources can be found almost anywhere, not just in the largest offices. The mayor's secretary can be an excellent source; she may know as much about the inner workings of city hall as the city council president. The woman who pumps gas outside the police station may know a lot about who passes in and out the station doors. Nurses in the hospital emergency room know who is getting sick and who is getting shot. "The wonderful thing about journalism," says Molly Ivins of the *Dallas Times Herald,* "is that it gives you a chance to talk to all kinds of people."

To do that, it's imperative that reporters get out of the office. Some of the best sources can be found on leisurely strolls through the territory, by stopping and chatting and learning who knows whom and who knows what. One source inevitably leads to another. And at each stop, reporters should pencil the names and phone numbers (home number, too, if possible) into their phone books, first alphabetically by name, then alphabetically under the subject—housing, unions, arson—that is that source's special area of interest or expertise.

Cultivating

There is no law that requires anyone to talk to a reporter. But most people will talk, and for a variety of reasons: Some like the publicity and the sense of self-importance; some want revenge against a political or personal rival; a few believe the public really ought to know what's happening. Reporters have to be prepared to exploit all these motivations, but they also hope they can find informed people who will talk for two additional reasons: because they respect that reporter's work and perhaps even because they like the reporter as a person.

"I think you have to see people out of the courtroom," says Walter Fee, who covers the courts for *The Milwaukee Journal.* "Jog with them, play racquetball with them, hike with them, anything you like. If you are really interested and not a phony, they do it. It takes time away from family, but I've found no alternative."

This is called *cultivating* sources. A jogging partner is much more likely to help you with a story than someone who doesn't remember your first name. Some reporters, including Bob Greene, make it a practice to jot down the names of the spouse and the children of the people they deal with on their beat. "Then," says Greene, "when you call the mayor and his wife answers, you say 'Hi, Charlotte, how are you? I feel like I know you. Can you tell me where I can reach Charlie?'"

Virtually all prospective sources have at least one thing in common—an appetite for good food. "There's a great American institution called lunch," says Leon Wynter, who covers banking and financial services for *The Wall Street Journal.* "I keep setting up those lunches whenever I can."

When things get too busy for lunch (the newspaper, incidentally, should pay), there's always the phone. The consistency of contact can be important. "The key thing with all sources is to call even when you don't have a story in mind," Greene says. "It shows sources you have a personal interest in them. If you have free time, why not just spin through the As and then the Bs and so forth."

Obviously some sources are more essential than others. Greene suggests compiling a primary list of the top 20 or so sources. "Those," he says, "you tickle every week."

Avoiding Being Cultivated

Walter Fee of *The Milwaukee Journal* was writing a story about a man accused of having organized crime connections when he came across the information that the alleged mobster had worked as a court commissioner for a district attorney. The district attorney was one of Fee's sources. Fee knew he risked losing this valuable source if he included high in the story the damaging fact that the DA had hired a reputed mobster. Still, the damaging fact appeared high in the story.

One of the dangers of cultivating sources is that they also begin cultivating you. Just as sources grow to like reporters, reporters grow fond of many of the people with whom they spend their days on the beat, especially if they've shared lunches or jogs. It is easy to soak up the perspective of these new friends, to begin taking their side—*cronyism* it's sometimes called. And it's hard to take the risk of alienating these friends or cronies with a tough story. More than friendship is at stake; an offended official can make a reporter's job difficult by withholding information.

But difficult though it may be, neither affection nor fear can be allowed to influence reporters' work. Journalists are ultimately obliged to their readers, not their sources. Fee's decision was the only decision a good reporter could have made.

"On any beat you will be working with people over and over," notes Saundra Keyes of Louisville's *Courier-Journal.* "You may like them and you may come up with a story they won't like. But that's never kept me from writing a story. You have to say, 'I'm sorry, but I have to write this.'"

Ground Rules

As a matter of course, reporters should expect the people they interview to attach their names to what they say (See Chapter 10, Attribution). When people say things *for attribution,* or *on the record,* their statements take on greater credibility. People also are likely to be more honest when they can be held responsible for what they said.

But sources are particularly valuable when they are willing to tell secrets—the boss is double billing his travel expenses, a superior has not been enforcing state conflict-of-interest statutes. Sometimes a source's name can't be attached to these secrets if the source hopes to stay employed. So reporters have developed a series of ground rules for their confidential dealings with sources. These are agreements—binding agreements—between a source and the journalist on how the information in question will be attributed (See Appendix D, Law).

Background

Information accepted on *background,* or *not for attribution,* can be used in a story but cannot be attributed to the source of that information by name. The reporter may, however, use some nonspecific description that gives readers a sense of the source's position without giving away who the source is. A deputy mayor might be referred to as a *high city hall official,* as a *source close to the mayor* or merely as *an official,* according to the ground rules worked out in advance. The coach of the local high school football team might be referred to as *someone familiar with the school's athletic policies* or as *a member of the athletic department* or simply as *one coach.*

Reporters press for permission to use the clearest attribution possible. Calling people simply *sources* may have a conspiratorial ring, but readers learn next to nothing about the importance, credibility or knowledge of that source. Be as specific as the source allows. A *high city official* presumably carries more weight than a *city official.*

Increasingly, newspapers are battling to convince sources to allow their names to be used. When they lose those battles, they are making an effort to tell readers why they are withholding a name. Here's an example:

A *White House official who did not want to be identified by name* said Reagan had told Carter in the call, "I was not suggesting that you or your administration were responsible for the declining intelligence capability . . ."
The New York Times

Deep Background

Sources who provide information on *deep background* will allow reporters to use the information they provide but without any attribution whatsoever. If the deputy mayor reveals on deep background that the mayor is planning to retire, the reporter could write no more than: "It has been learned that Mayor Cassidy is not planning to run for reelection when her term ends next year."

Reporters dislike stepping out on a limb like this . . . and for good reason. Deep background allows government officials to test new policies without taking any responsibility for them. If Mayor Cassidy changes her mind, she doesn't look bad; the reporter who wrote the story does. Reporters can't afford to have their credibility undermined like this very often.

Information obtained on deep background can be useful when reporters are trying to confirm statements they obtained with attribution elsewhere, or when they are looking for leads to further investigation. Bob Woodward and Carl Bernstein of *The*

Washington Post used a deep background source—referred to in the newsroom as "Deep Throat"—for these purposes in their Watergate investigation.

Off the Record

If sources say, "this is *off the record,*" ask what they mean. The term is frequently confused. "Sometimes people really mean background when they say off the record," notes Fred Barbash of *The Washington Post.*

Material that is really *off the record* cannot be used in the story, period. On routine stories, many reporters will simply walk away if a source insists on staying off the record. Others will stick around in the hope that their new knowledge will help them with future stories. Only if off-the-record material is developed independently, from *another* source, can it be used. Then the information should be attributed—but to the second source only. (When reporters receive off-the-record confidences they should honor them in personal conversations as well as in print. Too often, beginning reporters tell colleagues of interesting off-the-record tales that they can't write. This is risky. Sources may be upset if they learn that their secrets have become newsroom gossip.)

Ground rules should be agreed upon *before* information is exchanged. In theory, reporters assume all comments are for attribution, *on the record,* unless a source sets some other condition beforehand. Sources who deal regularly with the press usually are held to this rule. But in interviewing people who are inexpert in dealing with the press, most reporters will be a bit more generous.

▪ **A** ▪

Find the name and telephone number of a person in your area who could provide each of the following types of information.

1. Information on what has to be done to get a name on the ballot in the state Democratic gubernatorial primary.

2. Information on the safety of nuclear reactors.

3. Information on licensing procedures for doctors in the state.

4. Information on local civil defense plans.

5. Information on the knowledge required to pass the state bar exam.

6. Information on the safety of local drinking water.

7. Information on the average income levels of welfare recipients in the area.

8. Information on the chances of severe drought in the area.

9. Information on the way the decision on which police cars to purchase is made in a local town.

10. Information on how international basketball rules differ from collegiate rules.

11. Information on the movie that was most successful at local theaters last year.

12. Information on the health consequences of a diet rich in cholesterol.

13. Information on fatality rates on local highways.

14. Information on what the French mean by *nouvelle cuisine.*

15. Information on state hunting regulations.

▪ **B** ▪

Write a list of the names and telephone numbers of officials, community group leaders or experts who should be contacted to report each of the following stories locally, and a list of places you might go to find any additional sources who would be useful.

1. How are the elderly responding to rising prices? Are their Social Security and pension benefits adequate? Are they having difficulty paying for food or housing?

2. Have local police departments invested in bullet-proof vests? Why or why not? How much protection do the vests provide? What are their disadvantages?

3. How have local school boards responded to health warnings against high-fat, low-fiber diets? Have the lunches they offer students changed?

4. How common is the use of marijuana among local teen-agers?

5. How serious is the injury problem in high school football? Are students suffering injuries that may have long-lasting health consequences?

6. What is the quality of the air in the area? What steps are being taken to monitor air quality? What are the main sources of local air pollution?

7. Who are the likely candidates in the next election for mayor in a local town or city?

8. Have television, cable television and videotape recorders hurt business at local entertainment places?

9. How does local unemployment compare with that in the state and in the nation? Is unemployment here increasing or decreasing? What factors affect the local unemployment rate?

10. Is the dog and cat population in the area decreasing or increasing? How serious is the problem of strays? When was the last reported case of rabies?

■ **C** ■

Write a story based on the following collection of facts. You are writing for a newspaper dated tomorrow and read in the city where the events occurred.

Alice Batsel, press secretary to Mayor Georgina Desjardin, a Republican, agrees to discuss the mayor's upcoming decision on whether to run for reelection to a second term, but only off the record. You agree. Here's what she says: "Of course, she's going to run. Desjardin just ain't the type to cut and run, not when there's work left to do in this city. But we've got some *T*'s to cross and some *I*'s to dot before we make the announcement, got to get a campaign organization in place. We'll announce sometime next month. But she's told me it's definite."

From interview with Desjardin: "Well, I'm sorry but I just don't have anything to say on that. Yes, I enjoy this job. Yes, there's still work to be done. But there are a number of personal and family considerations that will go into the decision as well as political consideration. I haven't made a final decision. I'll be sure to let you know when I do."

From interview yesterday with Robert Barkley, the mayor's executive secretary: "Okay, I'm willing to talk about this with you, but only on background. You can call me someone who works in the mayor's office. Just don't say a secretary. Okay, you can say that I am familiar with her thinking. That's for damn sure. Yes, she is going to run. Yes, it is going to be announced next month. No, I don't think a date has been set yet. Yes, I'm sure she has no doubt about it. She told me separately and all of us together that it's definite."

From interview with Deputy Mayor Jacob Ambler: "I will discuss this subject only on deep background. You heard right — Georgina's running again. She told me a few days ago. I don't know any details about the campaign, just that she'll be heading our ticket in the city."

The Republican mayoral primary will be held Sept. 9. No other candidates have announced that they will run yet.

CHAPTER 20

Interviewing

The best answers regularly get saved for reporters who ask the best questions.

Those questions take preparation.

Not that reporters don't have to think on their feet. But more often than not, good interviewers have done plenty of thinking before they ever get on their feet to go to an interview, and they'll do some more after it ends.

Indeed, interviewing really is a three-step process: First a reporter spends considerable time finding the right people (See Chapter 19, Sources), reading about them and their views, and plotting a rough line of questioning. Next comes the actual face-to-face, or voice-to-voice, interview. And finally, in the minutes and hours that follow, reporters sort through their notes to see what's missing and whether a follow-up call is needed to fill in holes.

The Preinterview

Inevitably, there is a direct relationship between how much the reporter knows *before* an interview and how much that reporter will find out *during* the interview. Reporters who don't know the politics of the politician they are interviewing, who haven't read the books of the author they are questioning, who haven't looked up the background of the business executive

they are profiling, are hardly in a position to persuade these people to be forthcoming.

Homework

Sometimes it is wise to build up to a key interview. When Stuart Diamond, a reporter for *Newsday,* wrote a series on the Long Island Lighting Company's difficulties in building the Shoreham nuclear plant, he didn't interview company officials until he already had most of the facts. "I literally brought 150 pounds of material to LILCO for the interview," he recalls. "You have to know enough already so that you can penetrate the answers you are getting and get to the truth. In my series I was able to get their admissions because I was able to say in response to some of their answers, 'You are wrong.'"

This isn't to say that reporters should never hazard an interview without first gathering several carton loads of documents. Those who are out to prove that they know more law than lawyers or more business than businessmen frequently will lose track of the simple things readers need answered to understand a story. Reporters should enter any interview ready to learn. They should never make believe they understand something when they don't. But learning, nevertheless, takes homework. It is one thing to ask the mayor to explain some of the ramifications of that new zoning ordinance; it is quite another to waste time asking the mayor how he voted on the ordinance two nights ago — a fact that appeared in yesterday's paper.

Writing out Questions

Preparation for an interview should also include thinking about what questions you are going to ask. Jot down a list of potential questions. These rarely will be used exactly as they are written out or exactly in the same order — good interviewers always are open to new avenues of questioning should they present themselves. But a list of questions serves as a guide to keep an interview on track, as a fall back should the reporter become momentarily flustered, and as a check at the end of an interview to determine if everything has been covered.

"I not only write down questions in the order I might ask them, but I think about what the answers might be," says Diamond. "I try to envision the course an interview might take."

Getting Through

Most people who participate in public life, or who find themselves in the news, will be glad to talk with a reporter. They want a chance to state their case or to gain a little publicity. But some people, generally people whose portrayal in the paper is likely to be less than flattering, just don't want to talk. Anyone has a right to remain silent, but aggressive reporters often won't accept an initial "no" as a final answer. (Such aggressiveness becomes obnoxiousness when dealing with victims of tragedies, of course. These people should be approached gently and never hassled — See Chapter 24, Police).

Sometimes the problem is simply getting to talk to the source. Many secretaries are programmed to intercept the timid and hesitant caller. It may help to sound confident and personable. Reporters also have learned to take an end run around secretaries by calling an office before 9 a.m., during lunch or after 5 p.m. — times at which the secretary is less likely to be around to intercept.

The closer a reporter can get to a potential source, the harder it is for that person to turn down an interview. That's one reason aggressive reporters can sometimes be seen interviewing associates of their targets — they hope that news of their inherent wisdom and fairness will filter back. Nor does it hurt to "just happen" to be walking by a prospective source's house about the time he or she usually heads for work: "Aren't you Ms. Honeycutt? What a coincidence. I've been trying to arrange an interview."

When all else fails, a bit of forcefulness can't hurt: "Ms. Honeycutt, the story will run whether or not you respond to the charge. I just thought it would be better and fairer if it gave your side as well."

Choosing Tools

The first decision every reporter about to conduct an interview faces is whether to do it in person or by telephone. The telephone has one advantage: It's fast. That's an important consideration when working on deadline or on a story that may require dozens of interviews. And if a source won't talk or has little to add, on the telephone you haven't wasted much more than the time it takes to say "hello" and "goodbye."

But for an important interview, there is no substitute for being there in person. It is easier to size up people when you can see their faces, and people are more likely to open up when they can see your face. Proximity builds trust. In addition, an in-person interview gives reporters a chance to observe and collect the descriptive detail that can enliven a story.

If the zoning board decides to postpone a monthly meeting, the telephone probably will do. But a feature on a trapeze artist shouldn't be reported on the telephone. Neither should a story about the closing of a welfare hotel.

Tape recorders also present reporters with a decision. Nothing can compare with a properly functioning tape recorder for an accurate and complete record of key interviews. On timeless stories — a feature or a long-term investigation, for example — tape recorders can be invaluable. For an article profiling a person, tapes may capture the eloquence or the idiosyncracies of the subject's speech and free the reporter to listen and look more closely. In investigations, tapes may provide evidence needed to protect the newspaper's and the reporter's credibility.

Still, few newspaper reporters use tape recorders regularly. Some argue that the physical act of writing down what someone says makes them more attentive. Others live in fear that the tape recorder in front of them will self-destruct. And some sources grow nervous at the thought of having their words recorded for all to hear. The main advantage of settling for pen and pad, though, is that they save time — the tape would have to be replayed. For shorter interviews, therefore, veteran reporters almost invariably trust in their handwriting.

Interview Strategies

The questions experienced reporters ask are anything but haphazard. Whether those reporters have had a chance to prepare or are responding to a breaking story, their interviews usually follow a strategy.

Ease in

There are many ways to conduct an interview. But one that almost never works is to open with an accusatory question. If your first question to the president of the Board of Education were to be: "How can you talk about improving education when the board has recommended a 10 percent cut in school funding?" the president is hardly likely to be forthcoming in answering the questions that follow.

Reporters instead should start with an easy, comfortable question that gets the source talking. The hope is that the source will keep talking later in the interview when it comes time to ask those tough questions. Get that board president to open up by asking, "What improvements do you think are needed in the school system?" By starting with a less confrontational question, reporters ensure that they'll leave the interview with some answers, even if the source clams up or walks out later when it's time for those hard questions.

In an in-person interview, there's often time to open with a little small talk. The offices or homes of people who sit for interviews are filled with potential conversation pieces — a picture of family members, a framed degree from the University of Hawaii, a piece of art from Mexico. A few minutes conversation about what interests the interviewee can make that person comfortable.

Telephone interviews often call for a different technique; it may make sense to be more direct. "The only way I can keep a high-powered person on the phone is to ask questions that might interest him," says *Newsday*'s Diamond.

An Overview

"The biggest mistake beginning reporters make," says Ron Harris, assistant metropolitan editor of the *Los Angeles Times,* "is that they arrive on the scene, interview someone and begin to ask a series of minor, picky questions. They end up with a series of disjointed facts. Instead, what they should do first is say, 'Hey, guy, what happened?' Let him tell you the story, then you can go back and ask questions to fill in the missing details."

In other words, if a dam has collapsed, don't begin by asking the person in charge, "How many gallons of water escaped?" then, "What time did the first crack appear?" then, "What is the dam made of?" Instead, open with "Tell me what happened," or "How did it start?" Let that official say, "We got our first warning that water had begun to leak at 8:45, then we looked out and saw the crack . . ." Get the basic scenario — preferably in chronological order. Make sure you un-

derstand essentially what went on. "You want to start by getting an overview," says Harris. Then you can worry about exactly how many gallons of water escaped.

Obviously, reporters will need an overview in a hurry when they first arrive at a breaking event like a dam collapse. However, getting an overview can also be a priority on more leisurely but more complex stories. Leon Wynter, of *The Wall Street Journal,* says he often opens with general questions when conducting interviews on his beat — bank regulation: "I have people explain the structure, background and philosophy to me before getting into the specifics."

The Goal

When they do get down to specifics, reporters are looking for information that suits the needs of the stories they will write. From an interview with the union leader, they may need facts on the position of workers in a dispute and a tough restatement of that threat to strike. From an interview with one of the workers, they may want emotional quotes and specific complaints. And from an interview with the company's president, they may seek a reply to those specific charges.

Reporters have a much better chance of getting what they want from an interview if they know what their goal is. If they're looking for subjective comments, the interview should be filled with questions like: "What was it like?" "What were you feeling at the time?" "How did you react?" "What would you compare the experience to?" If the goal is expert analysis, however, most of the questions will use words like "explain," "interpret," "predict" and "analyze."

It's important that reporters attempt to clarify their goals as they plan an interview, but it's just as important that they remain flexible enough to respond to unexpected, but newsworthy, information that may come up as the interview progresses. If that worker whose union is threatening a strike happens to mention that the company routinely dumps chemical wastes in a local pond, reporters have to be ready to put aside their plans and goals and head off in a new direction.

A Trap

Despite what the movies and television shows would have you think, not every journalistic interview is an attempt to make a person sweat, twitch, tremble, and break down and admit guilt. In fact, the majority of interviews are just friendly attempts to get some helpful information and some usable quotes. But sometimes you do want to get newsmakers to say something that they might not have wanted to say. Sometimes you're laying a trap.

In *Interviews That Work: A Practical Guide for Journalists* (See Additional Reading), Shirley Biagi discusses a few possible strategies for trapping newsmakers. When interviewing a police officer said to have beaten a suspect, for example, a reporter might open with some general questions about suspects and the proper way to treat them . . . and then get more and more specific about what is alleged to have happened. The strategy is to force the subject into a corner, to place on the record general statements that will make it more difficult to evade the specific questions that follow—"Then how can you justify the rough handling that someone obviously gave that accused murderer?" Biagi calls this a *funnel* interview.

In the *covertly sequenced* interview the trickier questions are spread throughout the interview to surprise the newsmaker or lead the newsmaker into contradictions. For example, the reporter might ask early on whether the officer has known of any police officers who have used physical force with a suspect already in custody, then, after some more innocuous questions, ask whether the officer himself has ever felt a desire or a need to use physical force with a suspect in custody, then, after another interval, ask about what happened with that accused murderer.

A third technique—we'll call it the *machine gun* interview—is to weigh in at some point with a series of tough questions, leaving little room for evasion: "When did that suspect arrive back at the station house?" "Were you ever alone in the room with him?" "Did he get you angry?" "Did you ever hit him?" But hold your fire! The *machine gun* technique should not be used at the start of the interview.

Which technique a reporter chooses depends on the person and the situation. For example, if newsmakers are threatening to walk out, the detective-like approach of boring in might not work. But if newsmakers are confident and evasive, it might make sense to hit them with a rapid-fire series of questions.

The point is not that reporters should announce to themselves, "I'm going to do a covertly sequenced interview." These techniques can be mixed and matched, their names ignored. The point is that beginning reporters, at least, should devote considerable thought to what they are trying to accomplish in an interview and how best to accomplish it.

Questions

A reporter's "body language" in an interview can make a difference, as Biagi notes in her book. Alert and attentive, leaning forward, head nodding—these are gestures reporters may use to encourage interviewees to open up. On the other hand, appearing stiff, uncomfortable, bored or distracted can easily turn off a source. "You want to establish a rapport," says Ron Harris. Small talk can help; so can flattery —in small, controlled doses.

Nevertheless, the success of an interview is more likely to rest on the quality of the questions reporters ask than on their posture or their ability to chat about the weather. Some questions do the job. Some don't.

Direct

The more convoluted the question, the more convoluted the answer is likely to be . . . if the subject is able to understand the question at all. If you want a clear, direct quote, don't ask: "So, if the toxic wastes from your company were diverted by the B & R Hauling Company, which we have discussed as a possibility, though not a probability, and if your company suspected that something was amiss in the terms of the contract, then, if I may backtrack a bit, about your original decision to sign on with them, how does it look?" Instead ask: "With the benefit of hindsight, what more might have been done to assure that all your wastes were disposed of properly?"

Open or Closed

If a reporter is looking for quotes, it's wise to ask questions that require some explication. These are called *open-ended questions.* Don't ask high school students whether they are for or against a local busing plan. Ask them what their views on busing are and why. "Yes" and "no" make lousy quotes.

But in the search for facts, or confirmation of facts, *closed questions* can be efficient tools. Ask the superintendent of schools what her feelings on the starting date for the busing plan are and you could be in for 15 minutes of soul searching. If all you need is confirmation of the date, ask: "Is the busing going to start on the first day of school, Sept. 7?"

Getting Specifics

Good interviewers get more than just facts and quotes; they get *the* facts and quotes that will best communicate to readers the meaning of a story. Abstract, vague responses won't do that job. Reporters are after *specifics.* They are constantly working to keep their subjects' feet on the ground, to force them to illustrate their ideas, theories and characterizations with concrete examples.

The bank president who has just reported that more than $10,000 was embezzled from his bank might be asked what *specifically* he remembers about the suspect teller. "He was always the first teller here in the morning, and he always brought his own lunch," tells readers a lot more than just, "He was a fine employee."

A reporter interviewing a rescue worker at the scene of a flood might ask for a description of some of the *specific* things that rescue worker saw. "All that was left of one house was the garage and the chimney," is a lot more powerful than, "A number of houses suffered severe damage."

When interviewing a local high school student who is making $35,000 a year as a model, ask her to try to recall a *specific* example of when her work and her studies conflicted. An anecdote usually makes the point better than a statement: "One day we worked shooting some jeans ads till 10 at night. Everybody else went home to relax, I went home to read a chemistry book. We had a test the next day."

"Could you be more specific?" "Could you give me an example of that?" "Can you describe exactly what it was like?" "Can you remember exactly what happened?" "Can you recall a specific incident?" These are questions good reporters will ask again and again.

Concrete examples aren't obtained only through questions. Sometimes all a reporter at an interview has to do is look around. In features in particular (See Chapter 26, Features), physical details — clothes, furniture, mannerism — can add to the picture painted by the subject's own words. Here are some of the details spotted by a *USA Today* reporter interviewing author Jackie Collins: "She is drinking pink champagne and eating smoked salmon. She touches a pink napkin to her peach colored lips. All her furniture is cream colored. There are prints, paintings and figurines of leopards everywhere in her house."

Follow-ups

Make sure you understand the answer. Sometimes newsmakers will hide behind an unclear answer. More often their answers are unclear simply because they have difficulty explaining themselves. In either case, reporters have to be prepared to ask *follow-up questions.*

Follow-ups can be used to translate jargon: "But what exactly is blood doping?" To clear up confusion: "Wait a second, so you're saying these blood transfusions did not violate Olympic rules?" Or to respond to evasions: "Okay, but let me repeat my original question: Did you or did you not see these athletes take blood transfusions before their races?" In addition, follow-ups are sometimes used specifically to get a better quote: "Could you tell me again, why you didn't tell anyone about the blood doping?"

Ask. Ask. And, if necessary, reask.

Note Taking

People being interviewed talk faster than most reporters can write. One way of keeping up is to learn shorthand. Many reporters even concoct their own shorthands. And even the large majority of reporters who have no such formal system for recording what people are saying will use abbreviations and leave out some words to save time. They learn to jot down information in clear, but compact form.

Here's part of a statement by Police Chief Brad Jovens:

We have information that Bernard Levin, a teller at the First State Bank here left for Brazil Friday evening. Bank officials suspect that he was the perpetrator of an embezzlement plot at the bank. The suspect, Bernard Levin, is 35 years old, with no criminal record.

And here's how that part of the statement might be recorded in a reporter's notes (handwritten, of course):

Chief Brad Joves:

Bernard Levin, teller, 1st State Bnk, left for Brazil Fri. eve.

"Bank offic. suspect that he was the perp. of an embezzlement plot at the bank."

35, no record

Ron Harris suggests another technique that can help the interviewer who is desperately trying to play catch up with a fast-talking newsmaker: "Throw in a throw-away question." The subject has just said something marvelous. You're struggling to get it all down in your notes, but you have to say something so that there isn't too long a lull in the conversation. Ask an unimportant, even irrelevant question, Harris advises ("I imagine you've had a lot of time away from your family on this one, huh?"), and, meanwhile, keep writing down that quote.

Nevertheless, the real secret for getting the important information mentioned in an interview down on paper is to learn to recognize what information is worth noting down, and what can be forgotten. The first words reporters will write in their notebooks are the name — with correct spelling — and exact title of the person they are interviewing. After that, what they take down will depend on what they might need in their stories. Beginners usually try to scribble down everything. While they are struggling to record the trivialities, the important points fly by. Good reporters think before they scribble.

Facts

Reporter: How much exactly did you lose?
Bank president: Let's see . . . I have that

information right here. I know it's over $10,000. Oh yes. Ten-thousand four-hundred and twenty-three dollars. Is that exact enough for you?

    Reporter: Yes, thanks. Do you know over how long a period the money was being taken?

    Bank president: Six months, approximately. From the beginning of January to the beginning of July. I can't give you exact dates. We've had police here every day this week, and those are the dates I told them . . . I mean that's the approximate period.

That bank president, discussing the embezzlement of some money from his bank, didn't say anything quotable in this section of the interview, so what he said can be boiled down to a few facts. Forget those that have no chance of making the story — of course, police have been spending a lot of time at the bank. Jot down the rest, being careful to indicate what the numbers and dates refer to and to include the qualifications — those dates are only "approximate." Here's what might have appeared in a reporter's notebook:

Amount lost — $10,423

Taken over approx. 6 months, begin Jan. to begin July. No exact dates.

Quotes

    Reporter: What did you think of Levin, before you heard he had left for Brazil?

    Bank president: He was a fine employee. We never suspected anything. We have a lot of fine employees; yes, I can certainly say that. And let me add, we hire people we think will be good employees.

    Reporter: What specifically do you remember about him?

    Bank president: He was, let me see, always the first teller here in the morning, and he always brought his own lunch. I remember that . . . yes.

    Reporter: What was your reaction when you heard he was in Brazil?

    Bank president: I was shocked. You can quote me on that. I mean . . . it was just . . . I'm a bank president not a . . . Well, what else can I say? It was shocking.

Besides facts, interviews are designed to produce quotes. Reporters will take the time to write out the exact wording of any potential quotes (minus such excess verbiage as, "yes, I can certainly say that"), but there's no need to waste time jotting down the irrelevant — "We have a lot of fine employees"; the obvious — "we hire people we think will be good employees"; or the poorly worded (See Chapter 11,

Quotations). Here's what a reporter might have noted about this section of that interview:

"He was a fine employee. We never suspected anything. He was always the 1st teller here in the morn., and he always brought his own lunch." When heard in Brazil: "I was shocked."

Staying in Control

You're in the newsmaker's office or living room, taking up the newsmaker's valuable time. It's easy, in gratitude, to let the newsmaker control the interview, to smile and say "thank you" a lot and then leave, still smiling, with a useless collection of digressions, reminiscences and lectures.

Forget how important that newsmaker is. Forget how thankful you are to have been granted this interview. You're the one who is asking the questions. You will have to write the story. You are in charge.

It's your job to make sure the interview stays on track. You certainly don't want to offend the person you're talking with, but you also don't want to listen to a 15-minute discourse on the value of hard work when you're there to learn about a holdup, either. You may have to politely but firmly break in — especially if pressed for time. Wait for the end of a sentence and then jump. If that doesn't work, it may be necessary to actually interrupt. And if newsmakers continually filibuster, you might suggest, in so many words, that they keep answers short and stick to the subject.

Reporters don't want to be perceived as boors, but they can't be so polite or so shy that time runs out on their interview before they get the answers they need.

Listening

Reporters have a lot on their minds during interviews. They might be thinking about their plan for their interview, about whether they are getting the facts and quotes they need. They may be trying to decide on their next question, or still mulling over the previous one. And all the while they're straining to take notes.

There's a limit to the number of things humans can do at once. Something's got to give. And often what happens, strangely, is that reporters forget to listen to what the person they're interviewing is saying. The mayor's last comment, that she has decided not to seek re-election, might even have made it into their notes, but their minds are too busy trying to think of what else to ask her about this waterfront development plan to have really *heard* what she said. So the next question is something about ports and parks when it should have been: "Wait a second! When did you decide that you weren't going to be a candidate next year?"

Ron Harris, who runs a minority internship program for the *Los Angeles Times,* says he often has to give inexperienced interviewers this seemingly obvious advice: "Listen to the answers." Reporters often have to forget the next question and the answer to the previous one for a moment in order to pay attention to the answer to the question they just asked.

If reporters have the time, they might ease up enough so that they actually lose themselves in the conversation. "I like to let the conversation run," says Karen W. Arenson of *The New York Times.* "In a lot of interviews I like to just follow people's logic, to find out why they are thinking what they are thinking."

Some reporters draw out their sources by allowing silences to linger. "I'm not afraid to shut up and let sources fill in the silence," says Tom French of the *St. Petersburg Times.*

Whether or not you choose to go this far, part of the art of listening is certainly learning when to hold your own tongue. It is foolish to start debating with an interviewee who happens to say something you disagree with. Reporters are there to elicit someone else's two cents, not to add their own.

The End

Here are two things to remember as the interview is drawing to a close:

End Tough

Now's the time. You saved the tough questions for the end; don't neglect to ask them. By the end of the interview you have less to lose by alienating subjects, and after a long interview they might be more inclined to let down their guard. In fact, Tom French says he sometimes gets his best material *after* the formal interview is over and his pad and pen have been tucked away.

The Last Question

Before "goodbye" always ask: "Do you have anything to add?" or "Is there anything else I should have asked?" Sometimes there is. Then warn your subjects that you may have to call back with a follow-up question or two, ask for their home phone numbers, and leave your phone number in case they think of something else.

The Postinterview

Many reporters start to collect their thoughts by typing up their notes soon after an interview ends. That way they also can decipher their scribbles before the words that inspired them have been forgotten, and they can check whether there are holes in the information that might necessitate a follow-up call or additional interviews.

Most sources will be impressed rather than annoyed by a diligent reporter who calls back to clarify points. It also is appropriate to read sources passages of a story to check the accuracy of what you have written, particularly about a complicated issue. However, reporters should never surrender final control of an article to sources by promising them a chance to retract statements, censor paragraphs or read a final manuscript before the article appears on the newsstand.

Additional Reading

Interviews That Work: A Practical Guide for Journalists, Shirley Biagi, Wadsworth Publishers, 1986.
The Craft of Interviewing, John Brady, Writer's Digest Books, 1976.
Creative Interviewing, Ken Metzler, Prentice-Hall, Inc., 1977.

▪ A ▪

For each of the following interviews, write a list of the questions you would ask in roughly the order you would ask them. Then note whom else you would talk to before writing the story.

ONE

There is a crowd outside the police station chanting, "Conrad must go!" They hold up signs saying, "Kid Killer" and "Murderers belong in jail, not in blue." Three days ago, Police Officer Frederick Conrad reportedly shot and killed a 12-year-old boy. Police Chief Alan Rouchet has said Conrad reported that he thought the boy — who was walking through an alley when he was shot — was pulling a gun on him. Conrad had responded to a call for help after a delicatessen was robbed three blocks away. The shooting took place at 7:30 p.m. at twilight. Police accounts have not made clear what Conrad was doing in the alley. The boy, Peter Cairns, was shot in the head. The bullet entered above his left ear. No gun was found near the boy's body.

Conrad has been suspended from the force with pay, pending the outcome of a departmental investigation. You've dealt with him before, three years ago when he climbed a tree to rescue a cat that had been up there for 24 hours. He liked the feature you wrote. Conrad has been on the force five years. His record is free of prior disciplinary actions.

You haven't been covering the story (your beat is now city hall), but Conrad's lawyer called to say Conrad will give one interview — to you.

TWO

The sculpture has been smashed into — the police say they counted — 132 pieces. Someone knocked it off its pedestal, in front of the Amville City Hall, late at night two weeks ago. Police say it was smashed with a hammer after it fell. They report no suspects, but the words "Amville art for Amville" were sprayed in red paint on the sidewalk where the pieces of the sculpture lay. A number of local artists had protested the awarding of the commission for the sculpture three years ago to Ellen Dinkins, who lives in Holland. The sculpture — a representation of a pioneer woman — had been in place for only 18 days when it was smashed.

Dinkins is arriving in Amville today to investigate the chances of restoring or reconstructing her work, and she has agreed to an interview.

THREE

School Board President Julia Hines has just made the following statement:

"As you know, my opponent in next week's School Board elections, Stanley Wise, has been running around saying, in essence, that he's going to turn Central High into a high school Harvard. Wise wants to change everything: If there's a computer in room 103, he'll move it to room 102. The football team will wear red shirts and white pants instead of white shirts and red pants. He says he's going to upgrade the level of education. Anyone familiar with education knows he's just going to create chaos.

"We've had a chance to look over Mr. Wise's record closely in the past weeks. He's certainly had a great career: president of his own trucking firm, director of the Ridge Road Country Club, father of two fine kids. The mystery is what he knows about education. He has a B.A. in Business; I've got a Masters in Education. He's worked in trucking; I've been a college professor. He's spent his spare time worrying about Ridge Road's sand traps; I served as president of the PTA. And I've had four years experience at this job.

"Does Stanley Wise know anything about science education, advanced placement programs, accountability in education, physics labs, fitness programs, *et cetera, et cetera?* If he does, he must have read it in the newspaper."

A story on Hines's charges and Wise's response will appear in tomorrow's paper. You're interviewing Wise.

FOUR

Yesterday an overpass of the Spruce Highway—the most used road in the city—gave way and a large truck fell 25 yards to Richard Road, below. The driver of the truck was killed, a section of the highway, in both directions, was closed, and traffic was backed up during the evening rush hour for more than five miles. The story in today's paper included speculation from Highway Department inspectors that rusting beams had caused the overpass to give way. City budget cuts have reduced the funds available for highway maintenance. Highway Commissioner Frank Elliott—who is responsible for local highways and traffic patterns—was not available for comment yesterday. He has agreed to an interview today.

FIVE

A student you know at the local high school calls with a tip: "Coach McKinley has done it again," he exclaims. "He just cut three of his best basketball players—of course, they happen to be the only Hispanics on the team."

You get a list of this year's players from your source and use the phone book to call the homes of as many as possible. You reach two, including Willie Alvarado, a starting forward and one of the players cut. "The man had two standards," Alvarado says. "Yes, I was late to practice a few times and I missed a curfew, but so have other players. But he didn't see it that way. Twice he said, 'Willie, you're different. It's going to be tougher on you out there so you've got to be that much better.' He also told me I'm talented but that talent needs to lead. Then he pretty much stopped talking to me, and after I came late one day he just said, 'that's it.' There's no room for discussion with that man."

You ask about the other two players cut, Albert Reyes and Juan Ramon. "I don't know what he had against them," Alvarado says. "He claims they just aren't good enough but I think that's bull. They may not be stars but they're solid players. I really think he sacked them because they stood up for me. McKinley can't tolerate anyone who stands up to him on anything."

The other player you reach is John Richman, a sophomore who sees limited playing time. "McKinley has always been fair to me," he says. "He's really hard-driving but that's why this school has had winning teams for the ten years he's been here. We're one of the smallest schools in the division, too."

He balks when you ask about the three players kicked off the team, but cautiously answers when you assure him his name won't be used in the paper. "McKinley's an egomaniac," he says. "He's a talented egomaniac but he's an egomaniac. He wants things done his way or not at all. All three of those guys wanted some basic respect. They wanted to be treated like individuals with individual needs. To McKinley, every player is a member of a team. They have roles, not personalities . . . But is the guy a bigot? I just don't think so."

You call McKinley and he says it's true that he dropped three members of the team: "It's a long story," he says. "Their behavior was simply not up to the standards that we require of people who are going to represent this school. Why don't you stop by and we'll talk about it."

You agree and on the way you check the clips. An article dated five years ago reports that students staged a sit-in in his office one afternoon to protest what they said was his policy of not playing the Hispanics on the team.

■ B ■

Write stories based on the following interview assignments.

1. Interview the person responsible for security at a local library or bookstore about the problem of book theft and its prevention.
2. Interview a successful student-athlete about the pressures involved in combining training with academic work.
3. Interview a local bar owner about how drunks and minors looking to buy alcohol are handled.
4. Interview a police official responsible for investigations about the problems of dealing with informants.
5. Interview a representative of a high school or college English or journalism department about reports of declining writing skills among students.
6. Interview the manager of a local supermarket or grocery store about changes in customers' buying habits.
7. Interview an official of a community or university counseling service about changing attitudes toward psychological counseling.
8. Interview the owner of a new business about the problems and challenges of getting started.
9. Interview the manager of a local movie theater about local tastes in films.
10. Interview a fire department official about the problems of false alarms.

■ **C** ■

Write a story based on the following collection of information. You are writing for a newspaper dated tomorrow and read in the city where the events occurred.

Text of an interview today with Pottstown Police Chief Daniel Workman:

Reporter: We just got a call saying you're quitting. Anything to that?

Workman: Well, yes. I just told my staff today. I gave my resignation today to Mayor Joseph Ashburn.

Reporter: Why?

Workman: Well, it's quite simple really. When I came here eight years ago I said my goal was to improve the morale of this staff and try to lower crime in this city. Well, it's been a tough eight years, even tougher than I expected, but they've been rewarding years, too. And the point is that I think I've done what I set out to do. Now it's time to move on.

Reporter: Can you detail how you think things have changed?

Workman: Let's see. We have a staff of 28 full-time officers here. They were quitting at the rate of four a year in the five-year period before I arrived. Only two officers have quit in the past five years. I think that says something about morale.

Reporter: And the crime rate?

Workman: Well, you know we instituted this "crime watch" program here six year ago — where citizens are encouraged to stay alert for crime, particularly burglars. Since then the rate of burglaries in the city has declined 31 percent.

Reporter: If you believe things are going so well, why leave?

Workman: As I said, it's time to move on. I'm 45 years old. I think there might be a couple of more challenges ahead for this old boy before he hangs them up for good.

Reporter: What kind of challenges are you looking for?

Workman: Well, you know, I don't think I want to get too specific on that just yet. I want to stay in law enforcement though.

Reporter: There's been talk that you're in line for the post of police chief in Omaha. Any truth to that?

Workman: Well, I've talked to them. But I assure you I have no definite job offers at this time.

Reporter: When will you be leaving?

Workman: I've told Ashburn I'll stay until my replacement arrives.

Reporter: Any idea who that will be?

Workman: No.

Reporter: Is there anything else you have to say about this?

Workman: No.

Reporter: Can I give you a call if any other questions come up?

Workman: Sure, glad to help.

Text of an interview today with Ashburn:

Reporter: How's it going? Heard you had a bit of a shocker today . . .

Ashburn: I'm with you there. It was bad news for this city. We're going to miss Dan Workman. He has been an outstanding police chief for us. But I understand his decision, and wish him the best of luck. You can say I accepted his resignation with a good deal of regret.

Reporter: Where's he going?

Ashburn: Hey, you know I couldn't tell you that, even if I knew. That's Dan's business.

Reporter: Who's going to get his job?

Ashburn: We'll begin working on that tomorrow. Right now I don't have any idea. It could be someone now on the force; it could be an outsider. Those are going to be hard shoes to fill.

Coverage

CHAPTER 21

Obituaries

Death is probably the oldest regularly covered news story. In some preliterate societies the relatives of the deceased immediately take to wailing. This serves both to satisfy the heavens and to notify everyone within wailing distance that a tribe member is no longer with them. We spread this news through obituaries.

Obituaries also serve as a final remembrance of a person's life. They provide, in the words of Alden Whitman, who turned obituary writing into something of an art form at *The New York Times,* "all the characteristics of a well-focused snapshot," capturing the character and personality of subjects, as well as their achievements.

Form

Obituaries are the most formalized stories in newspapers. Most follow a standard pattern, which is why they often are the first stories assigned many news clerks and beginning reporters. But the form can be as entrapping as it is reassuring. Just as young composers can follow the design of a fugue to perfection and still create bad music, obit writers can master the form of an obituary and still fail to capture the essence of a subject's life. "Many obituaries suffer from dullness," warns Whitman in his book *Come to Judgment* (See Additional Reading). "They are little more than . . . a *curriculum vitae* wrestled into print."

Still, learning the form of a fugue or of an obituary is a starting point to composing one successfully.

Claim to Fame

For the purpose of our obituaries, each of us is assumed to have had a *claim to fame.* That fame may not be particularly widespread, in fact it might not extend beyond immediate family and business associates, but we all have some attribute or, as would be the case with a noted criminal, some flaw worth noting.

Jane Fonda's claim to fame will probably be that she was an Academy Award-winning actress known for her outspoken support for liberal political causes and her energetic and commercial advocacy of physical fitness. Bud Miller, a long-time grocer in Shamberg, will be recorded as "a grocer who worked for 38 years in Shamberg."

This is no time to get nasty. Miller's claim to fame is not that he had a reputation for drinking too much. But obituary writers do have to be honest. Richard Nixon's claim to fame, in large part, will be that he was the only president of the United States ever to resign from that office. ("Saints we are not in life," writes Whitman. "Nor should we be in death.")

The claim to fame, however unusual, goes in the lead:

Sybil Leek, who proclaimed herself a witch and wrote and lectured widely on the occult, the mystical and the supernatural, died of cancer yesterday at the Holmes Regional Medical Center in Melbourne, Fla. She was 65 years old.

The New York Times

People's claims to fame may have nothing to do

with their recent past. When Alice Huyler Ramsey died in 1983, she was remembered for an event that had taken place 74 years earlier:

Alice Huyler Ramsey, . . . who in 1909 became the first woman to drive across the United States, has died.

Los Angeles Times News Service in *The Boston Globe*

Age and Cause of Death

These are two topics about which people get secretive. Age is still a touchy subject for some of us, and some causes of death, particularly cancer, strangely are viewed as something of an embarrassment. Reporters have to press, firmly if politely, to get this information from a funeral home or from family. Obituaries are news. Readers deserve to know at what age and why someone died. One problem with the practice, for example, of listing all cancer deaths as simply the result of "long illnesses" is that it masks the toll of cancer in our society. A few newspapers have now gone so far as to refuse to print obituaries unless relatives are willing to divulge age and cause of death.

When age and cause of death are included in an obit, they belong in, or right after, the lead:

Frank Reynolds, the ABC News anchorman since 1978, died yesterday in Washington. He was 59 years old.

Reynolds had been ill with multiple myeloma, a form of bone cancer, for several months, but his death was attributed to acute viral hepatitis.

The New York Times

Developing the Claim to Fame

If an obituary is long enough—some run only a few grafs—the reporter's next job is to provide some more details about that claim to fame. In essence, the reporter supports the lead just as is done in any news story (See Chapter 14, Organization):

Leek, a native of Stoke-on-Trent, Staffordshire, England, once described herself in an interview as "just an ordinary witch from the New Forest of England," saying her family had been involved in witchcraft since 1134 . . .

Leek wrote more than 60 books, including "The Diary of a Witch," published in 1968, and works on numerology, phrenology and astrology. One of her most recent books, written with Bert R. Sugar, was "The Assassination Chain," which discussed theories behind the assassinations of President Kennedy, Robert Kennedy and Martin Luther King.

The New York Times

Chronology

At some point the obituary, again providing there is sufficient space, will jump back to the beginning of

someone's life and detail major events—such as birth, marriage, degrees and jobs—in chronological order.

Frank Reynolds was born in East Chicago, Ind., dropped out of Wabash College after a year and, after Army service in World War II, during which he won a Purple Heart, worked for CBS and ABC stations in Chicago. In 1965, he decided to take a 50 percent cut in pay to work as an ABC network correspondent in Washington.

In 1967, ABC offered him the anchor post on the "Evening News." He declined. "I felt they could find someone else to sit there and read the news," he said. A year later, however, he relented and moved to New York to share the anchor duties with Howard K. Smith . . .

The New York Times

Survivors

Any obit, at the end, will include a paragraph naming the person's closest relatives and often telling where they live. Newspapers generally have their own rules on who is mentioned and who is left out. Wives and husbands, children and parents always are named. Siblings usually are. Grandparents and grandchildren generally are not, although the number of them surviving sometimes is mentioned.

Pet dogs, no matter how beloved, don't make the list, nor do cousins. Either a spouse who has died previously or the closest living relative—usually a spouse, parents or children—comes first in the list of survivors. Previous marriages normally are noted, but the names of divorced husbands and wives aren't included among the surviving family members.

Sybil Leek's husband died before she did:

Her husband, Brian Leek, died in England in 1974. She is survived by two sons, Stephen, of West Palm Beach, Fla., and Julian, of Melbourne Beach, Fla., and two grandchildren.

The New York Times

Funeral Arrangements

Particularly in smaller cities, a significant proportion of readers may want to know what they can do to pay their respects. The final paragraph or two of a local obituary almost always will be devoted to information on who is handling the funeral, when it will be and whether the family would appreciate donations to a favorite charity.

Here is how Frank Reynolds' obituary ended:

The funeral will be held Saturday at 11 a.m. in St. Matthew's Cathedral in Washington. A White House spokesman said Mrs. Reagan would attend the requiem mass and that the president would attend "if his schedule permits." Reynolds will be buried in Arlington Cemetery with full military honors.

The New York Times

Getting the Information

During his 12 years as an obituary writer at *The Times,* Alden Whitman traveled across continents interviewing movie stars, prime ministers, authors and presidents, and returned to write obituaries thousands of words long that were stored in *The Times'* files until the subjects died. (*The Times* has about 1,000 advance obituaries on file.)

However, few obituary writers have the luxury of getting to know the people they will eventually be asked to write about. Instead they usually rely on facts phoned into the paper by the local funeral director handling the arrangements. These facts may be the only information available or necessary for a three- or four-paragraph obituary. But reporters should still remember to check the clip files just to make sure some newsworthy fact about a person is not being missed (See Chapter 18, Research).

If there will be room for a story more than a few paragraphs long, a reporter should push for more information. In some cases, magazine articles or books have been written by or about the person who has just died. That person also may be listed in the *Who's Who* series (See Chapter 18, Research) or some other biographical index. And there is no substitute for calls to family, relatives, friends, doctors and business associates to gather facts, anecdotes and quotes that help develop that "well-focused snapshot" Alden Whitman always tried to take.

The New York Times drew on printed material and on past interviews with Frank Reynolds and colleagues in compiling its obituary of Reynolds.

> According to Barbara Matusow's book "The Evening Stars," Reynolds's liberal views irritated many owners of ABC affiliate stations around the country. The network itself became uneasy about him, she relates, when Vice President Spiro T. Agnew, in excoriating the media, singled out Reynolds's commentaries for special criticism . . .
>
> The television newsman Sander Vanocur once described Reynolds as "a kind of James Cagney character." He came out of the Chicago school of journalism, Vanocur said, "which means you have paid your dues in one of the toughest journalistic towns in the world and you don't have to take anything from anybody."
>
> *The New York Times*

Enterprise

The term *enterprise* is used in this book to refer to stories on which reporters spend extra time and effort, stories in which they attempt to give readers a deeper look into events than may be possible in routine newsgathering under deadline pressure. There is room for such enterprise even within the confines of a format as tight as that of the obituary. The best obit writers distinguish themselves through the thoroughness of their research, through the quality of their description and quotes, and through their ability to communicate the texture, as well as the highlights, of someone's life.

This is from an obituary on the newspaper publisher Samuel I. Newhouse:

> Despite the vast scope of his holdings, Newhouse was an unobtrusive man, with no central office except his battered brown briefcase. He preferred to live and do business relatively quietly. "That's the advantage of being a shrimp," the 5-foot, 3-inch, self-described "newspaper businessman" once said. "Nobody notices you."
>
> Moreover, unlike some press lords, Newhouse did not use his newspapers as a megaphone to expound his thinking on public matters.
>
> "I am not interested in molding the nation's opinion," he said. "I want these newspapers to take positive stands of their own; I want them to be self-reliant . . ."
>
> *The New York Times*

Additional Reading

The Obituary Book, Alden Whitman, Stein and Day, 1970.
Come to Judgment, Alden Whitman, Viking Press, 1980.

▪ A. Writing Assignments ▪

Write obituaries based on the following collections of facts. In each case, the obituary is being written for tomorrow's paper in the town in which these people lived. All of them died on the day you are writing.

ONE

The editor tells you Charles L. Maxwell, a photographer who used to own The Photo Shop on Dexter Street here in Easton, has died. He tells you to take down the information from Funeral Director Frank Mansfield at Oberhurst Funeral Home:

"Charles L. Maxwell, 83. He died after a long illness. What illness, well, I guess the family won't mind. He had lung cancer. Lived at 207 High St. He was born in Springfield, Wisconsin, and went to high school there. Attended U. of Wisconsin in Madison and served in the Army after he graduated. He married June Bailey in 1934 and moved here that year. He'd learned photography in the Army apparently. Anyway, he worked as a free-lance photographer for eight years and in 1942 he opened The Photo Shop. Ran it by himself for five years and gradually expanded to where it had seven employees when he sold it in 1981. His wife, June, would help in the summer. She taught English at the high school.

"Maxwell was an active guy. He was a member of the Masons and a former vice president of the Rotary Club. He also helped design stage sets for the local theater group, The Prime-Time Players. Nice fellow. A couple of hundred people came to his house a few years back when he and June celebrated their 50th.

"June's still alive. He also had two sons; Brock lives in Houston and Larry lives at 12 Pepper Drive right here in town. Brock has three kids, Daniel, Susan and Leila. His wife's name is Anna. Larry has no kids. Isn't married for that matter. Maxwell is at the funeral home now. Friends can stop by here Friday from 9 to 11 a.m. and 3 to 6 p.m. The funeral will be Saturday at St. Luke's Catholic Church on Sellars Street. It's at 10 a.m. Oh, our address is 95 Hanneman Road. Burial will be for the family only."

You check the clips and find the only piece on Maxwell was a brief that appeared on the People Page in 1967. Seems his hobby was photographing kids. He is quoted there as saying: "Their faces are alive. The joys, the anguish, the love are there for everyone to see."

TWO

From Sheila Benson, the funeral director at Van Saun Funeral Home, 69 Webster St.:

"Esther Randolph. She died in a head-on automobile accident on Route 7 near Bennington, Vt. She was spending the week with her son. Her home here in Croton Lake was at 17 Roundabout Drive. Here's what we have: Born, July 9, 1916, in Pottstown, Penn. She was married in 1944. Her husband, Lionel, died in 1980. She has two sons, Jack Randolph of Bennington, Vt., and Lionel Randolph Jr. of Philadelphia, Penn. Neither has kids. Her maiden name was Bell and her parents' first names were James and Elaine. They're both dead. Background? She went to high school in Pottstown, Penn. Earned a degree in nursing from Thomas Jefferson University's School of Nursing and did graduate work at Johns Hopkins University. Worked at the Veterans Hospital in Philadelphia during World War II. She got married in 1946, I see. In 1952 she joined the Red Cross in Philadelphia and served as its director of nursing services.

"Later she became a specialist in, what do you call it, nursing recruitment. Let's see, she moved to this neck of the woods in 1959. In 1960 she became director of the Red Cross in the southeast portion of the state and then six years later, that was in 1966, she took a job with the state Health Department, where she was hired to set up the Community Nursing Services in the state. I've got here that this was the first time anyone had found a way to help the elderly poor people who were sick with home nursing. Here is how it was set up: Elderly people who couldn't afford a private nurse could contact the state and arrange for a nurse to visit them at their home. The service was for up to eight hours a day and the nurses would do all sorts of things — prepare meals, change bedding, you name it. It kept a lot of people out of the hospital. Mrs. Randolph ran the program — she was its director — from 1966 to 1970, coming over from the Red Cross. Then she supervised all community health programs for the state from 1970 to 1980, but still spent most of her time on that Community Nursing Services. Other programs were flu clinics, an educational program for the high schools, the Doctors on Wheels clinic. She retired in 1980.

"Awards? She got lots of awards. The latest was a leadership award from the American Association for Nurses when she retired. Let's see. She was a charter member of the National Association for the Advancement of Colored People and a member of the American Civil Liberties Union and the American Association for Nurses."

You check the newspaper's clips and find an article on the Community Nursing Services from 1972. It quotes Mrs. Randolph: "No one wants to fill a hospital bed. If we can bring nursing care to people in their homes, we'll cut medical costs, free hospital beds and help make the elderly healthy. There's no better medicine than to live in your own home." Article confirms funeral director's information.

You call M. Fremont Louis, commissioner of the state Department of Health, and a colleague of Mrs. Randolph for many years. He's glad to talk.

"It's hard to think of Esther as dead," he says. "She was a dynamo. Always helping people and never looking for credit for it. I saw her last month and she was still running rings around people half her age. She did everything to start that Community Nursing Services program. She wrote the federal grant proposal, she recruited the nurses to work in it and she publicized it through the senior citizens' community centers. The elderly and public health care in this state owe her a lot."

A call back to the funeral director is necessary to confirm that she will be buried Friday at All Saints Cemetery on 12th St. That's after they hold the service at 10 a.m. at All Saints Episcopal Church on 12th Street. The family says it doesn't want any flowers sent. Instead, it suggests donations be made to the National Health Council.

THREE

From Fred Logan, funeral director at Logan Funeral Home on 499 Broadway:

"Sun Tang Koo died in his home here in Redwood City . . . lived at 3144 Shore Blvd. He was 92. Quite a fellow. He graduated from the U.S. Army Corps of Engineers college equivalent training program in 1921 . . . traveled to China by ship the next year . . . Taught at Tsing-Hua University in Peking from 1924 to 1926. Then he taught at the University of Shanghai from 1926 to 1948. He taught civil engineering at both places. He was an elder at the First Presbyterian Church in Shanghai. He was actually born in the U.S., incidentally. In San Francisco. Anyway, he returned to the U.S. in 1948 and taught Chinese studies as a lecturer at San Francisco State University from 1948 to 1970. He was something of a self-taught expert on China. His book, "The Rise and Fall of Nationalist China" was published by Putnam in 1958 . . . He contributed articles on civil engineering, China and Christianity to a number of international journals. He was also a member of the Chinese Christian Fellowship and president of the Fellowship of Chinese-American Understanding from 1962–69 in San Francisco. He was a member of the West Side Presbyterian Church here. Services will be at the church on Wednesday at 10 a.m. That's at Geiger Square. Burial's going to be after the service at Willows Cemetery on Route 46. The family doesn't want flowers. Suggests that contributions be made to the Fellowship of Chinese-American Understanding in San Francisco instead. His wife, Kim, is still alive. He also leaves three children, two sons, William and Peter, and a daughter, Ellen Alpert. All of them live in San Francisco. He had seven grandchildren and three great-grandchildren."

You call Lois Richmond, a long-time professor of Chinese Studies at San Francisco State: "Yes, I knew him. We still corresponded, occasionally. He was something of a legend when he taught here. A true renaissance man. He didn't have any of the degrees of the rest of us, but I've never known anyone who knew more about China and its people. He also did a great deal to improve Chinese-American relations in the Bay Area. He personally worked out a compromise busing plan when the Chinese community downtown objected to being bused five miles to school in the suburbs. Instead an exchange program was worked out with another city school."

Kim moved here in 1975.

FOUR

You are in the office of Mayor Tom Jackson when you learn that Michael Lazar, chairman of the planning board, has died of a heart attack. He was just 63. Died in his home at 9 Dickerson Terrace here in Ducayne.

Jackson: "He should have listened to his doctor. He's been telling Mike to lose 45 pounds for a number of years now. But Mike did everything in excess. He ate well, he drank well and he fought hard for this town. Mike Lazar loved this community like few people do. He understood the history here and, I mean, practically convinced the merchants single-handedly to restore the downtown. Look at business today. Up 50 percent from five years ago. I'd like to take the credit but I can't. He'll be sorely missed and impossible to replace."

You stop down at the Planning Office and tell Martha McCarthy, the office secretary, the news. She says: "His temper did him in. Boy, could he blow. But he was as tough on himself as anyone. If we didn't have something for a meeting he could go through the roof. But he was just as quick with praise as he was with criticism."

You call John DeLuca, a Republican council member, because you know Lazar, like Jackson, was a Democrat. He says: "It's a real loss. Mike fought hard but clean. And he was full of new ideas. Frankly, we asked him to run for council as a Republican but he didn't want to hold elected office for anyone."

DeLuca agrees that Lazar was instrumental in restoring the downtown business district. So does Rita Tandy, who owns Tandy's Antiques. "He'd come by and say, 'Look, you want business, then help yourself. Strip off this ugly paint, put some trees out front, get some nice storefronts.' After awhile the Merchants Association began to listen and he helped us get some state Historical Preservation funds. He was the fireplug who got us started."

You call Hannemann Funeral Home, 88 Sickles Ave., for more information. Find out Lazar has lived here since he was 5. Moved with his family from Durango, Colorado, where he was born. Went to the local elementary and high schools and then to University of Chicago and University of Chicago Law School. Served in the Air Force. Saw action in Korea during that war. Returned in 1952 and opened his own law firm. Mainly does real estate and personal law. Appointed to the planning board in 1977. Chairman since 1980.

His wife and one daughter, Anne, live at home. His son Thomas lives in Nyack, N.Y., and another son, Peter, lives in Boulder, Colorado, where he's in graduate school. A second daughter, Heather Wilson, in St. Louis and owns a boutique. Lazar also has three sisters. We don't know their names. And three grandchildren.

He is going to be buried at Friends of Israel Cemetery Friday but the public is not invited. There will be a memorial service at City Hall Saturday at 10 in the morning.

■ B. Story Assignments ■
---

1. Write an obituary of yourself. Assume that you died yesterday of a heart attack and that services will be held at a local funeral home. Otherwise, stay true to the facts of your life. You can interview friends, relatives, employers and teachers for quotes.

2. Choose a person from your area in one of the following categories and write an obituary of that person based on interviews with people who know him or her. (You might tell people you are working on a profile rather than an obituary.) Choose a sudden heart attack as the cause of death and a local funeral home for the funeral.

   a. a mayor
   b. a school superintendent
   c. a barber
   d. a chef
   e. a judge
   f. a corporation president
   g. a minister, rabbi or priest
   h. an artist
   i. a scientist
   j. a professor

CHAPTER 22

Meetings, speeches and press conferences

Things got out of hand at the Sherrodsville, Ohio, Village Council meeting:

> The mayor was attacked, the village solicitor was pummeled, the fire station's pool table collapsed, a village councilman was charged with assault and the councilman's father was hospitalized with a heart attack.
>
> "I'm not used to having that kind of breakdown in authority," said the solicitor, Brad Hillyer, after last night's council meeting [at the fire station] in this northeastern Ohio village.
>
> Associated Press

The meetings that government bodies, school boards and other organizations hold; the speeches their officials make; and the press conferences that these officials call generally are quieter — and safer — affairs than this tumultuous meeting over a proposal to disband the two-man Sherrodsville Police Department. Mayors are not usually attacked. Village solicitors are rarely pummeled. Still, these functions are major sources of news. This chapter explains how to cover them.

Meetings

Most of the business of organizations, from the U.S. Senate to the Ridgewood Shade Tree Commission, is taken care of at meetings. That means reporters, inevitably, will spend much of their time sitting in the audience.

Reporters covering their first meeting are often so impressed by the attention the participants are paying to matters ranging from the selection of a new deputy assistant parks commissioner to the proper hour to begin next week's meeting that they return to write a thousand-word stenographic account of what went on. Usually it will end up being reduced to a few paragraphs by a grim-faced editor. Obviously, it's better to exercise news judgment beforehand.

What should be included in a story about a meeting? What's important to look for? Here are a few tips:

Keep a Tight Focus

The council may have passed three ordinances last night, but unless they were awfully important, the lead and most of the story are going to be devoted to the fact that council members voted to fire the police chief. Reporters have to remember that their job is not to keep the minutes of the meeting but to pick out one or two newsworthy developments to share with readers.

UNACCEPTABLE:
The Wilmar City Council last night voted unanimously to rename Carter Street, hired a new secretary and defeated a plan to monitor downtown with closed circuit cameras.

ACCEPTABLE:
The Wilmar City Council last night rejected a plan that would have made Wilmar the first small city in the United

States to use closed-circuit TV cameras to monitor its downtown area.

The Minneapolis Star and Tribune

It's always a mistake to return to the newsroom from a meeting with a couple of paragraphs worth of information on each of the five or ten items that were discussed. A coherent story can't be constructed out of such a hodgepodge of facts. At some point as the meeting progresses, reporters have to decide what their story is likely to focus on. Then they must gather enough information on that subject to make sure they can treat it thoroughly, even if that means some less newsworthy agenda item gets slighted.

Don't Just Sit There

The news at a meeting will usually be found in the more heated debates between participants and in the votes that follow those debates:

The Los Angeles City Council voted 9 to 4 to approve an agreement over noise control with the Burbank-Glendale-Pasadena Airport Authority despite strong objections from some members of the council that the agreement has no teeth.

Under the terms of the agreement, the airport authority will attempt to reroute departing flights away from city neighborhoods . . .

Los Angeles Times

Nevertheless, covering a meeting well will require more than just jotting down who says what and tallying the votes. Reporters will want to have prepared themselves before the meeting begins with information from sources and documents, and they will use breaks in the meeting to solicit additional quotes and explanations from the participants. Participants can also be corralled when the meeting ends. And after the meeting, good reporters will attempt to contact anyone who was directly affected by a decision taken there but was not in attendance—the police chief who was fired, for example. (With deadlines approaching, these follow-up interviews are usually conducted by telephone.)

Shortly after the council vote on that airport noise control agreement, the *Los Angeles Times* reporter was able to speak with a particularly important source:

Charles Aalff, the Federal Aviation Administration's air traffic manager for the airport, said in an interview that the change in direction requires aircraft maneuvering, to get quickly above nearby mountains, that many planes may not be equipped to do safely . . .

Don't Ignore the Audience

Sometimes the audience's behavior is the most interesting aspect of a meeting. If the audience is unusu-

ally large or small, count it. The number becomes part of the story. And note applause, jeers, catcalls or unruliness. The reporter who covered that Village Council meeting in Sherrodsville also had to note that a councilman's father, sitting in the audience, had a heart attack; that the councilman's wife, also in the audience, then began yelling, "Are you people satisfied?" at the mayor; and that the councilman allegedly jumped at the mayor causing both men to fall on a pool table, which collapsed.

At more orderly meetings, there is often a special slot in the agenda for audience complaints or suggestions. These comments frequently lead to stories, whether they represent the views of one frustrated citizen or of an organized and indignant group:

Rosemary Donohue called it an incentive to clean out her garage.

Barney Walsh called it a constitutional right.

And to another Glen Rock resident, a garage sale seemed "as American an institution as apple pie."

A coalition of private property protectionists, weekend browsers and peddlers joined forces in Glen Rock last night to win at least a temporary victory over a Borough Council attempt to restrict that bastion of free enterprise —the garage sale.

The (Bergen County, N.J.) *Record*

Find Out What's Next

There is often a long distance between a council or board's discussion of a proposal and a final decision. Sometimes discussions drag on without any formal action. Sometimes organizations vote to *table* issues —postpone them to another date. And even if a proposal is passed the first time it is considered, it may have to go through a public hearing and a final vote.

Reporters must always find out what happens next: When will the issue be reconsidered? When is the hearing scheduled? Is the mayor's signature required before the proposal becomes law? This information should be placed prominently in stories (See Chapter 15, Context and Background):

A proposed $17 million bond issue to pay for a five-year capital improvement program apparently will be submitted to Roanoke voters in a November referendum.

The City Council voted yesterday to schedule a public hearing to get citizens' views on the proposed bond issue . . . The hearing will be June 25 at 2 p.m.

Roanoke (Va.) *Times & World-News*

When a meeting is covered, the work often begins well before the meeting actually takes place. Reporters will want to call some of the participants to see what is scheduled. Sometimes there's news in the fact that something controversial is on the agenda:

Paramus Mayor Joseph Cipolla wants to rid his community of smut. He thinks it offends the "average person" with average community standards. But a tough pornography ordinance that he and the Borough Council are expected to introduce tonight has sharply divided many presumably "average" people.

The (Bergen County, N.J.) Record

The best way to cover a meeting, of course, is to attend it. But reporters staring at a list of the meetings held in a large town — meetings of the waterfront board, the environmental commission, the Memorial Day committee — quickly realize they will not be able to cover every meeting in person. They will want to keep tabs on any meetings they miss, however (with the possible exception of that Memorial Day committee).

Jim Flagg, who covers city hall for *The Express* in Easton, Pa., gets agendas of all city meetings sent to his offices as soon as they are printed. He follows up by checking with people who will attend or have attended. The best practice is to place two phone calls — one before the meeting and one after. The first call — "What am I going to miss?" — might go to someone on the board that's meeting or to the public official that board oversees. (The full-time health officer might know more about what the Board of Health will discuss tonight than the citizens who volunteer for the board.) The follow-up call after the meeting — "What did I miss?" — obviously must go to someone who attended.

If something newsworthy did in fact take place, many additional phone calls will follow.

Speeches and Press Conferences

People give speeches when they want to sell themselves, their organizations or their ideas. These two leads reported on speeches made during an election year:

DUBLIN — President Reagan, declaring "America is prepared for peace," announced yesterday he will consider a Soviet proposal to renounce the use of force in Europe if Moscow agrees to consider specific Western proposals to reduce the chance of war on the continent.

Associated Press in the Roanoke (Va.) Times & World-News

SAN FRANCISCO — Walter F. Mondale, accusing Ronald Reagan of virtually abandoning efforts to stop the spread of nuclear weapons, said yesterday that the future of the human race hinged on the outcome of the November election.

"Reagan has opposed every arms control agreement by every president of both political parties since the bomb went off," he said . . .

St. Louis Post-Dispatch

People hold press conferences when they have an announcement to pass on and when they have decided it's time to face reporters' questions:

Mayor Marion Barry said yesterday that competition for the district's lucrative cable television franchise is so intense that the losing bidders almost certainly will attempt to overturn the D.C. City Council's decision in the courts.

"I suspect the contract will end up in court," Barry said *during his monthly news conference.* "There's too much money involved with it. It's too far-reaching."

The Washington Post

Reporters have two jobs: They have to pass along the speaker's message. But they also have to help readers examine that message.

Preparation

Speeches and press conferences are sometimes scheduled so close to deadline that reporters won't have time to pursue thoroughly whatever news the speaker makes. As with meetings, it helps to find out beforehand what's likely to be said. "If you can get the person holding it to preview for you — off the record — what *will* be said, it's a big help on deadline," says Jim Flagg, whose deadline for *The Express* is 11 a.m. "It allows you to prepare, check clips and line up a few people for interviews ahead of time."

Reporters may be able to obtain a draft of a major speech in advance — with the understanding that no story will appear on that speech until after it is given. This can be a help, but reporters must make sure they still follow what the speaker actually says. Big news can be made in variations from prepared texts.

Finding the News

Politicians and officials always have a purpose when they give a speech or hold a press conference. But reporters are there for their own purpose — to find the news. There are occasions when the news that reporters find in a speech or press conference is not what the newsmaker intended them to find:

Without offering specifics, [Sen. Hart] pledged also to strengthen the program . . .

The New York Times

Sen. Hart obviously did not intend to have his lack of specifics highlighted.

There also are occasions when reporters include relevant background information (See Chapter 15, Background and Context) that casts the event in less flattering light:

Frank Wicks, taking his third shot at Rep. Samuel S. Stratton's 23rd District seat, asked the congressman yesterday to decline political action committee campaign contributions . . .

The numbers are clearly against Wicks. He lost so badly to Stratton in 1980 and 1982 that this year the Republican Party leadership virtually disowned him.

Wicks is non-plussed.

"I view that as a non-issue," he said.

(Albany, N.Y.) *Times Union*

The lead in a story about a speech might come from a remark two-thirds of the way through the address that contradicts something that person said one month ago; or reporters might choose to emphasize the reaction of the crowd or comments from the audience; or their stories might be based on answers to questions, not the speech or announcement itself.

Often the newsmaker's purpose and the reporter's purpose do coincide: The mayor has called a press conference to announce that the city will be constructing a new municipal swimming pool. Fine, that's news. But if the police chief emphasizes in a speech that the local burglary rate is down 3 percent and lets slip afterward that armed robberies have doubled in the last year, the reporter's story is going to focus on robberies, not burglaries.

Getting information and quotes from a speech or press conference, especially when no prepared text is available, will provide a stern test of reporters' note-taking abilities (See Chapter 20, Interviewing). The secret is to apply news judgment while taking notes and to jot down only potentially newsworthy material. The reporter's notes should not turn into a transcript or even a summary of all the points the speaker has made. Forget the governor's rhapsody on the beauty of this part of the state in springtime. Forget her tribute to the state's "hard-working law enforcement officials." But make sure you return from that speech prepared to write *in detail* about her attack on the mayor for wasting state funds.

Questions

Once the questioning begins at a press conference or after a speech, a well-prepared reporter sometimes takes over. This is no time for timidity. Good questions are concise and to the point (See Chapter 20, Interviewing); they may be used to force the newsmaker to clarify or defend points that have been raised or to pursue issues the newsmaker seemed to ignore.

When the applause starts or the questioning stops, good reporters will usually be dashing for the podium to conduct a brief private interview with the politician or official. If possible, they will have arranged beforehand for such an opportunity to talk alone. Alone with the newsmaker, reporters can pursue new angles, check quotes or ask questions they might not have wanted to share with competition.

Follow-up

And the reporting of a speech or press conference often is not complete when the reporter leaves the room: The mayor has to be contacted for a reaction to the governor's charges. The clips have to be checked for background on the dispute.

When Easton's mayor and police chief held a press conference to announce that they had broken a *police* burglary ring, they dutifully disclosed the charges that had been filed against police officers but said little else. Only by checking the affidavits filed with the village justice was Jim Flagg able, in a follow-up story, to include details of what had been stolen and how:

Two Easton policemen described by their peers as quiet and uncontroversial used their positions on the night shift to carry out a series of bold burglaries, according to Easton police investigators.

On several occasions, the two patrolmen, Fred Curry and Harvey Gogek, allegedly filed police reports on crimes in which they had played a role. Sometimes, police officials say, the target of the crimes was the department itself.

That portrait of an extensive crime ring *is sketched in affidavits filed this week* by Easton police with an Easton district judge.*

The (Easton, Pa.) *Express*

In writing up a speech or press conference, reporters should be particularly careful not to clutter the lead with too many details (See Chapter 8, Hard Leads). What's most important usually is who was speaking and what was the most newsworthy point that person was making:

Rep. Barbara Mikulski, D-Md., said yesterday that the idea of a woman vice presidential candidate should not be the top priority of Democratic voters and that the news media have mistakenly pinned the issue on the wrong party.

The Washington Post

Usually, such details as where the speech was given and how many people attended are worked into the second or third paragraphs, along with information that supports the lead (See Chapter 14, Organization). Here is the second graf of the *Washington Post* story:

Speaking to about 300 members of the National Women's Democratic Club, Mikulski, who has been mentioned as a possible nominee, said the idea is important but that voters and the media should focus more attention on the Republican Party's failings on women's issues.

Speech or press conference stories should waste no time taking advantage of the abundant number of

---

* The names in this story have been changed.

quotes available. The *Washington Post* story began quoting Mikulski in the third graf; some start even sooner.

"Why don't they [the Republicans] nominate a woman vice president?" Mikulski said during a 30-minute speech in which she discussed how the so-called "gender gap" will affect the 1984 elections. "Why don't the Republicans support the Equal Rights Amendment?"

Finally, when writing up a story about a speech or press conference—or a meeting, for that matter—the secret is to remember that the news is usually what was said, not the event itself (See Chapter 8, Hard Leads):

UNACCEPTABLE:
President Reagan held a televised press conference yesterday.

ACCEPTABLE:
President Reagan—vowing not to "pull the rug out . . . instantly" from farmers—said yesterday he would send Congress a plan expected to heat up the raging farm debt debate.

"We've got to get the government out of the agriculture business," Reagan said in a televised press conference.

USA Today

▪ A. Writing Assignments ▪

Write stories based on each of the following collections of information. In each case you are writing for a newspaper dated tomorrow and read in the town where the events occurred.

ONE

The following is a transcript of tonight's meeting of the Plainfield City Council:

Council President Shelly Shumar, Democrat, called the meeting to order and asked that the minutes of last week's meeting be approved. They were.

Councilman Greg Hawthorne, Democrat, Chair of Council Police Committee: "I don't have too much to say here. We had a robbery and a handful of burglaries this week. It looks like we're going to need at least one new police car soon though. One of those old Dodges seems to have blown its transmission. I would suggest that we consider replacing them all at once, rather than just handle the problem piecemeal. We could get rid of all 4 of those five-year-old Dodges, and probably get a good deal on some new cars. Save ourselves a lot of problems. If it's okay with you folks I'll have the chief start looking at prices." (Other councilmen and women nod their heads.)

Councilman Robert Reese, Democrat, Chair of Council Department of Public Works Committee: "Okay, we have the second architect's report on the new DPW garage and it's pretty much the same as the first one two months ago. Ardmore and Penn Inc. is the firm's name. Headquarters in Boynton. I'll read you the last paragraph: 'We conclude that renovation of the existing structure would be inadequate to handle the department's current and future needs. We believe a new structure should be constructed on the site. And we believe the new structure could be completed for approximately $400,000.' Okay? The original firm said $380,000, they say four-hundred. Both say we have to do it. There's danger to men and equipment in that old garage. I say let's go."

Shumar: "Are you introducing a motion, Bob?"

Reese: "I move that we authorize the Department of Public Works Committee to begin accepting bids on the construction of a new DPW garage on the present site, completely replacing the current garage."

Hawthorne: "Second, Shelly."

Councilman David Fayles, Republican: "Wait a second, Bob. We're just not with you on this one. Three-hundred and eighty to four-hundred thousand dollars. That's going to raise our property taxes, Bob. You know that. These consultants just love to take things down and build. I've looked that building over, and it looks to these eyes like it can be easily renovated. How old is it anyway?"

Reese: "28 years."

Fayles: "I say let's get another one of these firms to tell us exactly how much a renovation would cost."

Reese: "Come on, David. Let me read to you from the report of the first architectural consultant — Main Line Designs of LaPort: 'A renovation of such a deteriorating structure would simply not be cost effective. The department now has 6 trucks in its garage. They barely fit, and it is reasonable to assume more trucks will be needed in the future. Even if the structure could efficiently be renovated, it is inadequate for the department's needs.' Roof tiles are falling down, David. We had a garbage truck scratched by one, last month. The roof leaks. It's an incredible eyesore. Let's vote."

The motion is carried by a 3–2 vote, with Shumar, Hawthorne and Reese voting in favor and Fayles and June Bryson, Republican, opposed. Mayor Jonathan Rose, Democrat, must still sign the proposal. Rose was at the meeting and said he would sign it as soon as it reached his desk. The meeting adjourned shortly afterward.

TWO

The following is the text of the public participation portion of tonight's meeting of the Dawson Town Council:

John Goldsmith, 42, of 271 Lanier Road: "Mr. Mayor, council members, I've come before you here tonight to question the town's recent increase in parking fees from 5 cents to 25 cents per hour. Ladies and gentlemen, that is a 500 percent increase. And I didn't get a 500 percent raise last year. Yesterday I parked for what must have been all of 2 minutes on Gedney Street to buy the Sunday paper. I didn't bother to feed the meter because who wants to spend 25 cents for 2 minutes? That comes to $7.50 an hour. Well, I came out to find a $5 ticket on my windshield. The cop must have been hiding behind a tree because he was gone. My question is this. Why don't you put in meters with slots that will take nickels for 10 minutes, dimes for 20 minutes and quarters for an hour? I'd really appreciate it."

Councilwoman Barbara Moffett: "I guess as chairperson of the Police Committee I'll speak to that. I would say, Mr. Goldsmith, that you had bad luck. I'd guess your chances of getting a parking ticket in 2 minutes are about as likely as your odds of winning a million dollar lottery. This town has a police force of 14 and I don't think any of them have been assigned to harass you. As for the change in the meters, yes, it is 500 percent. But look where we started. Can you make a 5-cent phone call today, buy a 5-cent candy bar? We'd like to keep taxes down in this town and one way to do it is get some revenue from all the shoppers who enjoy the personal attention they get on Main Street. I'm sorry you had bad luck, but I'm afraid there isn't much we can do about it."

Averill Worshom, 78, 12 Decatur Ave.: "Mr. Mayor. As you know, sir, I've lived in this town 43 years now. When I first came here Decatur Avenue was a rural road with so little traffic that you hardly had to look both ways before crossing the street. No more. Dawson has grown, which I don't mind, but I do mind not being able to cross the street to visit with my neighbors. I'm not as spry as I once was and those kids from Upper Regional High School don't seem to care a hoot about the speed limit or about being polite. Would you please look into the matter? It would help, I think, if you would consider putting in a stop light or at least a stop sign at Decatur and Meadow-view Road. And unlike the gentleman who just spoke, I'd like to see a few more traffic tickets around here."

Mayor Russel Todd: "Mrs. Worshom, it's good to see you. I don't know about the part of your being less spry. You still keep one of the best vegetable gardens in town. Joking aside, though, we are well aware that traffic is getting to be a serious problem out your way. The council appointed a Traffic and Advisory Committee last month to look into just the kind of problem you are talking about and we expect a report in another two or three weeks. I know the intersection you are speaking of can get very busy and I expect it will be one of several that will get close consideration for a stop sign or stop light."

Angela Barbaro, Chairwoman of the Town Parks Committee: "Last year I came before you at this time to urge you to consider lifting all curfews at Landers Park. It seemed particularly appalling to us that kids could not use the park in the summer after 8 p.m., and you agreed. I'd like to say the trial we agreed to has been a resounding success, but I'm afraid at best I'd have to call it a mixed bag. Use of the park in general is up this year and the new playground for preschoolers is simply packed during the day. Vandalism also has increased again, though. Last week we took an inventory at the playground for older kids next to Ridge Road and I was truly shocked. Five of eight swings had been ripped from their support. The large slide was covered with some of the foulest graffiti I've ever seen, and there must have been a dozen shattered beer bottles under the jungle gym apparatus. I've discussed this with [Police] Chief [Eugene] Banks and he says he simply does not have the manpower to assign a patrol car fulltime to the park in the evening. Reluctantly, therefore, I'd like to ask you, on behalf of the Parks Committee, to reinstitute a dusk to dawn curfew at the park. I hate to do it because most of the kids in this town would benefit from fewer constraints on their lives and more breathing room, but the minority in this case has ruined it for all of them."

Councilman Robert Lansberg: "Mrs. Barbaro, thanks for your forthright report. I agree with you that the situation at the park has gone sour again and, as you know, we can't buy a new set of swings every month. I'd therefore like to propose a motion that the council reinstitute a curfew at Landers Park on Wilson Boulevard from dusk to dawn. We can't take away the park of parents and younger children in this town so a pack of unruly teen-agers can have a place to break beer bottles."

Councilwoman Moffett: "I second."

The council votes 5–0 in favor of the motion.

THREE

The following is the text of a speech delivered yesterday to unemployed people, in meeting hall at headquarters of Local 14 of the Fast Food Workers Union at 748 West Humphrey Street in Columbus, by Dolores Mandel, executive director of the new National Union of the Unemployed, founded just three months ago:

"Hello, brothers and sisters. We've gotten some press coverage lately, so you probably know something of what this is all about. The media can't handle things if they get too complex, so we've been keeping it simple. The simple version — are you listening, reporters? — is that we're starting a union of unemployed people. That we're uniting a group of people who tend to disappear for the 29 days of the month between the monthly releases of unemployment figures. That we're going to make a lot of noise and maybe even cause some trouble — the media just eat up that kind of talk — until people, one, start to recognize that the statistics have families and feelings and real human needs, and, two, until people start to listen to our demands, instead of just calling us names.

"Here's the complicated version: We aren't going to wait around for the do-gooders to have their periodic pangs of conscience anymore. We aren't going to wait around for our brothers and sisters in the other unions to think of us anymore. Though we thank the Fast Food Workers for the use of the hall, these other unions represent people who are lucky enough to keep a job in these crazy days. Those of us who have gotten the pink slip are an afterthought to them. We aren't going to wait. We're going to do what people have always done when they were oppressed and ignored. We're going to organize. We're going to unite. We're going to tell the world that we aren't going to be the doormat on which this insane, high-tech, global economic madness wipes its feet. We're going to shout a simple message — here we go, reporters — We want jobs! We want jobs! [Crowd joins in chant.] We want jobs! We want jobs! And we're going to get the millions of others of our unemployed brothers and sisters to shout it with us until . . . until . . . until they listen."

Crowd of 125 cheers wildly. They line up at tables in the back of the hall to sign up for new union. Later Mandel announces that 97 unemployed people joined her union at the meeting.

From interview after speech with Walter Hall, former worker with Atlas Ballbearing here, laid off three months ago, unemployed: "Are you kidding? Of course, I'm signing up. This woman talks sense. I haven't heard so much sense come out of anybody's mouth in a long time. We want jobs! I need a job."

From interview after speech with Mandel: "What power do we have? Would a couple of hundred thousand unemployed people sitting down on Wall Street have power? Would a couple of hundred thousand unemployed people paying a visit to those computer whizzes in the Silicon Valley have power? We can't go on strike, but we have lots and lots of power. We just have to decide how best to use it. Our demands? We want jobs to become a priority in this country again. We want a tax system geared to creating jobs not getting people to buy more computers. We want an economy geared to creating jobs not raising the rate rich people can earn on their investments. We want a government putting its money into job programs not missile programs."

▪ B. Story Assignments ▪

1. Watch a televised presidential press conference or a Sunday morning interview show. Write a news story based on the newsmakers' comments.

2. Attend a meeting of a local government body such as a city council or school board. Write a story.

3. Find someone giving a speech in your area by calling the local Chamber of Commerce, political clubs, a local college or the public school system. Attend the speech and write a story based on what is said and, if possible, on a follow-up interview.

CHAPTER 23

Government and politics

James Reston writes a column on Washington and the world for *The New York Times*. Don Melvin covers city hall for *The Burlington* (Vt.) *Free Press*. Both subscribe to the same philosophy of covering government and politics.

"You study the record," Reston advises. "You start by finding out what the officials have done. You look at the clips (See Chapter 18, Research). You find out where politicians came from, what their districts are like, what people know them. You call up their offices and say you'd like a copy of their speeches."

Most beginning political reporters will find themselves covering officials who "came from" no place more exotic than the other side of town and who have not necessarily preserved copies of their speeches. For the beginning reporter, covering government and politics almost always means covering *local* government and *local* politics. Still, when Don Melvin was sent to city hall in Burlington, he followed a routine quite similar to that Reston prescribes. Melvin checked clips on local politics and politicians in his newspaper library. He sought out some political science professors at the University of Vermont who had studied local politics in Burlington for more than a decade. He took the leaders of each of the city's three political factions out to lunch. He set up weekly meetings with the mayor. And he spent as much time as he could wandering around city hall, meeting and talking with officials and people who knew those officials. All this "homework," to use Reston's term, was hardly done at his leisure. Melvin was assigned to the beat just three months before a hotly contested local election.

Covering government and politics generally re-

quires keeping up with an endless parade of meetings, speeches and press conferences (See Chapter 22, Meetings, Speeches and Press Conferences). It also requires deciphering budgets and audits, and following campaigns and polls—skills discussed in this chapter. Whatever the task, however, our strongest suggestion is that beginning reporters do the homework—talk to the sources, read the records and documents—that will help them make sense out of the rush of politically charged events.

Sources

Professors moan about "politics" at universities. Business people complain of "politics" in corporations. What they are lamenting is a style of behavior that emphasizes manipulation of others, self-promotion, the creation of false appearances and the selective application of power. Politicians are often people devoted to the public good, as they perceive it. But they are also people who have chosen to spend much of their lives engaging in "politics." This is true as well of elected officials, who are, after all, just the politicians who managed to win the last election.

It is difficult to report on these people, whose behavior is often so controlled and rehearsed, simply by showing up at their public performances. Fortunately, in the privacy of their offices or their favorite hangouts, most politicians love to discuss the "game" of politics with reporters whom they've come to know personally. That's why when Jim Flagg was assigned the City Hall beat for *The* (Easton, Pa.) *Express,* he set out to meet potential sources away from the public gatherings where their posturing is likely to be most pronounced.

"I went around to almost every office at City Hall and tried to make contact with the people there face to face, from secretaries to the mayor," he recalls. And, as Flagg became more experienced, he began to look beyond those in office to the people who try to influence their decisions and to the people affected by those decisions. "As I've progressed as a reporter, I've begun to shy away from stories that start with 'City Hall said last night . . .'" Flagg explains.

The Chief Executive

Within the limitations imposed by the "checks and balances" of the Congress and the judiciary, the president runs the federal government. The governor, with similar restraints, is in charge of a state government. Finding the boss on the local level may not be that easy, however. Often *county executives* have a major say; often the elected mayor is just a part-timer and the city or town is run by a full-time appointed *city manager.*

The first thing any reporter on the beat must do is find out who holds the *real* power: Who makes the day-to-day decisions? Who hires the people who occupy the government offices? Who draws up the budget?

The Council or Legislature

Councils and legislatures can be great sources of information because they are filled with a bunch of politicians each of whom is struggling to gain recognition and a say in policy. The two or more sides to an issue that reporters usually look for (See Chapter 6, Objectivity) are frequently represented on the council or in the legislature. For example, when Mario Cuomo, New York State's Democratic governor, presented his 1985 budget proposals, legislators of both parties — but particularly Republicans — were quick to react. Articles in *The New York Times* that recorded these reactions gave readers a glimpse of what they could expect in the legislative battles ahead:

"I don't anticipate the governor's education package in its totality going anywhere," said Sen. John H. Donovan, a Chadwicks Republican who is chairman of the Senate Education Committee. But, he added, "there are components in the package that I want to discuss and pursue."

Reporters should review past votes and election statements to determine where the divisions lie in a council or legislature, so they know whom to approach to get a fair range of views.

Other Government Officials

The people who pass laws aren't necessarily the people who know the most about how they are carried out. Reporters will want to get to know the heads of city departments, from the police to the health department, to monitor how well policies are working in practice and to keep in touch with problems that may grow into issues (See Chapter 27, Municipal Services).

The *city attorney* is another important source. In this age of litigation, few governments refrain from suing or escape being sued. The city attorney is privy to information on all legal disputes affecting a government and is responsible for advising officials of the limitations and requirements imposed by various laws. And the *city clerk* is a valuable source for background on issues and for access to city records.

It's also crucial to know who keeps track of the money and who is spending it. Most cities have a full-time *financial officer* or budget officer. It's wise to know who heads the finance committee of the city council, too. And the *tax assessor* can be useful because he or she keeps track of property values in town and of how much each property owner is paying in taxes.

Boards

Boards or commissions are usually appointed by the mayor, council or some combination of the two. Boards often function as advisory bodies, and don't have the final say:

The Richmond Planning Commission *recommended* yesterday that the city transfer ownership of Parkers Field to the Richmond Metropolitan Authority as part of the plan to replace the ballpark's decrepit stadium.

Richmond Times-Dispatch

Two of the most important boards in any municipality are the *board of adjustment* (in some areas called the zoning board) and the *planning board* (or commission), which between them monitor development. A variety of additional boards, often staffed by volunteers, oversee everything from the operation of the library to the preservation of historic sites. Controversy can crop up on the library board just as it can on the council, and such controversies generate news.

Former Elected and Appointed Officials

Politicians lose as well as win elections. And top appointed officials are likely to be swept out of office with them when a new party or new administration takes power. These former officials understand how government works from the inside, and are often anxious to share their views. Some former officials, of course, sound off just to get even. Their charges, nonetheless, help balance the self-congratulations of those in power:

The former head of New York City's Off-Track Betting Corp. charged yesterday that Mayor Koch was attempting to "rewrite history" by claiming that OTB is free of political patronage.

(New York) *Daily News*

Power Brokers

Possibly the single toughest task in covering government and politics is discovering who holds power —and manipulates the visible politicians—behind the scenes. Candidates and officials are buffeted by a variety of interest groups on a wide range of issues. The people whose interests regularly prevail, or who broker the deals between the politicians and the interest groups, often prefer to keep themselves out of the limelight.

The first place to look for these *power brokers* is in the local political parties. Find out which members of a party have served as county committee people and are most active at party functions. The presidents or political liaisons of the Chamber of Commerce, the local board of realtors, the merchants association and any local banking organization also are likely to be influential behind the scenes. These people have a considerable stake in their communities and often provide financing for candidates.

Are candidates required to make public lists of campaign contributors? It is always interesting to keep such lists in mind as government favors and contracts are handed out.

Community Groups

The influence of various community organizations ebbs and flows with the news. Some, like the League of Women Voters, are worth contacting periodically. Though the league commonly avoids partisan positions on issues, its members often attend and monitor meetings reporters might miss. Active league chapters also prepare reports on a variety of problems in government.

The importance of most other groups varies. A local merchants association might suddenly emerge as a major force during a council dispute over whether to build a downtown parking garage. Taxpayer groups are most vocal and visible at budget time. And block associations, some of which grow up overnight, are heard from when there's a perceived need for better police protection or snow removal, or they might be there to voice complaints over intersections without stop lights and parks that have become hangouts for teen-age beer drinkers. In New York, members of the Good Old Lower East Side preservation group turned out in force to oppose a proposal for a city shelter for the homeless in their neighborhood:

"We on the Lower East Side have never turned our back on the homeless but it is unfair to expect our community to absorb most of the city's homeless population," said Susan Leelike of the Good Old Lower East Side preservation group.

The New York Times

Reporters should try to maintain some contact with these community groups even as they hibernate, waiting for an issue. The people in these organizations can help reporters penetrate the streets and homes where governmental decisions are actually felt.

Records and Documents

"Whenever anything comes up, I ask, 'Is there anything on paper,'" says Jim Flagg of *The Express* in Easton, Pa. "A ruling from the attorney, memos between departments . . . if it's on paper it saves time." Certain documents have to exist in government, and they do more than save time. They can be the basis for major stories.

Ordinances

Ordinances are the laws on the books in a locality. Typically they become news when they are proposed and debated before a council or legislature. But old laws, too, can become a source of fresh controversy (is it illegal to sell beer in town on Sunday?). And study of a town's ordinances—its ban on massage parlors, for example—can help reporters become acquainted with the issues that have been important in the area they are covering.

Development Plans

Development plans can spark fierce controversy in communities. Some people invariably favor attracting more businesses and industries to town because they bring jobs and pay taxes, lowering the residential tax rate. Others oppose development, fearing that it will change the character of a community or will bring traffic and pollution. These battles inevitably generate reams of paper.

Every municipality has a *master plan* designed to set out, in broad terms, how the community should grow. In theory, but not always in practice, that plan is reflected and enforced by *zoning regulations,* which establish areas, or zones, restricted to such buildings as one-family homes, apartments, businesses or factories.

Anyone interested in building anything from a

one-story house to a 1,000-unit apartment complex must submit a *site plan* to the planning board or commission even if the development conforms to existing zoning. Planners will review whether the proposed project conforms to requirements on lot size, height and distance away from roadways. Those whose projects conflict with existing zoning regulations must file for a *variance,* or exemption. Such requests usually are reviewed by a *board of adjustment.* Decisions of both the planning board and board of adjustment often must be ratified by the town's governing body.

If projects are controversial, they can be fodder for stories. Site plans and variance requests on file with the municipality's planning office inform reporters about who has asked to build and where. Reporters also should talk with the people who keep the files to find out if the city has received any written opposition to the proposed construction:

> A Moslem congregation has proposed that a $1.5 million marble mosque be built near Seven Corners . . .
>
> The proposed Dar Al-Hijrah mosque, with a 60-foot minaret and a one-story administration building, is planned for the corner of Leesburg Pike (Rte. 7) and Row Street, near two churches, a shopping center and high-rise apartment buildings.
>
> Two letters of opposition and one of conditional support already have been received by the Fairfax County Board of Zoning Appeals, which will hold a public hearing April 17 . . .
>
> *The Washington Post*

Tax Records

Reporters can't go poking around in people's income taxes — these are private. But the value at which various properties in town are assessed for real estate taxes is public information and that information can lead to important stories.

Jim Flagg says he regularly goes through the tax roles in Easton to see who pays *no* taxes. The issue is controversial in Easton because huge chunks of property are tax exempt. Flagg used the city's tax records to report this story:

> Here's a moot question: If the City of Easton could collect taxes on tax-exempt property [this year], how much richer would the city be?
>
> Answer: $925,000 — enough to balance the 1981 city budget without hiking the property tax and water-sewer fees.
>
> Here's another question, and it's not moot: How much longer will Lafayette College, the YMCA, cemeteries and every church and synagogue and non-profit institution in Easton enjoy freedom from property taxes?
>
> Answer: Maybe forever. But sides are forming in a test debate between two administrations — that of Dr.

David Ellis at Lafayette College, and that of Mayor Philip Mitman at Easton City Hall.

> *The* (Easton, Pa.) *Express*

Tax assessors often have two sets of tax records: One shows the taxes on each property, lists the owner of the property (or the person paying taxes on it) and is arranged by location. The other shows *all* the holdings and taxes paid by a particular property owner. Reporters who want to see how much the chairman of the local Republican Party pays on the properties she owns (and that should include all government reporters) can easily find the answer in this latter set of tax records. The other set of records can be used to find out what her neighbors pay on similar property.

Audits

It's always worth finding out what *audits* are done on government programs and when. Audits are economic report cards. They tell whether a program — welfare, aid to farmers — is being well managed or has problems, and they judge whether that program is operating within its budget. State and local governments along with various independent agencies have to be audited if they receive substantial funding from the federal government.

"The real news is when you get a critical audit," Flagg notes. "But you always get tips on what's going on, even from a positive audit." Flagg says he routinely reviews several audits a year, including an audit of city financing, an audit of the federally funded Community Development grant program and audits of three employee pension funds.

Budgets

The budget is a blueprint of a city's costs and revenues in the coming year. A superficial reading of the budget tells how much taxes will increase, whether state and federal revenues are increasing or decreasing, whether more or less money will be allocated to different city departments, and whether the city's debts are mounting. A detailed analysis can offer a wealth of information about the quality and quantity of services, such as how much it costs to collect a ton of garbage and how many police officers the city has for every 1,000 residents.

Reporters should not think of budgets as documents that miraculously appear one day at a city council meeting. Instead they should look at a budget as a process that goes on for months and should be written about all along the way.

This process begins when city department heads draw up what they consider to be their budgetary needs. Beware: The tendency at this stage is to inflate requests because all the players in the game know that budgets end in compromise. Next these requests are reviewed by the finance committee of the city council and a tentative budget is drawn up. Only then is it introduced to the public at a council meeting and discussed at a series of public hearings. There are stories all along the way.

"I try to track what kinds of increases each department is asking for and what kind of effects increase will have on taxpayers," says Doug Rainey of the *La Crosse* (Wis.) *Tribune.* "I try to put it on a level the taxpayer can understand."

The single most important budget issue to most local readers is whether and by how much their taxes will rise, or, in rare cases, decline. Readers should be told of the change in general terms:

The proposed tax increase in the municipal portion of the budget is $348,000 or 5.5 percent.

More importantly though, readers also should have the changes in the tax rate translated for them into terms they can use in thinking about their own budgets. Such changes are reported in terms of *assessed value,* which is a determination of a property's relative value for tax purposes and is typically lower than a property's real, or *market,* value.

If the proposed budget is adopted, taxes will increase from $4 to $4.22 per $100 assessed property value, or an increase of $220 on a home assessed at $100,000.

Such translations require the command of one powerful mathematical technique — long division. The "average" reader might not get that excited about the fact that municipal taxes are going up $348,000. But tell readers that taxes on a typical house in town will increase $220, or 5.5 percent, and the public hearing might be packed.

In addition to keeping track of changes in taxes, reporters should ask other, basic questions about each year's budget:

1. *How much have expenses increased or decreased both in dollars and as a percentage of the total budget?* Expenses will fall into three broad categories. Every city has *operating expenses* — the day-to-day costs of providing services and maintaining equipment. Salaries invariably make up the largest single such expense. Cities also have *capital costs* — money spent on major new equipment and on construction. And finally, like most of us, cities have debts. The *debt service* shows how much money the district must pay as principal and interest on old loans, typically bonds issued for construction projects.

2. *Where will revenues come from and how have the sources of money changed?* Though cities rely primarily on local taxes, they also get help from the state and the federal government. Cuts in state and federal programs can be a direct cause of tax increases on the local level.

3. *What changes in services or staffing will result from budgeting changes?* To answer this question, reporters first must compare this year's figures with those from previous years. Is the city library getting more or less money? The next step is to find out what effect this change in funding may have:

City Library Director James White says he plans to recommend reductions in services and hours of operation in response to budget cuts.

La Crosse (Wis.) *Tribune*

Remember, budgets affect people — people who use libraries, for example.

4. *Did department heads request additional funds that were left out of the final budget proposal?* What will the consequences be? Is the department head complaining?

5. *How much money does the budget set aside for salaries?* Does the salary line reflect anticipated raises or money for more personnel?

Bids

The city council, tired of wearing overcoats during its meetings, wants to install thermopane windows in city hall. Who should get the job? Most of the council members would be happy to give the job to the mayor's brother-in-law, who owns No-Draft Windows. But the law requires that any major public purchases be put out for competitive bidding. Municipalities must advertise for *bids* and must supply *specifications* that make clear the type of material or work it needs. In their sealed bids, competitors for the contract set out what they can deliver and at what price. All things being equal, the low bidder should get the job.

But, as in any process in which someone stands to gain substantial income, the chances for abuse are considerable. Occasionally, overt corruption dictates who is awarded a bid. More often, a governing body will draft "exclusive specifications" designed to favor a particular company. That city council might insist that the window company be located in town and have a staff of at least six people — a specification that only No-Draft Windows meets. Such exclusive specifications are illegal.

In covering the bidding procedure, reporters should seek the help of an expert not competing for the job. Among the questions worth asking: Are the specifications exclusive? Did the low bidder meet the specifications? Does the contract drawn up after the awarding of a bid require the contractor to purchase a *performance bond* (a sum of money put aside as an assurance to the city that the work will be completed as promised)?

The awarding of many contracts is routine. But when the low bidder is denied the contract or when only one bidder applies for a job time after time, a story—and further investigation—may be warranted.

While large contracts require advertised bidding, many day-to-day purchases, from toilet paper to thumb tacks, are simply written up on *purchase orders.* The dollar limit on such unadvertised—and unpublicized—purchases varies from city to city, but it can be in the thousands of dollars.

It's also not unknown for city officials to treat themselves to fringe benefits in the form of expensive lunches, junkets to check on services in other cities and exorbitant dry-cleaning bills for clothes ostensibly soiled in the line of duty. Such lavish spending would show up in expense and travel *vouchers*—statements of money spent.

Sometimes surprising corruption can show up in surprising ways and in surprising places:

When he was hired last summer as a $63,150-a-year deputy administrator in New York City's Human Resources Administration, he called himself Courtney Isaac Saunders. His colleagues knew him as "Ike" and say he spoke well, dressed well and worked well.

Yesterday, city officials announced that the former official had been arrested Thursday night in Washington under his real name . . . The New York City warrant accused him of falsifying his past history and relying on his city title to run up thousands of dollars in personal debts he charged to the city.

The New York Times

If they had looked into "Saunders" expense accounts when he was asked to resign four months before the story ran, reporters wouldn't have had to wait for the city's announcement.

Campaigns

Politicking is a year-round occupation for most elected officials. Whether they are in Washington, D.C., or Burlington, Vt., they try to stay in the news by issuing press releases, leaking information or scheduling events such as speeches, press conferences and ribbon cuttings that the media are likely to attend.

But politicking takes on a special fervor in the months preceding an election. Even the most close-mouthed officials suddenly have something nice to say to potential supporters or something nasty to say about the other side. And, as Don Melvin found after

"parachuting" into the middle of a hotly contested local race in Burlington, politicians are just as comfortable working reporters as they are working a crowd. "Certain folks tried to lean on me a little at first to see what I'd do," says Melvin. "They were testing me. What they were doing was a little like yelling at the umpire and hoping for a better call next time."

Fairness

It is difficult enough to cover a campaign fairly, even when the politicians are not leaning on the reporters. Charges and countercharges must be balanced, if not in a single story, certainly in the course of the campaign's coverage (See Chapter 6, Objectivity):

LOS ANGELES—Sen. Gary Hart, challenging Walter F. Mondale in debate yesterday on the eve of the final Democratic presidential primaries, accused the front-runner of conducting a distorted, personal campaign. Mondale responded that it was Hart who had raised [personal] issues.

Richmond (Va.) *Times-Dispatch*

Attention in the newspaper must be divided among the various candidates on the basis of some consideration of the newsworthiness of their respective pronouncements, the excitement they seem to be generating *and* the public's right to hear what they each have to say (See Chapter 6, Objectivity).

Political reporters must be particularly careful not to allow their own political and personal opinions of the candidates to color the stories they turn out. "It's inevitable that if you travel with a candidate, you'll develop some feeling one way or another for that candidate," notes David Espo, who has followed presidential candidates for the Associated Press. "You have to check yourself." And, of course, reporters can't allow themselves to be influenced by politicians who attempt to "lean on" them.

What They're Saying

Political reporters get themselves in trouble when they begin to place too much emphasis on their feeling that they've seen it all and that they know it all. After covering a candidate for a few weeks, a reporter may have heard the same speech a dozen times. It is easy to forget that readers probably have not heard the speech once and that they may never have been presented with that candidate's major proposals. Similarly, it's easy for reporters to become so entranced by their own speculations about *why* candidates are saying what they're saying that they forget to report *what* the candidates are saying (See Chapter 16, Facts).

An important part of the reporter's job is to pass on

the candidate's message to readers so that readers can evaluate it *themselves:*

> Jesse Jackson yesterday urged Hispanics to form a powerful "new majority" with blacks and suggested that such a coalition could defeat Mayor Koch in the 1985 mayoral election.
>
> "When we come together, we can win," Jackson said during a morning speech to the National Hispanic Leadership Conference, meeting in Washington.
>
> (New York) *Daily News*

What They're Not Saying

In addition to this basic "he-proposed, she-proposed, he-charged, she-charged" coverage, good political reporters will provide their readers with the facts to place candidates' statements in perspective. They might try to pin down politicians by measuring their campaign statements against their records—legislative and spoken. The candidate may be promising to upgrade the schools, but if he voted against the past three aid-to-education bills and attacked school spending in a speech last year, that claim sounds rather hollow.

Reporters might also try to sum up the major themes in a campaign or to discuss how candidates are communicating those themes. During the 1984 presidential campaign, a *Washington Post* reporter looked at Walter Mondale's advertising:

> They are children, bright-eyed and innocent, playing ring-around-the-rosy, coloring pictures and climbing onto a chair to stare out of a window and into the future.
>
> They are selling Walter F. Mondale for president . . .

Political coverage might also include a look behind the curtain at what's going on backstage in a campaign: Who is running the campaign? Who is paying for it? How is it being organized? What is the candidate's strategy? This isn't easy to do. It requires extremely thorough reporting to determine the strategies of rival candidates as they jockey for position. An interview or two won't do.

And there are dangers in these analytical stories. Too often, when the facts aren't there, the analysis disintegrates into conjecture (See Chapter 16, Facts). Also, in concentrating on what's happening backstage, reporters tend to lose sight of the politician's actual performances. They forget their responsibility to report what the candidate *is* saying.

"Political writers can focus so much on the strategies and aims of the candidates' staffs that they lose track of what the candidates are trying to do," says Steven R. Weisman, White House correspondent for *The New York Times.*

One of the most basic, and one of the best-read, election stories is the announcement of the results. The lead of that story obviously should tell who won, for what office and by what margin. The vote totals, the turnout and a quote from the winner and loser usually follow close behind. Space permitting, some of the major issues of the campaign also are recapitulated. As in any story, the unusual alters the basic formula. If it is an election outcome that defies the pollsters, the lead should note that it was an upset.

Even in such seemingly straightforward stories as these, reporters can get in trouble with characterizations or judgments. Note these two accounts of the results of the same New York City primary election:

> Chalking up large margins in many of Brooklyn's black neighborhoods, former Rep. Elizabeth Holtzman headed for a narrow victory early today over Norman Rosen in the hotly contested Democratic primary for Brooklyn district attorney.
>
> With 99 percent of the 1,519 election districts reporting, Holtzman had slightly more than 52 percent of the vote to Rosen's 48 percent . . .
>
> (New York) *Daily News*

> Former Representative Elizabeth Holtzman won the Democratic nomination for Brooklyn District Attorney last night with a comfortable margin over Norman J. Rosen.
>
> With 1,504 of 1,519 districts reporting, the vote was:
>
> Holtzman 93,788
> Rosen 85,084
>
> Miss Holtzman pieced her victory together by showing strength in the Flatbush and Park Slope sections of the borough, which made up her old Congressional district.
>
> *The New York Times*

Both these reporters would have been on firmer ground had they stuck to the facts—the percentages of the vote—and left to the reader the decision on whether that was a "comfortable" or a "narrow" victory.

Polls

Many reporters have written, and many readers have read, stories about the reaction of a few members of the public to an event in the news. Should the mayor run for governor? Should the United States develop weapons in space? Who should win an Academy Award? This is the proverbial person-in-the-street interview. In the following example, from a feature about the political views of recent immigrants, an immigrant from Korea is speaking:

> "Some people, they like Mondale, some people like Gary Hart, and of course, some like Reagan," he said. "I like the Democratic Party—it seems more helpful with

our side, the middle-class side. And I'm going to be sooner or later a citizen. But now I can't vote."

The New York Times

Such reaction stories are people stories. They can be colorful, poignant, funny. They are filled with quotes and descriptions. And they are next to useless as a measure of the greater public's views.

Reporting of polls, informal and formal, has progressed in the last few decades. Few reporters these days will make the mistake of presenting street-corner, come-as-you-will interviews as anything more than cute color stories. Those who try to treat them as some kind of serious reflection of opinion are quickly dressed down by their editors.

Recognizing the need to look for a scientifically representative sample of the population, some large news organizations such as *The New York Times* and CBS, *The Washington Post* and ABC, have hired experts to design regular polls gauging public reaction to a wide range of issues. And newspapers regularly write up the results of polls by such large organizations as those founded by Louis Harris, George Gallup and Burns Roper.

In fact, polls have come to dominate national political campaigns. Every candidate in a presidential campaign with a wisp of a chance has hired his own pollster. Candidates listen . . . and so do reporters. Barely a week passes without a new assessment of who's in first:

President Reagan has opened the election year with strong public approval but Sen. John Glenn of Ohio, once feared by the White House as potentially his most dangerous rival, has faded badly because of public doubts about his experience, a New York Times/CBS poll showed yesterday.

The New York Times

And state and city news organizations are also weighing in with their own surveys:

If the struggle between Mayor Washington and Alderman Edward R. Vrdolyak for control of city government were reduced to a popularity context, Washington would win easily, according to a Sun-Times/ Channel 2 News Poll.

(Chicago) Sun-Times

But if journalistic use of polling has improved, it still has a long way to go. Polls today are better designed and more frequently used; they may not be better understood.

Reporters too often tend to suspend their natural skepticism in reporting polls. They are dealing with numbers, which they may treat as if they are authoritative and meaningful — more meaningful than even the pollster would claim. Take the *Sun-Times* poll reported above. It said that 46 percent sided with

Washington and just 28 percent with Vrdolyak. But, as the newspaper noted, 26 percent said "neither" or "no opinion," suggesting an awful lot of prospective voters didn't much care or didn't understand the issues. The poll, based on 303 interviews with registered voters, also had a moderately large margin of error, 6 percent, meaning that among those with an opinion, Washington's lead might have been as little as 40 percent to 34 percent, perhaps not enough to "win easily" with a 26 percent undecided vote. Finally the poll question began with "Mayor Washington has been challenged . . ." and ended with "Ed Vrdolyak." Did the framing of the question and the positioning of the two men's names change the response? They often can.

Polls can be weapons during political campaigns. An optimistic poll might cause a candidate's supporters to become overconfident and stay away from the polls. A pessimistic poll might scare away voters who don't want to waste their vote on a loser. That's why candidates *selectively* feed poll results to reporters. It is also why the misreporting of polls is of such concern.

The best advice for reporters writing about polls is simply: Be cautious. Even though a poll has been conducted "scientifically," its results should hardly be treated as absolute truths. During the 1984 presidential campaign, for example, *The New York Times* ran a front-page article noting sharp discrepancies in the findings of major pollsters. It noted, among other things, that on the same day a *New York Times*/CBS poll found President Reagan with a substantial 18 percentage point lead over Walter Mondale, an ABC poll found Reagan a single percentage point ahead. Noted the author of The *Times* article: "Despite efforts in recent years to make opinion sampling more scientific, the task remains almost as much art as science."

For one thing, polls deal with people, not test tubes. Sometimes people do not have firm views on a subject. Embarrassed to appear ignorant, they may offer an answer to a question they have limited interest in and little knowledge about. And people without firm views can quickly change their minds. "The results of polls are unstable when the property they measure — opinions — is unstable," one pollster told *The Times*.

In addition, people can be influenced by who asks a question and how it is asked. "Do you support the mayor's plan to provide equal education for all children?" will undoubtedly get a different response than, "Do you support the mayor's plan to bus white students into black schools?" In discussing the limitations of polls, Burns Roper of the Roper polling organization has reminded journalists of the old saying, "Ask a stupid question; get a stupid answer."

It is not enough that reporters themselves be aware of the limitations of a poll. They must make sure their readers have the same opportunity to evaluate and question the results. That's why stories about polls should include the following information:

1. What is the poll's margin of error—the amount, according to statistical formulas, by which the poll can err? A 56 to 44 percent lead with a 4 percent margin of error might be significant; 56 to 44 percent with a 15 percent margin of error means little.
2. How many were undecided? A large group of undecided voters means the electorate is, to use one of the pollsters' favorite words, "volatile"—in other words, don't place your bets.
3. What group was being sampled? A sample of "likely voters" might have opinions different from a sample of "eligible voters," for example.
4. What was the size of the sample? Readers deserve to know that this prediction, however scientific the survey, was based on interviews with only 537 people. Such numbers help keep poll stories humble.
5. If findings are presented for any subgroups—people with incomes of under $20,000 a year, for example—what was the size of the subgroup sample and what is the margin of error for conclusions about it? Undoubtedly, that sample will be smaller and the margin of error higher.
6. When was the poll taken? For example, was it before or after that debate between the candidates? Might the results be dated?
7. What key questions were asked and how were they worded?
8. Who paid for the poll? If it was candidate Smith himself, that should give readers pause.

The New York Times regularly answers most of these questions for readers in a short article titled "How the poll was taken" that runs alongside all its poll stories. Here is the beginning of one such article:

The New York Times survey of Democratic delegates is based on telephone interviews conducted June 14 through July 9 with 1,561 delegates. This includes 523 of the 568 unpledged delegates and 1,038 of the 2,276 pledged delegates. The pledged delegates interviewed were those reached among a randomly selected sample of 1,125 such delegates . . .

Polls are probably the best device available for finding out what that amorphous Public, with a capital *P*, is thinking, but reporters and their readers must keep the limitations of those polls in mind.

Additional Reading

"How To Read a Budget," Frederick O'Reilly Hayes, *Columbia Journalism Review,* January/February 1976.

The Reporter's Handbook, An Investigator's Guide to Documents and Techniques, ed. John Ullmann and Steve Honeyman, St. Martin's Press, 1983.

Municipal Yearbook, International City Managers Association, published annually.

Reporting: An Inside View, Lou Cannon, California Journal Press, 1977.

The Boys on the Bus, Timothy Crouse, Ballantine Books, 1972.

Making Sense of the News, A Modern Media Institute Ethics Seminar, 1983.

"'Trust Me' Journalism," Gerald Lanson and Mitchell Stephens, *Washington Journalism Review,* November 1982.

▪ A. Research Assignments ▪

ONE

Using research materials or interviews with people familiar with government, write explanations that could be used in a newspaper article for the following terms.

1. Run-off election

2. Fiscal year

3. Block grant

4. Line item

5. Zero-based budgeting

6. Grandfather clause

7. Mill rate

8. Matching grants

9. Spot zoning

10. Non-conforming use

TWO

Using research materials or interviews with people familiar with local government, obtain answers to the following questions.

1. What form of government does the municipality have? Is the mayor elected by the public or by the council? Is the mayor a part-time or full-time employee of the municipality? Is there a city manager who runs day-to-day affairs?

2. How many council members are there? How often are they elected?

3. Is the government partisan or nonpartisan (in other words, are there competing political parties or no political parties)?

4. What council members are responsible for overseeing which departments of government? What formal and informal system exists for this oversight?

5. How often does the council meet, when and where?

6. What were the last five ordinances passed by the council? Who voted for them and who voted against them?

7. Who are the presidents of the local Democratic and Republican clubs? Have they ever held elective office?

THREE

Using research materials or people familiar with the financing of local government, obtain answers to the following questions.

1. When must department heads submit their budget requests to the municipality's principal financial officer?

2. Who draws up the budget?

3. When is it first submitted to the mayor and council?

4. By when must it be adopted?

5. What percentage of the current budget is spent on salaries? What are the salaries of the mayor, the council, the chief of police and the chief administrator of the municipality? How do these compare with their salaries five years ago?

6. How much money will the municipality receive this year from the federal government? From the state government? As specifically as possible, find out what it is being spent for.

7. What major construction projects are planned in the current budget year? How much is being spent on them?

▪ B. Writing Assignments ▪

Write stories based on each of the following collections of information. In each case you are writing for a newspaper dated tomorrow and read in the town where the events occurred.

ONE

The following budget information was just released by the town of Kalispell. An interview with Town Manager Robert Wajsblat follows.

Town of Kalispell Budget Revenues

Source	Actual Budget Current Fiscal Year	Proposed Budget Next Fiscal Year
Water Commission	58,790	61,230
Building Permit Fees	21,500	22,575
Municipal Parking	3,250	3,250
Fines and forfeitures	12,768	13,200
Delinquent Tax collection	27,890	33,000
Other Revenue	83,645	85,300
Tax Levy	590,000	700,000
Total Revenue	797,843	918,555
Federal Revenue Sharing	146,500	89,000
Prior Year Surplus	27,000	0
Grand Total	971,343	1,007,555
Property Tax (per thousand dollars assessed valuation)	$28.10	33.33

Expenditures

Salaries		
Town Manager	— 30,000	— 31,500
Police Chief	— 30,000	— 31,500
Supt. Public Works	— 27,500	— 28,457
Water Commissioner	— 25,000	— 25,825
Mayor & Council	— 9,000	— 9,000
Police	—112,200	—123,420
Public Works	—122,000	—126,270
Town Clerk	— 18,000	— 18,630
Waterworks	— 76,000	— 78,660
	449,700 (total)	472,362 (total)
Utilities	22,800	28,500
Streets and Roads	28,615	21,500
Insurance	62,900	65,035
Legal	2,700	3,500
Buildings & grounds	7,950	7,950
Municipal Court	14,500	14,500
Recreation	5,700	5,700
Fire	17,635	17,635
Planning Office	7,500	7,500
Waterworks	27,890	27,890
Plowing	3,750	3,750
Overtime pay	42,000	42,000
Other expenses	25,000	25,000
Debt service	253,625	253,625
Grand Total	971,343	1,007,555

Wajsblat: "What do I think of the budget? Frankly, I don't much like it, but this town is paying for cuts in the federal budget. Look at our federal funds next year. They are almost being cut in half because of cutbacks passed by Congress. Where are we supposed to go? That's more than $50,000. More than 5 percent of our budget in one fell swoop. Yes, I think it would be fair to call this an austerity budget. Take a look at expenditures. They'll be rising all right—3.6 percent. But it's beyond our control again. You know as well as I that the police department held us all up for a 10 percent pay raise. Ten percent. Heck, everyone else in town is getting 3.5 percent and the mayor and council haven't asked for a penny more, even though $1,500 is a joke for the time they put in. And when utility bills and insurance go up we either pay the piper or shut down. We already have to cut back on street repair—sharply. And most other items are stuck where they were, which with inflation will have to mean some cutbacks. Yes, it is unusual to have no surplus. Don't blame me, though. I just got here this year. Maybe, just maybe the town shouldn't have borrowed what it did for the new fire engine last year and the expansion of the municipal building the year before and the new fire station the year before that. Maybe our debts are coming back to haunt us. No, I don't think the residents of this town are going to like the looks of the tax increase they face. Hey, the average house here is assessed at $70,000. That means everyone will have to pay a bit more. You figure it out. When they complain though I'll just show them the numbers . . . tight as a drum. The only other choice to raising taxes is to cut the uncuttable. Sure we could save a few thousand getting rid of the summer recreation program. Or we could let the snow pile up when it snows. Or we could fire one of our six police officers. But I wouldn't suggest any of them. The waterworks. Yes, that could become an issue. Our expenses for it were nearly double revenues last year but it could be inevitable. If we raise water rates to lower taxes, then the public is just paying another way. It's possible though that we should sell all 12 wells and the treatment station to County Waterworks. I've suggested that the council consider it. You hate to see that though, if for no other reason than that the commissioner and four men in the plant could lose their jobs."

TWO

1. Thomas Staney, Republican, is running against Ruth Paps, Democrat, for sheriff of Camden County.
2. Incumbent George Director, Republican, is retiring.
3. Three weeks until the election.
4. Staney in speech yesterday before county Republican Club in Briarsville: "It's time we brought the great unstated issue in this campaign onto the table. It's time we discussed whether this woman—Ruth Paps—is really qualified to be sheriff. A sheriff has to run a large county department. Ruth has been a community activist for a few years. I've been a deputy sheriff for five years. A sheriff has to wear a gun and be ready to arrest dangerous persons. Ruth has raised three children. I've personally arrested two bank robbers—with gun drawn. We're not electing someone to the school board here. We're choosing the county's top law enforcement officer, the man who will help protect all of us against lawless elements. Voters have to consider the qualifications of the candidates for that job."
5. Al Lansan is campaign manager for Staney.
6. Lansan in interview after Staney's speech: "Yeah, I think it's fair to say this is a change of tactics on Tom's part. We've been trying to be chivalrous up to now. But this is starting to look like a close election, and we felt it was time to play some hardball. To start making clear to voters exactly what choice they're facing here. We laid off of Paps till now. But now she's going to have to take the heat."
7. Paps in interview a few hours after Staney's speech: "Yes, I heard about his speech today. I don't want to get into a name calling contest here. Tom has

every right to be proud of his work as a deputy sheriff, but the point is who will do the best job of running this department, not who has arrested the most people. Let me just say that my experience as head of the Neighborhood Protection Association — which has worked closely with the Sheriff's Department and other law enforcement agencies — is a pretty strong qualification. If a woman can be a Supreme Court justice, she can be a sheriff."

8. A check of the clips confirms all the facts mentioned by Staney and Paps.

THREE

Evelyn Anderson is running for city council in Rahway as an independent. Her opponents, Democratic incumbent Keith Parkins and Republican Alice Jones, have come out in support of a 137-unit, eight-story luxury apartment complex with accompanying arts, crafts and clothing boutiques proposed for four acres of city-owned land a quarter mile east of downtown by KBC Developers. Anderson opposes the project. She has been invited by the local Preservation Council, a non-profit group interested in preserving the town's heritage, to give a speech explaining her views. About 85 people attended the speech this evening at Volk House at 343 Jefferson St.

Anderson: "Good evening. It is nice to speak this evening at a place that stands for the history and traditions of our fine town. I'd guess that if he were alive today Erasmus Volk would have trouble identifying with the town he helped incorporate 123 years ago. Yet the changes — expensive townhouses, boutiques catering to the wealthy and the tourist, too much pavement and too little greenery — have only begun. There's still time for us to stop our town from becoming a haven for the wealthy urbanite instead of for the families of many religions, races and cultures who have called it home for the past several generations.

"When I was a school girl here — dare I say 35 and 40 years ago — North Tucker was still a wooded grove. A 65-acre farm occupied what is now the Crescent Drive development. And the biggest building in town stood four stories. Times have changed, and when KBC Developers moved to speed that change by building an eight-story apartment in the only remaining wild parkland, I decided someone had to speak for those who have long lived in and long loved this town. Unlike my opponents I have no vested interest in this town. Unlike Mr. Parkins, I do not own a real-estate firm that stands to benefit if property values in this town are pushed beyond the reach of its average citizens. Unlike Mrs. Jones, I do not own an antique shop that relies on wealthy tourists for business. I am a native of this town. I've put three sons through its public schools. And I've taught in those schools for 12 years now, teaching some of your children in elementary school art, in fact.

"Let me make my position clear. I am not against development per se. Far from it. I am for the preservation of this town's independent and heterogeneous character. Over the years as you know I've been a member of your organization and, from 1978 to 1982, its vice president. I was part of the committee that lobbied the council to seek grants to restore and upgrade the turn-of-the-century brick buildings along Main Street. I have long fought to get the council to put a town recreation building on the very four acres KBC now wants to turn into a luxury apartment complex.

"Why should we oppose the KBC plans? My opponents say it would bring down taxes in this town by attracting wealthy residents. I say hogwash. Our schools already are filled to capacity. What will the cost be to build a new elementary school for the complex's children? Who will pay those costs? What will the cost be to provide additional sanitation and snow removal and police protection for this complex? Who will pay those costs? The answer frankly is that no one knows. At the council's urging, the Planning Board already has pushed through the KBC proposal without the benefit of an economic or environmental impact statement. Is this sound development?

"I say let's look at impact, let's look at alternatives. This town has proven unique in its ability to mix people of different socioeconomic backgrounds. Bring in an exclusive apartment complex designed to lure the wealthy from the cities and it is only a matter of time before those of us of moderate means will be forced to move elsewhere, only a matter of time before a horde of like-minded developers turns our once-rural town into a high-class asphalt playground.

"What about the specific four acres in dispute? It is an informal playground to dozens of children on the east side of town. As you know, it is the only open play area east of Main Street. Isn't that something worth preserving? Isn't that something worth developing — as a playground, a nature walk, a teen recreation center? At the very least, I can promise you that if elected to council I will be an independent voice — independent of the developers, independent of the party hierarchies and independent of the commercial interests who would stand to gain customers. I ask for your vote. Thank you."

A check of the clips confirms Mrs. Anderson's information about the KBC development plans and the current use of the property. It also shows that KBC's plan has been approved by the Planning Board but still must be approved by the Town Council. No date has been set for the council's vote.

The clips further confirm that Perkins owns High Road Realtors and that Mrs. Jones owns The Highboy antique store.

FOUR

Three candidates have been running for a single seat on the Granby Village Council. On the basis of the following interviews with the candidates, clips and election returns, write a story for the local paper. Your deadline is before all the votes have been counted.

The candidates are: Douglas Jermack, incumbent Democrat of 5 Cedar Lane, 46, first elected to council in 1978; Republican Glen Armaleo, 52, born in Granby, lives at 19 Garth Boulevard; Sandra Liscomb, 34, independent, of 23 Moonshine Terrace . . . 96 percent of the vote has been counted. Here are the returns so far — Liscomb 124 votes, Jermack 4,729 votes, Armaleo 6,412. Voter turnout, 46 percent. Previous low turnout, 51 percent.

Armaleo, at Republican headquarters: "What do you say, quite a herd of elephants, huh? We've come a long way, baby, ya know. I'll tell you, I'm ecstatic. This vote shows that the public wants fiscal responsibility and fiscal restraint. There are just so many extracurricular school and recreation activities this town can afford to support."

Jermack, reached at his home: "I'd like to congratulate Glen for campaigning hard. I have already conceded defeat. Frankly this hurts pretty bad, but I'll be back. If the Democrats had cared enough to vote, I'd be serving four more years. Still, the people have spoken and I accept their verdict. Perhaps I took my opponent too lightly."

Liscomb can't be reached for comment. Clips show the following:

Jermack operates an antique store at 256 N. Broadway and is a member of the Elks, the Rotary Club and the Granby Softball League. He is married and has two sons. In the race he spoke in favor of the high school budget and of building six new tennis courts in Riverview Park. He argued from time to time that the courts would pay for themselves within 15 years as a result of the fees that the village would collect for their usage. He also supported a 9 percent raise for the town's 25 police officers.

Liscomb works part-time for John Henneman, a C.P.A. in neighboring Spring Valley. She is a tax clerk. She has three sons and two daughters and is divorced. She ran primarily to oppose a new shopping center planned in her neighborhood. (No mention is made in the clips of Jermack's or Armaleo's views on the shopping center.)

Armaleo is a partner in the law firm of Jones & Armaleo, Esq. on North Main Street. He is a scout leader of Boy Scout Troop 83, an American Express Gold Card holder, and a member of the Rotary Club. He is married and has a daughter and a son. Armaleo supported the police raises. He campaigned for increased police protection in The Cross Arms Apartment complex, which is a place in which there have been two dozen burglaries in six months among the 256 units. He opposed plans to build the six tennis courts to be operated by the village and he led a successful effort in September to defeat the school budget.

FIVE

The following poll was conducted by Wilson Lynch Inc., a major national polling organization, for your paper, the *Burnsville News*. According to Harrison Stewart, a senior poll analyst for the company, the poll was conducted among 945 adults (over age 18) in the state selected at random from the telephone book. The poll was conducted by telephone between last Tuesday and Friday. The margin of error — 5 percent. Last Monday, the federal government announced plans to build a nuclear waste repository 200 feet underground in a salt bed 45 miles west of Burnsville. The repository would store radioactive wastes from nuclear power plants in this and neighboring states. The paper commissioned the poll to measure public response to that announcement. Here are the questions and responses.

In your view, can nuclear power help eliminate U.S. dependence on foreign oil?

Yes	*No*	*Don't Know*
54 percent	33 percent	13 percent

Do you support the construction of more nuclear power plants in the United States?

Yes	*No*	*Don't Know*
48 percent	46 percent	6 percent

Would you support a plan to build a nuclear power plant in Burnsville?

Yes	*No*	*Don't Know*
42 percent	56 percent	2 percent

Did you know the federal government has proposed building a repository for nuclear wastes 45 miles west of Burnsville?

Yes	*No*
73 percent	27 percent

Would you support construction of such a waste site?

Yes	*No*	*Don't Know*
28 percent	69 percent	3 percent

Comment by Stewart: "We've seen similar patterns in a half-dozen cities in other states. The message seems to be 'it's not so bad in principal but . . .' Certainly nuclear waste continues to be the Achilles heel of the industry from the public's point of view."

■ C. Story Assignments ■

1. Find out what, if any, federal grants a local city or town has received. Track down the last audit of the largest grant program and write a news story based on that audit. If the municipality has not applied for or has not received any major federal grants, write a story about why it hasn't.

2. Find out how much a local city or town has borrowed in the last five years, why it has borrowed the money and what the repayment terms are. Check the last five municipal budgets to determine whether the service, or repayment, of the municipality's debts (this is found in the debt service line of the budget) has increased or decreased. Interview the chief financial officer to determine why. Also find out what percentage of the municipality's expenses go toward servicing the debt. Write a story based on your findings.

3. Write an article on a meeting of a local planning board or planning commission. Stop by the planning office the day before the meeting to get a copy of the agenda. Ask to see any letters or communications about the projects on the agenda and also ask to see site plans. Interview people familiar with or affected by items on the agenda before or after the meeting.

CHAPTER 24

Police

A jewelry store had been robbed and a detective with the Austin Police Department was making a statement for the microphones of the local broadcast media. Mike Cox, a reporter for the *Austin American-Statesman,* listened as the officer announced that a white male had come in, taken an as yet undetermined amount of jewelry and escaped. The reporters with the microphones said, "thanks," and left.

Cox stayed. "How did it go down in there?" he asked the detective, now that they were alone. Cox learned that the robber had come in with an attaché case and had pistol-whipped the store manager. He also learned that three other store employees had been locked in the restroom.

"Did he tie them?" Cox asked. The detective acknowledged that the employees had been handcuffed by the robbers. After getting a few more details, Cox had his story—a better story than the competition's.

Mike Cox's father also was a police reporter. So was his grandfather. Cox knew that was what he wanted to be before he could even type. "I grew up hearing stories about how exciting it is to cover police," he recalls.

It is the rare reporter who hasn't spent some time coaxing details out of the police or counting the survivors and the victims of a fire. On modern newspapers this may not be a glamour beat, but there are few sterner tests of basic reporting skills—the ability to obtain and care for facts, to turn often difficult people into useful sources, to function efficiently with blood, smoke or tears flowing around you.

"You do get kind of callussed," Cox says. "The other day I was bantering with a homicide detective just three feet from the body of a dead wino."

Beat Checks

Police reporters probably spend more time than any other reporters worrying about the stories they might have missed . . . and with good reason. It's a small city, indeed, in which a day goes by without a crime, a fire or an accident serious enough to make news. And crime and disaster are unpredictable. They can occur at any time. To protect themselves, almost all reporters on the police beat devise a system of regular checks, a monitoring system they use to ensure that no murder or major fire somewhere on the fringes of their beat escapes them.

Calls

One morning each week Doreen Carvajal, a police reporter for the *St. Petersburg Times,* takes her turn calling every one of the 20 or so law enforcement agencies in the area—various local police departments, the highway patrol, the Coast Guard. The next day another reporter will make the calls.

Beat calls are so much of a ritual in the lives of police reporters and of police and fire departments that both sides could probably play the game in their sleep: "Got anything for me? Anything up?" asks the reporter. "Nope, quiet, just the way we like it," comes the typical response. Reporters will be lucky to get one solid lead in a few dozen such calls. But that lead can wake them up in a hurry: "I'd come right down to the station if I were you. We had a little visit from the mayor early this morning, and it wasn't exactly in his official capacity. The charge was drunken driving."

Telephone calls have definite limitations: Controversial stories are often reserved for reporters whose faces as well as voices are familiar. Beat calls are no substitute for efforts to cultivate sources. And officers are often telephone shy to begin with. They know that in many cases their calls are being taped by their departments. Nevertheless, these regular phone calls provide one important way for reporters with a lot of departments to cover to help protect themselves against missing stories.

The Radio

Next to Carvajal's desk is the speaker of a police radio. There's also one next to a copy clerk's desk and those of the other police reporters. The exchanges on the various police frequencies in the area crackle away in the background as these journalists go about their business. Carvajal listens with some fraction of an ear for a tightening of someone's voice or for a code number indicating something serious has happened, such as a robbery in progress or a murder.

Records

Police keep a running log, traditionally called a *blotter,* of the events of the day. Though the amount of detail in them varies greatly from city to city, blotters should always include at least a line or two noting a suspect's name, the charge and the time of an arrest; the time, place and parties involved in any accident; and the source, time and nature of any complaint. The blotter is open to the public and typically is maintained by the sergeant at the main reception desk. Reporters scan blotters for unusual complaints, prominent suspects or repeat offenders.

Other police reports that may or may not routinely be made available to reporters are *investigation reports, arrest reports* and *accident reports.* These give details about what happened, and the names of the witnesses, suspects and officers involved. Much of Doreen Carvajal's day is filled with tracking down these reports and police memos, which under Florida law are generally open to the public. "Did anyone write about the shooting that occurred a couple of days ago?" she might ask an officer. If someone did, she should be able to get a copy and with it, perhaps, additional information on witnesses and on the police investigation.

The records of the Austin police are on computer. So Mike Cox checks the blotter each morning by call-

ing for information on a computer terminal. He punches in the code 01 to learn if any murders have been committed; 02 for rapes; 03 for robberies. "I usually won't go beyond robberies," Cox says. "Austin's so big I wouldn't generally even write about a robbery unless someone was killed, a bank was hit or the robber was wearing a Mickey Mouse suit."

The Rounds

At 5:30 every morning, Mike Cox walks into the press room at police headquarters. An officer will be waiting to brief him on what's happened overnight. Later, he might stroll by the criminal investigations bureau, stop by homicide to see what they're working on and poke his head in to check with robbery detectives. This is the "in person" equivalent of beat calls.

Reporters keep regular rounds to get access to those police reports only the trusted reporters see and to pick up on bits and pieces of the news the printed record doesn't hold. They listen to police investigators gripe about their problems in gathering information and their frustrations when they end up with not quite enough evidence to make a charge stick. And in the process reporters begin to understand better the workings of a police department, and they begin to replace the formal relationships of routine news gathering with something warmer and, most likely, more productive.

In smaller cities, police reporters regularly stop by all the divisions. They might learn from "traffic" about plans to install lights at two hopelessly congested intersections. The officers at "juvenile" may peddle a "nice" story about a special program designed to encourage vandals to work off the damage they've done. "Operations" may want to show off a new computer linking the town with national crime data from the FBI or Law Enforcement Administration.

These visits lead to legitimate news. They also can lead to valued sources.

Sources

Doreen Carvajal recalls that she was once asked by police to hold a story on a hospital employee being held on narcotics charges. The police said they were hoping to turn the employee into an informant. Carvajal checked with her editors, and they decided, properly, to go with the story. Unless they are convinced people's lives are at stake, newspapers can't get into the habit of censoring themselves when it suits the police.

"Everyone seemed to understand that that's the rules except this one sergeant," Carvajal says. "He ended up blaming me. When I had to deal with him a few weeks later on a story about a man arrested for trying to get minors into porno films, he wouldn't return my calls. I had to go to an assistant chief who ordered him to talk."

Police officers operate in an extremely tense, occasionally dangerous, highly insular and highly politicized world. Many police officers aren't sure just what place reporters have in that world. It's not hard to find officers who believe they've been burned by reporters and who are antagonistic toward them. Reporters have to try to win these officers over. They also have to know their rights, and they have to keep an eye out for sources outside the police ranks.

Local Police

Long-time police reporters often reach the point where they can count on officers to supply them with the information they need. "When there's a two-alarm fire at 2 a.m., if somebody doesn't call me at home, I'm going to be angry," says Mike Cox.

Newer reporters have to work to build up that trust. "You can't go in with a chip on your shoulder," says Carvajal, who faced special problems as a working woman dealing with what she calls "macho" men. "You have to try to develop a style that uses a sense of humor, because that's the way they deal with their job. If they can identify elements in you that they find in themselves, then they'll talk to you. I think you can still ask the tough questions, but you can ask them in ways that make clear you aren't screwing them."

Carvajal also goes out of her way to do legitimate news stories about the police that aren't confrontational. "When I first came, I did a story on the canine school and spent some time with the guys training new dogs," she recalls. "People like dog stories and I also made some contacts that way."

Some officers by the nature of their job are more likely to have newsworthy information and more likely to share it than others. Detectives generally are the most helpful people on the force. They are experienced officers, often less concerned about what their boss will think than street patrolmen and more knowledgeable about ongoing investigations. Their job also isn't that different from that of the reporters who cover police stories. They, too, call strangers and try to piece together information.

Other important police sources are the head of the local Patrolmen's Benevolent Association—essentially the police union—and the attorney for the association. They're often willing to air their members' gripes about departmental policies.

Other Law Enforcement Officials

Just as the branches of the armed services like to outdo one another, law enforcement agencies with overlapping jurisdiction tend to compete. A reporter who has been "stonewalled" by the local police department should consider whether any other officers might be involved. Once, when the public information officer of the St. Petersburg police refused to release information about a strange child abuse case, Carvajal developed the story with the help of other sources—including the Sheriff's Department. "You can rely on rivalry between the agencies," she says. "It's important to talk to all of them."

Witnesses, Victims and Suspects

"Too many police stories rely on just one source," says Carvajal. "Always try to avoid using *just* what the police say about an incident. Go back and talk to a neighbor or someone who was involved. You can usually flush things out."

There are risks here. Reporters must be careful not to accuse someone of a crime on the basis of an account by some guy who happens to have been standing across the street. But what that witness saw, in his own words, can help dramatize the more formal account provided by police. Quotes from non-official sources—friends, relatives and neighbors of victims, for example—help communicate the tragedy of an event. This is from the neighbor of a 13-year-old boy who was found dead after having been missing for almost a week:

"I prayed for him every night, for the dear Almighty
God to let him come home safe, let him come home
safe . . . You can't trust nobody today, it's the God's
truth."

The New York Times

The danger of cronyism (See Chapter 19, Sources) is at least as great a risk on the police beat as on any other. It is all too easy to parrot the perspective of the police on their work and on the people they arrest, especially since police can be so sensitive to criticism. One way to preserve a balance is to maintain a wide range of outside sources.

Crime

It is not for reporters to try to create a new race of humans who do not want to read about pistol whippings or murders; that would be like trying to create people who do not stop to rubberneck at the scene of gory accidents. The ability to cover a jewelry store robbery or a murder is a skill all reporters—even the most serious minded—must have.

Basic Facts

Crime stories are about emotion and drama, but they are also very much about detail: names, addresses, ages, times (See Chapter 13, Information Selection). Reporters covering a crime will want to make sure that by the time they are ready to write they have made an effort to obtain *all* the relevant basic facts. In covering the murder of a South Philadelphia man, three *Philadelphia Inquirer* reporters clearly made that effort. Here was their lead:

> The body of a man who had been shot to death was found early yesterday on a back road in Camden County, about a mile from the site where reputed organized-crime figure Salvatore Testa was found slain Friday, police said.

The following is a list of the information that reporters should *try* to gather. (The examples are from *The Inquirer* story.)

1. Name, age, address, closest relatives and profession or claim to fame (See Chapter 21, Obituaries) of any victims.

> The victim was identified as Marvin T. Wicks, 21, of the 400 block of Bar Street, South Philadelphia, by Luis A. Rodriguez of the homicide division of the Camden County prosecutor's office . . .*

2. The exact time and place of the crime and of the discovery of the crime, including a description of the scene.

> Wicks' body, found near Hickstown and Erial Roads in Gloucester Township . . . at 6:48 a.m., was lying on a 3-by-4-foot pallet just off the shoulder of Hickstown Road, in front of a roofless, gray, concrete structure at the edge of the now-closed Gem's Landfill . . .
> Wicks was found lying on his back with his right arm by his head, according to [Gloucester Township Police Chief Seth] Stichler, who said $170, including $50 bills, was scattered on the ground inside the crook of his arm.

3. Detailed description of the circumstances of the crime, including any weapon used, method of entry, method of escape, and, in the case of death or injury, the official cause and time.

> An autopsy by the Camden County medical examiner's office showed that Wicks died of the two bullet wounds from a small-caliber handgun. There was no estimate of the time of death.

4. Description of any damage to property or loss of property — with dollar amounts if possible.
5. Name and identification of any witnesses, particularly the persons who discovered the crime. (Wicks' body was found by "an unidentified bicycle rider.")
6. Description of the police investigation of the crime, including any possible motivation for the crime, any possible clues and the names of officers involved in the investigation.

---

* The name and address of the victim in this story have been changed.

Assistant Camden County Prosecutor Dennis Wixted said officials were investigating whether the two slayings were linked. Philadelphia police, cooperating with Wixted's investigation, said the second slaying was not connected with Testa's gangland-style execution . . .

Stichler said investigators had made impressions of what appeared to have been automobile tire tracks near the site where Wicks' body was found.

7. Name, age, address and profession of suspects, if any, plus exact charges against them.
8. Description of the circumstances of the arrest, if any, and of the *booking* — when suspects are brought to the police station and information about them and their alleged crime is recorded. Reporters should also know the schedule for the *arraignment* — when charges are presented before a judge and bail is set.
9. The response of suspects to charges against them, if available (perhaps through their attorneys).
10. Any additional consequences of the crime resulting from death or injury, loss of or damage to property.
11. Any unusual circumstances involved in the crime (to use Mike Cox's example, the fact that the robbers were wearing Mickey Mouse suits).

Not all the preceding information, of course, will be available on every crime in time for reporters to make their deadlines. The point is that they should try to get as much of it as *is* available or pertinent. All the important questions readers might have about a story must be answered even if the only answer police can provide is "we don't know" or "no." *The Philadelphia Inquirer* reporters covering that murder told readers that "no weapon was found at the site." They also made clear where police were stymied ("There was no estimate of the time of death") or holding back ("An item had been found there, but [the chief] declined to describe it.").

Can police be expected to cooperate with reporters as they search for these facts? Generally, yes. Groups of journalists and law enforcement officials in most states have agreed on certain basic guidelines for helping the police determine what they should and should not say to reporters about arrests. Reporters should be able to get a copy of these guidelines from a local press or bar association, and they should be able to hold police to them. Here are some standard rules on what information officers should be expected to release:

1. The defendant's name, age, residence, employment, marital status and similar background information — unless the defendant is under age.
2. The substance of the charge as contained in the complaint or the indictment (See Chapter 25, Courts).
3. The circumstances immediately surrounding the

arrest, including the time and place, resistance, pursuit, possession and use of weapons and a description of items seized.

4. The identity of the person filing the complaint—unless that person is under age or the victim of a sex crime.

Such guidelines also generally discourage officers from releasing information that may prove prejudicial to a defendant, such as statements about the character or reputation of the accused person, admissions or confessions the accused may have made, and speculation or opinions concerning the evidence that might be used in a trial.

Terminology

The facts about crimes will often be communicated in legal jargon. These terms can be tricky. Here are some pairs of terms that police reporters must be particularly careful not to confuse (See Chapter 25, Courts, particularly the chart on pages 304–305, for discussions of additional legal terminology):

1 Charged/indicted

Charges are accusations made before a judge at arraignment. A *grand jury*—a deliberative body of citizens—usually must decide whether there is enough evidence to pursue the *charges* before someone is *indicted.*

2 Felony/misdemeanor

Felonies are more serious. Violent crimes—murder and rape, for example—are *felonies.* So are major crimes against property, such as robbery, burglary or car theft. Reporters rarely will be concerned with *misdemeanors* such as shoplifting. People convicted of *misdemeanors* generally face only fines. People convicted of *felonies* often are sent to prisons or penitentiaries.

3 Robbery/burglary

Robbers threaten or use force. *Burglars* sneak in and out. (See Chapter 1, Meanings, for more discussion of terms for stealing.)

4 Murder/manslaughter

Murder means killing with malice: *first degree* if it was premeditated, *second degree* if it was not. *Involuntary manslaughter* means it was an accident; *voluntary manslaughter* that it was intentional but done without malice—in the heat of passion, perhaps. All these killings are *homicides.*

5 Parole/probation

Only people who have been serving jail or prison terms can be *paroled,* but people can be placed on *probation* after they are convicted of a crime *instead* of being locked up. Both are forms of conditional freedom that can be retracted if the person fails to meet the terms of the parole or probation.

6 Suspect/criminal

This is the most crucial distinction reporters covering crime will confront. No one is a *criminal* until he or she has been proven guilty of a crime. People who have been arrested and charged with crimes are *suspects* to be considered innocent until proven guilty. And *suspects* are not arrested *for committing* crimes. They are arrested *on charges* of having committed crimes, or, if no charges have yet been filed, *in connection* with crimes. Similarly, all allegations of potentially criminal behavior are just that—*allegations*—whether they come from police, from witnesses or in that rare case, from the reporter's own observations. And such allegations must always be carefully attributed (See Chapter 10, Attribution).

Fires, Accidents and Disasters

When something is burning down, crashing or collapsing, reporters don't want to have to rely on the telephone or police reports. They want to be there. But "there" more often than not will turn out to be a chaotic scene of smoke, shattered glass and sirens. Drawing a coherent story out of that frantic confusion is quite a different task from conducting interviews across desks and coffee tables.

Upon arriving at the scene of a fire or disaster, the first job facing a reporter is to determine what is most *perishable*—what is least likely to stick around. If the fire is still burning, a reporter will want to begin by jotting down some observations before it goes out. If overturned cars are still on the highway, blocking traffic, a reporter will note the scene and try to determine how long the backup is. Then it's time to start talking to people.

Officials

A reporter's most important official source will be the person in charge. The chief or captain, if there's one there, will have access to the most information and will have authority to release the most information. If you don't know the chief, ask any officer or firefighter. Or just head toward the person in the white hat.

From this interview, and supporting interviews with other officers or firefighters who may be able to supply more first-hand information, reporters primarily will want a rundown of the basic facts (See Chapter 13, Information Selection). But the professionals who handle tragedies can occasionally provide a dramatic quote as well:

Trooper John Pfanz of the Pennsylvania State Police, who spent yesterday morning sifting through the charred rubble, said: "It's devastating to stand there in someone's home and know that a few hours earlier, there was a family and now there's nothing, and to know that a battery could have saved them."

Firefighters found one smoke detector, without batteries, on a wall in the second-floor hallway.

The Philadelphia Inquirer

The facts reporters are looking for start with the dead, the injured and the property damage. These usually will appear in or near the lead, with death always taking precedence:

Two children, aged 7 and 9, who apparently had been left unattended, were killed last night in a fire in their Brooklyn home that they may have set themselves by playing with matches, officials said.

(New York) *Daily News*

Notice the cause of the fire in the *News* lead. That's the next question, though fire officials won't always be willing to speculate.

East Whiteland Fire Chief Donald Fonda . . . said the fire may have been started by an overloaded electrical outlet, a malfunctioning television or video game, or by a cigarette.

The Philadelphia Inquirer

Questions aimed at filling in other details follow: What's the address? When did the fire start? How many people lived in the building? How many escaped? How many fire companies responded? How quickly did they respond? When was the fire brought under control? What are the names and addresses of the dead? Officials can help piece together these facts by recounting events chronologically (and reporters may decide to employ that chronological organization at points in their stories — See Chapter 14, Organization):

A few moments later, the first fire truck arrived, and Brunstetter and other firefighters entered the front door, where they found Mary Catherine's body. Her brother was lying at the top of the stairs.

The Philadelphia Inquirer

The fact-gathering pattern is the same at car accidents and plane crashes as at fires, though the exact questions asked of officials obviously will vary somewhat. In an automobile accident, reporters would want to know the types of cars, their speeds and destinations and the conditions of the road. (Reporters should be cautious about using speculation from police at the scene of an accident that implies criminal intent — "it appears she was drinking.") The necessity

to get down all the details, though, remains, no matter what the incident:

Police say Hatridge apparently lost control of the car on a curve in the 17200 block of New Halls Ferry Road about 9:15 p.m.

St. Louis Post-Dispatch

Survivors and Witnesses

Interviewing survivors and witnesses is no fun, but it has to be done — delicately. Survivors of a fire, an accident or a disaster usually can be spotted by their glazed appearance. "Was anyone in there?" "Did anyone see what happened?" These are two questions reporters may ask everyone they see until they find someone who answers "yes, me."

Sensitivity obviously is all important when interviewing someone who has just lived through a horror. "So how does it feel to have lost everything you own?" won't do. Reporters have to be sympathetic and gentle; there's no substitute for real human compassion. A touch of someone's hand, an offer of coffee or a blanket, can help. Survivors and witnesses also need room to gather their thoughts and express their feelings. An initial question followed by silence can be much more effective than a barrage of staccato questions. Vivid memories should require little prompting:

"There was just a huge ball of flames coming from the rear of the house. I came out thinking I would take the family into my house. But nobody came out."

The Philadelphia Inquirer

Reporters want emotions and descriptions from the people at the scene. Facts will have to be checked later with officials.

Hospitals

After checking with survivors, witnesses and officials at the scene, reporters covering an accident, fire or disaster will likely head for the hospital where the injured were taken. There may be more interview possibilities at the hospital, usually in the emergency room, where survivors who were not seriously injured and the relatives of victims may be gathered. Afterward, hospital officials should be consulted for the facts on the injured.

Most hospitals have established procedures for releasing information. Often the supervising nurse or the head nurse in the emergency room will be responsible for handling the press. Reporters should expect to be given the following information within a reasonable amount of time:

1. The name, address, age, occupation and marital status of patients.

2. The general nature of the injuries.
3. If the person is dead, the time of death, the person's name (pending notification of next of kin) and the cause of death, if it has been confirmed (this may require waiting until after an autopsy).
4. The condition of patients—usually expressed by one of these terms (in order of increasing severity): good, satisfactory, fair, poor, serious or critical.

The terms used by hospitals to label a patient's condition are one set of jargon reporters can*not* attempt to translate. "Stable," another word that's often used, can be applied to a person with a cracked ankle or a person with a cracked skull. Reporters don't have the expertise to make sense out of this confusion. If they can get through to a doctor, they might be able to wheedle out details of the injuries, but otherwise all they can do is pass on what the hospital is saying:

Two passengers were admitted to Christian Hospital-Northwest, where they are listed in serious condition.
St. Louis Post-Dispatch

Hospital officials should *not* be expected to speak to legal questions: Was he drunk? Was he shot from close range? Was it a suicide? While hospital officials may offer a tip, the official word on these questions should come from police.

Enterprise

The police beat has plenty of room for more challenging reporting, too. Though they will make few friends in doing it, the best reporters on the beat eventually will turn their attention to the police department itself. Are its crime statistics accurate? Are its salaries competitive? Does it offer equal protection to all parts of town? Are there any crimes that seem to be overlooked? Are suspects treated properly and victims treated with kindness?

Sometimes police officers are too callussed; sometimes they get nasty; sometimes they are accused of being corrupt:

Indian County Sheriff Keith Stephans and his department's investigations chief, Sgt. Alvin Crews, were indicted yesterday on charges of stealing weapons from the department's evidence locker . . .*
(Denver) *Rocky Mountain News*

* The names and county in this story have been changed.

These can be tough stories that may cost reporters friendships and blow useful sources. At a few papers, like the *Los Angeles Times,* "police politics" has been made a separate beat in recognition of this problem.

In an article in *feed/back,* a San Francisco journalism review, David Johnston, the *Los Angeles Times* reporter assigned to cover police politics, lamented a "failure [by newspapers] to look upon the police with the same questioning viewpoint that is routinely applied to elected politicians, school administrators and others who work for government." Yet, Johnston noted, "police costs often consume one-third of a city's operating budget."

And serious reporting on the police beat needn't be limited to stories of overspending, malfeasance and brutality. In-depth features have traced the lives of criminals in an effort to explain "why," have reconstructed the trail of clues police have followed to solve complicated crimes and have taken a closer look at the victims of crimes:

Two days before she was killed, Alison Jay wrote an essay for her English class in which the young woman described her frustrations about violence in Des Moines.

At one point in the essay, the 18-year-old senior at Technical High School said she was becoming scared to walk the city's streets.

Her fears came true last weekend. Jay's nude body was found Saturday morning about four blocks from her home. Authorities said she had been strangled.

Her classmates and teachers at the school said Monday the essay was typical of Jay, who did not share her thoughts or concerns easily . . .**
The Des Moines (Iowa) *Register*

Additional Reading

"On the Police Beat," David Johnston, *feed/back,* Winter 1983.
"Crime Doesn't Pay, Except on the Newsstand," Mitchell Stephens, *Washington Journalism Review,* December 1981.
Police Magazine, a bimonthly published in New York City by Criminal Justice Publications Inc.

** The name in this story has been changed.

▪ A. Research Assignments ▪

ONE

Using research materials or interviews with people familiar with police and fire department work, write explanations that could be used in a newspaper article for the following terms.

1. Reckless endangerment

2. Saturday night special

3. Controlled substance

4. DOA

5. Released on own recognizance

6. Airplane's black box

7. Miranda rights

8. Third-degree burns

9. Three-alarm fire

10. Triage

TWO

Using research materials or interviews, obtain answers to the following questions for a police department in your area, and illustrate some of the answers with quotes.

1. How many police officers are on each shift?

2. How many of those officers are actually on patrol at any one time?

3. Are all parts of town regularly patrolled?

4. How many people work for the police department and how do they break down by rank?

5. What are the salary scales for the different ranks?

6. How many women and members of minority groups work as police officers?

7. What training is required to become a police officer?

8. Do police have special procedures for dealing with rape victims?

9. What percentage of reported crimes lead to arrest?

10. What percentage lead to convictions?

THREE

Using research materials or interviews, obtain answers to the following questions for a fire department in your area, and illustrate some of the answers with quotes.

1. Is the fire department volunteer or paid?

2. If it is paid, what are the salary scales for the different ranks? If it is volunteer, what clothing or other expense allowances are the firefighters entitled to?

3. How many firefighters are on duty or available to respond to alarms at various times of day and night?

4. What is the average response time to a fire? Has that response time changed in the past five years?

5. What kind of equipment does the department have? What is the oldest and what is the newest piece of equipment?

6. What training is required to become a firefighter?

7. What is the name and background of the fire chief?

8. What percentage of its time does the department spend answering false alarms?

9. What was the most serious fire the department was called to in the past year?

■ B. Writing Assignments ■

Write stories based on each of the following collections of information or police reports. In each case you are writing for a newspaper dated tomorrow and read in the town where the events occurred.

ONE: Robbery Report

POLICE DEPARTMENT

Complaint No. 57693	2. Mun. Code 0207	3. Phone No. 768-5000	4. UCR	21. Prosecutor's Case Number	22. Department Case Number

Crime/Incident Armed robbery	6. NJS	23. Victim/s/ Frank Berry DOB 7/9/43	24. Age 43	25. Sex M	26. Race Blck

DATE AND TIME	7. Between	8. Hour 10:30pm	9. Day Today	27. Victim/s/ Home Address 47 Michaels Way	Phone 968-4482
	At			S. S. No. 109-75-1327	

. Crime/Incident Location Keough's Pharmacy, 13 Castle Heights Rd.	28. Employer Albert Keough	Phone 968-1843

14. Municipality Lawrence	15. County Dubuque	16. Code	29. Person Reporting Crime/Incident Frank Berry	30. Date and Time 10:48 p.m.

17. Type of Premises Pharmacy	18. Code	19. Weapons–Tools Handgun	20. Code	31. Address	Phone

2. Modus Operandi

Went to Keough's Pharmacy in response to phone call from Frank Berry, the night pharmacist. Berry said he had been robbed, at gunpoint, by a white female as he was counting receipts for the day at closing time. Arrived at store at 10:45. Berry gave following account:

He was alone in the store at 10:20 when a caucasian woman of medium height and build entered store. Suspect was wearing black leather pants and motorcycle jacket, a helmet and goggles. Took off goggles and stood for five or ten minutes looking at rack of birthday cards. Suspect then glanced out front door and walked to register with two cards after slipping goggles back on. Upon reaching register pulled out silver pistol with right hand and told Berry to empty the register into a paper back. Suspect apparently knew of store's alarm system. Warned pharmacist not to push silent alarm to right of register. After Berry handed suspect bag, she told him to lie face down, close his eyes and count to 500 if he wanted to see his kids again. She apparently escaped on foot. Berry gave this description: "She was a cool customer, polite but real scary. Her voice was honey but she said,'this shoots bullets.

33. Vehicle	34. Year	35. Make	36. Body Type	37. Color	38. Registration Number & State	39. Serial Number or Identification

VALUE STOLEN PROPERTY	40. Currency $425	41. Jewelry	42. Furs	43. Clothing	44. Auto	45. Misc.

46. Total Value Stolen $425	47. Total Value Recovered	48. Teletype Alarm	49. Technical Services	50. Technician–Agency

51. N.C.I.C. Check	52. Rein Check	53.	54.	55.	56.

57.	58.	59.	60.	61.	62.

List Accused – List and Identify Additional Victims – Describe Perpetrators or Suspects – Action Taken Include Findings and Observations of Investigator – Physical Evidence Found – Where By Whom – Disposition and Technical Services Performed – Interview of Victims – Witnesses – Persons Contacted – Accused Suspects – List – Describe Stolen Property – Value – Court Action – Attach Statements.

63. No. of Accused	64. Adult	65. Juvenile	66. Status Crime	67. Status Case	68. UCR Status Month ——— Year ———	69. Date Cleared
70. Name		Address			71. Age 72. Sex 73. Race 74. DOB	

75. Name Sgt. Charles Birns Signature	76. Badge Number 36	77. Page —— of —— Pages	78. Date Report 12/15	79. Reviewed By
		80. Weather	81. Car No. 54	82.

TWO: Accident Report

NEW JERSEY POLICE ACCIDENT REPORT

PAGE 28 OF _____

| 41 CASE NUMBER 725 | 42 POLICE DEPARTMENT OF Perkins | CODE | 43 STATION PRECINCT |

45 DATE OF COLLISION — 46 DAY OF COLLISION — 47 TIME (USE 2400 HRS) 23:12 — 48 NO. OF VEHICLES 1 — 49 NUMBER KILLED — 50 NUMBER INJURED 1 — 51 COUNTY Silver

52 MUNICIPALITY Perkins — 53 ROUTE NUMBER OR NAME OF STREET Route 45 — 54 MILE POST 14 — 55 INTERSECTING STREET, ROAD OR RAILROAD 100 yrds n. of Allen St.

56 IF NOT AT INTERSECTION & NOT MILE POSTED Allen St. — 57 DISTANCE FROM 1 OR 2

VEHICLE 1 — 58 POLICY NO. 12-44-89 — 59 INS CODE 03 — VEHICLE 2 — 80 POLICY NO. — 81 INS CODE

60 DRIVER'S FIRST NAME Brian — INITIAL R. — LAST NAME Kelly — 82 DRIVER'S FIRST NAME — INITIAL — LAST NAME

61 NUMBER AND STREET 241 Valley Avenue — 83 NUMBER AND STREET

62 CITY Perkins — STATE — EXPIRES 9/88 — 84 CITY — STATE — EXPIRES

63 DRIVER'S LICENSE NUMBER M064 119 924 — 64 STATE — 65 DOB MO. DAY YR. — 66 EYES B1 — 67 SEX M — 85 DRIVER'S LICENSE NUMBER — 86 STATE — 87 DOB MO DAY YR. — 88 EYES — 89 SEX

68 OWNER'S FIRST NAME [X SAME AS DRIVER] — INITIAL — LAST NAME — 90 OWNER'S FIRST NAME [SAME AS DRIVER] — INITIAL — LAST NAME

71 MAKE AND MODEL Toyota Tercel — 72 YEAR 83 — 73 LICENSE PLATE NO. 105HDK — 74 STATE

75 VEHICLE REMOVED TO Perkins Police Station — 76 AUTHORITY 1 OWNER 2 DRIVER 3 POLICE

78 INITIAL IMPACT — AREAS DAMAGED
10 UNDERCARR. DAMAGE
11 OVERTURNED
12 TOTALLED
13 NONE OR UNKNOWN
14 OTHER

SPD. ZONED 35 — V1 SPD. 50 — V2 SPD.

79 DIAGRAM — Rte 45 — vehicle

100 ALCOHOL DATA
DRIVER NO. 1 — TEST GIVEN YES / NO / REFUSED — TEST TYPE BLOOD / URINE / BREATH — TEST RESULTS
DRIVER NO. 2 — TEST GIVEN YES / NO / REFUSED — TEST TYPE BLOOD / URINE / BREATH — TEST RESULTS
PEDESTRIAN — TEST GIVEN YES / NO / REFUSED — TEST TYPE BLOOD / URINE / BREATH — TEST RESULTS

101 ACCIDENT DESCRIPTION

Driver failed to negotiate left-hand turn on Route 45 just north of Allen St. Car veered off road and crashed into oak tree. Driver did not have seat belt on and was thrown forward. Protected head with right forearm. Taken by patrol car to Perkins Medical Center. Driver, age 20, identified himself as the quarterback of the Colby State College football team here in Perkins.

(See attached for additional description)

102 DAMAGE TO PROPERTY OTHER THAN VEHICLE (GIVE OWNER'S NAME AND ADDRESS)

103 SUMMONS TO Brian Kelly — SUMMONS NUMBER 0579268 — CHARGE Speeding — NAME OF COURT Silver Cnty Court

104 OFFICER'S SIGNATURE — 105 BADGE NUMBER — 106 REVIEWED BY (BADGE NUMBER) — 107 STATUS

24 NAMES · ADDRESSES OF INJURED · IF DECEASED ALSO INCLUDE DATE & TIME OF DEATH

NJTR-1 (R8/83)

STATE COPY

Officer Stanton Charles:

Clocked driver going 50 in 35 mph zone as he passed Allen St. Pulling out to ticket him when he hit the tree. Impact sheared off right side of car. It probably would have killed a passenger, but driver was alone. Driver appeared stunned but only serious injury was right forearm which apparently hit and cracked windshield.

Said he was returning home from Ricco's Pizzeria on Water Street where he and friends had gone to celebrate victory over Butler College today. Said he had argued with a teammate over his game plan and was distracted. Driver apparently had not been drinking. I drove him to the hospital for X-rays. Police tow truck took car to police station.

From call to hospital: Nurse Clara Milkey: "Kelly has broken two bones in his right forearm. He is in stable condition but is being kept overnight for observation. Yes, he will have to wear a cast. No, I don't know how long, but he surely won't be throwing footballs again this winter."

From clips: Colby State had a record of 3 wins and 3 losses this year in football. (You know the team won 16–13 this afternoon.) Kelly, a junior and the first-string quarterback, had passed for 8 touchdowns and 1,037 yards and run for 268 yards. He is the team's dominant offensive player. The team was 2–1 in the Small College Conference and had six games remaining, all in the conference. Kelly is righthanded.

THREE

The Movies, a movie theater complex that shows seven films at once at 77 Transom Road here in Burlington . . . From an interview with Officer Janet Flannery: "We had a report of an incident at The Movies at 10:45 p.m. this evening . . . we arrived and found that the theater's cashier Amos Rob had experienced a robbery at 10:30 p.m. in which he lost all the funds in his cash box — an amount totaling $346. The perpetrators, Rob has told us, were two white males . . . one of whom was wearing glasses, the other of whom we are told was wearing what appeared to Mr. Rob to be a black Mickey Mouse hat. There were no patrons in line at the time . . . the theater's last show begins at 10:15 . . . Mr. Rob said the robbers came up to his ticket window. One aimed a black revolver at him and demanded all the money he had. Mr. Rob said he turned over the money quickly. The robbers stuffed it in a white plastic bag and then ran off . . . Rob said he did not get a good look at the two men, because he was nervous, but that the one without the hat seemed to have dark hair and they both seemed to be in their early 20s. He said he did not recognize them as patrons of the theater. There were no other witnesses. We have no record of this theater being robbed before. The theater's guard and ticket taker were both inside the lobby at the time of the robbery. We have no suspects at this time, but we are investigating. Yes, the Mickey Mouse hat is a possible clue . . . though I would imagine the fellow has taken it off by now."

Amos Rob in interview gives his age as 22. Confirms Flannery's account, and adds: "The robbers' exact words? 'Let's have all the money!' That's all they said. Yes, I'm sure it was a Mickey Mouse hat. I've seen them at Disneyland, actually. It was black, with two, large, black, round ears and a picture of Mickey Mouse on the front. I think I'm going to have nightmares about Mickey Mouse hats. Let me tell you, this was the scariest thing that ever happened to me."

One of the seven theaters that makes up The Movies is showing a Disney film "Snow White," with a Mickey Mouse cartoon called "Mickey Goes Camping."

FOUR

Smoke streaming out of the top story of factory . . . Orange flames dance out of the bottom floor . . . it's 6:23 a.m. Chief Robert Salant of the Turnbull Fire Department says the fire began at about 5:25 a.m. . . . four trucks are here aiming water at the factory . . . it is the Regal Fire Alarm plant . . . Salant: "Yeah, the alarms went off and all, but when we got here the fire was pretty well along." Can still hear occasional fire alarm going off inside (Salant confirms that that is the noise) above the din of workers and flames . . . Salant: "Our information is that there were two watchmen inside the place when she went up. Both men got out without injury. No firefighters have been injured either."

It's 7:10 a.m. . . . still smoking like a chimney from the top floor, some of which is charred and eaten away. The flames are gone though . . . firefighters climbing ladders, knocking out windows and pushing in smoldering walls. The building is brick and timber.

Firefighter Alan Caldwell: "No, we didn't find any sign that there was anyone else in there, but there are certainly a lot of melted fire alarms. The whole place is black and the machinery looks useless."

You are told some lady from Regal has arrived . . . Hildy McGomery, vice president of Regal Fire Alarms: "It's awful, just awful. We're just glad our two men got out on time. This was a $3 million plant. We'll have to see what's left of it. Our fire alarm system might have saved the life of those two men, but it just goes to show that fire alarms can't prevent fires."

The two watchmen already have left scene, you discover. At 7:30 Salant says the fire is completely out. He says the fire trucks arrived at 5:40 but that the fire already was going strong. Salant: "It's obviously much too early to determine for sure what caused this thing, but we're going to look very closely at the electrical wiring. This had all the signs of an electrical fire." He summarizes the damage: bottom floor gutted, structure seriously damaged; other floor, top floor, contents about half gone. Address of plant 62 Commerce Street in an industrial park in Turnbull.

FIVE

1. Frank Richards is the 21-year-old son of Councilwoman Celeste Richards, a Republican and a close friend and political ally of Republican Mayor Ralph Hamilton.

2. Frank is a student at the University of Chicago. He's in his junior year and returned to Dayton yesterday for a short vacation.

3. Late last night attendants aboard US Air flight 505 flying Frank to Astor Airport near here informed the pilot that he was in some trouble.

4. Lucille Audrey, a flight attendant aboard the plane, a 727, said the following in an interview: "All I can tell you is what I saw. This well-dressed young man . . . we later learned that his name was Frank Richards . . . suddenly slumped over in his seat and began moaning quietly. About 15 minutes later he vomited in his lap. The woman sitting next to him . . . her name was Adora Campis . . . called me over in something of a panic. It was clear we had a medical emergency. I checked his pulse and made sure his breathing passages were clear. Then I notified the captain—who radioed ahead for an ambulance on the ground—and I stayed with him until we landed half an hour later. By then he was awake, though groggy, and he refused medical help and made his way off the plane, where a friend helped him to a car. He didn't even get his luggage. Look, I'll tell you what I told police—it looked to me like a drug problem."

5. Sgt. Gerald Stern, a detective with the police here, said in an interview: "We had reports of a medical emergency that looked like a drug problem aboard US Air flight 505 from Chicago, which landed here at 11:55 last night. We went before Judge Elliot Robinson in Superior Court early this morning and obtained a warrant to search the luggage of Frank Richards, the man in question. The bags were clearly labeled and he had left them at the airport. We searched and found some suspicious materials which were analyzed for us this morning at the police labs on Center Street. Our report states that his luggage contained a significant quantity of heroin, I can't say exactly how much right now, but enough to keep even a moderately heavy user happy for a week or so.

"We have notified Mr. Richards, whom we reached at his mother's house at 10:30 a.m. today, and he arrived at police headquarters with his parents at 11:45. He was fingerprinted and booked on one count of possession of heroin, a felony. He was released to the custody of his parents and told to appear in court at 2 p.m. this afternoon for formal arraignment.

"No, I haven't discussed the case with either of his parents. Yes, normally we would set bail in such a case but we know Mr. Richards' family and we are confident he will report as required."

6. A call to the Richards house at 63 Chestnut Drive. The man who answers the phone says no one there wants to talk to the press, but the family lawyer — Walter Fields — can be contacted.

7. Walter Fields, in an interview, says: "Look, this is a good kid, from a good family. He's never been in trouble in his life. I don't know what this business is all about, but we'll be there at 2 p.m. tomorrow and give our views to the judge. That's all I have to say."

SIX

You are making your morning telephone checks and the guy who answers at Fire Department headquarters has put you on hold. To your surprise, Chief John Crowley comes to the phone. Here's what he says.

1. A fire broke out at 5 a.m. this morning in a three-story frame apartment building in Lambertsville. Brought under control at 5:46.

2. 12 residents escaped uninjured.

3. "We don't know how it happened," said Crowley. "But we know it seemed to start by the front porch. Anytime a fire starts outside a house at 5 in the morning, well, you can't help being suspicious."

4. Three people were killed in the fire. They were all children. Three sisters who lived in a third-floor apartment: Cynthia Evans, 12; Lynette Evans, 8; and Tania Evans, 1. The building was at 29 Mercer St.

5. Crowley: "Tania almost made it. Her mother had her in her arms but then she stumbled in the heavy smoke and dropped her as she was groping down the stairs. The kid was pulled out a few minutes later but she died on the way to Good Samaritan Hospital. Apparently smoke inhalation. The other two kids were trapped in their third-floor bedroom. The mother, Alicia Evans, 33, is okay now. She's with relatives. The father, Mark, he's 32, was rescued from a third-floor ledge by firemen. All the other residents lived on the first two floors and managed to escape through the doors or out windows."

6. Crowley: "We had three trucks and 15 men there within four minutes of getting the alarm but it was hopeless. This thing went up like tinder. One more thing. We've cited the landlord for negligence for failing to install smoke detectors. His name is Arthur Hopkins and he lives on McDonald Avenue. I don't have his exact address. The city code here in Lambertsville requires all landlords to install fire detectors in any multiple dwelling building. The fine will be $500. It doesn't seem like much for three lives."

7. By now deadline is just an hour away and you know you have time for just another call or two. You run to the reverse directory and get through to two people living in the adjacent apartment at 27 Mercer St.

8. Jennifer Markus, 53: "I woke up coughing and ran to the window. I thought *our* house was on fire. The smoke was just pouring out the windows. You could hear the flames popping inside."

9. Jon Kaunitz, 29: "I heard people screaming that there were kids in there. I wanted to help, but the smoke was so dense I couldn't get close."

SEVEN

It's 11 p.m. Halloween night and you've just finished editing a feature on Rent-A-Costume, a new store specializing in monster outfits. The newsroom is nearly empty. The night rewrite man went home with a stomach ache after eating too much candy. Only your boss, the night city editor, and a clerk remain. That means you get to do the police checks.

You reach Sgt. Stanley Richman at Marion police headquarters. He's just returned from the scene of an accident. You are only an hour from deadline so you know you'll have to cover it by phone. Here is what he says:

1. The accident occurred at 10 p.m.
2. It involved two cars, a green 1985 Toyota Corolla and a black 1984 Volvo 142 S.
3. The Corolla was being driven by Margie Simmons, 32, of 14 Bashaw Terrace in Marion. Her sons, Paul and Stephen, both 9, were in the back seat. Mrs. Simmons was driving northbound on Route 9W in Marion and had just crossed Arlington Road when the crash occurred.
4. The Volvo was being driven by Maurice Vialle, 43, of Garden Road in Marion. He had no passengers in the car.
5. Mrs. Simmons and her two sons were killed in the collision. They were pronounced dead at Parsons Valley Hospital but actually probably were killed on impact.
6. Vialle was taken to Parsons Valley Hospital as well. Richman isn't clear what his condition is.

You ask how the accident occurred.

Richman says that Route 9W is lined with trees and barely two lanes wide for about a one-mile stretch just north of Arlington Road. Vialle, driving south, apparently never completed a sharp curve to the right, Richman says. His car, obscured by the curve, crossed the divider and entered the northbound lane directly in the path of the oncoming Toyota.

Richman said of Mrs. Simmons: "She never had a chance to swerve, if you know what I mean. It must have all happened in seconds." He said that when he arrived, the Toyota had rolled onto its side. Its crushed roof was leaning against a pine tree beside northbound lane. The front end was caved in. The door and fender on the passenger's side of the Volvo were caved in and the car, blocking both lanes, was spun around so that it was facing northbound. Richman: "This is what we have: It appears as if Mrs. Simmons hit Vialle as he crossed in front of her."

You ask whether any charges will be filed. He replies that the accident is under investigation. You ask how fast the cars were traveling. "It's impossible to judge exactly," Richman says. "But from the violence of the impact, I would have to guess at least one of them was speeding. The speed limit there is only 35 miles per hour and those cars were totaled."

Richman says he knows nothing about Mrs. Simmons or Vialle. As you're about to hang up, you remember reading an article about two months ago. "Haven't there been accidents on that stretch of road before?" you ask. "Yes, a couple," he replies. "Mayor Long has been applying for state money to widen the road there for a couple of years."

You call Parsons Valley Hospital and learn that Vialle is in critical condition. The night nurse won't disclose the nature of his injuries. You call the Simmons home. No answer.

You rush to the reverse directory and call a phone listed under the name of Charles Balint, of 16 Bashaw Terrace. A woman answers. Hesitantly and gently, you identify yourself and tell her that her neighbor and her neighbor's children have been killed in a car crash. You ask whether you might ask a few questions so that your story can be as accurate and complete as possible.

"I'm in shock," says the woman, who later identifies herself as Janice Balint. "The police called about 10 minutes ago. Margie was my best friend. She was always kind, always ready to listen and help out. It makes no sense."

She continues. You learn that Margie Simmons is a former fashion model who gave up her career 11 years ago when she married her husband, Alfred. She was frequently on the cover of top fashion magazines before leaving modeling. She had carrot-red hair, green eyes and was of medium height.

"She was an excellent seamstress. In fact, she made both the boys' Halloween costumes. That's why they were on Route 9W. They went to the south part of town to go trick-or-treating with friends, and they must have been on the way home. Margie was so proud of the witch costumes she made. She wanted to see the expressions of the people when they opened the door. She was in a cheerful, bubbly mood when she left off Alice."

You ask who Alice is and find out that Alice, 6, is Mrs. Simmons' daughter. She had a bad cold so Mrs. Simmons left her with the Balints to take the boys trick-or-treating. You also learn that Alfred, an executive for Exxon, is in Houston on a business trip. The boys, freckle-faced, red-haired twins, were classmates at Douglass Elementary School. They were good students but a "bit mischievous." They would sometimes switch identities to confuse substitute teachers.

You hang up and try the Vialle house and one or two neighbors. No one answers. You rush to the library and pull out the clips for accidents. You find that this is the third fatal accident at the same location in six months. Two months ago, four people were killed when seven teen-agers in a car driven well above the speed limit (at 50 miles an hour) failed to complete the same curve and crashed into the trees. Four months ago, one person was killed and another critically injured when their cars collided during a rainstorm.

You have a few more minutes and then you absolutely must start writing. You decide to call the mayor. It turns out to be a stroke of luck. He says he had met Vialle, who moved to Marion six months ago from Paris, France, leaving his family behind. He worked in foreign trade and had planned to return to France at Christmas to move his family to this country.

"The senselessness of it, what a disaster, what a mess." he says. "They should name that stretch of road 'death curve.' The state's supposed to maintain it and I've been writing to them and calling them for several years. There's not even a sign warning of a sharp curve. If they don't do anything this time, I'll go out there with a pick and shovel and widen it myself."

▪ C. Story Assignments ▪

1. Check the blotter at a local police station. Ask to see the report on an incident that interests you and write a news story based on the report and interviews with police officers and others connected with the incident.

2. Compare this year's crime statistics in a town with last year's. How have things changed? Are the numbers of certain crimes up or down? Is the number and percentage of crimes solved up or down? Develop a story from some aspect of the reports.

3. Write a story on some aspect of police procedure. How are the officers assigned? How frequently do their shifts rotate? How much overtime do they work? Do they have any quotas to fulfill? Has new technology changed the way the station operates? What reports do officers have to fill out? Do they feel as if they are buried in paperwork?

CHAPTER 25

Courts

Few institutions are as formal and tradition-bound as the courts. Judges—in their old-fashioned black robes—*hand down* decisions, grand juries *hand up* indictments. Bank robbers and drug smugglers, few of whom presumably have any Latin, find themselves seeking *writs of habeas corpus* (statements from the judge that they are being illegally held). Companies, not anxious perhaps to fight a government charge that they polluted nearby water supplies, plead *nolo contendere,* meaning that, while they do not admit guilt, they do not contest the charge against them.

Reporters wandering around a courthouse will confront many such unfamiliar rites and obscure terms each day. Each offers reporters an opportunity to err, and the consequences of such errors can be particularly severe here, where people's money, reputation and freedom are so often on the line. That plea of *nolo contendere,* a reporter may learn too late, was not exactly a *guilty* plea after all.

To make matters worse, procedures can differ from court to court and from state to state. A reporter trained in California, where the Supreme Court is in fact the *top* state court, might be taken aback to learn that in New York the Supreme Courts are superseded by the state Court of Appeals.

Most reporters approach the courts without the benefit of any legal training. Tom French says he did not even know how many people sit on a jury (12 on most criminal juries) when he took over the court beat at the *St. Petersburg Times.* Beginning court reporters have to get hold of any documents they can find on the structures and procedures of the courts in their jurisdictions. (The chart on pages 304–305 provides a rough outline of the path suspects might travel through the criminal justice system.) Reporters also must consult a good legal dictionary (See Additional Reading) to help penetrate the legal jargon. And they must be prepared to sit down with a notebook and some friendly lawyers or court clerks to run through the structures and practices of the courts they are covering.

"Look up everything! Ask about everything!" advises Fred Barbash, who covers the Supreme Court for *The Washington Post.* When I have trouble writing something clearly is when I don't really understand it." Tom French echoes Barbash's advice: "Don't feel stupid. Lawyers are good at explaining things. They're anxious that you get it right."

Reporters covering the courts must stay on top of all the jargon and ritual, but at the same time they can't allow it to set the tone of their reporting. For behind the Latin terms and the rigid customs are some of the rawest, most compelling events and decisions in our society. "Courts are a repository of human drama, a window on everything!" Barbash exclaims.

This is a difficult beat. It should not be a dry beat:

Allen Paul Henry, weeping on the witness stand, admitted yesterday that he had stabbed a waiter to death with a kitchen knife last summer, but he pleaded that it was a "tragic misunderstanding" born of his lifetime of exposure to prison violence."*

The New York Times

* The name in this story has been changed.

Records

First, says Ted Rohrlich, who covers the courts for the *Los Angeles Times,* "you want to learn where the records are kept and which are open to public inspection and which are not." These records include *search warrants* (statements that there is enough cause for suspicion to search someone), *arrest warrants* (statements that there is enough evidence to arrest), *affidavits* (sworn statements), *indictments* (formal charges by a grand jury), *depositions* (sworn statements by witnesses), *civil suits* (complaints filed by one private person or company against another) and the *transcripts* of hearing or trials.

The court clerk usually has responsibility for keeping track of most of these pieces of paper and should be asked for help in determining where they are filed. Court clerks also should have information on which of these papers the public, and therefore a reporter, has a right to see. It's wise to double-check, however. Clerks can be a bit more protective of the privacy of their files than the law is.

Some courts have boxes where material of interest to reporters—major decisions and indictments, for example—are filed. All court reporters routinely check the court's *calendar* of scheduled cases and the *docket* (a listing of cases on file). But, warns Walter Fee, who covered the courts for six years for *The Milwaukee Journal,* "depending on the calendar is like depending on a New York City subway schedule. It's written in Sanskrit."

Often armed with tips from sources, reporters go beyond boxes and calendars and dockets to the files of warrants, indictments, suits and other documents themselves. Ted Rohrlich calls it "the mundane process of regularly checking the records." As Rohrlich knows well, what is in those court records can be anything but mundane. It was during one of his regular visits to the files that Rohrlich discovered allegations of a scheme to sell phony tickets to Dodger games (See Chapter 7, News Judgment). There are exclusives hidden in those files.

"So many stories are there on paper," says Tom French of the *St. Petersburg Times.* "You can get a lot of great human detail and emotion and quotes from the records."

And most court records are *privileged*—they can be quoted in a story without fear of libel (See Appendix D, Law). As a result, even when other sources are available, court reporters stick as closely as possible to the printed word. "Documents are absolutely crucial," says *The Washington Post*'s Fred Barbash. "Since you are reporting things that are terribly damaging to people, the only way to protect yourself is to rely on privileged information."

Sources

It was a case no one was supposed to find out about.

"It wasn't on the court calendar," Walter Fee of *The Milwaukee Journal* recalls. "No reporters or members of the public were in the courtroom." This mystery hearing, Fee says, was a contempt of court proceeding against a juror, an unemployed veteran, who had arrived late in court after calling and explaining that his car had broken down.

"The judge took umbrage, cited the juror for contempt and fined him $3,000," Fee says. And the public never would have found out about this severe action had Fee not had a source, a *bailiff,* one of the court officials in charge of taking care of prisoners and guarding jurors.

Courthouses are filled with people worth knowing: not only the judges who hear cases and the lawyers who argue them, but the court clerks who file them and the judges' law clerks who help review them. A major part of a court reporter's job is cultivating these people (See Chapter 19, Sources).

Judges

Many judges will agree to talk periodically with reporters on background (See Chapter 19, Sources). Some, Fred Barbash has found, "like a little publicity." "Every now and then they will want to call a reporter with a story," he says. "You want to be the one they think of calling." When Barbash was assigned to the United States Supreme Court, the first thing he did was introduce himself to each of the justices.

Lawyers

The law is an adversarial proceeding. In court, prosecutors and defense lawyers try to influence the judge, play the jury and play the press. But the reporters who ultimately gain the respect of both sides are the ones who listen carefully to the arguments and write their stories "down the center." "I think some reporters tend to side with defense lawyers and others side with prosecutors," says Walter Fee. "Try to avoid that."

Most of the news originates with prosecutors—the district attorneys and U.S. attorneys who conduct investigations, announce indictments and prosecute trials. Reporters want to get to know them and their staffs, particularly their investigators.

Defense lawyers tend to be, as Rohrlich puts it, "a little defensive" and therefore more reticent than prosecutors. Nonetheless, as the prosecutor begins to weave a web of evidence implicating someone, particularly if that evidence is leaking out on background, it is crucial to at least attempt to get the accused's version of events into print. Fairness; innocent until proven guilty: These are the operative commands here.

In civil cases the attorneys for both sides, obviously, need to be approached. And even lawyers who are not directly involved in a particular case can be useful as sources of legal information, gossip or general guidance.

"Most court reporters make rounds," Barbash says. "They take a little walk around the building every day. You walk into the U.S. attorney's office, and he'll say he's got an important indictment coming down. Almost all stories come that way."

Suspects

Usually lawyers will try to protect them from the press, but if suspects will talk, what better source is there for an account, however one-sided, of the events in question. One warning though: Accepting such information *off the record* (See Chapter 19, Sources) can be very risky. If someone were to confess to a crime off the record, the reporter would be left with knowledge of a crime and no ethical way to report it.

Witnesses

After a crime or disaster (See Chapter 24, Police), witnesses can be crucial sources of information and quotes. But court reporters see the witnesses who are about to testify in court somewhat differently. Attempts to beat the court to prospective testimony leave reporters with an additional responsibility: the burden of checking and balancing what witnesses say, a job that during a trial would be handled by the adversarial process. Unless there is a compelling reason to move faster—a reporter's own investigation, intense competitive pressure, a suspicion that the prosecutor is holding back—reporters generally will wait to hear witnesses out during the trial.

Clerks

Court clerks and judges' clerks are repositories of information on new cases, on schedules of hearings and trial dates, on the whereabouts and availability of courtroom exhibits (which generally are kept separate from the rest of the files), and on the operation and, sometimes, the finances of the court. They are the best source of tips on new cases and a good source of tips on when decisions are about to be handed down. When a new law reducing the waiting period for marriage licenses went into effect unannounced in Flor-

ida, Tom French was the first reporter in the state to get the story. His secret: A clerk, whom he had befriended, called and told him about it.

Courtroom Regulars

Most courthouses attract a group of people, usually retired, who entertain themselves by spending the day watching trials. Fred Barbash often has taken advantage of their expertise. "They are remarkable for their knowledge of what's going on, who is going to testify, and where," he explains.

Criminal Court

This is where people accused of threatening the well-being of society end up. This is where prison and occasionally even death sentences are handed out. The road from criminal charges to sentences is long and has many possible turnoffs, detours and roadstops. The chart on pages 304–305 has a detailed outline of the criminal justice system. Each turnoff, each detour, each roadstop may contain a story.

The first story—the arrest and charging of a suspect—is discussed in Chapter 24, Police. Police reporters often stay with the story through the initial court hearing at which the suspect is *arraigned,* or formally charged, before a judge. From then on court reporters usually take over.

Indictments

In serious cases, or *felonies,* the prosecutor usually must develop the case twice: First, a grand jury, a panel of citizens, decides behind closed doors whether there is enough evidence to formally charge or indict an individual. (In some states, a prosecutor can file charges directly through an *information.*) Then, the case is presented in open court before judge, jury, spectators and the press. The release of a grand jury's indictment often makes news:

A suspended Boston plumbing inspector was indicted yesterday by a federal grand jury on charges of racketeering and extortion.

The Boston Globe

So, too, should a decision by a grand jury *not* to indict, a decision by a prosecutor *not* to pursue a case or a decision by a trial jury *not* to convict. Newspapers have an ethical responsibility to follow up the outcome of any case in which they report that someone was arrested and charged with a crime:

A charge of arson was dropped yesterday in the case of Paul D. Searford of Dorchester, a 23-year-old roofer

This chart, prepared by a presidential commission, shows how cases move through the criminal justice system—from detected and reported crimes to prosecution, the courts and the corrections system. Procedures in some states may vary from those outlined here. The varying weights of the lines reflect estimates of the relative numbers of cases that reach each stage in the system. (The President's Commission on Law Enforcement and Administration of Justice, *The Challenge of Crime in a Free Society*, 7-12; 1967)

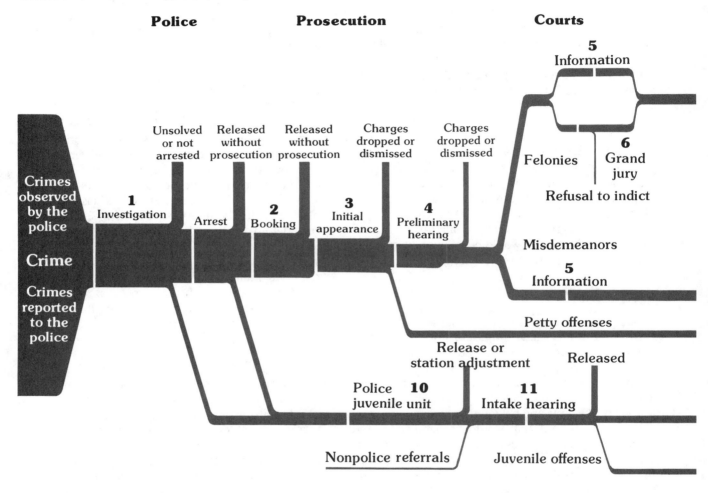

1 May continue until trial.

2 Administrative record of arrest. First step at which temporary release on bail may be available.

3 Before magistrate, commissioner or justice of peace. Formal notice of charge, advice of rights. Bail set. Summary trials for petty offenses usually conducted here without further processing.

4 Preliminary testing of evidence against defendant. Charge may be reduced. No separate preliminary hearing for misdemeanors in some systems.

5 Charge filed by prosecutor on basis of information submitted by police or citizens. Alternative to grand jury indictment; often used in felonies, almost always in misdemeanors.

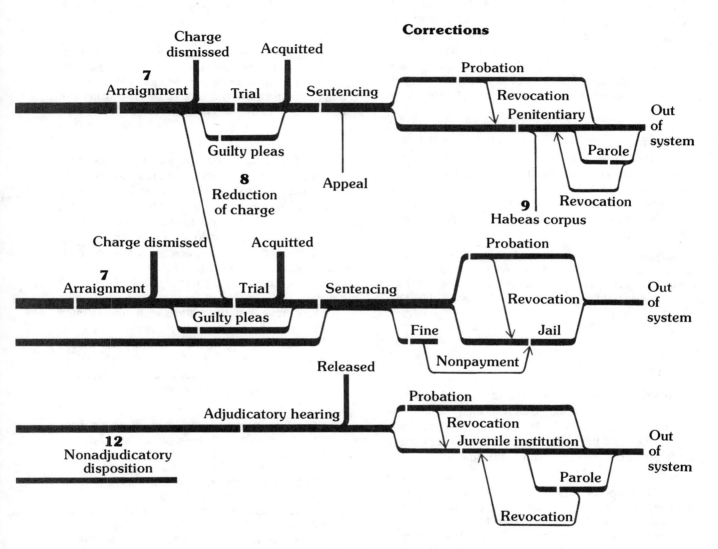

Corrections

6 Reviews whether government evidence is sufficient to justify trial. Some states have no grand jury system; others seldom use it.

7 Appearance for plea; defendant elects trial by judge or jury (if available); counsel for indigent usually appointed here in felonies.

8 Charge may be reduced at any time before trial in return for plea of guilty or for other reasons.

9 Challenge on constitutional grounds to legality of detention. May be sought at any point in process.

10 Police often hold informal hearings, dismiss or adjust many cases without further processing.

11 Probation officer decides desirability of further court action.

12 Welfare agency, social services, counseling, medical care, etc., for cases where adjudicatory handling not needed.

who had been accused of setting the fire that destroyed St. Bartholomew Church in Newburyport on Jan. 24.*

The Boston Globe

Pleas

The vast majority of cases never get to a jury. In some major cities, it's been estimated that as many as 90 percent of all cases are dispensed with through *plea bargaining*—a process in which prosecutor and defense attorney agree to allow the defendant to plead guilty to a lesser charge. A suspected drug pusher might be allowed to plead guilty to possession of narcotics, which carries less severe penalties. A murder suspect might accept a five-year sentence for manslaughter.

The reasons for plea bargaining are complex. Sometimes it results when the evidence is not as airtight as the prosecutor might like. Often it's a means, however imperfect, of meting out some form of justice in a criminal courts system that is suffering from too many cases and too few judges.

Guilty pleas, whether or not to a lesser charge, make news:

A Hancock Park mother of four who police believe is responsible for distributing 80 percent of the nation's child pornography pleaded guilty yesterday to a felony pornography distribution charge in Los Angeles Superior Court.

Los Angeles Times

Trials

No criminal court story generates as much interest and electricity as a major trial, especially a trial involving a prominent defendant. In this story previewing a major trial the writer used a soft lead (See Chapter 9, Soft Leads) to bring out the drama:

NEWPORT, R.I.—Uncharacteristically for him, Claus von Bülow is spending the winter season here in Newport, which is gray and cold this time of year.

Usually, he and his wife, the former Martha Sharp Crawford, have come here in the warm months, closing up their large apartment on Fifth Avenue in New York to pass the summer at their estate, Clarendon Court, as members of Newport's fabled summer colony.

But Mrs. von Bülow is now in Columbia-Presbyterian Hospital in New York, in a coma that began on the night of Dec. 20, 1980, while she was visiting Clarendon Court. And as a consequence, von Bülow and his attorneys must be in Superior Court here at 9:30 a.m. Monday to begin the selection of a jury that will try him on charges of attempting to murder her.

The New York Times

*The name of the roofer, the church and the town have been changed here.

Covering a major trial can be emotionally draining for any reporter. Days are spent in court: watching as the defense and prosecution lawyers develop their cases; listening to a parade of experts who try to build or undermine the case for conviction, who try to erase doubt or plant enough of it to sway even a single juror. Reporters, notebooks open in front of them, will be listening for the gist of the arguments and for good quotes. One of the early witnesses in the trial of Claus von Bülow was his wife's maid:

Miss Schrallhammer testified that on the morning of Dec. 27, 1979, "I heard Mrs. von Bülow moaning" in the bedroom. "I knocked on the door and just walked in," she said. "Her right arm was hanging off the bed; her arm was limp. I touched her and she was ice cold."

The New York Times

Evenings during a trial are spent writing: news stories on the day's witnesses, features describing the scene in the courtroom (See Chapter 26, Features), background stories that examine how each side is building its argument. Weekends and days off may be spent following up a lead found by digging through new exhibits and motions. The case can become all-consuming, and it can drag on for months. Still, few good reporters covering a hot trial consider asking off the story.

Trial coverage sometimes starts with jury selection as it did in the von Bülow case. It may include mention of the motions lawyers file—asking that a trial be moved to another jurisdiction, asking that charges be thrown out for lack of evidence, or seeking to widen or narrow the scope of the evidence introduced:

[von Bülow's] attorneys are trying to get the judge to suppress the key evidence in the case, a black bag containing hypodermic needles and vials of drugs. It was taken from von Bülow's locked closet at Clarendon Court by his stepson, Alexander von Auersperg, and a private detective the night of Jan. 23, 1981, after Alexander, his sister and his grandmother had grown suspicious about the origin of the coma into which his mother sank on Dec. 21, 1980. She remains at a hospital in New York, and her doctors say she will never recover.

The New York Times

Eventually the prosecution will present its case, with the defense attorney cross-examining the witnesses. Then the defense will call its witnesses, with the prosecutor cross-examining them. Each side will also get an opportunity to bring back witnesses to rebut the opposition's arguments. (And reporters will be trying to give approximately equal play to the arguments of both sides.) Finally, after closing speeches to the jury by both attorneys, the jury will consider a verdict. That verdict generally is the biggest story of all:

> As Claus von Bülow sat flushed, still and expressionless, a jury today pronounced him guilty, as charged, of twice trying to kill his wealthy wife, Martha von Bülow, by injecting her with insulin.
>
> Twenty-four times, as the seven men and five women rose one by one to be polled by the court clerk, von Bülow heard the word "guilty" roll out. He showed not a flicker of emotion at the verdict, which was delivered by Barbara Connett, foreman of the jury. The 55-year-old businessman faces a maximum sentence of 40 years in prison.
>
> *The New York Times*

Notice that verdict stories mention prominently not only what the defendant has been cleared or convicted of but also what the maximum (and often the minimum) sentence is. The date of sentencing, if set, also gets prominent attention. Quotes from the judge, jurors, defendant or attorneys, if these people are willing to be interviewed, can be invaluable in bringing out the emotions that fill a courtroom on verdict day:

> "I think I can speak for the other jurors and myself in saying that it was a painful experience," said David Taffs, a computer analyst and their selected spokesman. "Other jurors have said they would be reluctant to repeat it, and I feel the same way."
>
> *The New York Times*

Any stories about a trial must also provide background information for those readers who haven't been following along (See Chapter 15, Background and Context). Here are two of the 12 paragraphs of background *The Times* included in the von Bülow sentencing story:

> The case sprang to public attention last July when a grand jury indicted von Bülow on two counts of attempting to murder his wife at Clarendon Court, the couple's mansion here. The charges relate to the comas she suffered in December 1979 and December 1980.
>
> Mrs. von Bülow's family, including two children by her first marriage and her mother, Annie-Laurie Aitken, spent almost $100,000 collecting evidence against von Bülow. Alexander von Auersperg, a son and the state's first witness, gave that amount in his testimony.

Many trials don't warrant the gavel-to-gavel coverage accorded the case against von Bülow. That's where reporters' sources come in. "Ideally you don't want to miss a minute of what goes on in court," says Ted Rohrlich. "But in practice, with 20 trials going on in the building at once, you may miss a lot. In that case you want to develop communication with the lawyers and court personnel so you can have a sense of when important or newsworthy witnesses will come up."

Appeals

Court coverage rarely ends when the verdict is announced. Readers will be interested in the sentence that is handed out if the defendant was found guilty. And readers should be informed if the verdict is overturned by a higher court on appeal. Claus von Bülow's conviction *was* overturned on appeal, and *The New York Times* reporter who covered the trial was there with the story:

> PROVIDENCE, R.I.—More than two years after the long and dramatic trial in which Claus von Bülow was convicted of twice trying to murder his wealthy wife, the Rhode Island Supreme Court overturned the jury's verdict today and ordered a new trial.

(Claus von Bülow was found innocent in that new trial in 1985.)

Good court reporters also try to keep track of the lives of the people they have been covering after the legal process has had its say. They may visit prisons for interviews, and they remain alert for parole board decisions determining when convicts will be released.

Civil Court

Civil court is where people and companies use the legal system to settle disputes. Often these lawsuits—filed by individuals or companies against individuals or companies—involve efforts to collect damages for injuries or for failure to comply with contracts. The prosecutor has no role here, and, unless someone is held in *contempt of court* for interfering with the process, no one goes to jail. Still civil court can make big news.

AT&T was dismembered in civil court and former Israeli Defense Minister Ariel Sharon lost a multimillion libel suit against *Time* in civil court. Johns-Manville Corp. filed for reorganization under bankruptcy laws in civil court in large part because of the hundreds of millions of dollars in civil suits filed against it by former employees who worked with the cancer-causing fibers of asbestos used in many of the company's products.

"Civil court is not as sexy as criminal court, but a lot more important to your readers," says Tom French, who has covered both. Yet, since it rarely is the setting for movie or television scenes, the workings of civil court may be more perplexing to reporters.

Fred Barbash says he has seen too many reporters write that someone was found guilty in a civil case. No one is guilty or innocent in civil court. If the plaintiff wins, however, the defendant may be liable for huge sums of money in *actual damages*—compensation for losses actually suffered by the plaintiff—and *puni-*

tive damages—additional compensation designed, presumably, to teach the defendant not to do it again.

> A jury has ordered the manufacturer of a one-ton robot that killed a worker at a Ford Motor Co. plant to pay the man's family $10 million.
>
> *The Philadelphia Inquirer*

Among the thousands of civil suits that may be filed, reporters look for cases in which unusually large amounts of damages are sought, in which unusually prominent individuals or businesses are involved or in which the issues seem particularly significant or likely to set a precedent:

> Television anchorwoman Christine Craft won $500,000 yesterday in a suit against her former employer, who she claimed demoted her for being "too old, unattractive and not deferential enough to men."
>
> (Chicago) *Sun-Times*

The need for reporters to stay with stories after verdicts is no less important in civil court. Craft's victory was overturned upon appeal, although she eventually won $325,000 in damages after a new trial.

Enterprise

"The main thing," advises Barbash, "is that there is always drama associated with the courts. It's important not to get so consumed with the legal issues that you neglect to dramatize and make relevant these cases."

Barbash has flown to South Carolina to interview victims of "brown lung" disease in order to dramatize discussion of a Supreme Court case on cotton dust and job safety. Tom French examined how effective Florida's new, supposedly tougher drunken driving law was by following through the courts the first two dozen cases to be prosecuted under the law:

> The law was clear about Alfred L. Aspiro, a jack-of-all-trades and three-time convicted drunken driver. Arrested in a Dodge van in July 1982 with a bottle of vodka at his side, he was supposed to spend at least 10 days in jail.
>
> Instead, a Pinellas County judge sentenced him to probation.
>
> He was supposed to be fined a minimum of $1,000. The judge fined him $250.
>
> He was supposed to lose his driver's license for 10 years or more. The judge suspended it for six months.
>
> What happened to Aspiro was no isolated case. Thousands of other drunken drivers in Florida are escaping even the minimum sentence required by a new, year-old law. And the ones who stand the best chance of escaping the minimum sentences are the most dangerous drivers—the ones who are repeatedly caught drunk on the road. . . .*
>
> *St. Petersburg Times*

* The name in this story has been changed.

Some of the drama in the courts lies in the legal system itself and in its weaknesses and blindspots. Here are some examples of questions reporters might ask about the courts they cover:

1. How do sentences for white-collar crimes compare with sentences for violent crimes?
2. Do judges differ in the sentences they impose? How significantly?
3. Which judges are frequently overruled by higher courts?
4. Who owns the hotels that sequestered jurors are sent to?
5. What is the average sentence actually served for different offenses?
6. How does plea bargaining affect sentencing?
7. How much do trials cost?
8. Are the fines defendants are being asked to pay actually being noted in the records?
9. What is the conviction rate of the prosecutors? How does that compare with that of prosecutors in other jurisdictions?
10. How are judges selected?

Here is how the *Los Angeles Times* began a story about one problem courts face—nuisance suits:

> Two Houston football fans, upset over a referee's call in a championship game which their team lost, sue the referee and the National Football League for "consumer fraud."
>
> A happily married woman in Boston, after falling and breaking her pelvis, sues her husband for $35,000 for failing to keep the sidewalk clear of ice and snow.
>
> A 24-year-old Boulder, Colo., man sues his parents for $350,000 because he doesn't like the way they brought him up.
>
> These are some examples of what many critics of the American legal system might regard as frivolous lawsuits, lawsuits that are increasingly clogging court calendars and delaying justice in more important matters . . .

Odd cases can make stories in their own right. When being interviewed for this book, Tom French, who has a taste for the offbeat, was pursuing a story about a doctor who was sued not only for malpractice but for stealing a patient's ligament.

Additional Reading

The Reporter and the Law, Lyle W. Denniston, Hastings House, 1980.

Black's Law Dictionary, Fifth Edition, Henry C. Black, West Publishing Co., 1983.

Gideon's Trumpet, Anthony Lewis, Random House, 1964.

Free Press and Fair Trial, a report of the American Newspaper Publishers Association, American Newspaper Publishers, Reston, Va.

▪ A. Research Assignments ▪

ONE

Using research materials or interviews with people familiar with the courts, write explanations that could be used in a newspaper article for the following terms.

1. Warrant

2. Surrogate court

3. The bar

4. Chambers

5. Summary judgment

6. Class action suit

7. Restraining order

8. Note of issue

9. Taking the Fifth

10. Eminent domain

TWO

Using research materials or interviews with people familiar with the courts, obtain answers to the following questions about a state court system.

1. What is the name of the highest court?

2. How many justices sit on the highest court? What are their names?

3. How are justices selected for the highest court?

4. What are the names of the other state courts?

5. Does the state impose the death penalty? For what specific crimes?

6. What is the penalty in the state for possession of less than an ounce of marijuana?

THREE

Choose a local municipal or state criminal court and obtain answers to the following questions through research materials and interviews with people who work at the court. Illustrate some of the answers with quotes.

1. What is the name of the court?

2. How many such courts are there in the state?

3. What are the names of the judges who preside at this particular court?

4. How were these judges selected?

5. How long must defendants at the court wait to stand trial? Is there any backlog of cases?

6. What is the name of the prosecutor or prosecutors at the court?

7. How were the prosecutors selected?

8. Do prosecutors at the court frequently engage in plea bargaining? Give an example.

■ B. Writing Assignments ■

Write stories based on each of the following collections of information. In each case you are writing for a newspaper dated tomorrow and read in the town where the event occurred.

ONE

You discover the following information from a source in the municipal building and confirm it with police and with court records:

1. Robert Lowry, 19, of Logan, Utah, has been sentenced to serve 30 days in the county jail on Blanchard Street here in Wheeling. He was sentenced three days ago, but no one found out about the case.
2. Lowry was arrested two weeks ago at a Wrigley's Convenience Store, 1400 Woodley Road in Wheeling.
3. Municipal Court Judge Helene Broussard heard the case and handed down the sentence.
4. Lowry was a Bible salesman for the New Order of Christian Hope headquartered in Austin, Texas.
5. He was sentenced for trying to steal three packages of Hostess Cupcakes and a package of cheddar cheese. The total value of the items was $3.45.

Both the judge and store officials refuse to comment on the case. You are, however, able to reach Lowry by telephone at the jail. Lowry: "I was starving, if you know what I mean. I had a place to sleep but it was going on two days that I hadn't eaten and my boss wouldn't advance me any money."

Lowry said he had lost his previous week's paycheck of $237 in a poker game. His boss wouldn't lend him money and his mother wouldn't accept a collect call, he said. He had no credit cards and the motel he was staying at, the Crestview on Calvery Lane didn't have a cafeteria or restaurant, he added.

Lowry said this is the first time he had asked his boss, Anne Jones, for an advance. When you reach her by telephone, she also declines comment.

TWO

1. Last day of trial here in East Brunswick of Andrew Doomas, 98 East Brunswick Ave., East Brunswick, for involuntary manslaughter. Trial had lasted three days, total. (Trial had been covered daily in your newspaper.) Doomas is 38.
2. Victim: Jennifer Jacobs, 7, of 34 East Brunswick Ave., in East Brunswick.
3. From closing statement of prosecutor, Asst. Dist. Atty. Joan Shelton, 58: "The defense has not contested the fact that the defendant's white Honda Accord hit young Jennifer as she was crossing East Brunswick Ave., at the corner of Mulberry Street, on August 28th. We have shown, through five witnesses—three of Jennifer's friends, Susan Shaw, Nicola Wainright and Georgina Wainright; one driver of another car at the intersection, Ralph Handleman; and one pedestrian standing on the corner, James Hampton— that Jennifer was walking, not running across the street and that if the defendant's car stopped at the stop sign there, it stopped very briefly. We do not mean to suggest that Mr. Doomas had any malice toward young Jennifer, only that he was careless in his driving, horribly careless. The only witness the defense offered to challenge any of what you heard from five people who were on the scene was the defendant. Think about that."
4. From closing statement of defense attorney, John Anderson, 29: "Yes, you have heard the testimony of the few obviously horrified and upset people who had fuzzy glimpses of the events on August 28th. But you also have heard the testimony of Andrew Doomas, the vice president of the First State Bank

branch in our city, the father of a three-year-old boy himself; a man whose life has been changed by this accident, by this unfortunate, horrible accident; a man who has had, as he told you, difficulty getting behind the wheel of a car again. Andy Doomas remembers events of those moments clearly. He remembers little Jennifer dashing out, running wildly, in front of his car, after he had stopped and looked both ways at that stop sign, before he could stop his car again. Andy Doomas certainly has suffered enough."

5. Jury talks it over for one hour and forty-five minutes. Returns to courtroom at 3:53 and jury foreman Janice Freedman says they have found the defendant guilty.

6. Tears can be seen on defendant's face after verdict.

7. Judge Judith Jones, 62, says she will announce a sentence next Monday.

8. According to the law books, maximum sentence for involuntary manslaughter in state is four years in prison and a $10,000 fine.

9. Defendant, his family and attorneys will not comment after trial, except Anderson says, "Don't worry, we are going to appeal this decision." Gives no details.

10. Shelton, interviewed after verdict: "Obviously, we're satisfied with the jury's decision. We have nothing against Mr. Doomas except that he and others like him must learn to drive properly and protect this city's children."

11. Freedman, interviewed after verdict (no other juror will talk): "It was pretty simple really. There was no real disagreement among us. We just went over the evidence and the evidence said he was guilty. We heard five people there say she wasn't running and that he didn't stop much at that stop sign. What could we do but believe them?"

THREE

The following printed statement was released today by the office of Robert McHenry, commissioner of the Department of Public Works here in Selma:

The Department of Public Works, under the leadership of Robert McHenry, as part of its unceasing efforts to serve the citizens of this area, is launching a suit, filed today in Superior Court, against the Reliable Tire Outlet, of 262 South Street here.

The cause of the suit is the unconscionable problem we are facing here with a shipment of 64 truck tires ordered one year ago for use on large vehicles employed by your DPW. In the year since we made the order, 16 of the tires have leaked air — a satisfactory rate of only 75 percent — well below any acceptable standards. We have removed all 64 tires from our vehicles and are asking them for, in our suit, damages of $9,450 to cover the cost of the tires and the labor involved in installing and removing them, plus $100,000 in punitive damages, so that this company never does likewise to another municipality.

We say that implicit in the contract we signed with Reliable Tire Outlet is the understanding that the tires would be acceptable. When the satisfactory rate is only 75 percent in a year, that is not satisfactory. It is breach of contract, and that is the ground of our suit.

We have tried for two full months to get Reliable Tire Outlet to relieve this problem in gentlemanly fashion. They have said "no." We have, consequently, no choice but the courts.

From interview with Jane Sheraton, president of the Reliable Tire Outlet: "McHenry wants to take this thing to court. Fine. We will say in court the same thing we have been saying in our talks with him and his people: Fourteen of those sixteen tires that leaked were on trucks that frequently visited the East Side Dump. The dirt path to that dump is covered with glass, sharp stones and plenty of old nails. No tires could stand up under such punishment. There is nothing wrong with our tires."

From interview with McHenry: "I'll tell you. When you buy truck tires from people, you got to think you are getting tires that are going to last more than a year. I'll tell you something else, I have never, in my fifteen years in this job, been so angry about a deal we made. She says the problem is the road to the dump. Sure, there's glass and sharp stones and nails on that road. It's a dump. What do you expect, a red carpet? I'll tell you, we bought those tires for "heavy duty use." Those words are used in the contract. We used them heavy duty. They didn't hold up. What did she think she was doing, selling tires for golf carts?"

A visit to the East Side Dump shows there to be many pieces of broken glass, many sharp stones and many nails scattered about on paths seemingly used by trucks.

A reading of the contract for the purchase of the trucks (a copy is provided by McHenry's office) shows the following paragraph:

These tires shall be consistent with standards for heavy duty work by large industrial vehicles.

From a second interview with Sheraton: "Is he talking about golf carts again? My Lord! As I've told McHenry time and time again, heavy duty use for tires does not mean driving them over glass and nails. We sell heavy duty tires — the best you can buy. We do not sell tires made of concrete."

FOUR

Julia Mead-Smith. She is twenty-seven. First day of trial in District Court. Judge Benjamin Roberts presiding. Tried on charges of robbery. Charges say she held up local welfare office — Department of Human Services here in Westport, 4 West Franklin Street, a state office, on September 28 at 3:45 p.m. Charges say that she walked in waving a gun, aimed it at cashier downstairs, that she ran away, that she made off with $768 from cashier . . . was arrested two days later . . . money not found . . . in opening statement District Attorney Shelly Fortrand, 45, the prosecutor, said: "Our case against Miss Mead-Smith rests on the testimony of the two people in the best position to say who robbed the Department of Human Services office here on September 28: the cashier who was robbed and the guard at the door." In his opening statement court-appointed defense attorney James Bronklin, 58, said: "We will show that Ms. Mead-Smith was not anywhere near the welfare office on the afternoon it was robbed. We will show that the two witnesses who claim they saw her there were mistaken." First witness called Susan Bolin, 38, cashier at welfare office. The following from transcript of her testimony:

Fortrand: Mrs. Bolin, what is your profession?
Bolin: I work as a cashier at the Department of Human Services.
Fortrand: Do you remember what happened on the afternoon of September 28th?
Bolin: Sure do. I was sitting at the counter. When this woman comes rushing up to the counter. Didn't take me long to see she had a gun. She said, "You better give me that money, honey, everything you got," in this weird, phonied up voice. I didn't think twice. I was shaking so bad. I just emptied out everything we had in the drawer, lots of fifties and twenties, and gave it to her in a plastic bag. Then she ran out. The whole thing couldn't have taken more than five minutes."
Fortrand: Could you describe the woman?
Bolin: "Well, she was white; she had straight brown hair; dark eyes; must have been about my height, 5'5". I couldn't see her clothes below the counter.
Fortrand: Had you ever seen this woman before?
Bolin: Yup. She was what we call a regular. One of those who never gets off welfare.
Bronklin: Objection, your honor.
Judge Roberts: Mrs. Bolin, please stick to the question.
Bolin: I'd seen her before. She was one of the people I worked with, cashed checks, gave out spending money.
Fortrand: Is this woman in the courtroom now?
Bolin: Yes.

Fortrand: Could you point to her?

Bolin: There. (Points in direction of defendant.)

Fortrand: Did you know this woman by name before you were robbed?

Bolin: I had to. I cashed her checks. Julia Mead-Smith.

Fortrand: No further questions.

Bronklin: Ms. Bolin. This woman you say robbed you. Was she wearing anything unusual?

Bolin: Yup. A mask.

Bronklin: Could you describe that mask please?

Bolin: Well, I don't remember what color it was, but it went from just below her eyes to, well it covered the rest of her face. You know, like the cowboys wear.

Bronklin: So all you saw of this woman was her eyes and her hair?

Bolin: Yup. She was wearing a mask, as I said.

Bronklin: You say she had dark eyes and long brown hair?

Bolin: That's right.

Bronklin: Do you know any other women with dark eyes and long brown hair?

Bolin: Sure, plenty. Hey, wait a second . . .

Bronklin: You say she was about your height, 5'5"?

Bolin: Yup.

Bronklin: You sit on a stool behind the cashier's counter, is that right Ms. Bolin?

Bolin: Right.

Bronklin: You say you couldn't even see this woman's clothes behind the counter, and you were sitting on a stool. How could you tell that she was about your height?

Bolin: Well, after a while you sort of can estimate.

Bronklin: So you sort of estimated her height, is that right?

Bolin: Okay. I guess so.

Bronklin: This long brown hair. How do you know it wasn't a wig?

Bolin: I don't know. Looked real enough to me, but I guess you can't really tell. It all happened so fast and I was nervous, of course.

Bronklin: Ms. Bolin, you say you knew the defendant. Did you like her?

Bolin: Oh, no. None of us do. She always gave us a hard time. Always was trying to get away with something.

Bronklin: So it's fair to say that you had a strong dislike for Julia Mead-Smith before you identified her as the woman who robbed you? Is that correct?

Bolin: Yeah, okay.

Bronklin: No further questions, your honor.

At that point court adjourned until tomorrow. No stories had been written on this case since Mead-Smith's arrest.

▪ C. Story Assignments ▪
---

1. Find a trial in progress at a local courthouse. Sit in on a day's activities at the trial, interview people involved in or familiar with the case, and write a story about events in the trial that day (remembering to include sufficient background on the case).

2. Find the records of civil suits that have been filed recently at a local court. Select an interesting case and write a story about it based on the records and on interviews with people involved in or familiar with the case.

3. How long does it take for cases to move from arrest to trial in a local court? Why does it take that long? What are the consequences of any delay? Write a story on this subject based on research in court records and interviews with people working in and served by the court system.

4. What sentences are people arrested for drunken driving likely to receive in your area? Do sentences vary from town to town? From judge to judge? Is there any connection between the sentence and the background of the defendant? Write a story on this subject based on research in court records and interviews with people at the courts.

CHAPTER 26

Features

Joel Brinkley had never reported overseas when his editors at *The Courier-Journal* in Louisville, Ky., sent him to Thailand in early 1982 to write about the thousands of Cambodian refugees massed in camps along the border. When he received the assignment, Brinkley knew almost nothing of the region's history. He spoke no Cambodian.

But Brinkley had one advantage over reporters who had watched events in the region for years: He had never before witnessed the squalor, the suffering or the starvation he was to find. His senses had not been dulled. And, as an investigative reporter, he possessed a keen ability to observe, to ask and to listen as the survivors spoke of courage, of cruelty and of lost hope.

After two weeks at the camps, Brinkley returned to Louisville. Still weak from a bout with yellow fever, he wrote a series of articles for which he won the Pulitzer Prize in international reporting.

Here is how the first piece began:

Gaunt, glassy-eyed and possessionless, they crouch in the heat amid thousands of others, hungry and diseased. They stoop over small, dry plots of rock-hard soil. And they wait.

They wait in tight lines for hours to get today's ration of food from international relief agencies: a bowl of rice gruel, two bananas, a bucket of brown drinking water.

They wait for doctors to heal them.

Some wait for news of family, though many know their relatives are dead; they remember watching brothers and sisters, parents and children being murdered, or struggling for a final breath before starvation.

They wait for another assault by Thai soldiers who come to rape their women. Or for the Vietnamese troops to launch an all-out offensive that would drive them across the border into Thailand.

And some wait to learn where the next steps in their miserable lives will lead them. Meanwhile they sweat, swat at mosquitoes and inhale the stench of hundreds of thousands of suffering and dying countrymen.

Death and destitution.

Seven million Cambodians have been caught between the two since 1975.

About 3 million are already dead, and many who remain alive could die soon from disease or starvation.

The lucky ones are the million or so Cambodian refugees who escaped the grip of the Communist Khmer Rouge, dodged gunfire from Vietnamese invaders and trekked hundreds of miles with little or no food to sanctuary in refugee camps on the Thai border.

But what kind of sanctuary is it?

For many, it's a rectangle of hard, bare ground the size of a desk top.

It's a plastic sheet for cover, so low overhead that it rubs the noses of some who sleep.

It's the searing odor of sweat, defecation and death. It's the ceaseless buzzing of a million flies and the hack of 10,000 coughs.

It's row upon row of blank-faced sufferers whose futures hold no promise or respite.

Life in a refugee camp is hellish, unbearable. The relief worker who ends his first day wet-eyed can't always blame the choking dust.

But compared with life in Cambodia since 1975, many

refugees say their present plight doesn't seem so bad. . . .*

Good feature writing is impossible without thorough reporting and precise communication. Brinkley heard the buzzing flies, the tubercular coughs, the wails . . . and made his readers hear them. He smelled the stench of raw sewage, of defecation, of dead bodies . . . and made his readers smell them. And he captured the blank faces of the thousands who were squatting on the hard ground.

"I sort of saw myself as a reader," recalls Brinkley, "I wanted readers to feel as if they were standing there, looking, listening and smelling what I was."

Every feature writer should want the same. Whether writing about the misery of starving people or the humor of a circus clown, a feature should challenge a writer to apply the highest level of observation and description.

Observation

It sounds relatively easy: "Just write a feature on that." The pressure of collecting facts on a breaking

event is off. You just have to get the "sense" of things. No problem.

Wrong. Getting the sense of something, as reporters quickly learn, takes at least as much work as getting the basic facts. All good reporters *overreport;* they collect much more information than they actually will use. But this is never more true than in reporting features. Then, writers will sometimes find themselves discarding five, sometimes 10 times as much as they use. That is because observations that speak to essences ("A rectangle of hard, bare ground the size of a desk top" is an example) can be difficult to find.

Look and Listen

During his first few days at the Cambodian camps, Joel Brinkley made no effort to interview the refugees. He just went to the camp and watched. Later, when much of his energy was concentrated on understanding the people and drawing out their stories, he continued to observe, jotting down the most vivid images

* This story is reprinted with the permission of *The Courier-Journal.*

in the margins of his notes at night. The power of his observations gave power to his story. A few pages of Brinkley's notes with those observations, sometimes scribbled in the margins, are reproduced here.

When working on features, reporters recalibrate the built-in-editor they use when taking notes for a deadline story on a speech or news interview. They jot down even seemingly unimportant details, recognizing that just such detail can help build understanding and interest in their story:

SAN DIEGO — They talk with their hands. One hand follows the other, swooping, diving, climbing, turning — the fingertips of one constantly seeking a kill shot on the other wrist.

Reliving the day's flights in the officers club at the Miramar Naval Air Station, fighter pilots are conspicuous — less for their olive drab flight suits or khaki uniforms than for their restless hands . . .

Los Angeles Times

If the observations are not there in a reporter's notebook, no amount of skill in writing can compensate.

Listen and Learn

Feature writers, like all reporters, will be looking for good quotes. More than other reporters, they will need snappy anecdotes.

Their job is not done, though, when they've gotten the lively quotes and telling anecdotes. They have to keep an ear out for deeper meanings that can enable them to step beyond surface appearances. They have to keep listening.

"If a reporter is writing about people readers don't normally know about," Brinkley explains, "he ought to get inside the heads of these people to understand what makes them tick, rather than just settling for recording what they say." Brinkley says it took him days of conversation with the Cambodian refugees before he grasped the essential point that they found their misery in the refugee camps was far preferable to the horror of life in their own country.

Description

Feature stories must live up to the same standards of proof and factuality as news stories (though the rules for attributing states of mind are a bit more liberal — Brinkley writes that the refugees *wait,* not that they *say they wait*). And features use the same language and basic format of news stories — words are simple and precise, sentences direct and concise, and paragraphs short and logically ordered.

How then do features differ? For one thing, they use soft leads (See Chapter 9, Soft Leads), like Brinkley's:

Gaunt, glassy-eyed and possessionless, they crouch in the heat amid thousands of others, hungry and diseased. They stoop over small, dry plots of rock-hard soil. And they wait . . .

Not:

The approximately one million Cambodian refugees who managed to escape the Khmer Rouge and Vietnamese invaders are facing disease and shortages of food in their overcrowded refugee camps in Thailand.

Then, feature stories differ in that they forsake the *inverted pyramid* form used in writing news. Instead, features tend to build to conclusions and to end strong (See Chapter 14, Organization). This is how Brinkley concluded his article on the refugees:

Once they're across the border, many refugees carry two thoughts with them.

Chamm [Peoum] offers the first with passion. "All the people want to kill Pol Pot. We want to kill him very much."

The second comes softly from Theam Den, his eyes downcast. "I can never, never go back to Cambodia. Never again."

And features differ from news stories in a third way: They usually rely much more heavily on description.

Color

Reporters working on features are trying to achieve a particularly intense form of communication with their readers. They frequently want their readers not just to *know* but to *feel*. One direct route to the feelings is through the senses, and good feature writers evoke images that refer to the sensory experiences of readers, bringing these readers to the scene.

Sight (aided here by analogy):

. . . bare ground the size of a desk top.

Touch:

. . . a plastic sheet for cover, so low overhead that it rubs the noses of some who sleep.

Sound:

. . . the ceaseless buzzing of a million flies and the hack of 10,000 coughs.

And smell:

. . . the searing odor of sweat, defecation and death . . .

It seems strange to refer to these grim images from Brinkley's story as "color," but clearly they take readers a step beyond a mere black and white recounting of the politically significant facts. They bring the story to life.

Such descriptions, of course, would not have been possible had Brinkley not put so much energy into observation. And the descriptions would not have been effective had he not communicated them in such simple, direct language (See Chapter 2, Plain English).

UNACCEPTABLE:
Their tawdry plastic sheets sagged precariously over their bodies at a height that frequently left them grazing the very tip of their noses as they lay in repose.

Anecdotes

We have already discussed the use of anecdotes as soft leads to stories (See Chapter 9, Soft Leads). They are equally effective in the body of a feature story. Little stories help make larger stories comprehensible. Here is an anecdote, told mainly through quotes, that Brinkley used to illustrate the horrors that had been inflicted on the Cambodian population by Pol Pot's Khmer Rouge:

Say [Khol], a handsome young man, had been a lieutenant in Lon Nol's army. But when the Khmer Rouge forces approached from Phnom Penh, "I threw away my

uniform, put on clothes to look like an ordinary farmer and tried to leave the city."

The executions had already begun.

"I saw many, many people killed, hit on the back of the neck with a bamboo knife. They threw the bodies into huge, big piles in the middle of the street. I saw my friends in those piles."

"Later, Pol Pot pushed me to Battambang Province (in western Cambodia), where we built a big water tank," Say said. "No machines or tools. Just people. We worked 24 hours a day, seven days a week until it was finished. Many people, old people and young people, they died, dropped while we worked, and we worked around them."

Specificity

Feature writers should frequently remind themselves to avoid abstractions, to make events real, to be specific. Instead of writing about industrial production, they might focus on events in a single steel mill. Instead of writing abstractly about hunger, they might focus on the story of a hungry person. Feature stories usually are most effective when ideas are discussed in terms of the people who hold those ideas and when organizations and movements are discussed in terms of their members.

One of the strengths of Brinkley's series was his constant effort to describe an almost incomprehensible tragedy through a series of real, easily understood images — the plastic sheet rubbing against noses, for example — and through the experiences and words of specific people. Readers may have some difficulty relating to massacres and refugee camps, but they can picture what it is like to live under a plastic sheet and they can sympathize with an individual like Say Khol.

Tone

News stories all have pretty much the same tone; they are straightforward recountings of the facts:

The Department of Housing and Urban Development said yesterday there are 250,000 to 350,000 homeless people in the United States.

New York Times News Service in *The* (Baltimore) *Sun*

Feature stories, however, give their writers the option of selecting whatever tone seems most appropriate to their material. Some tongue-in-cheek humor, for example, seemed called for in this account of efforts to mate two lowland gorillas at the Houston Zoo:

On Wednesday, in their first appearance before the local news media, Vanilla countered Abe's romantic moves with a couple of punches to her 350-pound suitor's head.

Houston Chronicle

A *Boston Globe* writer approached this story on "the new face of work" produced by technological changes with a sense of informed wonder:

This is the first industrial revolution to be covered and analyzed in the newspapers. It is also the first whose agenda has been published in advance.

Short, fast-paced sentences can set the tone, and help bring out the drama, in more emotional stories. This feature accompanied longer news stories on the attempted assassination of then President Gerald Ford:

SACRAMENTO, Calif. — The day was sunny and beautiful, and the tiny woman in red waited with other spectators for President Ford to walk by.
Most of the well-wishers wanted to shake Ford's hand. The woman in red had a gun.

United Press International

Brinkley enhanced this dramatic effect in his series through the use of repetition:

They wait in tight lines. . . .

They wait for doctors. . . .

Some wait for news of family. . . .

They wait for another assault by Thai soldiers. . . .

In choosing a tone, feature writers are establishing their *point of view* in the story—*point of view* in this case meaning perspective, not opinion. In choosing to use humor, the author of the *Houston Chronicle* article expressed a decision to concentrate on the funny aspects of efforts to mate two gorillas in captivity rather than on the brutality or pathos that might conceivably have been found in the situation.

Once they select a tone or point of view for a feature story, reporters must be careful to stick to it. One word in this paragraph of *The Boston Globe* story quoted above seems to violate the story's tone:

For, say, 6000 years, work was mostly a matter between men and the soil; then, for 200 years, it was symbolically a confrontation between men and machines, though, of course, many *folks* still farmed.

The word "folks," which might have been appropriate in a less formally written story, seems too colloquial amidst the knowing historical pronouncements here. (The word *men* is objectionable for an entirely different reason—*women* have worked, too.) A feature should not suddenly switch from informed wonder to folksiness or from humor to drama.

Another way to go wrong is to lay it on too thick.

WEAK:
. . . Vanilla, no loose woman she, countered Abe's ape-like romantic moves, made with all the subtlety of a bulldozer, with a couple of well-placed punches to her

350-pound Romeo's love-addled head. It looked more like tag-team wrestling than romance.

Types

Features are opportunities for reporters to step back from breaking events and to concentrate on the people and issues behind those events, to step back from the insistent and timely and to focus on the offbeat and timeless. The main account of the death of 35 illegal aliens abandoned in the desert without water would be written as a news story. But a survivor's recollection of events would be written as a feature, so might follow-up stories on the routes taken by illegal aliens, on the problems faced by border patrol officers, on the hardships encountered by aliens even if they succeed in their journey, on the legislative confusion over how to handle illegal immigration and on a legendary person who guides illegal aliens across the border.

Profiles

A *profile* is a portrait of a person in words. Like the best painted portraits, the best profiles capture the character, spirit and style of their subjects. They delve beneath the surface to look at what motivates people, what excites them, what makes them interesting. The problem is that lives are hard to fit into newspaper articles, no matter how much space is allotted for them.

Reporters who simply try to cram into a profile all the facts they can come up with inevitably end up with something more like a résumé than a story.

UNACCEPTABLE:
Laurel Coburn has operated The Tea Shop on Smith Street for 28 years. She has lived in Weston her entire life and graduated from high school here before enrolling in Smith College in 1951. It was there, as a magna cum laude English major, that she first developed an interest in tea.

Like all other stories, profiles have to have an angle, a primary theme (See Chapter 8, Hard Leads). That theme should be introduced in the lead, it should be explored, and often it will be returned to at the end of the story. Something of a person's character, spirit and style will then be revealed through that theme.

Often the theme of the profile will be obvious the moment it is assigned. This woman is in the news for one reason: She sells machine guns.

SALEM, Va. (UPI) — The first thing you notice when you enter Joan Davis' office is her friendly smile. Then you see the machine guns.

The (Memphis, Tenn.) *Commercial Appeal*

Through an exploration of her interest in machine guns (done mainly through quotes), the writer is able to give readers insights into this 38-year-old mother of four:

"I absolutely love it but I look crazy sometimes," Ms. Davis said, referring to the stares she draws when moving the guns from her office to a bank vault. "It's about like fishing. If you ever get into it, it doesn't let go of you."

The craftsmanship and history of each weapon are what fascinate her, not the gun's destructive capability.

"A lot of people think you're dealing with instruments of death," she said. "I don't look at it that way at all. People who collect old cars don't think of them as things to travel in, they consider them as pieces of history, and that's the way I feel about machine guns . . ."

At other times, the theme will require some thought. It would be easy in profiling peace-activist David Dellinger to write a stereotypical article about one man against the system. But what interested Henry Allen in this profile for *The Washington Post* was how Dellinger, son of a Republican lawyer, and president of his high school class, had fought for radical change with an idealism consistent with the American way. Here is how his piece began:

Mom.
Apple pie.
David Dellinger.
At 64, after 40 years of astonished, saddened insistence that the American capitalist system is madness; after three years in jail for refusing to fight in World War II; after countless hunger strikes, sit-ins, arrests and visits to Cuba, Hanoi and China; after helping lead the anti-Vietnam-War movement, and after returning to this little hotel lobby at 10th and H streets NW following his address at the No-Nukes rally on the Mall, David Dellinger is All-American.

It takes a thorough understanding of a person's life to create a revealing sketch of that life. If they are given the opportunity, reporters will want to spend time with their subjects in their private as well as their public lives. In this profile of stripper Tempest Storm, William Burrows led his readers backstage:

When she first appeared, the woman might have been dressed for an inaugural ball, looking and moving with the controlled grace that is often called "class."

But she is perspiring under the spotlight now, and if those watching from the darkness have noticed, they do not care. The black, full-length coat, the velvet gown, gloves, rhinestone necklace and fur stole have been discarded, leaving the woman in a white negligee. Three musicians grind out "Stormy Weather," which is her song, as the negligee—almost all that is left to separate her from the people in the darkness—slips off her shoulders.

The people have been waiting to see that negligee fall away, so its removal is celebrated with loud applause and some whistling. They look up at her body with varying degrees of appreciation as she sways and twists with the piano, saxophone and drums for a few seconds more.

Lips that glisten a moist, mandarin orange part and smile warmly back at faces her dark blue eyes can barely see. She is absorbing the applause like a sun worshipper basking in the heat, knowing that she has brought her audience to its peak just moments before the curtain takes her away, leaving the people out there alone again.

Then Tempest Storm, the reigning queen of a dying art, picks up her clothes, climbs to a small, electric blue and white room, and drops onto a folding bed whose soiled sheet is marked with a predecessor's lipstick. She uses a tissue to mop the perspiration from her face and from under her long, red hair, while a single fan tries to dislodge thick dust and push around hot, stale air.

The Wall Street Journal

Good profiles are spiced with the words of family, friends, enemies and the subjects themselves. Tempest Storm told Burrows she had little use for the explicit sex of X-rated films:

"I think taking off all your clothes—and I've never taken off all my clothes—is not only immoral but boring. There has to be something left to the imagination . . ."

In a profile of another master of a dying art, Burrows talked to the wife of Hungarian-born Vincent Nemeth to capture the passion Nemeth held for making barrels.

"Working on barrels doesn't pay much," says Mrs. Nemeth, "but with Vincent, it's a labor of love. My Vincent is a barrel nut."

The Wall Street Journal

Sidebars

It's snowing. It's been snowing for six hours already. Twelve inches on the ground, and the storm shows no signs of letting up. The weather bureau is now predicting that 18 to 22 inches will collect on city streets before the storm finally moves up the coast. The previous record snowfall here was 20 inches.

A storm of this magnitude clearly deserves a hard news story—detailing how much has fallen and is likely to fall in various parts of town and summarizing the effects of the snow on the city. But along with this news story—the *mainbar*—editors will assign a series of *sidebars*—stories discussing in detail one aspect of the larger story. One sidebar might consider people stranded at local airports and hotels; another might investigate, using clips and reference materials, the other large snowstorms that have hit the city. A third sidebar might focus on people who make money from a storm—snow shovelers and plowers; another might look into why weather patterns have been unusual this winter.

Most sidebars are written as feature stories. The mainbar here was about a primary election in Tennessee. The sidebar began this way:

It was something, said Dwight Foster, that he had always wanted to do.

At 24, however, he had just never gotten around to it. But yesterday he took off from work at a local steak house and went to the Waverly Belmont School here and exercised his franchise.

He pulled the lever next to the Rev. Jesse Jackson's name, adding another vote to the Chicago minister's tally . . .

The Philadelphia Inquirer

Backgrounders

The story has been in the news. Readers have heard about the confrontation between the British prime minister and the coal miners, but the hard news stories have not allowed reporters much chance to write about the historical background of the dispute. To add depth to readers' understanding, a *backgrounder* was assigned. Like sidebars, backgrounders are usually written as features:

LONDON — There is an old saying here that British politicians should not tangle with three institutions. One is the monarchy. Another is the church. And the third is the British coal miner.

Coal's centuries-old role in British energy and the miners' militant tradition has turned their periodic confrontations with British governments into dramatic struggles. Those struggles frequently upset economic policies, and in 1974 a miners' strike for higher wages brought down the Conservative government of Prime Minister Edward Heath, by forcing him to call an election, which he lost.

Despite these risks of tangling with the miners, Prime Minister Margaret Thatcher is making it abundantly clear that she is willing to take them on rather than back away from a policy of layoffs and a growing number of mine closings intended to revitalize the state-owned coal industry . . .

The New York Times

Reporters might be assigned to write a backgrounder on the safety record of nuclear power during an ongoing dispute over a nuclear power plant. They might be assigned a backgrounder explaining exactly what the Consumer Price Index is at a time when increases in the index are making news. Backgrounders rely heavily on research. They may be the closest reporting comes to scholarship.

News Features

If researchers at a local university make a major discovery today about the causes of cancer, that would be a hard-news story in tomorrow's paper. But if a reporter decides to look into new approaches to cancer research at several institutions — even though there has been no major discovery — that story, a *news feature,* could run tomorrow or it could run a month from tomorrow. Such a story is newsworthy, but it needn't appear on any particular day. It is looking at a trend, rather than at a breaking event. This is probably the major factor that distinguishes news features from hard news.

News features are used to investigate subjects that simmer instead of exploding. They may take on one of the larger issues of the day — abortion or drug use, perhaps — or they may focus on changes in lifestyle — from the spread of break dancing to the "gentrification" of Hoboken, N.J.

HOBOKEN, N.J. — In this town of steel-toed work shoes, shot-and-a-beer taverns and an occasional beehive hairdo, the invasion of the quiche-eaters continues.

Lured by rows of relatively inexpensive brownstones convenient to Manhattan, young professionals and artists have been moving in droves to the left bank of the Hudson River. And Hoboken, which some local residents look upon with pride as perhaps the least fashionable city in the country — if not all of New Jersey — is becoming positively trendy.

The New York Times

Human Interest

Profiles paint pictures of individuals. Human-interest stories, or slice-of-life stories, tell about particularly interesting circumstances in people's lives. A child's 100-mile walk to raise money for the Muscular Dystrophy Foundation is a human-interest story, so is a man's decision to donate one kidney to an ailing twin or a fireman's rescue of three children from a burning building. Human-interest stories often can be written either as hard news or as features. But stories about human beings' aspirations and achievements usually are more interesting when a feature approach is used.

WEAK:

A 14-year-old Odessa girl walked 100 miles in the last three days in order to raise $4,500 for the Muscular Dystrophy Foundation.

BETTER:

Mindy Sackler says she's already forgotten the blisters, the muscle cramps, the endless roads.

Yesterday the 14-year-old 9th grader sat exhausted in the rain for nearly 45 minutes after finishing a 100-mile, three-day walk that took her from the high school hockey field in suburban Odessa to a ranger station in the wilds of Stockton State Park.

Today she was fresh and smiling as she presented a check for $4,500 to the Muscular Dystrophy Foundation, compliments of 112 friends and supporters, some of whom were betting she couldn't finish . . .

Brighteners

Newswriting can be awfully solemn. As their name implies, brighteners are designed to provide relief from the earthquakes, crimes, fires and recessions that often seem to fill the papers. Their goal is usually to elicit a smile if not a laugh.

The world, fortunately, is filled with potential brighteners: hot-chili-eating contests, attempts to set a record for non-stop pingpong playing, parakeets that escape and then fly back home, mock presidential elections in elementary schools, a Halloween parade.

In the first part of this century, many newspapers would mix in a few short brighteners to lighten up their front pages. *The New York Times* once ran a short front-page story about the president being hit by a pea.

Like all feature stories, brighteners are opportunities for reporters to loosen up, to show a little style, to experiment. If reporters are self-critical enough to throw their failed experiments in the garbage, their successful experiments can add charm and humor to a newspaper.

Here's the start of a brightener about a raccoon who became a regular visitor to the apartment of a former police detective:

In the early-morning darkness, the masked burglar huddled on a ledge outside the open window. Slowly, stealthily, he parted the drawn drapes and slipped silently into the room.

Little did he know he was walking into the presence of a man who, in 24 years of service with the State Police, had captured many a midnight marauder.

Little did he care.

In fact, Roscoe the Raccoon didn't even notice the astonished occupant of the East Greenbush apartment . . .

That was two months ago . . . Roscoe has been dropping in two or three nights a week ever since . . .

(Albany, N.Y.) *Times Union*

Additional Reading

A Treasury of Great Reporting, eds. Louis L. Snyder and Richard B. Morris, Simon & Schuster, 1962.

Best Newspaper Writing 1985 (1984, 1983, 1982), ed. Roy Peter Clark, The Modern Media Institute, St. Petersburg, Florida.

How I Wrote the Story, ed. Christopher Scanlon, *Providence Journal,* 1983.

On Writing Well, 2nd edition, William Zinsser, Harper & Row, 1980.

■ A ■

Go to one of the following places and spend a few hours there as a *passive* observer. Ask no questions, but take notes on what you see, smell and hear.

1. A hospital emergency ward
2. A local welfare office
3. City hall
4. A police station
5. A park
6. A busy store
7. A factory
8. An athletic team's practice
9. The lingerie department of a store
10. A pawn shop
11. A church on Sunday
12. A 3rd-grade classroom
13. A dance school
14. A gymnasium
15. A disco

■ B ■

Write down a list of features you might write if the following events took place in your town.

1. A tornado tears through a trailer park, killing two people.
2. Unemployment rises 2 percent in town to 10 percent overall.
3. A water-main break leaves Main Street without electrical power for two days.
4. Next week is Halloween.
5. A girl from the local high school wins the Miss Teen-age America Pageant.
6. The Federal Aviation Administration issues a report saying training and safety standards at many airports around the country are subpar. Assume there is a small airport in your county.
7. Drought damages the corn crop in the area.
8. The mayor proposes a plan to develop the waterfront.
9. The mayor proposes an ordinance to ban garage sales in town.
10. Town to celebrate its 100th birthday.

■ C ■

Write a profile of one of the following people.

1. A chimney sweep
2. A stamp collector
3. A bird watcher
4. A long-distance runner
5. A disc jockey
6. A bartender
7. An airplane pilot
8. A magician

9. A person on welfare
10. A police officer
11. A housewife
12. An undertaker
13. A garbage man
14. A professional musician
15. A pool shark

▪ D. Story Assignments ▪

Write stories based on the following assignments.

1. Assume a local police officer shot and killed a suspect in a minor crime. Write a sidebar on local police regulations for using guns.
2. Write a human interest story on the strange things local garbage collectors find in people's garbage.
3. Write a seasonal brightener about a local resident who takes on the role of Santa Claus or the Easter Bunny.
4. Assume a local zoning board has decided to allow industrial development in a previously all residential area. Write a backgrounder on the history of local planning and zoning.
5. Write a news feature on the problem of teen-age pregnancy locally.

▪ E. Writing Assignments ▪

Write feature stories based on each of the following collections of information. In each case you are writing for a newspaper dated tomorrow and read in the town where the events occurred.

ONE

It's summer and it's hot—been in the low 90s for three days. Local boy, aged 11, Danton Roberts, 33 Randolph Street, in Delmore, set up a stand in front of his house yesterday. He's selling fresh orange and grapefruit and carrot juice. Uses parents' juice maker, charges 50 cents per glass, 8 ounces in glass. Says this is his first business venture. It's working. Randolph Street is a through street to Delmore's downtown business district. Plenty of shop owners and shoppers drive and walk by. Yesterday Roberts made $21. Today he's made $16.50 by 2 p.m. He says he paid $9.65 for both days' supply of fruit and carrots, thinks he'll have enough to last until end of day ("My parents don't charge for the juice maker"). Sign on his table reads: "Fresh Juice—Cheap." He's rigged up an orange and yellow pool umbrella to keep off the direct sun.

Roberts in an interview: "I thought this over carefully, but I never thought I'd be this busy. I might keep going all summer. My first thought was how hot and thirsty everybody standing at the bus stop at the corner looked. So I figured I'd set up a lemonade stand. Ya know. There's always these cute stories about kids selling lemonade. But I thought, 'Who do I know who really likes lemonade? It's either too sour or it's half sugar.' So I decided on fresh juices. Everybody seems to like it well enough. What will I do with the money? That depends on how long I stay at it. I've already got enough for a new video game cartridge but I might save up for a new bike."

Roberts says he and his family are health conscious. He says there are lots of joggers in the area and some of them have been customers in the evening. So have his friends, but about half his customers are drivers who stop when they see the sign. Roberts is "almost 5 feet tall," has dark brown hair that hangs in bangs over his forehead, wears blue jeans, running shoes and a tee shirt reading: "I love nature."

At 2:05 two customers are lined up. One is Mildred Kaye, 31, of 14B Bothels Way on the west end of town. She works part-time at Andrews Antiques three blocks away on River Road and catches the 2:20 p.m. bus at Randolph and Perkins, a half block away. Kaye, smiling: "I guess you could call me a regular. Yesterday I bought the orange. Today I think I'll be really brave and try the carrot. No, I don't drink carrot juice at home. But you don't have to be a health food nut to want a cool drink after walking up from River Road. My boss may have to sell me as an antique if this heat keeps up. Maybe I can convince this kid to sell fans to the bus company as well."

Second person buys an orange juice, waves away questions and drives off in car by curb. "Need those vitamin Cs man. It's a busy world," he says.

TWO

Guess who is playing second base for Kennedy High School's varsity baseball team? Christine, that's right, Christine Malley. And Christine Malley, your editor has just informed you, is to be the subject of a feature you are to write this evening.

You stop at the athletic director's office on the way to the practice field at Kennedy, and, wouldn't you know it, they've put out a press release. It reads:

Kennedy High School's Athletic Director Richard Mooney announced today that Junior Christine Malley has made the school's varsity baseball team and will be the starting second baseman in the side's first contest, against Johnson Industrial High, next week.

Miss Malley, who survived tough competition for the squad, under the leadership of Coach Rod Saunders, will be the first female to play on a varsity baseball team in the history of the state.

End of release. Before you left the newsroom, you checked through the clips and called the state education department. She *is* the first in baseball. A girl named Virginia Rogers played on Wheatley High School's varsity *basketball* team for two weeks in 1983 before she quit the team.

There's the team, all decked out in the school's colors—purple shirts and white pants. And there's Malley fielding grounders to the right of second base, her uniform fitting snuggly. You watch for a few minutes. She handles seven balls . . . makes no errors. Talks a lot on the field, too. In those few minutes you hear her say, "This one's mine." "Hit it to me will ya." "Look alive everybody." "Come on, try to get one by me." "Can't you hit 'em any harder than that?"

You head for the man with the gray hair. Here's what Coach Rod Saunders, 5′6″, 47, has to say: "Hi, you know you're the first reporter that's come by. Look, my position on this was simple: I simply chose the best men, oh, I mean the best peoples, ah persons, for the team. I had talked to her gym teachers. I knew she could pick it, but she had to prove it during the tryout and she did. Made my decision yesterday. Do you see her out there? She's really something. A real pepper pot. Keeps the whole team alive with her chatter."

You ask the coach who the second-string second baseman is, and you head for him, by the batting cage. Name, John Accosta, senior; says he started all last year, doesn't seem anxious to talk with you: "Coach thinks this lady's better than me, okay? What am I gonna say? We finished 12 and 8 with me out there last year. Let's see how we do with the lady, okay? That's all I got to say."

You wander out to the outfield and find starting shortstop and number three hitter Ted Mostrieli shagging flies. Mostrieli: "I have nothing bad to say about her. Can she handle the pivot on the double play? Yes. Can she go get balls in the hole? Yes. Me and Johnny felt like a real comfortable team out there. But I guess me and Christine will do fine, too. I tell ya, she is one tough little woman. And I'll tell you something else, too: If anybody on another team says anything nasty to Christine, there are gonna be quite a few of us who are going to quiet them down."

You can hear her chatter louder now: "Throw that ball." "Let's see some hustle." "Come on, hit it to me." You watch her for a while and again she fields without errors, gracefully. Then she starts walking toward the batting cage, and you get ready to watch her swing.

She looks less comfortable hitting: mostly ground balls, one fly to short center that Mostrieli catches easily. You walk back over to Mostrieli and ask about her hitting. "That's a problem," he says.

You walk over to the coach and ask the same question. Saunders: "Well, we're batting her at the end of the order, and we don't need much production from the number nine spot. But Christine is going to have to work on her hitting."

Practice is ending and you catch up with Malley as she heads toward the locker room. "These last few days must have been pretty exciting for you," you say.

"Sure have, and now I'm having the time of my life." Malley, who says she is 16, looks to be about 5'5". She has light brown skin, dark brown eyes and black, curly hair.

"Where did you learn how to play?"

"My dad taught me, though he died when I was 10. Been playing baseball with the boys in the lot down the block since I was 7. Played little league with the boys, too."

"Why did you decide to do this?"

"Cause I love baseball. There wasn't much thrill playin' intramural softball with the girls last year. I think I batted about .990. These guys can play and I think I can play with them."

"Anybody give you any trouble?"

"I got plenty of dirty looks when I showed up for the tryout. Got some more when Saunders announced I made the team. But a lot of the guys congratulated me, and nobody's said anything."

You're getting near the locker rooms, so you ask the obvious question.

"Hey, Saunders says he'll arrange for me to use the girls locker to change everywhere we go."

And finally: "Having some trouble hitting this pitching?"

"Working on it. I'm working on it."

While you're waiting outside the locker for Malley to shower and change, you meet Al Reynolds, a senior here, who you soon learn is her boyfriend. You ask him how he feels about all this:

Reynolds: "Great, great, think it's great. I'm not much of an athlete myself, but Christine's good at it, and she deserves to play with the best. I've never seen her so happy as last night after she got the news." Malley comes out, wearing black pants and a metallic green blouse, and you ask if she sees this as an important step for women. Malley: "I'm glad if this will help some other girl somewhere, but I gotta say I did it for me. I wanted to play, and now I'm playing. What could be better?"

"You make a lot of noise out there."

"Love the game. I really get into it. Look, I'm having the time of my life."

Malley and Reynolds walk off together. You go to a pay phone and call her mother, Sally Malley, 43. Mrs. Malley: "Of course, I'm happy for her. I would never keep her from doing what she wants to do. She's always been a strong-willed girl. She gets what she wants. She's also always loved baseball. Can't say any of this surprises me."

Finally, you visit Mr. Mooney, 46, in his office. "Did this cause any problem for you?" you ask.

"Life is full of problems. Life is full of change, too. Out with the old, in with the new. Go with the flow. These aren't the 1950s. The girl wanted to play. Coach Saunders says she was good. Her grades are okay. Who am I to stand in her way?"

"Did you consult with the district's attorney?"

"Hey, there's no law problem here. This is baseball. This is modernity; the new generation; women's lib; femininity. No chauvinist pigs in this school. I didn't ask anybody's permission. Just got to read the papers. The times are changing. McKerney saw the press release and he said, 'good job, Mooney.' Told my wife last night and she said, 'Good job, Mooney.' So I guess all Mooney's done is a good job."

You head back to the newsroom hoping you won't start writing like Mooney talks. One last call to Supt. Gene McKerney at home to get the following: "We support the girl 100 percent. We support Coach Saunders 100 percent. And we support Mr. Mooney 100 percent. I personally think this is a wonderful development."

Now you write . . . for tomorrow's paper.

THREE

Stats out today . . . unemployment up 1 percent nationwide in last month . . . call unemployment office in town . . . get name of man laid off this month for feature on human side of statistics. . . . unemployment center director Jill Roberts: "Joseph Schwartz is the kind of man we love to help, and the kind of man it hurts not to be able to help. He is supposed to come in here once a week; sometimes he comes when he doesn't have to just to check to see if we have any jobs." She says Schwartz was fired from the Hastings Pipe factory in town three weeks ago.

Bob Hastings, president of the company, on the phone: "No, I don't know Joseph Schwartz by name. Why did we fire him? Same reason we fired 146 other workers this month. We ain't selling enough pipes. Our orders were down 43 percent last month from the same month a year ago. I ain't running a charity, and frankly I can't say chances are good these folks are going to get their jobs back."

Schwartz okays an interview. Sitting in living room of small, Cape Cod style house. Has beard, blond hair, blond beard, no hair on top of head, says he is 6'6", looks it, says he is 36. Schwartz: "I have never been fired from a job in my life. I worked at that factory for nine years, before then I did some traveling in Europe and the States. We knew business was bad but no one expected this. Why am I so gung ho on finding a new job? Because I have three young kids: Jeremy, 4, Theodore, 2, and Katherine, 3 months. We haven't saved anything recently. I'm not saying we're going to starve, but I got to build a family." Schwartz's wife, Susan, 36, enters the room with a baby. Her husband continues: "One of us has got to find a job soon, and Susan is breast feeding the baby. It's too early for her to go to work. I've been to every factory in the area. They all say they're firing not hiring. I'll take anything at this point." Susan Schwartz: "We're not trying to get sympathy. We're not starving. There's plenty of food in the house. My parents have helped us out some. I have diapers for the two little ones. But you've got to buy new clothes, school things. We believe in nursery school. We may want summer camps, someday. We just want to live normal lives, and this sort of throws those plans out the window, in a sense."

Next day . . . with Schwartz as he visits local supermarket that advertised packing job . . . ten people on line for interview . . . while on line Schwartz says: "You know, when I was a kid, I thought work was a joke. I traveled and lived off my wits. But, this hurts me. I look at those kids and this hurts me. What kind of a father am I if I can't buy them what they want?" Man in front of Schwartz on line turns to him and jokes: "I hear they're paying packers $40 an hour here." Schwartz: "Yeah, and expense account lunches, business trips to Paris, retirement at full salary at the age of 55." Schwartz's turn to interview comes and he learns they are paying $6.50 an hour. Made $10.50 an hour at Hastings. Schwartz, while walking home: "Fun, looking for a job, huh? Looking for a job is the worst job I've ever had in my life. Begging, I always feel like I'm begging. Asking for favors. All these lines. I want to go to work in the morning, that's all, and come home every week with a little pay check. Look, I believe that the economy will turn around. Has to, right? I'll find something, or I'll move. We don't own our house. I'll rent in Dallas or Phoenix or Kuwait." Walking slower as he gets close to home. Walks in door. Susan Schwartz: "So? What happened? " Joseph Schwartz: "What always happens. They said I should call tomorrow. I'll call tomorrow. Anything else in the paper this morning?" Next day on phone Schwartz says that he called and that he did not get the supermarket packing job. Call to Kile Dobson of Fresh and Fast Supermarket, who is in charge of hiring and who says:

"Yes, I remember the tall guy. He was nice. I liked him. But the guy we hired seemed really excited. Can't hire everyone can you?"

▪ PART SIX ▪

Specialized Coverage

CHAPTER 27

Municipal services

Some newspapers do little more in reporting on municipal services than to react to crises—a drought cuts water supplies, a building collapses, garbage collectors go on strike or a snowstorm ties up the city. Readers deserve more than this mad scramble, under deadline pressure, to figure out what went wrong.

If the press is to be a watchdog on government, the basic services provided by government should be high on the list of things worth watching. Day in and day out, little that governments do has as much effect on citizens as such municipal services as garbage collection, public transportation, street and highway maintenance, housing inspection and regulation, park operations and the supply of water.

On smaller papers, the important task of covering these services may be left to already overburdened city hall reporters (See Chapter 23, Government and Politics). Larger papers may assign a reporter specifically to the transportation beat or to housing. General assignment reporters pick up the rest.

Sources

All municipal services should be reported from the inside, that is, through interviews with officials and workers, and from the outside, through interviews with the people who regularly use and are affected by those services.

Many of these "inside" sources can be found in the same building—city hall, the municipal building—

as sources for political or governmental stories, but they tend to inhabit smaller offices. A reporter will probably want to visit the mayor for a comment on a story about the city's failure to fill last winter's potholes, but the head of the Department of Public Works will know more about the story, as might the DPW's purchasing agent, its public information officer (if there is one) and the men and women who drive the trucks and lift the shovels.

Reporters responsible for evaluating government's performance in providing these basic services will want to know their way around all levels of the sanitation department or the traffic, transportation, parks, health or housing departments. Housing or health inspectors, for example, are in a particularly good position to be helpful, as are the scientists who test the quality of local water or the engineers who check the safety of bridges. Their jobs are to evaluate services, and although their work is not always publicized, they may have the most precise answers to reporters' questions.

It is also wise to cultivate sources in the county, state and federal governments as well as at city hall. County, state and federal officials are themselves responsible for maintaining some services (some roads and parks, for example) and for evaluating the city's performance on others (water quality, for example).

Remember, government officials won't always be the best or most honest judges of the quality of the services their governments provide. Citizens groups and professional organizations that monitor services offer a different and valuable perspective. Reporters covering traffic and transportation will want to know the leaders of the local AAA as well as representatives of commuter groups that might be affected by changes in bus lines, construction of roadways or new schedules for commuter trains. When reporting on housing, landlords, tenant groups and community activists are essential sources. And these are areas in which individual citizens, too, can be of invaluable assistance. The sanitation commissioner can explain why Wednesday garbage pickups were ended. The head of the local community association can protest. But the best quotes on the effects of that decision are likely to come from some frustrated homeowner who is staring at a collection of overstuffed garbage cans at about 6 o'clock Wednesday evening.

Records

The reports filed by city inspectors after they check the safety of buildings or elevators, the sanitary conditions in restaurants, or the quality of air or water can be a fertile source of stories about municipal services. The findings of these inspections are announced only sporadically, but they are available to reporters. They can lead, for example, to stories about an outbreak of food poisoning at a local restaurant or a landlord who has shut off the heat at a nearby housing project.

Inspection reports also provide evidence of how well—or how poorly—health and safety standards are being enforced. Before examining the reports, find out what inspections are required under state and local statutes and when they must be carried out. It may turn out that the building or restaurant or elevator that has *not* been inspected in a decade is more newsworthy than the building, restaurant or elevator that's been cited for minor violations of code. The question may become, "Why hasn't it been inspected?" and "Who owns it?" The potential for graft is evident here.

There are other records municipal reporters will have occasion to pore through: maintenance records of city buses, records of public hearings (a good place to look for potential sources), hiring records and, of course, ordinances, zoning variances and budgets (See Chapter 23, Government and Politics). The city or town clerk should know where most of these are filed in a smaller municipality. In larger cities, reporters may have to search out the records at each department.

Basic Stories

The municipal services beat is not without its breaking news. Sometimes these services cause contro-

versy. Sometimes they break down. And the public also has to be told about efforts to keep them in shape.

Controversy

Black clergymen said yesterday they will "jump the tracks" of subways during the morning rush hour Wednesday to protest what they call a lack of minority representation in the search for a new head of the Metropolitan Transportation Authority.

(New York) *Daily News*

Such controversies should automatically send reporters off in search of the other side, in the case of this *Daily News* story that meant a spokesman for the governor:

The spokesman said the governor is considering two minority candidates for the MTA post and that "if Rev. Sharpton [one of the leaders of the protest] has the name of one or more candidates, the governor would be personally delighted to review the qualifications."

Breakdowns

That same day the *Daily News* ran another breaking story about a municipal service. In this case the news was that something had gone wrong:

A 12-inch water main beneath 28th Street and Eighth Avenue burst early yesterday, disrupting subway service and cutting off water to dozens of businesses in a one-block area.

(New York) *Daily News*

Since the basic services governments provide—sanitation, transportation, water—are so crucial to readers' lives, the extent as well as the location and time of the interruption in service becomes a crucial part of these stories. The *Daily News* reporter considered these questions in his lead and then again in later paragraphs:

Yesterday's water main break spilled hundreds of gallons of water onto uptown subway tracks on the IND Eighth Avenue line. A Transit Authority spokesman said local trains were rerouted onto express tracks between West Fourth Street and 34th Street, bypassing the 14th Street stations, between 6:20 a.m. and 7 a.m. . . .
Arturo Lopez, of 213 W. 28th St., one of the few residents on the block, said he was forced to take buckets to a nearby hydrant to get water. "The situation could have been worse," he said. "At least most of the businesses on this block are closed for the weekend."

"Why" is always an important question when the government or its equipment fails:

[Department of Environmental Protection spokesman Andrew] McCarthy said the cause of the break was not immediately known, but he noted that "traffic and subway vibrations, combined with the old age of some of the mains, is the usual diagnosis in that part of Manhattan."

Projects

Alongside these controversies and calamities, the municipal services beat has its share of news stories that inform readers about the plans for, or progress of, municipal projects—the digging of a new municipal well, rebuilding of a playground or the improvement of a road:

The facelift of U.S. 31 in Hoover is half complete and should be finished in April, according to the Alabama Highway Department.

The Birmingham (Ala.) *News*

These stories must be covered—people need to know when they can expect some improvement in traffic on U.S. 31. But reporters interested in government services must also find the time to dig deeper.

Enterprise

It is not possible to measure the adequacy and efficiency of municipal services merely by writing about subway protests, water main breaks and highway improvements. Here are three basic questions reporters might pursue to get beyond such disconnected events:

How Have Things Changed?

Is service better or worse than it was? If available, statistics are an important starting point for such investigations, though they must be elucidated and illuminated with interviews and observation. Has traffic on local roads increased or decreased in recent years? Are parks used more or less frequently? Is mass transit more or less reliable?

Service on the New York City subway system deteriorated last month to what appears to be the lowest level on record. More than three times as many trains either failed to leave their terminals or broke down en route this January as in January 1977, according to Transit Authority data.

The New York Times

The news isn't always bad:

A $1 parking fee, new permit rules and a new gate were successful in decreasing traffic and other problems at Willamete Park last summer, city and neighborhood association officials said yesterday.

The (Portland) *Oregonian*

How Are Services Perceived?

Compare the points of view of officials in charge of services and inspections with those of the people whose homes and businesses are being affected. Such an effort often will uncover wildly conflicting points of view. Good reporters try to verify who is correct through further research, but even the feelings themselves can provide the basis of a lively story:

The elderly who once spent much of their time in their neighborhood parks now sit on benches at their perimeters and say the dirt disgusts them and those who use the parks frighten them. Young people say they have known the parks only as disreputable gathering spots and see no reason to protect or preserve them.

The New York Times

How Do Conditions Vary?

Are parking regulations the same in upper-class, middle-class and poorer areas of town? Are streets plowed as quickly and maintained as well? Are building codes enforced as strictly?

Despite the fact that there are more people on the West Side, there are fewer sanitation men and trucks than on the East Side and only three pickups a week compared to five on the East Side.

The Westsider (a weekly in New York City)

Story Approaches

Here are some more specific questions that might be worth pursuing for each type of municipal service:

Transit

1. What proportion of funding is local, and what proportion is state or federal?
2. If a transit company is privately owned, what is its history? Who is on the board of directors? What firm provides its insurance (and who owns the insurance companies)?
3. What is the local history of fares, and what are the procedures for increasing fares?
4. How many people work for the company, and how does their pay compare with that at other companies?
5. What is the system's safety history, and how does it compare with that of similar transit systems?
6. How old is the equipment and what percentage of the time is it out of commission?
7. How often are the buses, trains or subways late and by how much? How frequently do they run?
8. What percentage of riders use the system during rush hour? What percentage of revenue is derived

from rush-hour fares? (Off-peak fares are lower, so these two percentages are not always the same.)

Sanitation

1. If the system is public, what is its operating budget and how much is it costing taxpayers? How do costs compare with those of neighboring communities? Ask a leading private firm what it would charge to pick up the area's garbage.
2. If the system is private, how is the franchise awarded? Is there usually more than one bidder?
3. What is the average daily pickup per truck (in tons)? How many workers are on each truck? How frequent are pickups?
4. What disposal system is used? If there is a town dump, are there any problems with odor or pollution of nearby water sources? Has it had an effect on property values? Is there enough room?
5. Has the town made any effort to recycle garbage? If so, has it been successful?

Traffic

1. Who is empowered to enforce traffic rules? Who decides where to put up signs?
2. Are traffic signs effective? Locating misleading or inaccurate signs can make a good news feature. If signs are missing, how long does it take to replace them?
3. Who decides where to put traffic lights? What input does the public have into the system (parents groups are chronic complainers about the inadequate lights near schools and playgrounds)?
4. Are there chronic traffic problems? What can be done? Ask experts. What is being done? Ask officials.
5. Is there sufficient parking? Do merchants believe that customers have easy access to the business district?
6. Where are the trouble spots in town? Are there bad curves or intersections that have been the scene of an unusual number of accidents?
7. Does traffic cause air pollution problems downtown? Have any planning studies been undertaken to improve the flow of traffic?

Water

1. Is the supply well water or surface water? Are the watershed or the wellfields (the places the water comes from) protected from pollutants?
2. What are the system's reserves? Are they adequate? In case of drought, how long could the system hold up?
3. What chemicals are tested for in the water? Does the water meet or surpass mandated federal or state standards?
4. How many inspectors are there to check the watershed and make sure it is pollution free?
5. What are the charges for water use and how do they compare with those of neighboring communities? Is the water company publicly or privately owned?
6. How is the water treated? What levels of chlorine and fluoride are added?
7. How old are the treatment plants and the lines? How much water is being lost to leaks throughout the system?

Public Works

1. Does the town have regular programs to fill potholes, to clean culverts (roadway drains), to repair curbing and to widen roads?
2. Where are the trouble spots in town (flooding usually is the most common public works problem)?
3. How old is the municipality's equipment and what is the equipment's repair record?
4. What is the town's reputation for clearing the streets after a snowstorm? Does it use salt and sand? How much of each? Any complaints about these quantities?

Parks

1. Is there an organized recreation program? Is there adequate equipment for recreation?
2. What other activities are offered in the park (concerts, plays, races, bingo)?
3. What is the town's park acreage? Is parkland evenly distributed around the community? Are there any plans to expand the park system by buying land?
4. What type of parks are there (conventional playgrounds, open space)?
5. Are the parks well maintained?
6. Are they safe?
7. Are they used?
8. How can they be improved?

Housing

1. What are the housing codes and how strictly are they enforced?
2. What are the town's zoning laws? Do they differ from the town's master plan? What do officials plan to do about any discrepancy?
3. Is there any public housing in the community? What is the community's attitude toward public housing? (Usually public housing proposals result in heated arguments between proponents of home

rule and those looking for financing from the state and federal government. Beneath the surface of such arguments are often strong sentiments about the social and economic integration of the community.)

Additional Reading

The Reporter's Handbook, ed. John Ullmann and Steve Honeyman, St. Martin's Press, 1983.
Municipal Year Book, published annually by International City Managers Association.

▪ A. Research Assignments ▪

ONE

Using research materials or interviews with people familiar with municipal services, write explanations that could be used in a newspaper article for the following terms:

1. gridlock

2. building permit

3. SRO hotel

4. paper streets

5. right-of-way

6. carbon filtration system

7. recharge basin

8. certificate of occupancy

9. roller-bearing failure

10. sewage sludge

TWO

Using research materials or interviews, obtain answers to the following questions for a city or town in your area, and illustrate some of your answers with quotes.

1. Where does the water come from? Who supplies it?

2. Who inspects restaurants and how often?

3. How many building permits have been issued in the last month? What types of projects are most of them for?

4. Who is the municipal official responsible for the parks?

5. How large is the staff of people who clean the parks? Are there more or fewer people than five years ago?

6. Which of the roads in the area are under the control of the city or town government? The county? The state? The federal government?

7. Who provides the bus service?

8. How many bus routes are there?

9. Are all parts of the city served equally well?

10. Does the town have a municipal pool?

11. How often is the water tested?

12. Where are the reports on water tests filed?

13. How many potholes were filled last year? Is that more or less than the previous year?

THREE

Select either an abandoned or particularly rundown building or a building that houses a pornography shop or a disreputable bar, and find out who owns it through the following steps:

1. Determine where the local property records are kept.
2. Locate the street address in a guide to lots and blocks in the city (property is catalogued in city records by lot and block, not address).
3. Take the block and lot number to a directory of deeds, mortgages and other papers. It is in reverse chronological order. You must go through it until you find the last time the property changed hands or was first registered. NOTE: Once you find the record of the last sale of the property, it may list the principal owner, or it may merely list a corporation. If it lists a corporation, proceed to step 4.
4. Find out where local records of businesses and corporations are kept. A list of corporations will provide you the names of the principal owners and officers.

FOUR

Call the local bus company and ask for the schedule of a bus that travels along a major thoroughfare, and a bus that travels an out-of-the-way route.

Stake out each route for two hours, with a watch, and observe whether the buses are on time. You might also observe whether they are crowded and in what condition they appear to be (dirty, falling apart, noisy, spewing fumes, or perfectly fine).

If the buses are *not* on time, call an official of the bus company and ask, "Are there any problems in running on time?" The answer should either provide an explanation for what you observed, or a revealing contradiction.

If the buses *are* on time, try to find out how long the schedule has been in effect. Do riders have to wait a longer or shorter time than they did five years ago?

(To extend this exercise, you might: try to locate through newspaper clippings critics of the bus system and interview them; conduct interviews with riders; or visit the company garage and talk to drivers, mechanics and supervisors about changes they've perceived.)

■ B. Writing Assignments ■

Write stories based on each of the following collections of information. In each case you are writing for a newspaper dated tomorrow and read in the town where the event occurred.

ONE

A press release issued by the Columbia Department of Highways today:

Highway commissioner Frank Rothman, as part of his continuing effort to improve the city's roads and bridges, announced today that a $35,000, six-month reconstruction program will begin next Monday at 11 a.m. on the four-mile-long stretch of the Westside Expressway between East 4th Street and River Road.

The program will make major structural repairs to the roadway, much of which is elevated, to repair damage caused by the 42 years of wear and tear accrued since the section was constructed.

"When this is done this section of the Westside Expressway — the most used road in the city — will be the par of any in the state," Mr. Rothman said.

From an interview with Rothman: "No, we're not adding anything new onto the expressway. Just fixing it up. Oh, traffic. Yes, traffic. Yes, we will have some problems there, of course. But Westside has six lanes. We may have to close two in each direction for much of the time, but we will always have at least one lane of the expressway open in each direction. Backups? Well, look, a lot of cars use this road, and we may have backups during rush hours. People might have to put up with quite a bit of inconvenience for a while, but if we hadn't done this we could have had some serious trouble with the Westside Expressway. Yes, I think it is fair to say that motorists who take the expressway home from the downtown area at River Street can expect some significant delays Monday evening. You got to break some eggs, you know."

From an interview with Ronald Coleman, president of the local Automobile Association: "Good news, that's what we call it. Sure, there are going to be traffic troubles. We will be urging our members to find other ways home from work from Monday afternoon on — 10th Avenue would be a good alternate route. But anyone who has driven on that stretch of Westside lately can see that it needs work."

TWO

You make a routine call to the Parks Department here in Lincoln and are surprised by what sounds like a non-routine piece of information: the department has decided to pave over all the grass area in Oak Tree Park . . . this according to public information officer Mike Chevra.

Chevra explains why: "This is the problem . . . The grass has just turned into a sleeping area for derelicts and drug users. We have decided that the park will be a cleaner place for all if we can get them out . . . And the first step is getting the grass out . . . at least that's how I understand the thinking here. The paving will begin on Monday and should be completed by the end of the month."

You call Pauline O'Shea, the parks commissioner. She says: "Look, I love grass. I wouldn't have taken this job if I didn't love grass, but I can't see a park turned into a dormitory for degenerates. If it takes getting rid of the grass to get rid of the degenerates . . . that's what we're going to do. This was my decision, and mine alone."

Time to visit Oak Tree Park. It runs between Lincoln Avenue and Jefferson Avenue on Forsythe Road. It's a half-block large piece of grass and trees with some asphalt paths winding through. It's two blocks west of the downtown shopping center and it's bordered by a row of shops on Lincoln, a three-story apartment building and some pretty ramshackle frame buildings on Forsythe and a warehouse on Jefferson. Not the nicest part of town, but you've seen worse.

It's sunny, about 11 a.m., and you spot one man sleeping on the grass. A woman seems to be sleeping on one of the couple of dozen benches scattered throughout the park. She's clutching a stuffed shopping bag.

Two women with strollers are sitting on a bench at the outskirts of the park. An elderly gentleman is on the bench next to theirs. Otherwise the park is empty. You try to talk to them all:

One woman with stroller: "Yeah, I come here most days. No, I hadn't heard they were going to take out the grass, but it's fine with me. Look, this is the only park for blocks around here . . . otherwise you wouldn't catch me here. There are some awful people who hang out in this park and maybe paving it over will get rid of them."

She reluctantly gives her name, Sheila Rhodes, but will say only that she "lives in the neighborhood." Her friend refuses to be interviewed.

Elderly gentleman: "Sure I'll tell you my name. I'm Fred Strauss, I live a block from here at 328 South Broadway, I'm 72 and I've been coming here almost every day since I retired five years ago. No, I don't sit in the middle of the park but I walk through it sometimes though. It's the only green place around here.

"They're going to what? Of all the bone-headed schemes. Let me tell you something. If they'd put a cop here during the day to shoo these people, they'd solve the problem easy enough. There's little enough grass. Let them use all that asphalt to fix some of these streets."

The woman with the shopping bag is sitting up now. The shopping bag is stuffed with clothes and papers. Her dress is stained and wrinkled. She gives you a suspicious glance but answers your question: "Nah, I don't need nobody knowing who I am and I have no address, but I do got something to say about what you're telling me. And that's that it's no surprise. They'd close the whole city down just to keep us from finding a lousy place to sleep. I know I'm not the prettiest sight but I haven't hurt anybody. They kick us out of here, where are we gonna go? You got a room at your place? You see the city finding any place for us? Let 'em pave over the whole city." She falls silent.

Man sleeping on the grass curses and refuses to talk to you.

You check with Friends of City Parks and reach the organization's president, George Myerson, who is also president of Fargo Bank, downtown: "Yes," he says. "O'Shea has discussed the plan for Oak Tree with me, and I'll tell you what I told her. It's ridiculous. Let them fight derelicts, if that's their problem, with police, not asphalt. Our organization believes this city needs more grass and greenery, not less."

You check with the mayor's office and confirm that the city does have an ad hoc program for providing shelter at night for homeless people. Anyone who shows up at the city's Greene Street unemployment office at 9 p.m. is taken to either a local church or synogogue. The office is at 49 Greene St.

You call back Chevra to check the details of the plan: "All the grass areas will be paved but none of the trees, bushes or benches will be affected," he says. "And it's a special playground asphalt like they use on some tennis courts. It's got more give than the old-fashioned kind and isn't as punishing if you fall on it. Yes, the plan is definite. We've already ordered the materials. As for Myerson, I can't comment on-the-record. Off-the-record, I think he wants to run for council so this will make him look good."

THREE

Someone on the phone who refuses to give her name. She says she works in the New City Transportation Department. Says: "Listen, you should look into this. Something terrible is happening. The new commissioner and his people have a new policy. They send the old buses to the black areas of town and the new buses to the white areas. Nothing on paper of course. But I've heard them discuss it with people who do the routing. As a matter of fact, I'm a dispatcher myself and they told me. But you can't say that. Just call me someone in the department."

You decide to stand on the corner of Blaine and Harrison streets in the middle of a predominantly black section of town. You count 21 buses in four hours from 2 p.m. to 6 p.m. None of those buses looks new, 10 look very old. The next day, also a weekday, you pick a corner—Elm and Spruce roads—in an almost exclusively white neighborhood. This time 25 buses come by during the same period. Twelve look almost brand new, none seem to look as old as the ones you saw the previous day.

You call up the transportation department and learn that the city purchased 22 new Japanese buses last year. It also owns 45 GM buses that are nine years old and 20 buses bought from GM 20 years ago. You ask if there's any way to tell the nine-year-old buses from the 20-year-old buses and are told the really old ones all are painted dark blue in the back, while the nine-year-old ones are painted light blue.

Next day you are back counting again, during the same hours, at Blaine and Harrison—no Japanese buses, 10 light blue backs, 10 dark blue backs. Next weekday at Elm and Spruce, same hours: 13 Japanese, 12 light blue backs, no dark blue.

You call a source at the transportation department and ask for names of some dispatchers, the people who send the buses out. The first three you call won't talk. A fourth, Gil Hawkins, agrees to talk—on background. He's willing to be identified as a dispatcher. Says: "Look, no one's ever come over to me and told me in so many words what buses to send where. But the commissioner himself came by about five or six weeks ago and said, 'You know we have a lot of important people riding these buses on some lines, and we also have some people who don't work too hard on others, if you know what I mean. Let's make sure the right people get the right buses.' He was saying the same sort of thing to other guys, also about three weeks ago. I nodded. I don't like it, but I want to keep my job. I have been sending the new buses mostly on the lines that go through Riverdale and Plainfield. Four Corners gets the older ones. Everyone I know here is doing the same."

Riverdale is where Elm and Spruce streets are; Plainfield is another well-off, predominantly white neighborhood. Blaine and Harrison are in Four Corners. You ask the dispatcher if there might be some other explanation for the difference in buses assigned to the different routes. His answer: "I wish I could say there was, but all the routes in this town are designed to be of roughly equal length and equal difficulty. The only difference between the route that passes through Blaine and Harrison — the number 4 bus — and the route that passes through Riverdale — the number 10 — is the people who ride the bus. They are both 12-mile routes and they both end up at the downtown Depot at Elm Boulevard and Jesse Road."

You try to interview some of the bus drivers on the 4 and 10 routes. Most won't talk. One on the 4 route does complain: "Of course we get the older buses . . . does that really surprise you?" He won't give you his name. Another driver, James Rosen of the 4 line says: "Yeah, I'll talk. Let them fire me if they want. Shortly after that guy Cransfield . . . is that his name? . . . took over, all of us noticed something was up. I have a lot of friends who are dispatchers, so I know exactly what's going on: the old buses go for the blacks and through the working class neighborhoods of town, white and black. The new buses go for the executives in Riverdale and Plainfield. The executives get to work on time, and the working people get stuck when one of those old GM jobbies breaks down . . . happened to me two days ago. A bus load of people had to wait for another bus because of a busted starter on one of these ancient number 4s."

Transportation Commissioner Herbert Cranston calls just before you were going to call him: "What's this I hear about your interrogating all my men?" he asks. You present your facts.

Cranston: "A — that's absurd. B — I would never say any of these things. C — if you print any of this garbage you will have one hell of a libel suit on your hands!" He hangs up.

Cranston calls back a half hour later: "Hey, I'm sorry I got so angry. Look, I checked with some of my people, and they tell me that it is possible that we do have more of our new buses on some of our lines, not because of any discrimination, of course, but because of the different needs of drivers on those lines. But believe me we will investigate this carefully, and if there is even the hint of any unfairness, I can assure, I will insist on changes in our bus scheduling." Cranston said he couldn't be more specific on the different needs of drivers on the routes. Cranston: "These are very technical issues."

You call three other people you know at the department, all of whom deny, on background, that there's any difference between the bus routes that might justify the imbalance of new buses and old buses. All are prepared to be identified as Transportation Department officials. Then you drive through Four Corners to Suffern and also take the route past Elm and Spruce to Riverdale. The first takes you past a few miles of apartments, stores and factories and then winds through a section of two and three-bedroom brick and stucco houses on tenth-of-an-acre lots. Most of the people along the route are black. The other route heads east along Main Street and then north through a wooded area, past the municipal golf course and into an area of split levels and two-car garages. Neither route seems to have very many hills. You return to the office and begin to write.

Cranston was appointed commissioner two months ago when the new mayor,

Republican Albert Fauk, took office. (You try to reach the mayor but he's out of town on business.)

▪ C. Story Assignments ▪

1. Obtain information on the schedule and record of a local city bus company or private bus line. How often are the buses on time? How many buses are there? How frequently are they supposed to come? Compare the current information with information about previous years. Write a story based on the comparison.

2. Interview municipal officials in charge of either transit, transportation, housing or parks and then interview the people who are affected by the services they provide. Write an article about different perceptions of the service.

3. Pick two areas of a city or town with roughly equivalent populations but sharply differing income levels. After interviewing local officials or officials of the companies that provide the services and after personal observation, write a story comparing one of the following services in each of the two areas:
   a. Sanitation
   - frequency of pickups
   - number of workers
   - cleanliness of streets

   b. Buses
   - number of lines
   - number of stops
   - frequency of service
   - crowds on the buses
   - quality of the buses in use

   c. Parks
   - number and size of parks
   - upkeep of parks
   - number of employees assigned
   - number of benches
   - athletic facilities

   d. Roads
   - state of repair of major streets
   - traffic
   - number of officers handling traffic
   - enforcement of parking rules

CHAPTER 28

Education

Few public issues command the attention of parents more than disputes over the quality of their children's education. And school policies also can stir up non-parents; homeowners in most towns pay more local taxes for public education than for anything else.

Yet until the last few years, many reporters dreaded an assignment to the education beat as much as a starting pitcher might dread being relegated to the bullpen. They saw no glory in it . . . and often with reason. Education coverage on many papers more often than not meant attending school board meetings and writing occasional fluff features on slow news days. Few education stories other than those on desegregation battles and teachers' strikes made Page 1.

But when journalists begin looking for the factors that most influence our society, they increasingly find themselves staring at the schools, especially as international competition in science and technology heats up. Many editors and reporters have begun to realize that the only thing wrong with the education beat is the way it has been covered.

"There are too many *school district* reporters and too few *education* writers," laments Dale Rice, education writer for the *Dallas Times Herald.* "Too many reporters get so caught up in the politics and infighting . . . that they forget the effect of policy when it filters down and hits the kids."

Rice, who spends more time in the schools than at the Board of Education, considers himself to be part of a new generation of education writers intent on opening what he calls "a real window to the school system." That takes time and effort. In late 1983, Rice and two other reporters from the *Times Herald* spent six months compiling a 55-part series on the comparative quality of education in the United States and other industrialized nations. The series, which received national attention, began like this:

A new academic achievement test, given to students in Dallas and seven other major cities around the world, indicates American children are among the worst students of mathematics in the industrialized world, and do not fare much better in science and geography.

It's rare for editors to give reporters a half year to look into anything. But most education writers can at some point manage to find a week or two to investigate some aspect of education from within the schools. For example, Jim Killackey, education writer for *The Daily Oklahoman* in Oklahoma City, visited the schools to look at how well laws designed to help the handicapped were working. He looked at the jumble of programs through the experiences of three children they served—a 13-year-old boy with cerebral palsy who attended "mainstream," or conventional, classes; a 12-year-old blind boy who divided his day between special and conventional classes; and a 17-year-old girl with muscular dystrophy who attended a special school for handicapped children.

"You really have to get out of the office and beyond the school board meetings," Killackey says.

Sources

Most teachers say they relish the independence of their job. Nonetheless, a complicated assortment of economic decisions and social pressures affect their ability to do their job well. Good education reporting requires an understanding of those decisions and pressures and of their impact on the classroom.

The Board of Education

"One of the first things you want to know is where educational policy is made," notes Saundra Keyes, a former English professor who covers education for *The Courier-Journal* in Louisville, Ky. No group will have more to say about that policy than the local board of education.

Members of the board are either elected or appointed by elected officials to make basic decisions about the schools and to oversee how they are run. Divisions among board members usually reflect disagreement in the community over the direction and financing of education. "Most school boards tend to be divided along some kind of line," says Rice of the *Times Herald.* He suggests that new education writers check clip files to get a sense of these factions and then meet individually with board members, perhaps, leaving pen and notebook behind. "Ask them what they think of the board and its problems," he suggests. "I think people are sometimes more relaxed when you don't approach them for a specific story."

Central Administration

Though they often are relied on too much, the administrators of a school system certainly can't be ignored. The superintendent and his staff interpret and put into effect the broad policies of the board of education. The system's purse strings also are opened and closed here. The superintendent and the deputy superintendent for curriculum usually top the hierarchy. But there are other important sources in the administrative offices.

An education reporter will want to know the district's public relations person, if it has one. Rice says he calls daily to keep tabs on breaking news. And the district's finance officer can help interpret and bring to life the mass of numbers in the budget. Staff assistants and secretaries also can help lead a reporter to news. Early in Rice's career, he says he befriended a school secretary in Syracuse, N.Y., who would often lend him books . . . with xeroxed copies of school documents hidden between the pages.

Teachers

Teachers should know more about what's really going on in the classroom than their bosses. They may be tougher to meet than administrators—most don't spend much time in an office—but it's worth the effort to track them down after class or at home, Rice notes. He suggests that new reporters on the beat ask leaders of the local teachers' union to arrange an informal get-together with several active teachers from different schools in the district.

Students

When an irate mother arrived in a Dallas classroom with a loaded gun, Rice knew of the incident—and of what led to it—before police had arrived at the scene. A student reporter saw the principal escort the woman from the room and called the *Times Herald.* "You will not believe the loyalty you can develop among school kids, especially among would-be journalists," says Rice. "Find out what the best student newspaper is, talk to the students on the staff and say, 'Listen, anytime you need information or help, call me and I'll get you information.'" Such favors get returned many times over, Rice adds.

Community Groups

Parents and taxpayers keep close watch on the schools. Irate parents have banded together to ban books, promote prayer and fight to keep French classes from being cut. They are a major force in debates on everything from crossing guards to lunchroom rules. Their views should be monitored before they surface at board of education meetings. Virtually every school has an active parent-teachers association, and education writers should develop sources on all of them. Organizations as diverse as the Chamber of Commerce and the local Council of Churches also keep tabs on the schools, and taxpayer groups often lead battles to defeat school budgets they judge excessive.

Other Officials

Schools nationwide are relying more and more on state and federal funds to support special programs and fill budget gaps. Some states, such as New Jersey, have set limits on how much school boards can spend in an effort to equalize educational opportunity in poorer and wealthier districts. Education writers need to know which elected officials at the local, state and federal level oversee education, and they must keep track of legislation coming before education committees in the various legislative bodies.

College and University Officials

"Higher education doesn't get nearly as much coverage but has just as much impact," says Jim Killackey of the *Daily Oklahoman*. College and university policy battles, especially at private schools, tend to be less public than those at the primary and secondary school level, but education writers are learning to uncover them. Their sources are administrators, teachers and students, along with the politicians who fund public universities and the alumni who help fund private universities.

While there may be fewer community groups battling for a say in higher education, disputes over financing, departmental expansion, accreditation, tenure, academic performance and admission standards can be just as heated and as newsworthy as battles for the 8-year-old's mind. Here is an example:

> The California State University campuses at Los Angeles and Dominguez Hills have the dubious honor of being the only colleges or universities in the state where fewer than half of the graduates who took the new basic skills test for prospective teachers have passed.
>
> *Los Angeles Times*

Documents

Important stories lie behind the dollar figures in school budgets and the statistics that fill reports on academic achievement. But to find these stories reporters need to know where to look and what to look for.

Budgets

The school budget determines how much money the schools will spend in the next school year, gives some details about how this money will be spent and tells where the money will come from. The budget process can have as much to do with the caliber of local schools as can the district's teachers. If test scores have dropped, for example, the explanation might be that classes are bigger. And if classes are bigger that might be because budgetary restrictions limited the number of teachers the school administration can hire.

New education writers *must* familiarize themselves with the intricacies of the local budget process. Who proposes budget items? Who evaluates these proposals? What time of year is the budget drafted? Who is responsible for approving it? Some school budgets are put up to popular vote. Others must be approved by the board of education or the city government.

Like most municipal budgets (See Chapter 23,

Government and Politics), school budgets are compromises between attempts to improve programs by increasing revenues and attempts to hold down taxes, usually property taxes, by limiting expenditures. This basic struggle, however, can be obscured by technical terms and jargon.

"I was sitting in a press briefing going through a two-inch thick school budget agenda, when I suddenly came to a paragraph saying federal Chapter 1 funds in the district would be cut $1 million," recalls Saundra Keyes of *The Courier-Journal*. "If I didn't know what Chapter 1 was, I couldn't have known what to ask. The bottom line is that it's extra reading and math help for poor kids. I wrote a story saying that 2,500 low-income kids in the city wouldn't be getting special aid."

Statistics

All school districts compile statistics. These might range from the number of hot lunches served each day to the percentage of students skipping school. This process is often formalized by the federal and state governments, which require reports on the results of programs they fund, such as aid for handicapped and underprivileged children. Occasionally, these statistics are publicized, but, more than likely, only when they show academic excellence or improvement: Educators are no more anxious than anyone else to air their dirty laundry. However, these reports should be available to the public and, therefore, to reporters, if specifically requested (See Appendix D, Law). Find out what reports your district is required to compile and when they are due. Each set of findings is a potential story.

In addition, the National Center for Education Statistics in Washington, D.C., publishes a vast array of statistics on American education from the number of students who have finished ninth grade to the average teacher's salary in each state.

> Students are likely to pay an average of 7 percent more to attend the United States' private colleges and universities in the fall, says the National Center for Education Statistics.
>
> *USA Today*

Comparisons of such numbers to local statistics can provide fertile ground for stories, too.

Laws and Regulations

Many of the activities of local schools today are dictated by federal and state governments. A knowledge of the relevant laws and regulations is necessary for reporters to be able to investigate local compliance with these rules. It may also be necessary simply to follow the conversation at a meeting or hearing in the principal's office.

"At a hearing there may be a quick reference to an amendment," notes Keyes. "If you know the amendment and you realize it could change funds to your district, you've got a front-page story. Some laws are referred to so commonly by educators they've become part of the jargon—like Public Law 94-142, which is a law funding programs for handicapped children."

Specialized Publications

A variety of academic journals cover aspects of education. Many education reporters find that reading *Education Week,* which reports on elementary and secondary school education, and the *Chronicle of Higher Education,* which covers college and university policy, helps keep them up-to-date on ideas and issues in the field and can lead to story ideas.

Keyes was education writer for *The Tennessean* in Nashville when she read an interesting story in the *Chronicle of Higher Education* on what happened to Iranian students after the American hostages were taken in Iran. "That day I was on the phone to all the college campuses in Tennessee seeing if they had any Iranian students and how they were being treated," Keyes recalls.

Basic Stories

Reporters on the education beat will spend much of their time monitoring the intricate and ever-changing relationship among educational funding, educational programs and educational performance. These are the issues that tend to dominate school board, PTA and community-group meetings, and these meetings tend to dominate the working days or evenings of many education reporters:

The Boulder Valley School Board decided last night to ask voters on Oct. 18 to approve a $4.3 million tax hike that would protect threatened programs and add some new ones.

The Denver Post

The trick is to leave the meeting with as detailed as possible an idea of how the decisions that have been reached or debated will actually affect readers through their taxes and through changes in the programs being offered their children. Good education reporters will ask, during or after the meeting, "How much will that cost the average property owner?" or "Will that have any effect on class size?" or "What programs will be cut if the increase is defeated?" The answers reporters

get to these questions will form the backbone of their stories.

If approved by the voters, the proposed tax hike would boost property taxes by $48 on a $120,000 house. That would increase the total assessment on such a home from $688 to $736.

The Denver Post

Next year's budget occupies a board of education for a few months each spring, but disputes about how children should be taught, how well they are performing and how the schools should be run fill more of the board's time. The reports on these subjects that administrators must make to the board give some sense of what's going on inside the schools:

The number of failures in four basic courses taken by high school students in the South Colonie School District has dropped by almost 50 percent since 1981, the district Board of Education was told last night.

(Albany, N.Y.) *Times Union*

Ultimately though, answers to questions about what and how students learn can be found only by visiting the schools themselves.

Enterprise

The Dallas school board had decided to institute a competency test that elementary school students had to pass before they could be promoted. What would its effect be on students? To answer that question Dale Rice and Linda Austin of the *Dallas Times Herald* alternated spending one day a week in a third-grade classroom for an entire school year. With the help of school officials, the reporters followed the development of five kids who seemed likely to pass the test and five whose prospects were poor. The result was a series of articles with an unusual and important perspective.

"What impact does the school board have when it makes a decision?" asks Rice. "What really happens in school? We showed the outcome of a policy in very human terms."

The last bell on the last day rang, and time ran out for third-graders in Sandra Warner's class.

"Pull your chairs up around the table," she told the 10 students remaining in her room, after 15 of their classmates had been dismissed. "I want to talk to you."

One of those left, a tiny girl, looked up with big, brown eyes. "We're gonna flunk," she said under her breath . . .

Dallas Times Herald

Dozens of enterprise stories can evolve by looking for the answers to Rice's question: What is the impact of school policy? Put another way: What goals does the school system set for itself? What goals do state and federal agencies set for it? How well are these goals met? And who benefits and who is hurt by these successes and failures?

Such questions don't have to be reserved for occasions when a new policy has been instituted. A school's performance in teaching math, for example, is newsworthy whether or not a new math curriculum has been adopted. Here are some examples of specific questions that might be asked about any school district at any time. Such questions are not asked enough.

1. How equitably are funds distributed in the school district? Compare programs at schools in wealthier and poorer sections of town.
2. How much state and federal money does the school district receive? Do comparable districts get more or less? Has the district been as vigorous as it should be in seeking outside funds?
3. What kind of programs does the school offer for students with special needs or abilities? What goals has it set for these programs? Have they been met?
4. How much does the school district pay each year to repair damage caused by vandals? Is vandalism increasing or decreasing? Are any comparative statistics available? Has the nature of vandalism changed? How does the system try to deal with it?
5. What efforts has the district made to integrate its student population? Are students bused? If so, what has been the educational impact of the policy? How do perceptions of parents, students and

teachers today compare with their perceptions when the practice was begun?
6. How much attention does the district pay to students who have no interest in attending college? Are their special needs for vocational training met?
7. Is the district strict or liberal in its tenure decisions? Are good teachers being lost? Are poor teachers being retained?
8. How effective do the students believe their education to be? What suggestions do they have for improving programs?
9. How does the district's college placement record compare with that of similar districts? How well do students do when they reach college? Do they consider themselves well prepared?
10. How successful has the district been in attracting quality teachers? What are the educational and professional backgrounds of its teachers?

Additional Reading

Covering the Education Beat, published by the Education Writers Association, 1980, Woodstown, N.J.

Condition of Education, Annual review of education statistics published by the National Center for Education Statistics.

Directory of Education Associations, Annual listing of national, regional and state education organizations, U.S. Education Department.

"How to Read a Budget," Frederick O'Reilly Hayes, *Columbia Journalism Review,* January/February 1976.

■ A. Research Assignments ■

ONE

Using research materials or interviews with people active in education, write explanations that could be used in a newspaper for the following terms:

1. Special education

2. PPBS budget

3. A criteria-referenced test

4. Grade equivalent score

5. Open classroom

6. Tenure track

7. Gifted child

8. Percentile rank

9. ESEA

10. In-service training

11. Resource teacher

12. Tracking

TWO

Visit a high school in your community and obtain the following information. Illustrate some of your answers with quotes.

1. Attendance. Find out what the school's policy is for class attendance and whether it has changed in the last five years.

   • Is class attendance up or down from the past? Why?

   • Are students free to leave during unscheduled periods?

   • Are parents notified if students miss class?

   • Who is in charge of monitoring attendance?

   • How does the school deal with chronic or repeated absenteeism?

   • What efforts have been made to improve attendance?

2. Enrollment. Find out whether enrollment has declined or increased in the last five years and what the effects of the size of the student body have been on educational quality.

   • Have any teachers been laid off because of a loss of students? Has that meant a loss of young teachers?

   • Have class sizes changed?

   • Have any teachers been assigned to subjects for which they haven't been trained?

- Does the school offer as many electives and extracurricular activities as it has in the past? Are facilities for these classes or activities overburdened?

- Have changes in enrollment affected student or faculty morale?

- What changes in the school-age population might be expected in future years?

3. Standardized tests. Find out what the standardized test scores for the school are for each grade in which such tests are given.

- Have these scores declined or increased in the last five years? Why?

- How do they compare with the scores in neighboring schools and school districts?

- How do they compare with national statistics?

- Why do teachers think they are increasing or declining? What do students think?

- What efforts have been made in the district to improve test scores?

- Is there any concern that too much stress on such scores interferes with rather than aids education?

▪ B. Writing Assignments ▪

Write stories based on each of the following collections of information. In each case you are writing for a newspaper dated tomorrow and read in the town where the events occurred.

ONE

The following press release issued by the Uniondale School District:

The winner of the annual Temple High School Outstanding Science Student Award was announced today. He is Mario Alvarez, a senior. The award — a bronze plaque — is given every year, on the basis of a vote by all the school's science teachers, to the student they consider the best science student at the school. Last year it was given to Susan George, who is now a freshman at Harvard University.

Mario is now in Esther Sampson's Advanced Biology class. Last year he studied Physics with Sam Victor. His hobby is Botany, and he has compiled an album describing all of the flowering plants grown in the Uniondale area.

From an interview with Sampson: "Yes, sure I'll talk about Mario. A fine, fine student. Did you know he was handicapped? Mario's a paraplegic. Lost the use of his legs in an automobile accident four years ago. He was one of three students moved to Temple last year from Lakeview School for the Disabled as part of that new main-streaming program — mixing handicapped kids in with other students. Mainstreaming sure worked with Mario. He's gotten the highest scores on every test I've given this semester. And his Botany project is great. He's got a half dozen friends scouring the neighborhood to find examples of flowering plants. He presses them and puts them dried in an album. Very impressive. One of the two or three best students I have had in 13 years of teaching."

An interview with Frederick Roland, assistant principal at Temple, and a check of the clips confirms Sampson's facts. Clips show that mainstreaming was quite contro-versial when first announced. It required the school board to spend $23,000 in ramps and other special facilities at Temple.

From an interview with Alvarez: "It was great news. All the kids were coming up to me in the halls today and patting my back and shaking my hand. And it has to help on my college applications. I still haven't been accepted anywhere. Schools? Well, I applied to Princeton, Stanford, Dartmouth and a couple of state universities. I think I sent out six applications in all.

"My disability you mean? I prefer that word to 'handicap.' Well, I don't see how that had anything to do with it. But if this helps show people that disabled students belong in class with everyone else, that's great. Lakeview was a nice place, but it didn't have an Advanced Biology class. Botany? Well, I guess my disability did have some-thing to do with that. When I first got my wheel chair I was so excited to be indepen-dent again I'd go on these long walks. You don't exactly fly along in a wheel chair and I noticed things I'd never noticed before. Then I just started keeping a record of things, that's all.

"No, I don't think I want to do research in Botany. It's a little early but I'm thinking pre-med. There's nothing like being sick to make you realize how important doctors are. My address: 666 First Street in Uniondale. I'm 17."

TWO

Press conference held at 10 p.m. tonight at Currier High School. Speaking: Charlotte Hall, president of the Clarkstown Education Association, union of Clarkstown's 187 teachers, and Charles Stewart, president of Clarkstown Board of Education.

Hall: "It's been too long coming, far too long, but tonight we can finally tell you that we've reached an agreement on a new contract for teachers in this district. For us it's not perfect, but in the end our students come first. The teachers in this district have been extremely concerned about ballooning class sizes. Classes of more than 30 were becoming quite common. Well, this contract won't allow that. And I hope the parents realize that this will be as much a victory for their children as for the teachers. All the studies I have ever seen have noted that overenrollment slows learning. As for the money, I'll let Mr. Stewart speak to it. No one got exactly what they wanted, but I will strongly urge my members to support our agreement when it comes up for a vote a week from today. Remember, this is a tentative agreement until the majority of the 187 teachers in our rank and file vote for it."

Stewart: "Miss Hall has been a tough negotiator, no doubt about it, but I think I can come before the taxpayers tonight and say, 'we've held the line on excessive raises while improving the quality of your students' education.' Here are the terms: All the teachers in the district will get a 6 percent raise. For the district that comes out to an average of, let me see now, $1,125 a teacher. One of the stumbling blocks was how much new teachers will get and we held the line there. Last year we started teachers at $15,200. We couldn't see a big hike here and Miss Hall finally agreed tonight to $500 for a starting salary of $15,700. Frankly, that leaves us quite competitive with the rest of the state. Frankly, knowing the tax situation in this town, we did the best we could do. We in essence split the difference in our demands and added a sweetener, which is the guarantee that no classes will have more than 30 students. It's worth it. A strike in our town would have been ugly."

Stewart, in response to a reporter's question: "Yes, we have had classes with more than 30 students in the past. No, I don't think it was a detriment to the quality of education, but we fully support this new policy. I can say we have never had as many as 40 students in a class but we may have had 35 once or twice."

Hall, in response to a reporter's question: "The average starting salary in this state last year, when we were at $15,200, was $15,350. I suspect a meager $500 increase will put us further behind. The key thing though was the class size and the fact that I can go to people already in the system and say, 'Hey, this is a decent raise.'"

Check of clips: Board and teachers have been negotiating for six months. Teachers originally demanded a 9 percent increase and class sizes of 25 or less. Pay scale in the district under the last contract ranged from $15,200 for a new teacher to $27,500 for a teacher with a master's degree and 12 or more years experience. Teachers last week voted to strike "within a month" if a contract could not be reached.

THREE

The Board of Education of Morrisville met tonight at Morrisville Elementary School.

1. Meeting began at 8 p.m. and ended at 11:30.
2. Board votes 9–0 to accept minutes of last meeting.
3. Communications: Dennis Allen's 6th-grade class raised $227 for the Muscular Dystrophy Foundation by organizing a car wash last week. Two students at Morrisville High School, Franca Stover and Gerald Loughlin, were Merit Scholarship semifinalists.
4. Report on Standard Reading Test scores by Board President Charles Brown. *Brown:* "As you can well see this test is not good news. For the third straight year, the reading scores of 6th graders in our system have declined. Three years ago the average reading score for sixth graders was 79, which means that by the end of sixth grade they were right on track, reading at a late sixth grade-beginning seventh-grade level. Two years ago the drop was to just 78 and last year 76, but this year our sixth graders got an average score of 73 at the end of the year. That means, ladies and gentlemen, that the average sixth grader completing elementary school in this system has the reading skills equivalent on a national basis to a sixth grader finishing his or her first semester. I find that appalling and think we've got to find a way to stop the slide. I've asked John Klein, who, as you know, is assistant superintendent for instruction to come here tonight and give us his views on these test scores."

Klein: "No doubt this is discouraging, but I think the scores have to be seen in perspective. For one thing, these scores represent an average for *all* sixth graders in this district. You may not know that we only had 57 this year. A few, frankly, are very slow learners and five have been retained. Some of these are reading at a second and third grade level and these bring the average down. Still, this raises some grave questions about an educational experiment we tried last year. We decided to go to an *open classroom* approach — all 57 students were taught in one large open area by two teachers and a teacher's aid. The idea was for teachers to have more flexibility in their planning and teaching approach, but one, Ethel Rosegrant, missed a good part of the year . . . I think seven weeks this spring . . . with pneumonia and we never did find a single substitute who could fit into that situation. One teacher can't keep track of what 57 students are doing and instead of individualized instruction I'm afraid there may have been too much wasted time. Personally, though, I would give the open classroom one more year to take hold. It hasn't really had a fair trial yet."

Trustee (board member) Jack Gantz: "I never liked all this experimental stuff anyway. Look, it is time we got back to basics — reading, writing and arithmetic. That's what I learned at school and the kids just aren't getting it. I move that we eliminate the open classroom at the elementary school next year so that this fiasco doesn't continue."

Trustee Alice Richardson: "I second."

Trustee Joan Dershowitz: "Isn't it a little extreme to be changing educational policy on the basis of a five-minute presentation? Mr. Gantz, I have friends with children in that open classroom. Those kids came home with beautiful work in arts and crafts. The brightest ones were able to meet in small groups to work on a wonderful social studies project that, as we bragged last month, was exhibited at city hall. The slowest kids got individual attention that would have been impossible with just one teacher. Sure, all that went by the board when Ethel Rosegrant fell ill, but don't cure the patient by killing it. I propose that we ask Miss Rosegrant and the other teacher in the class, Paul Moore, to give us a report next meeting."

Board votes. First vote, 6–3 against Gantz's motion to eliminate open classroom in sixth grade. Gantz, Richardson and Bob Shaeffer vote to end open classroom. Second vote, 9–0 to ask teachers in open classroom to present a report.

5. Board votes 9–0 to spend $875 for a new tuba for the band.

FOUR

You hadn't remembered those chairs being so little, but the 15-year-olds do seem to fit in them just fine, and undoubtedly you did too at their age. But you're no longer 15 and you sat, with the principal and superintendent, in one of those little chairs for about an hour today in Rodney Markham's 10th-grade biology class at Randall Regional High School as he quite deliberately got himself suspended.

Markham did exactly what he had told his principal he was going to do, exactly what he said he'd do when he called the newspaper. In a clear violation of district policy on sex education, he had shown his students, male and female, a series of large, full-color pictures of humans engaged in sexual acts. The district's regulations on sex education, you had learned, say: "Sex education should be conducted for boys and girls separately. Sketches of people may be employed briefly in the lessons, but under no circumstances are potentially pornographic photographs to be shown to these teen-agers."

The district's regulations say teachers may be suspended and, after full investigations, their contracts terminated, for "clear and willful violations of district policies." At 10:32 this morning, a couple of minutes after Markham's class had ended (it ran from 9:30 to 10:30 a.m.), District Supt. Max Whelan got out of his little chair, walked over to Markham and said: "You have clearly and willfully violated district regulations in teaching this lesson. I am therefore suspending you without pay effective immediately, and I will now institute procedures that I hope will lead to the termination of your contract. Please collect your belongings."

You didn't know who to grab first, but you decided to go for the man himself: Rod Markham. He's a little guy, about 5-foot-6, he wears granny glasses, he's prematurely bald and he says he's 28. Master's degree in education from University of Minnesota . . . He's been working here in Randall five years . . . says he never taught anywhere else.

Your first question: "Well, you did it. How does it feel?"

Markham: "You can go over these things time and time again in your mind but still not be prepared for them when they finally happen. I would say the lesson was even more successful than I had imagined. You could see a look of real interest on those kids faces as they learned from the pictures. You sensed that mysteries were being cleared up in their heads by getting a chance to see what these acts looked like. But I also have to say that Whelan's little speech hit me harder than I'd expected. It's no fun to lose your job, even temporarily. But the ACLU [American Civil Liberties Union] has gotten me a fine lawyer and I think we're going to give them a hell of a fight."

You had written a story about this a week ago, when Markham first announced his plan. He said then: "In the years I've worked at this school I've grown increasingly frustrated and concerned by this policy. I do not believe any good can come from denying these young men and women full information on this crucial subject. I have decided to take a stand." This time you simply asked him whether it was worth it.

Markham: "I believe an important lesson was taught in this classroom today, both for these young men and women and for this community. I'm willing to pay whatever price is necessary to help take people out of the dark ages and to help the children of this area learn how to deal with the problems and joys of sex intelligently."

The students had been mostly quiet during Markham's lecture. They certainly seemed more interested in the five pictures of sex acts he showed them and in his lecture on love and caring than in the three adults sitting in the back of the classroom. Incidentally, those pictures were as explicit as could be — if they had been in a movie it would have been rated X.

After the lecture was over, every one of the 23 students — 13 girls, 10 boys — seemed to stand and clap or cheer. Some booed as Whelan walked over to Markham. You started interviewing some of the students before they filtered out into the hall. The other adults could wait.

Susan Korniche, 15, . . . lives in Westwood: "That was good. It was really fine. Look, no problem . . . the poor guy."

Alan Jacobs, 14, . . . lives in Westwood: "No, I wasn't at all embarrassed. The girls didn't bother me. The pictures didn't bother me. I learned something today from a great teacher. This is awful."

Katherine Emmers, 15, . . . lives in Fort George: "Yeah, it made me feel a little uncomfortable, but we're not babies. We can handle it."

Steve Smith, 15, . . . lives in Westwood: "The bastards. Hey, I've seen pornography. You think I can't buy *Hustler*? That wasn't pornography. It was graphic but it was for good teaching. Just good teaching."

Jill Condor, 15, . . . lives in Westwood: "No, of course I didn't mind having boys around. This wasn't giggle time. This was serious. Mr. Markham treated it seriously, and we took it that way." You could confirm that. There were no giggles or snickers.

The principal, Astrid Kane, had returned to her office. You found her there, but she said you'd better talk to Whelan. Whelan was in his office and first you asked him about the students' applause and their comments.

Whelan: "We're not at the stage yet where we're going to let 15-year-olds make policy in this district."

You asked for the record why Markham was suspended.

Whelan: "This district draws a strict and important line between sex education and pornography; we have for ten years. You and your readers have to understand that. We do not believe that 15-year-olds should be exposed to material like what we saw today. Do you see the point? We believe that this type of instruction — and it should never be so graphic — should be done with boys and girls separately, so they won't be embarrassed and so it won't lead to anything. And we believe in the right to enforce the regulations that the board, the community, and I believe in. Those pictures, let me tell you, were even worse than I expected. I really wish we could have stopped that teacher before he did what he did to those kids, but I'm glad at least that we can stop him before he does it again.

"He even waited until the last 10 minutes to show them just to spite us," Whelan adds.

As you were getting in your car, you saw Markham loading his car with papers and books and notebooks. He looked back at Randall High School and seemed to smile.

Back at the office, you called Joyce Jamison, Markham's ACLU lawyer. Jamison: "Hi. I just got back from the high school. I told Whelan we're going to fight this thing all the way to the Supreme Court, if we have to. The state ACLU is clear on this: Students and teachers have the right to talk intelligently and openly about sex."

You recalled that Kane had said there were 28 students in Markham's biology class. Only 23 had attended. With Kane's help, you got the numbers for the other five students. Two parents just said their kids were "not feeling well." Two refused to talk. But Celia Zimmerman, of Westwood, the mother of Saundra Zimmerman, 15, said: "I'm just not that kind of a mother, and Sandy's just not that kind of a girl. Of course they were right to fire that man. We don't need pornography in our schools. No, you can't talk to Sandy, and yes, we forbid her to go to school today."

▪ C. Story Assignments ▪

1. Write a story on a meeting of a local school board. Before the meeting stop by the school district's offices to get a copy of the agenda, and contact sources within the district to brief yourself on the issues that are scheduled to be discussed.

2. Obtain a copy of the most recent budget for a local school district. Assume the budget has just been released. Based on interviews with sources in the district and research materials (such as the previous year's budget), write a story about that budget and its potential effect on the district.

3. Through interviews with faculty and students at a local public school, find a teacher who has a reputation for doing outstanding work in the classroom. Write a profile of that teacher that demonstrates why he or she is so successful. Try to obtain permission to sit in on some classes.

4. Write an article on facilities and programs for disabled students at a local public school or college. Find out how much the programs cost and whether the school receives state or federal funding to help pay for them. Spend some time with disabled students and ask them about the adequacy of the facilities and programs that are available. Contact the leaders of any on-campus organizations of disabled students. You might also talk with leaders of off-campus organizations that represent the disabled to get their views on what should be done.

5. Write an article on the writing skills of undergraduates at a local college or university. Interview teachers and students at the school. Do they believe writing skills have declined? Why? Look for test scores that might offer evidence of a change in writing skills.

Business and labor

Corporations determine what products will appear in our homes and how much of our income we will have to devote to buying those products. The economic conditions under which those corporations operate — and how they respond to those conditions — help determine the environment in which we earn, spend, pay taxes, and get fired or hired.

In recent years, newspapers have been paying more and more attention to such matters as government statistics on retail sales, the interest rate on government bonds and the rate of corporate borrowing. They've also allocated more and more space to such stories as Sony's latest quarterly earning report, the Union Pacific Corporation's decision to sell a gas pipeline company or fashion designer Anne Klein's decision to start a new business.

Newspapers are devoting additional pages to business and economic news in part for a *journalistic* reason: Editors are increasingly aware of the impact such news can have on many aspects of our lives. But business is also getting more attention for a *business* reason: The readers most interested in this news are the readers most attractive to advertisers — the well off.

If business coverage is focused on the world of corporate executives, labor coverage looks at the situation of the less affluent but more numerous people who work under these executives — people who are, alas, less attractive to advertisers. "Many newspapers now have large business staffs," notes William Serrin, who covers labor for *The New York Times.* "But I know of no paper that has a large labor staff."

The labor beat — Serrin suggests it be called the "work beat" — offers a chance to report on some of the consequences of business and economic decisions. It looks at how people spend their eight or so hours each day on the job, at struggles to organize and protect workers, and at the periodic battles between employers and employees over wages and conditions:

GRAND PRAIRIE — Members of United Auto Workers Local 276 made plans yesterday to continue their walkout at a General Motors plant in Arlington as negotiators worked to end the strike at 13 GM assembly plants nationwide.

The Dallas Morning News

Labor reporters usually can find their way through the offers and counteroffers of contract negotiations without a course in accounting. Though a sense of labor history helps, many of the challenges of the beat involve dealing with people rather than poring over texts. It's essential, for example, for labor reporters to overcome any stereotypes they may have about people who work in clothes that get dirty. Otherwise, it will be difficult to go beyond stories relaying the rhetoric of labor leaders to stories relating the reality of working conditions and attitudes on the job.

Business, on the other hand, is a difficult beat to walk onto without some training. Karen W. Arenson, who covers business and economics for *The New York Times,* majored in economics in college, but when she got a business reporting job she took additional night courses in accounting and in finance. Arenson wanted to be sure she understood all the numbers and terms through which businesses report on their performance and on which businesses and financiers base their decisions. "These courses tell you what a company is about and how to think about a company," she says.

Still, as much as an understanding of the numbers and the jargon can help, business and economic reporters, like all others, ultimately must turn to knowledgeable people for help. For example, Leon Wynter came to *The Wall Street Journal* with an MBA in economics, experience in banking and graduate training in journalism. But in struggling to understand the complicated workings of the banking regulatory system he was covering, he needed sources.

Business Sources

A reporter assigned to cover business in a city or town will want to start by figuring out what businesses the people in the area are engaged in. The local Chamber of Commerce can provide a basic list. There also are books that categorize and list businesses by something known as the *Standard Industrial Code.* Finally, the newspaper's library may have a separate, alphabetical file on businesses to help fill out the list and fill in the reporter on what's been written (See Chapter 18, Research).

Then it might be time to focus on a particular company. "You want to know: What is the company doing?" advises Arenson. "Who does it compete with? How successful is it? How profitable is it? What is its growth potential? What problems does it have or might it have in the future?" Business reporters also should be thinking about whom the company employs, where it releases its wastes, how it determines its price structure, what new products it might be introducing, and, in general, what role the company plays in the economy and environment of the area. At the very least, the answers to these questions will give a reporter key background information to tuck away until the company finds its way into the news. Often, though, the answers can lead directly to an interesting story. Here are two paragraphs from the middle of a story about a fast growing company in what its president perceives to be a growth industry:

The firm, which has headquarters in Springfield, Ill., and employs more than 1,100 people in the St. Louis area, has become No. 1 or No. 2 nationally in five of its product markets. Sales zoomed 68 percent to $210.96 million last year, making Amedco one of Wall Street's darlings.

The company began by offering consulting and accounting services to the funeral trade, and then

moved into manufacturing and supplying items such as embalming liquids and biers for that industry.

St. Louis Post-Dispatch

Analysts

It often makes sense to start reporting from the outside. Among the most knowledgeable sources a reporter interested in a company or industry can find are the *securities analysts* and *investment bankers* responsible for monitoring it. These are the people whose job it is to determine the attractiveness of these companies or industries for potential investors. They can help make sense of the statistics the company releases and give a reasonably objective assessment of the company's strengths and weaknesses. Fortunately, they're usually happy to publicize their expertise by talking with reporters, as was the case in this excerpt from a *New York Times* article about wholesale changes at Aetna Life and Casualty Company:

"It's been time for them to shake things up for years," said Donald E. Franz, an analyst at Smith Barney, Harris Upham & Company.

Securities analysts can be found with brokerage firms like Paine Webber and Merrill Lynch. W. R. Nelson and Company in Rye, N.Y., puts out a directory listing the analysts that follow specific industries and companies.

Company Officials

In approaching a company itself, reporters either can start by contacting a public relations person and working their way up to the chief executive — getting smarter as they go along — or they can begin at the top and enlist the boss's help in leading them to other people with whom they should talk. Certainly, the person who runs the company should be somewhere on every reporter's list of sources. Here, the chairman of the board of Fotomat discusses efforts underway to turn around the company's financial problems:

"While the refinancing we seek is a prime ingredient in reshaping Fotomat, I believe we are making progress," he said. "Our current results indicate that our marketing and cost control programs are working."

St. Petersburg Times

Many businessmen and women are wary of reporters, and it's often best to get to know them while working on a relatively non-controversial story. Kathryn Harris's first assignment for the *Los Angeles Times* was to cover the semiconductor and computer industry. To get her feet wet in this unfamiliar area, she decided to "wade in" with a general story about the housing problems in "Silicon Valley," the area in

California where many of these firms are located. This story gave her a chance, she says, to meet the people in the industry in a "non-confrontational" situation. Then Harris waded in a little deeper with a profile of a major corporation in the area—Tandon. "It's a good exercise," she says. "You talk to the competition, to the suppliers, to the customers, as well as company officials. If it's a company you're going to cover for awhile, it helps to get to know it inside out."

The Other Side

After spending much of their day talking with business people and then writing stories that in many cases will be read primarily by business people, reporters may be tempted to assume the perspective of the men and women they cover. That's dangerous. The suppliers, customers and competitors Harris suggests talking to provide a broader point of view on the operations of a company. But reporters must also seek out non-business people: union leaders, environmental groups and public interest and consumer groups of the type spawned by Ralph Nader. And reporters should keep track of people who have left companies in their area; these sometimes disaffected employees can add balance to a story . . . if, that is, it's clear that they aren't just selling sour grapes.

"You want to cover as many bases as possible and get different points of view to the full extent that there are different points of view," says Arenson. She begins each story by jotting down what angles might be developed and what range of viewpoints might exist on each point. Then she decides what sources she might find to represent those viewpoints. "You can help define a story that way," Arenson says. You also can —if your selection is broad enough—ensure that your information won't be too one-sided.

Regulators

A month after joining *The Wall Street Journal* to cover bank regulation, Leon Wynter found himself embroiled in one of the hottest stories on his beat in years. The Continental Illinois National Bank, ninth largest in the country, was on the brink of failing. Wynter had to find out why and what might be done about it, a task he soon learned meant penetrating the bureaucracies of three federal regulatory agencies. "How much was the bank borrowing? How much were its deposits falling down?" These are among the questions Wynter needed answered. "I was calling a lot of people I didn't know to find out," he recalls.

The Federal Deposit Insurance Corporation was designing a package that would keep the troubled bank afloat. Wynter found himself in the unenviable position of having to get acquainted with the FDIC's

chairman by calling him at home on the weekend. He also needed sources at the office of the controller of the currency, a division of the Treasury Department, that was keeping a watchful eye on the books of Continental Illinois, and at the Federal Reserve, which pumped in funds to rescue the bank.

All businesses are subject to some regulation by federal and state agencies. An airline, for example, might deal with the Securities and Exchange Commission when it is selling its stock, with the Federal Aviation Administration when it tries to schedule flights at busy airports, and with the National Transportation Safety Board should one of its planes crash. The owner of a funeral parlor might obtain a low-interest loan through the Small Business Association but might also be challenged by the Occupational Safety and Health Administration for exposing workers to unsafe conditions or by the Federal Trade Commission for misleading customers.

Business reporters should know who is keeping tabs on the businesses they cover. They also should keep in mind, as Wynter did, that the best information often doesn't come from the top regulators but from the lawyers who get the complaints, the investigators in the field and the middle-level bureaucrats who write the reports.

Labor Sources

Labor reporters should start by tracking down the union leaders who are active in their towns, but it is important that they not stop there. The head of a union of local clerical employees can discuss the workers' salary structure, their benefit packages, their organizing efforts and the union's likely demands in the next contract negotiations. He or she cannot give a first-hand account of what it is like to be a secretary in a firm in the process of installing word-processing equipment.

"You can't cover labor just by writing about John Doe, who is head of Local 33," says William Serrin. "If you want to cover work then you'll be in the offices and the department stores and the factories finding out what's really cooking." Serrin calls this "bottoms up" reporting.

For some reporters, interviewing workers means going to a local bar dressed in a faded pair of blue jeans. Serrin believes this is condescending: "You don't interview executives at their clubs, why always interview workers at bars? Like everybody else, some workers drink, but x times as many others just go home in the evening and mow the lawn."

When reporters are covering events in union headquarters or halls, they should keep an ear tuned to possible dissident groups. And, of course, management officials are crucial sources for the other side on labor stories.

Labor reporters also should be aware of union activities that are not related to formal negotiations: health plans, community involvement, legal and educational services, and political support for candidates. And additional stories about work can come from government agencies such as the federal Occupational Safety and Health Administration and its state equivalents. It's important to remember that the large majority of the workers in the United States, particularly service employees, are *not* unionized. Their problems with salary and working conditions should not be ignored.

When Jim Kadera of *The Oregonian* in Portland wrote a story on logging accidents, he interviewed a wide range of sources, including officials of the state Workers Compensation Department, a consultant to the State Accident Insurance Fund, a vice president of a lumber company and the safety manager for an association of loggers. Here is Kadera's lead:

> When Delton Reich Jr., a 32-year-old choker setter was crushed by a rolling log yesterday, he became the 15th logger to die in an accident in the state this year.

There's one other good place to find sources on the local labor situation — an unemployment office.

Documents

No matter how good they are with people, reporters haven't earned their pinstripes on the business beat until they've learned to make sense of all the numbers with which companies measure their performances. Some are found in the reports and statements issued by *publicly held* corporations (companies in which the public can buy stock). Numbers hold the keys to an understanding of the company's profits, its debts, the cash it has on hand, its taxes and the payback investors can expect for their dollars. These numbers also may reveal a company's troubles: inventory that's piled up or has been depleted, capital investments in new plants that are being underused, profit margins that are lower than the competition's.

"There is no more fundamental skill required in doing well in this field than understanding corporate financial statements," says Chris Welles, a freelance business writer and the director of the Walter Bagehot Fellowship Program in Economic and Business Journalism at Columbia University.

The federal government's securities and exchange laws require corporations that sell stock to the public to produce *annual reports* on how much they've earned, how much they've spent, how much they owe and how their performance compares with that of past

years. These reports include a *balance sheet,* listing the company's assets (what it owns) and its liabilities (what it owes) at a specific time and a *statement of income and retained earnings,* comparing the company's sales and operating profits for one year with those of past years. The charts on pages 366 – 368, drawn from a New York Stock Exchange publication, *Understanding Financial Statements,* provide an example and an explanation of typical versions of these reports.

"Some people look at balance sheets as dry," notes Arenson. "But they tell you how the company has used its money and where that money came from. If you don't get interested in that, perhaps you shouldn't be covering business."

Financial statements may supply reporters with straightforward stories, supported by quotes from company executives and outside analysts, about a company's performance. This story, based on a company report, must have been easy for the writer to find:

> The Tribune Co. reported profits of $21.6 million in its second fiscal quarter as gains from its newspaper and broadcasting groups more than offset losses in its Canadian newsprint and forest products operations.
>
> *Chicago Tribune*

In attempting to understand a business, however, reporters must often do more than simply report whether it is making a profit. Like potential investors, they will look for comparisons between the company's performance in this year or quarter of the economic year and past years or quarters:

> The beleaguered Fotomat Corp. said yesterday that it had its first profitable quarter in a year and a half during the accounting period ended July 31.
>
> During the quarter, the St. Petersburg company earned $1.5 million, or 15 cents per share, on revenues of $50.8 million. During the same quarter last year, the company lost $2.6 million, or 30 cents per share.
>
> *St. Petersburg Times*

Like investors, reporters will often be interested in *ratios* within a financial report. Welles advises that business reporters investigate such things as *profit margin* — a company's profit as a percentage of sales (after taxes) — and *return on equity* — a company's net income as a percentage of all the money that has been invested in it. (The higher the return on equity, the more money investors are likely to make.) These methods of analysis won't always make it into a story. But they may be useful in getting a broader view of the company's performance.

The next step might be to look beyond the performance of one company to the performance of an industry as a whole. "Let's take a company whose earnings dropped 22 percent last year," suggests

Welles. "If its major competitors dropped 10 percent, that's bad. But if its major competitors dropped 40 percent, that might not be such a bad performance."

While annual reports and quarterly financial statements include lots of information about a company, neither is as complete as the *10K statement* publicly held companies must file with the federal Securities and Exchange Commission. These statements include information on everything from the legal proceedings that may be pending against a company to the salary of its top executives. They may be made available by a company; they will be made available by the nearest regional office of the Securities and Exchange Commission.

When a company wants to issue more shares of stock, it must provide potential buyers with an additional document, called a *prospectus*. This will include information on the company's earnings, its major stockholders, its lines of business and its competition. The company is legally responsible for the accuracy of the information it includes in a prospectus. This document can be as valuable to a journalist trying to report on a company as it is to an investor thinking of buying a piece of it.

Numbers, of course, don't tell the whole story on businesses, and reporters keeping track of trends and people read a lot more than financial statements. Most top business and labor reporters keep up with *The Wall Street Journal* and *Business Week* to track national events and patterns that will affect business and, therefore, also affect workers. Reporters with specialized business beats, such as Leon Wynter, also follow the trade press in their area of expertise. (Wynter's regular reading includes the *American Banker* and *Bank Letter*.)

In addition, research publications such as *Business Information Sources* and the *Encyclopedia of Business and Information Sources* can help reporters find and sort through piles of paper generated by business. Others like Standard & Poor's *Register of Corporations, Directors and Executives* offer basic information on major corporations and a starting point for compiling a list of the top people in an industry nationally. And for reporters mired in the jargon of business, the *Modern American Business Dictionary* offers hope.

Labor reporters needn't worry as much about preferred stock or sinking-fund debentures, though they should become familiar with the wage scales, benefits and pension plans that might be discussed in a contract. A union's own newspaper can be a useful source of this and other labor information. While many union newspapers are little more than public relations sheets for union presidents, some are powerful voices for the political and economic interests of their members. One New York City union paper, the *Public Employee Press,* regularly provided the local dailies with leads to stories on subjects ranging from the deterioration of the city's bridges to generous real estate tax breaks being given local builders.

Basic Stories

The business pages on a typical day will be filled with stories about new (and, if the company is to be believed, improved) products; plans to open or close plants; reports of higher or lower sales or profits; news of bankruptcies, acquisitions and mergers; stock, bond and commodities market reports; and the by-now almost daily statistics that the government releases about the state of the economy. The most common labor stories discuss strikes, negotiations, layoffs and, upon occasion, new hirings.

Here are some basic questions to keep in mind when reporting and writing these stories:

How Will It Affect Consumers?

Will the larger company created by the merger continue to offer the same services, and prices, to customers? What does the fall in the value of the dollar in relation to other currencies mean for American consumers? How are changes in the *prime interest rate*—a rate paid only by some favored corporations —likely to be felt by individual borrowers?

Not every story offers such an angle. Not every article has room for it. But business and labor reporters who want to interest a wide variety of readers in their stories must pay attention to the interests of this wide variety of readers. Here is a paragraph from a story on a possible strike by employees of Continental Airlines:

A strike is not expected to present a major inconvenience to Los Angeles passengers because Continental operates only about 12 flights per day here.

Los Angeles Times

How Will It Affect Investors?

In a long-awaited announcement, Sears, Roebuck & Co. said yesterday that Chairman Edward R. Telling has agreed to postpone his retirement until the end of 1985 at the request of the company's board of directors.

Chicago Tribune

Gulf and Western Industries, *in a widely expected streamlining move,* said yesterday that it would take a $470 million write-off in its just ended fiscal year to divest itself of several major lines of business . . .

The New York Times

Both these leads raise the same question: Why did

Balance Sheet

"Your Company"

Millions

Assets	As of December 31	1985	1984	The Company Owned
Current Assets				
Cash..........................		$ 9.0	$ 6.2	Generally bank deposits.
Marketable securities..............		—	2.0	Government or corporate bonds or stocks that can easily be sold.
Accounts and notes receivable........		12.4	11.4	Amounts owed the company by its customers and others less amounts considered uncollectible.
Inventories.....................		27.0	24.6	Raw materials, work in process and finished merchandise, stated at the lower of cost or realizable value.
Total Current Assets.............		$ 48.4	$ 44.2	
Property, Plant and Equipment				
Buildings, machinery and equipment, at cost....		104.3	92.7	
Less accumulated Depreciation........		27.6	25.0	Loss of value through wear and tear.
Land, at cost....................		.9	.7	
Total Property, Plant and Equipment....		$ 76.7	$ 67.7	
		$ 77.6	$ 68.4	
Other Assets				
Receivables due after one year.......		4.7	3.9	Amounts due to be owed the company, and likely to be collected, in the next year.
Surrender value of insurance.........		.2	.2	Value of insurance policy if cashed in.
Other........................		.6	.5	
Total Other Assets...............		$ 5.5	$ 4.6	
Total Assets....................		$131.5	$117.2	

The Company Owed

Liabilities & Stockholders' Equity

Current Liabilities

Accounts payable	$ 6.1	$ 5.0	Money owed for raw materials, supplies and services.
Accrued liabilities	3.6	3.3	Unpaid salaries, wages, interest and commissions.
Current maturity of long-term debt	1.0	.8	
Federal income and other taxes	9.6	8.4	Amount due in next year on money that has been borrowed.
Dividends payable	1.3	1.1	Promised payments to stockholders.
Total Current Liabilities	$ 21.6	$ 18.6	
Other Liabilities	3.6	2.5	Other liabilities due after one year.
Long-Term Debt			
5% Sinking-Fund Debentures, due July 31, 1987[1]	26.0	20.0	Long-term debt is the amount due next year on money borrowed.
Stockholders' Equity[2]			
5% Preferred Stock[3] ($100 par: authorized and outstanding—60,000)	6.0	6.0	Amount originally invested in the company computed by multiplying the number of shares held, or outstanding, times the par value—an arbitrary stated value—of the shares.
Common Stock[4] ($10 par: authorized—2,000,000; outstanding—1,830,000)	18.3	18.3	
Additional Paid-In Capital	9.6	9.6	Money received from the sale of stock at more than par value.
Retained Earnings	46.4	42.2	Earnings not paid out in dividends but reinvested in the business.
Total Stockholders' Equity	$ 80.3	$ 76.1	
Total Liabilities, and Stockholders' Equity	$131.5	$117.2	

[1] 5% *sinking-fund debentures* are a type of long-term debt, or long-term borrowing, which must be repaid by setting aside a certain amount out of earnings at stated intervals. A debenture is a certificate of debt issued by a corporation—a corporate IOU. In this case the company is paying 5 percent interest on that IOU.

[2] *Equity* is the amount of money that has been invested in a company.

[3] *Preferred stockholders* have first call on dividends and their dividends are fixed—in this case at 5 percent a year.

[4] *Common stockholders* are paid dividends only after preferred stockholders have been paid.

* *Source:* New York Stock Exchange

Statement of Income and Retained Earnings

"Your Company"

Millions — Year ended December 31

	1985	1984	1983
Sales	$115.8	$110.0	$104.5
Less:			
Costs and Expenses:			
Cost of goods sold	$76.4	$73.2	$70.2
Selling, general and administrative expenses	14.2	13.0	12.1
Depreciation	2.6	3.5	2.3
	$93.2	$89.7	$84.6
Operating Profit	$22.6	$20.3	$19.9
Interest Charges	1.3	1.0	1.3
Earnings before Income Taxes	$21.3	$19.3	$18.6
Provision for Taxes on Income	11.4	9.8	9.5
Net Income (per common share: 1985—$5.24; 1984—$5.03; 1983—$4.97)*	$9.9	$9.5	$9.1
Retained Earnings, Beginning of Year	42.2	37.6	33.1
	$52.1	$47.1	$42.2
Less Dividends Paid on:			
Preferred Stock ($5 per share)	(.3)	(.3)	—
Common Stock (per share: 1985—$3.00; 1984—$2.50; 1983—$2.50)	(5.4)	(4.6)	(4.6)
Retained Earnings, End of Year	$46.4	$42.2	$37.6

Callout notes:

- Amount received or receivable from customers.
- Part of income used for wages, salaries, raw materials, fuel and supplies and certain taxes.
- Part of income used for salespeople's commissions, advertising, officers' salaries and other general expenses.
- Provision from income for the reduction of the service life of machinery and buildings.
- The remainder after deducting the above expenses from sales, but before providing for interest charges and taxes.
- Amount required for interest on borrowed funds.
- Amount paid or payable for taxes.
- This amount was earned for stockholders.
- Earnings reinvested in the business. Usually not all of the year's earnings are paid out in dividends. Some are retained in the business for expansion or other purposes.

* After preferred share dividend requirements.

these reporters choose to emphasize the *predictability* of the announcements they are reporting on? The answer is that many of the people who turn to the business pages do so to gather information on which to base investment decisions—whether to sell their stock in Sears, for example—and the fortunes of such speculative investments may hinge on how events live up to expectations as much as on the events themselves. Bad news may be interpreted as good news by investors if they expected worse. *In a long-awaited announcement* tells investors and potential investors that Sears's move is not likely to jolt the stock market.

Often the information for investors is more direct:

> The First Chicago-American National announcement drew positive reactions from bank stock analysts and from other bankers in Chicago . . .
> . . . It will be an exceptionally good deal for both parties," said Robert Wilmouth, chairman of LaSalle National. "First Chicago is making an excellent acquisition, and the price is very good also."
>
> *Chicago Tribune*

How Will It Affect Workers?

The answer to this question will be of interest not only to a company's employees but to their family and friends, and to the merchants who sell to them. This story about the decline in the shoemaking business focuses on the fate of workers at one local plant:

> . . . At the Gardena Shoe Factory, there are about 200 piecework employees—a third less than at peak operating capacity—all working four-day weeks. The plant made 3,000 pairs of shoes a day last year; it now turns out only 1,800.
> The Gardena plant could be gone in one or two years, says Arthur Hirshberg, who runs it for Desco Shoe Corp., its New York-based parent.
>
> *Los Angeles Times*

How Will It Affect the Economy?

We may not use that product. We may not know anyone who works at one of those stores. We may prefer piggy banks to stock markets. But it is difficult to find anyone who can claim to be a disinterested observer of the waves of recovery and recession that raise and lower inflation, unemployment, profits, wages and interest rates. As a science, economics seems about at the stage medicine was 150 years ago. The predictions of economists often seem to go awry. Their prescriptions often seem about as effective as leeches applied to cure a fever. But readers need clues to the future course of the national and local economy, and reporters—as humbly and as unpretentiously as possible—must try to provide those clues:

> WASHINGTON—The economy has slowed in the current quarter to a 3.6 percent annual rate of growth, substantially below the pace set during the first half of the year . . .
> Although sharp drops in growth normally are cause for concern, some economists said the 3.6 percent growth rate for July through September was just what was needed to prolong the recovery.
>
> Associated Press in *The Philadelphia Inquirer*

Enterprise

The best business and labor stories seem to be written by reporters who can step back and provide some perspective on changes brought by new products, new markets and new technologies.

William Serrin convinced his editors to allow him to wander around Pittsburgh in, as Serrin puts it, "expanding circles" for three or four weeks in search of stories about the effect on workers of the decline in smokestack industries. Few newspapers can give their staff such luxuries, but Serrin says his "serendipity expedition" eventually led to dozens of stories.

Kathryn Harris, in an effort to "be the first in the nation to report on trends" in a trendy field—video games—suspected that the entry of so many companies into the field would bankrupt some of them. She vowed that she would do a story on the field every six weeks just to keep up. Her close monitoring of the industry helped her write one of the first stories on sharp price cutting in the industry as the market for games softened.

Karen Arenson was reading through *The Wall Street Journal* when she came across an article reporting that Kraft had lost a lot of money and had taken an $18 million tax write-off on cheese. She investigated and came up with a good story—the national cheese industry was suffering because of a failure to plan properly for highs and lows in milk production.

Leads to enterprising business stories are all around us—on the shelves at the local supermarket, for example: Why did the brand name suddenly change on the milk cartons? How are these new sugar-free cereals selling? And leads to labor stories may be standing behind the counter at the supermarket: Have those new computerized checkout machines that talk changed the training required of store employees? Do they result in fewer errors? Why do so many men seem to be taking the checkout jobs?

Many business stories will simply report on a company's earnings. Many labor stories will detail the progress of negotiations. But good reporters on either beat are too curious to restrict themselves to such routine coverage.

Additional Reading

Financial and Economic Journalism: Analysis, Interpretation and Reporting, Donald Kirsch, New York University Press, 1978.

How to Read a Financial Report, 4th edition, Merrill Lynch Pierce, Fenner & Smith Inc.

Understanding Financial Statements, The New York Stock Exchange, 1981.

Business Today, 3rd edition, David Rachman and Michael Mescon, Random House, 1982.

Financial Handbook, 5th edition, Edward I. Altman, John Wiley & Sons, 1981.

Where to Find Business Information: A Worldwide Guide for Everyone Who Needs Answers to Business Questions, David M. Brownstone and Gorton Carruith, John Wiley & Sons, 1979.

▪ A. Research Assignments ▪

ONE

Using research materials or interviews with people active in business and labor, write explanations that could be used in a newspaper article for the following terms.

1. Attrition

2. Commodities index

3. Gross national product

4. Stopping the clock in negotiations

5. M1

6. Eurodollars

7. Market share

8. COLA

9. Tax shelter

10. The morning fixing of the price of gold

11. Shop steward

12. Fixed assets

13. Chapter 11

14. Liquidity ratio

15. Capitalization ratio

TWO

Choose a corporation active in your area. Obtain answers to the following questions about that corporation, and illustrate some of those answers with quotes:

1. Who is the chief executive officer?

2. Who is the chief operating officer?

3. Who is the treasurer?

4. Who is the marketing director?

5. Is the corporation publicly or privately owned?

6. What business is the corporation involved in?

7. What was its net income last year?

8. What was its operating profit last year?

9. Who are its major competitors?

10. What are its major challenges in the next year?

11. What waste products, if any, does it release into the area's environment?

12. If its employees are unionized, to what unions do they belong?

13. How many jobs does the company provide in the area?

THREE

Choose one of these groups of workers:

orderlies and nurses' assistants at a nearby hospital
interns at a nearby hospital
secretaries at a local college
professors at a local college
sanitation workers in a nearby town
police in a nearby town
workers at a nearby factory
teachers in a local school district
workers at a nearby fast-food restaurant
clerks at a nearby supermarket

Obtain answers to the following questions about these workers, and illustrate some of the answers with quotes:

1. What, if any, union do they belong to?

2. What is their average starting salary?

3. What benefits are they entitled to?

4. What percentage salary increase did they receive last year?

5. How does this compare with the increase in the cost of living in your area?

6. What educational background and training is required for their jobs?

7. How frequently are workers fired?

8. What chance for advancement is there?

9. Have there been any major layoffs in recent years?

10. If they leave their jobs, how difficult would it be for them to find comparable positions?

■ B. Writing Assignments ■

Write stories based on each of the following collections of information. In each case you are writing for a newspaper dated tomorrow and read in the town where the events occurred.

ONE

A press release issued by the McDermitt Industries Corporation today:

McDermitt Industries Corporation, known for its leadership in the pest control business, was pleased to announce today that they have purchased the Get Em company, one of the nation's leading makers of rodent traps.

MIC purchased 100 percent of Get Em, a privately owned company from its president, Harvey L. Mainsprig, for $2.6 million.

MIC, with headquarters in Houston, Texas, is a publicly owned company with $6 million in assets. Their well-known products include: Watch Out bug sprays and Oh No You Don't insect traps. MIC also sells agricultural pest controls under the MIC NIX label. MIC ranks number four among the nation's leading pest control companies.

Get Em, which is exclusively in the rodent trap business, and which makes the popular Get Em mousetrap along with other rodent traps, presents new challenges to MIC's aggressive management team because of Get Em's $27,000 loss last year and $12,000 loss in the previous year.

From interview with Mainsprig: "Yeah, I have a comment. Not a happy one. I've owned this company since its birth 31 years ago this month. Get Em has been my life. But we were losing money, and I just didn't have the capital to keep Get Em alive by myself. I owed it to our employees to find someone who did. MIC fits the bill, yes, they do. It's one fine, well-managed company."

Get Em's central office and its only factory are located here in Cedar Spring on South Main Street. Get Em employs 56 workers.

From interview with Mayor Susan Apt: "Well, our goal is to save Get Em and the jobs it provides. McDermitt has the capital that Harvey apparently didn't have, but frankly we're a little worried about this. Harvey Mainsprig had a commitment to this town and its people. These new owners, some Houston corporation, could easily move the plant away from here. That's what we're going to have to make sure doesn't happen. I hope they didn't just buy Get Em for the brand name. I hope they bought the fine employees."

From an interview with George Gold, executive vice president of McDermitt, in Houston: "No, we have no plans to move Get Em. We are going to look very closely at their operations, but this is an exciting acquisition for us. We have great confidence in the company's future in the rodent trap field. Beyond that I wouldn't want to speculate."

TWO

1. DNA-Tec is a firm here in Watertown, working to develop commercial applications for gene-splicing techniques.

2. Three months ago, DNA-Tec introduced its first product, a widely publicized new bacteria that can increase the resistance of soy beans to certain types of insect damage.

3. Yesterday DNA-Tec's public relations director, Albert Devito, announced that the company had lost $3.2 million in the most recent quarter. Its sales were $5.1 million.

4. *Devito:* "Yesterday DNA-Tec's stock closed at 16 and a half."

5. *Devito:* "The company has lost money every quarter since it was founded three years ago: $5.2 million in the quarter before this; $10.2 million last year; $3.3 million in this quarter last year."

6. *Devito:* "We invested more than $10 million in a new laboratory to produce our soy-bean fortifier this year."

7. *Devito:* "We have sold a considerable amount of the product this month: there is no doubt that it is off to a fine start."

8. DNA-Tec's President Fred Strausberg is interviewed: "Let me emphasize that this is a fine, strong, promising company. We have expected some losses in these initial quarters as we begin to establish our product, but there is no doubt that this will soon be an extremely profitable company."

9. Harry Beuno, securities analyst with Andrews, Smith, Jones, who specializes in the new biotechnology companies: "To be honest, we expected a little more from DNA-Tec. So far from what we have seen, their soy production just hasn't taken off like we had expected, but there is no doubt that it is early in the game. Farmers may need more time to discover the product."

10. Reynold Smith, who sells the DNA-Tec product at his chain of local farm stores, Seth Smith's Supplies, says in an interview: "So far they haven't proven to our customers that this stuff works better than the pesticides we've been using for decades. It ain't cheap, and to be frank, some of our people are plain scared of it. We've sold some to folks who like to try something new. A lot of people will be waiting to see what they have to say."

11. Devito after he's called for one final question: "The product is not cheap. Yes, it may be more expensive than standard pesticides, but there is no doubt that farmers will save money on it in the long run, because it provides stronger protection against crop damage and is non-toxic."

12. Beuno says the cost of treating an acre of soy with DNA-Tec's product is $14. The cost, using the organophosphate pesticide, Parnagion, is $12.50.

13. After announcement, DNA-Tec stock was down 1 point by closing time on the American Stock Exchange.

14. Sharon Wolfer, securities analyst with Irving, Frank, who specializes in biotechnology companies: "Of course, I heard the news. No, it didn't surprise us. We knew they were having start-up troubles. But it's time for them to begin convincing investors that they will turn it around."

THREE

Paula Fortino is president of the National Office Workers union. Four months ago it won an election to represent 103 clerical employees at DNA-Tec here in Watertown. Fortino calls a press conference yesterday to explain that she will ask her DNA-Tec people for authorization to strike if she can't reach a contract settlement for them with DNA-Tec by next Friday.

Fortino: "You can quote me on this: These are some of the hardest working employees in this company. These are some of the hardest working employees I have ever seen. Yet here they keep roping in biology graduates who are still in diapers from every university in the country and paying them $100,000 a year, and my people, who are keeping the place running while they play with their test tubes, are making a lousy 15 Gs a year. Have you tried living in this community on that?"

Fortino is asked when the union might strike: "I will ask that my people call a strike Monday morning at 6 a.m. Let them try to run the place without us, that's what I say."

Fortino is asked if she knows that DNA-Tec lost $10.2 million last year and $3.2 million last quarter: "They keep saying that we should hang in there, that this thing is going to take off; well, my people can't pay rent with potential and promises. If they want to be a serious company, let them start paying like one. Strausberg hasn't exactly been suffering for the cause; he's bringing in $250 Gs a year, plus perks, during this so-called start-up time."

Fortino is asked what she is demanding: "Simple, give us a 5 percent hike in wages this year; 5 percent again next year; and then when all the bean bugs are in their graves

[DNA-Tec introduced a new bacterial product designed to increase resistance of soy beans to certain types of insect damage three months ago], we can open this thing up and start again."

Papers filed with the SEC report that company President Fred Strausberg earned $246,000 last year. There are no records available on the salaries of scientists. Strausberg does not return phone calls to his office.

DNA-Tec PR man Albert Devito says in an interview: "All I can say is that we have been negotiating in good faith; that we have made an offer of a 5 percent salary package over three years, that this is a company that is still in the starting stages and that with the losses we've suffered (confirms figures) we are in no position to pay more; and that we are outraged at Mrs. Fortino's attempt to hold a gun to our heads. That's it. No more questions."

In 20 interviews with DNA-Tec clerical workers in the cafeteria, none say they oppose the strike. Here are some representative quotes:

Ginnie Steward, secretary in the marketing department: "Look, most of us are here because this looked like an exciting place to be; but I support a kid, and on this salary I can't even buy him a bike. Nobody else around here is suffering. We're tired of being the heroes. We're ready to strike."

Ovidio Torres, secretary to the company president: "This is a good company. Mr. Strausberg's a fine man. But if he won't start paying us something approaching what we're worth, he's going to have to learn to do his word processing for himself. I say let's strike."

▪ C. Story Assignments ▪

1. Choose a publicly owned corporation and write a story on its performance last year based on the company's financial statements and interviews with people in and out of the company.

2. Write an article about the gardening and landscaping business in your area, focusing on one particularly successful company.

3. How difficult is it to start a restaurant in your area? Write about the obstacles that must be overcome and the chances of success based on interviews with a number of restaurant owners, workers and patrons. Focus on one restaurant.

4. Write an article on the unemployment situation in your town based on interviews with city officials, business leaders, labor leaders and unemployed workers.

5. Find a local union that is attempting to organize a new group of workers in your area and write an article on their efforts based on interviews with union leaders (there may be more than one union competing for the workers), workers and management.

CHAPTER 30

Science

Those who equate science with sour memories of pop quizzes on the periodic table need to take another look. "It intrudes everywhere," wrote Henry Grunwald, editor in chief of Time Inc., in the first issue of the general-interest science magazine *Discover.* "Airplanes crash and their designs are changed: science. The computer garbles your bank account: science. The atmosphere is polluted: science. It is cleaned up: science. Radiation hurts: science. Radiation heals: science."

For the most part, newspaper editors have been slow to recognize the far-reaching impact of science on readers. Several major newspapers, including *The New York Times, The Boston Globe* and Long Island's *Newsday,* have started weekly science sections within the last decade. But on most medium- and small-sized papers—and on some large ones—science, medicine and the environment still are among the last frontiers of largely unclaimed territory. More than likely a lone science writer or environment writer or medical writer has staked out some portion of this territory. The remainder, however, is there to be explored by any enterprising reporters eager to separate themselves from the horde of journalism school graduates.

Preparation

Whether they have degrees in science or not, science writers can't afford to stop studying. "It can be fun to pick out a challenging story you know nothing about . . . and learn," says Jim Detjen, science writer for *The Philadelphia Inquirer.* As an undergraduate at Rensselaer Polytechnic Institute in Troy, N.Y., Detjen took courses in physics, chemistry, biology and earth sciences. But, he says, "most of my expertise has been picked up along the way while researching stories."

Detjen notes that he spends about eight hours a week scanning two dozen popular and professional science journals ranging from *Physics Today* to *Science.* He clips articles in areas he plans to write about and in areas he suspects he might have to write about.

Stuart Diamond, an English major in college, says he devotes two or three hours a *day* to sorting through the mail he gets as environment writer at *Newsday.* He says he gets 50 to 75 letters and magazines a day and has filled about 30 file drawers with clippings and notes he can turn to for background information. "A story on solar energy eventually has to explain how solar energy works," says Diamond, adding that at times he has read hundreds of pages or more just to glean "a few crystal clear paragraphs on how something functions."

All this takes patience. "If you aren't interested in learning for learning's sake, you shouldn't be a science writer," Diamond counsels.

Complexity and Uncertainty

What scares reporters away from science stories is what scares students away from science courses: They seem so complicated, so abstract. That is a problem. Many scientists, for one thing, work in a language most of the rest of us don't understand—higher mathematics. There is no way a reporter without graduate-level training is going to be able fully to understand recent developments in subatomic particle physics.

Science news is also filled with a level of uncertainty that can trip up all but the most careful reporters. City councils, eventually, vote yes or no. Juries decide either to convict or acquit. Unemployment rates go up or down. Scientists, on the other hand, frequently get results that *if confirmed, suggest* a *relationship* between two things.

Science reporting presents more problems than most other kinds of reporting. There's no way around that. But good reporters who have mastered the skills outlined elsewhere in this book can succeed in helping the public understand how scientists are changing the world. Here are some suggestions on how that can be done.

Ask

The key to reporting and writing science is breaking codes (See Chapter 2, Plain English). At some point reporters must force scientists to leave the equations and the statistics and try to explain in plain English what they've found and why it's important. Reporters may not be able to master the physics of subatomic particles. But, with work and help, they can understand something about the implications of these particles.

To build understanding, science writers must be prepared to ask simple questions and to persist in pursuing those questions until scientists respond in language the reporter and, therefore, the reader, can understand. "If need be, I'll spend a half hour trying to get an understanding of a single phrase," says Stuart Diamond. If one source can't explain the point, Diamond will turn to another.

Explain

The next job is making sure readers will understand, too. Analogies can be invaluable for making sense out of the complex, as in the *New York Times* story that described a "magnetic gun" as so powerful that it was like "launching a bullet with a lightning bolt." (See Chapter 5, Analogies, Metaphors and Clichés.)

Specific examples, written in simple language, can help make the abstract or complex easier for readers to grasp. The following paragraphs from a *New York Times* story on the use of robots in brain surgery make clear just how delicate the procedure has to be:

. . . he said it is important to secure any robot used in an operating room so that "some glitch does not injure the surgeon or patient."

Such a glitch, which did not cause any damage, occurred in the second operation here, Dr. Ceverha said. A fleeting power surge while the computer was sending its instructions resulted in the robotic arm being off target by an inch. In the brain, Dr. Ceverha said, an inch is as good as a mile.

The neurosurgeon working with the robotic arm that day recognized there was a problem before the drilling started, and the device was reprogrammed.

Qualify

No matter how significant a step forward they represent, few if any advances in scientific knowledge are reached without some lingering doubts remaining. Will the link between that virus and certain cancers prove merely coincidental? Can the work establishing the link be duplicated? If the connection stands up, will it lead to any progress toward a cure?

Reporters must make sure they are aware of what doubts the researchers, and their critics, hold. And in writing up those researchers' findings, they must be sure not to overstate their significance. That means using words like *suggests, indicates* and *points to an association,* rather than *proves.* And it means informing readers of the questions that remain to be answered.

Scientists in New Jersey *have reported progress* in developing an unorthodox form of nuclear power that they say avoids radiation hazards and does not depend on radioactive fuels.

However, the optimistic progress report by United Sciences Inc. of Princeton, N.J., . . . *was greeted with some skepticism* by other physicists. They said while the process might eventually be useful, its success appeared technologically remote.

The New York Times

Bring out the Significance

Without being oversold, the importance of scientific findings *does* have to be made evident—and right away. In a murder story, a reporter doesn't have to take time out to explain why death is important. But a science writer, dealing with esoteric and seemingly remote developments, almost always has to sell the story, to make clear why the reader should care. Sometimes this job is done in the lead itself, sometimes in the second paragraph.

The author of this piece devoted his lead to explaining what experts—his sources—considered to be the implications of research efforts with brain-dead lab animals rather than to detailing what scientists had accomplished:

> Doctors who have been looking for ways to prevent the severe brain damage that follows stroke say they may be on the verge of success, offering some victims for the first time the hope of resuming normal lives.
>
> *The New York Times*

Of course, interpreting significance entails risk. It forces reporters to sort out which "experts" really are expert and which are merely promoting their work.

Whom Do You Trust?

Reporters usually are skeptical people, trained to doubt, to question, to see the other side. Yet some reporters seem to undergo a change of personality on the science beat. "A sort of spreading of the gospel theme has always been a part of science writing," laments Nicholas Wade, who writes editorials on science and technology for *The New York Times*. "A reporter in another field would be horrified if someone told him his primary responsibility was to get across his source's message clearly."

Part of the explanation for the lack of skepticism of some science writers is that science can seem so intimidating: It's difficult for a reporter who barely passed freshman chemistry to challenge the interpretation of some scientific issue by a professor of chemistry. Another part of the explanation is that science can seem so pure. Aren't we taught from grade school onward that scientists are people who have devoted themselves to the rigorous and selfless pursuit of knowledge?

The best science writers, however, never forget that scientists, in fact, are far from infallible. Scientists can make errors in gathering the data on which they base their conclusions. They can make errors in interpreting what their findings mean. And they frequently disagree among themselves, sometimes sharply, on subjects ranging from the origin of the universe to the impact of manmade environmental pollutants on the cancer rate.

Again, scientific findings are based on *evidence*—which is not the same as *proof*. Scientists interpret evidence differently, and different experiments can produce seemingly contradictory evidence. This is healthy. The history of science is the history of old theories being proven wrong.

It also helps to remember that scientists, like the rest of us, can have their blind spots caused by political, economic and professional interests. A scientist whose work is funded by tobacco companies, to pick an obvious example, may be a little extra cautious about conceding a relationship between smoking and cancer. And scientists, no matter what degrees or prizes they have been awarded, are no more likely to make sense on political questions—the nuclear arms race, for example—than others of us who have thought deeply about these subjects.

This is not to say that science reporters must live in fear of charlatans and blowhards; it is only to say that they have to make the same judgments about the credibility of their sources that other reporters make. They must be cautious. Who is funding the research? What has the scientist accomplished before? How have other scientists reacted to the findings? What evidence does the scientist provide? Has the research been accepted for publication in a reputable journal or presented at a reputable conference? Who has competing theories?

The fact that a new theory is unpopular does not make it wrong. Ask Galileo! But the fact that an idea is not receiving support certainly must be considered and reported. In the end, the best means of gauging the credibility of sources is to talk to a lot of them—try to hear out the full spectrum of views. Careful and thorough reporting won't necessarily uncover who is right, but it will protect the reporter from being intimidated and the public from being misled.

Sources

The day news of a serious accident at the Three Mile Island nuclear plant made front-page headlines nationwide, *Newsday*'s Stuart Diamond began telling his readers what had happened and why. Diamond's first article about the crippled plant said human error played a major part in causing the accident. It was an assertion the Nuclear Regulatory Commission, the agency in charge of regulating the industry and investigating the accident, denied and would continue denying for a week, Diamond recalls. But it was correct.

How did Diamond know more than the NRC and have the confidence to take on the experts? He had sources inside the plant. According to Diamond, a scientist at Brookhaven National Laboratories whom he knew called a friend who was working for the utility and told him to trust Diamond.

A former investigative reporter, Diamond collects sources as an entomologist collects insects. He keeps the name and phone number of every person he interviews; he adds to that file the names and numbers of experts in various fields drawn from the mail and the articles that cross his desk. In all, Diamond estimates he has amassed the names and phone numbers of 20,000 sources, enough to fill a modest-sized city telephone directory. As a result, he says, he never finds himself dependent on the availability of a single source at deadline time. "When I get a story at 3 in the afternoon, the first 10 people on my list may be unavailable," Diamond explains. "You need 15 names, just in case. You need depth."

Science reporters might begin building that depth with visits or calls to the following places and people:

Universities

University and college science departments, laboratories and research hospitals are full of one invaluable resource — experts. The list of science faculty at a nearby university will give new science writers their first list of potential sources. Reporters should get to know these professors and be aware of their areas of expertise. "When I was working on a series on toxic wastes awhile ago," Jim Detjen recalls, "I approached a toxicologist at a local university and asked him to give me an impromptu lecture on basic toxicology and a list of what to read."

University scientists also make news in their own right:

> Scientists at the State University at Stony Brook have found what may be the first major evidence that homosexuality and heterosexuality are at least partially biological in nature.
>
> (Long Island, N.Y.) *Newsday*

When Detjen began as a science writer for *The Philadelphia Inquirer,* he spent two weeks meeting the public relations person for every major university and research center around Philadelphia. "Getting stories from PR people at major universities is one of the main ways of getting stories in science," he says.

Two directories put out by the American Association for the Advancement of Science (AAAS) help reporters find out whom to contact. One, the *Public Information Contact Directory,* lists the addresses and phone numbers of public relations contacts at universities and public and private research centers. The other, the *Reporter's Guide to Key Research Activities in Science and Engineering,* summarizes research activities at 250 university, government and private research facilities.

Conferences

While science reporters obviously can't attend every major conference at which scientists meet to discuss their research, it is certainly useful to visit some. Conferences are a good place to learn about recent advances in a field and to meet some of the top experts. At times, a conference's list of participants can be as valuable — as a guide to sources — as the conference itself. (These lists are available to reporters whether or not they attend.)

Findings presented at a conference can be reported in a breaking news story or lay the foundation for a broader look at a problem, as was the case with this story in *The New York Times:*

> The world's seas and oceans, already polluted with spilled oil, toxic chemicals and radioactive waste, are now being fouled by a new and insidious form of pollution — plastic waste.
>
> . . . The problem has become so serious that 150 marine wildlife researchers from 10 countries met recently at the University of Hawaii in Honolulu for the *first international conference* on the issue.

Government Agencies

It's important that the science beat not be reduced to the "Gee! Wow! What'll they think of next?" beat. Science writers must remember that the rewards of science — superstrong plastics, genetically engineered plants, nuclear power — carry attendant risks. One way to stay on top of the problems associated with science is to get in touch with the government agencies that are supposed to monitor and minimize many of those risks.

A reporter investigating a tip that workers in a local plastics plant are being exposed to toxic chemicals might turn to the federal Occupational Safety and Health Administration or the state department of health. An investigation of records at the local OSHA office, for example, would help determine whether the plant has been visited by federal regulators. Further information on that plastics plant might be obtained from OSHA's sister agency, the National Institute of Occupational Safety and Health in Cincinnati, which puts out hundreds of documents that discuss the uses and potential abuses of various chemicals in the workplace.

Reporters sniffing around a local nuclear power plant would want to be in touch with people at the Nuclear Regulatory Commission. Reporters following a flu epidemic would contact the Centers for Disease Control in Atlanta, which keep detailed information on epidemics nationwide and try to trace their cause. (Most federal and state agencies publish directories that define the responsibilities of their key personnel and provide phone numbers.)

Regulatory agencies should not be a reporter's last stop, however. The Nuclear Regulatory Commission proved a less than reliable source during the accident at Three Mile Island; the Environmental Protection Agency moved slowly in cleaning up toxic wastes. Indeed, at times a regulatory agency's foot-dragging in enforcing its own rules becomes a major story in itself. A good place to start on such a story might be the General Accounting Office, which conducts investigations for Congress into how well certain federal programs are functioning.

Trade Groups and Professional Organizations

In contacting sources at trade organizations, it's important to find out who funds them and which economic and political interests they represent. Don't be fooled by independent-sounding names. During the debate in the 1970s over whether saccharin should be labeled a carcinogen, the Calorie Control Council was widely quoted attacking research that showed that the artificial sweetener caused cancer in laboratory animals. Few such reports bothered to identify the Calorie Control Council as an organization representing the manufacturers of artificial sweeteners, including saccharin, according to the *Columbia Journalism Review.*

Representatives of trade organizations—the Atomic Industrial Forum and the Chemical Manufacturers Association are two of the most vocal—sometimes can be helpful sources as long as their views are carefully attributed and the other side is contacted. "Industry groups are more useful than people think," Diamond says. "People tend to distrust them, but they know more than anyone thinks because their livelihood is at stake." Certainly it's worth getting on the mailing lists of these organizations.

Professional organizations, such as the American Medical Association, are less likely to push a product, as the Atomic Industrial Forum pushes nuclear energy. But these organizations have their biases, too. Reporters shouldn't expect an unbiased response from the AMA on an issue affecting the income of doctors.

Public Interest Groups

Public interest groups—the Natural Resources Defense Council and the Environmental Defense Fund are two that are well known—also have an ax to grind. Nevertheless, they play an important role as watchdogs of government and industry. Reporters will want to be on the mailing list of a wide range of these groups. The scientific data behind their arguments is sometimes incomplete, but they can be quite useful in identifying potential stories. For example, environmental groups complained long and loudly about poor enforcement of toxic-waste laws under the Reagan administration before Congress began investigating. (The *Conservation Directory* published annually by the National Wildlife Federation in Wash-

ington, D.C., provides an excellent list of public interest groups.)

Media Resources Service of the Scientists' Institute for Public Information (SIPI)

This non-profit organization has tried over the past decade to find responsible scientists in a range of fields who are willing to talk to reporters. SIPI attempts to identify what areas scientists have expertise in and what biases they might bring to an interview. When a reporter calls, the service, located in New York City, acts as an intermediary, supplying the names and backgrounds of scientists who might be helpful on the story.

"If something comes up in the news and I need to write a story but don't know much about it, I'll call them," says Detjen. "Once a truck overturned and a beehive on it fell off. The bees went wild. They swarmed into a nearby development and stung enough people so badly that 25 or 30 went to the hospital. I needed a bee expert and I needed one quickly . . . They helped me track one down and I was able to write a spot-news story explaining the bees' behavior."

SIPI's service can be reached by calling (800)223-1730.

The Hastings Center

If the story is not how terminally ill patients can be kept alive but whether it is *ethical* to artificially prolong their lives, reporters will want to give the Hastings Center a call. The Center, located in Westchester County, N.Y., has a staff of philosophers, political scientists and sociologists who specialize in *bioethics,* the ethical ramifications of science.

Journals

Too much science writing is really just the rewriting of articles that have appeared in science magazines and journals. Reporters seem to wait hungrily for the arrival of the latest issue of *Science* or the *New England Journal of Medicine,* probably the two most prestigious American journals, in the hope that they will contain an article that can be popularized—perhaps a new development in the struggle to understand cancer, perhaps a new study on the relationship between alcohol and illness.

There is nothing wrong with using journal articles. In fact, reporters would be remiss if they failed to keep up with these important sources of information and ideas. But reporters who use a journal article as the basis for a story must be conscientious about making phone calls to its author and others in the field to verify, clarify and expand on the findings it reports.

This story by science writer Richard Knox of *The Boston Globe* is based on a paper published in an issue of the *Proceedings of the National Academy of Sciences:*

> Scientists at Stanford University have gotten their hands on the elusive chemical "switch" that activates the machinery of cell division.
>
> The feat should make possible a long-sought goal of geneticists: To sort out the component parts of this crucial biochemical signal so they can understand how it works — or fails to work — in normal growth and in disease.
>
> In a scientific paper published yesterday, the researchers said . . .

Knox's research began in a journal, but it didn't end there. In the paragraphs that followed, he went on to quote not only from a telephone interview with one of the paper's authors but from an interview with Dr. Gerald Selzer of the National Institutes of Health, whom he identified as a leading researcher in the field. Selzer called the findings "an important step in understanding the origin of replication in the bacterial cell."

One problem with covering science by reading journals is that journals are slow. Much of the news released in journals could have been available to the enterprising reporter months earlier. "By the time a story gets to *Science,* it's not fresh," says Stuart Diamond. "I've traced stories from a draft, to a research paper, to a technical journal to *The New York Times.* It usually takes six to eight months."

Diamond and other aggressive reporters try to learn the results of major studies and experiments *before* these findings are published in a journal. They hope their sources will lead them to potentially newsworthy research or that they will spot interesting projects when they are first presented as papers at conferences. There is a danger in trying to beat the journals, however. The major scientific journals employ strict checks in an attempt to weed out sloppy research. Reporters working with unpublished findings assume more responsibility for evaluating the credibility of that work themselves.

Old journal articles, of course, also make excellent background reading for a reporter tackling a new subject. Rather than trying to search all the many journals that write on a field, reporters often will rely on indexes of journals to find articles of interest. Probably the most useful science index for journalists is the *General Science Index,* which 10 times a year lists by subject area the articles run in nearly 100 English language periodicals, from the scholarly *Science* to the general interest *Science Digest.* Many other indexes or abstracts exist that cover specific areas of science.

References

No science writer, no matter how well trained, can avoid stumbling on unfamiliar terms, names and designs. That's why most try to keep a good selection of reference books handy. Here are a few that are particularly helpful:

1. *Van Nostrand's Scientific Encyclopedia (6th Edition).* What exactly is a quark? Quark (a subatomic particle) and more than 20,000 other scientific terms and concepts are discussed in this two-volume work. For more detailed explanation: McGraw-Hill publishes a 17-volume *Encyclopedia of Science and Technology.*

2. *The Way Things Work: An Illustrated Encyclopedia of Technology.* How are you going to explain to readers why the airplane crashed on takeoff if you don't really understand how any plane gets off the ground? This multivolume work is filled with explanations, for non-scientists, of how devices ranging from the artificial heart to airplanes work.

3. *McGraw-Hill Dictionary of Scientific and Technical Terms.* This can be the first step in translating scientific jargon into plain English. Among the 98,500 terms in the 3rd edition is *agitator body,* which is no more than a drum, mounted on a truck, for transporting freshly mixed concrete. *Black's Medical Dictionary,* now in its 33rd edition, will aid in penetrating the vocabulary of medicine.

4. *American Men and Women of Science.* Want to know something about the background and research interests of that scientist you are about to interview? This seven-volume set is a good place to start. It provides current biographical information on thousands of leading researchers in all disciplines of science. It will explain, for example, that Stephen J. Gould, noted for his theories and writings about evolution, has been a winner of the no-strings-attached McArthur Fellowship, a cash award allowing recipients to do whatever they please.

5. *The Handbook of Toxic and Hazardous Chemicals.* This is a useful desk manual for any reporter covering occupational and environmental health stories. It contains concise health and safety information on some 600 of the most commonly found chemical pollutants in air, water and wastes. Readers can quickly learn, for example, that creosote is a flammable, heavy oil with a sharp, smoky smell; that it is absorbed through the skin; and that

the Environmental Protection Agency considers creosote a carcinogen.

Basic Stories

Science seems to make news more and more frequently: An electrical engineer figures out how to squeeze more circuits onto a silicon chip; another pesticide is found to cause cancer in animals; a new artificial organ is tested; radio astronomers think they can "hear" the Big Bang, which is generally believed to have given birth to the universe. This news usually falls into one of the following categories:

New Regulations

The federal government and state governments periodically revise regulations affecting the environment, energy pricing and exploration, and occupational health. Less frequently, they set standards for research in other areas of science, such as recombinant DNA (the replicating and rearranging of genes) and cryptography (the use and deciphering of secret codes). The most important regulations make news when they are announced and, if reporters are following their beat closely, some time after they are implemented when reporters should examine whether they've worked.

> In an attempt to curtail the flow of chemical pollutants into New Jersey's rivers and underground reservoirs, the state Department of Environmental Protection next week will propose standards for disposing of hazardous wastes.
>
> *The (Bergen County, N.J.) Record*

Reports

Government agencies, congressional committees and private organizations periodically release reports or studies evaluating the latest scientific information available about a controversial subject:

> Acid raid could be reduced significantly with a 6 percent increase in consumer electric bills if utilities pursue the least costly pollution measures, *according to a new government study.*
>
> *The Providence (R.I.) Bulletin*

Stories on these reports should be discussed in the context of the ongoing debate to which they contribute. The *Bulletin* drew on an earlier study to provide context for its story:

> The National Academy of Sciences last month issued a report linking coal-burning boilers to acid rain in the Northeast and Canada.

Discoveries

Firsts always make news, whether in sports or in science:

> A satellite carrying an infrared telescope has discovered swarms of large particles around the star Vega, and scientists say they think the particles and the star make up a complete solar system like our sun and the nine planets and thousands of asteroids and meteorites that surround it.
>
> *The Washington Post* News Service in *The Philadelphia Inquirer*

Understanding a first in sports — "the first woman to win three gold medals in cross country skiing" — is rarely difficult. But in science it may take considerable work to pin down just what makes the story significant:

> If true, it is the first evidence that the universe contains a second solar system like this one. Though scientists have speculated for years that the earth and its eight sister planets are not alone in the cosmos, they have never had evidence that their speculations were correct.

Advances in Knowledge

These may be reported in scientific journals, announced at conferences or uncovered by an enterprising reporter. Their news value often depends on their potential applications:

> SAN FRANCISCO — A new drug that was isolated from a fungus may significantly increase the success rate of organ transplants and enable surgeons to replace organs they couldn't transplant before, according to a panel of medical researchers.
>
> *Chicago Tribune*

Threats

And now the bad news:

> San Diego drinking water contains two to four times the levels allowed under new federal regulations of a group of suspected cancer-causing agents, according to chemical analysis performed for The San Diego Union.
>
> *The San Diego Union*

Chemicals pollute air and water; "swine flu" seems to threaten, then the swine flu vaccine threatens; satellites tumble down from space; fallout from Chinese nuclear tests drifts down on the land where Pennsylvania cows graze. Science reporters owe readers the same thoroughness and the same care on these stories that they apply to scientific advances.

It is easy to alarm people. It is harder to help them to evaluate just how dangerous those chemicals in their drinking water are. Science writers often must tread a thin line between a desire not to spread unwarranted panic and an equally strong obligation to give readers the whole truth. Some also must resist editors who, perhaps panicked themselves by the news of traces of a pesticide in food, aren't interested in the qualifying sentences explaining that the risks to humans are unknown and that the acceptable levels of consumption allowed by regulators are somewhat arbitrary.

Enterprise

There are few, if any, beats on which reporters devote more time to stories that are not about breaking news. Science writers frequently step back from the rush of the new or the scary to give readers a more leisurely look at science at work or at the science that explains how the world works.

Explaining

The New York Times had a news story detailing the death and destruction unleashed by a major earthquake in Mexico, but it shared the front page with an article, by science writer Walter Sullivan, that tried to explain *why:*

It was an earthquake that had to happen.
The epicenter of the earthquake that devastated parts of Mexico yesterday lies along the front where the Pacific Ocean floor drives under the Mexican coast, tearing at the underpinnings of the continent.
The relentless pressure has caused scores of earthquakes along the line, much like firecrackers on a string. It was just a matter of time before the next one struck . . .

The New York Times

A subject doesn't have to be as alarming as an earthquake to warrant an explanation. Scientists are working to understand aspects of the world as diverse as ice ages, human memory and honeybees. What they have learned can be fascinating.

Informing

The readers of science articles, whatever else they may have in common, all are consumers. They may want to know how to buy a personal computer and how to find out if their drinking water is safe; whether to buy generic drugs and whether to feed their babies on demand. The answers to such questions, which often center on how to stay healthy and how to treat illness, are the basis of numerous articles, called *service articles* because they provide consumers with a

service—information they may be able to use to improve their lives:

The first prescription pill approved to fight genital herpes—Zovirax—reaches drug stores today, and already doctors are deluged with inquiries.
Doctors say the drug, known generically as acyclovir, will be a boon to many herpes sufferers. But it should be prescribed only for those who have at least six outbreaks of herpes sores a year.

USA Today

The pool of questions service articles might answer is deep. What can be done to reduce the pollution caused inside our homes by heating and cooking? What foods cause the least buildup of cholesterol? What's the most effective way of treating breast cancer?

Of course, in providing answers, reporters must take great care not to become inadvertent mouthpieces for those who profit by overselling a less-than-perfect remedy. In 1982, for example, the drug accutane was promoted in the media as a cure for acne. What some of these reports failed to note, according to the *Columbia Journalism Review,** was that the drug was suspected of having the potential to cause birth defects in the babies of women who took it during pregnancy.

Research

Science writers don't always just sit back and wait for scientists to finish their research. Often the research itself is interesting, whether or not it has produced conclusions. What efforts are now being made to conquer AIDS? How are scientists studying the increasingly tiny particles they have found inside the atom? How do scientists investigate theories that brain chemistry can cause mental illness?

Jim Detjen decided to see what researchers were up to with the world's fastest laser:

HOLMDEL, N.J.—It's a slow day for the world's fastest laser at Bell Laboratories.
Tiny strings of glowing red and green light beams zigzag across the darkened room causing dust particles to dance in the air. A steady "Beep! Beep! Beep!" hums rhythmically in the background.
The researchers are firing their laser, a device that emits intense beams of focused light, at a relatively ho-hum pace. Since it is merely a demonstration, they have adjusted the laser to shoot out pulses of light that last for a leisurely 80 femtoseconds, or 80 millionths of a billionth of a second.
. . . A revolution is under way in the way people communicate . . .

The Philadelphia Inquirer

* "Pushing New Drugs—Can the Press Kick the Habit," Jim Sibbison, *Columbia Journalism Review,* July/August 1985.

Public Policy

The intersection between science and society is always worthy of attention by reporters. Jim Detjen again:

PITTSBURGH — The robot is marching steadily from the pages of science fiction into the nation's factories. Already about 6,000 are in place, and the number could climb to 100,000 by 1990.

But as robots slide, swivel and twist their way into the nation's work places, some experts are worried that the nation is not adequately prepared for this industrial invasion.

Two researchers at Carnegie-Mellon University here argue in a new book that the United States had better start paying attention to robots, or else there could be significant disruptions to American society.

The Philadelphia Inquirer

Many such scientific advances create questions for public policy: Could genetic-splicing techniques produce dangerous organisms? Might faster, more powerful computers pose a threat to privacy? Is manned space flight a useful investment of the nation's resources? Of course, the most serious of such questions are posed by weapons research.

Follow-up

It's important in science, as in any area of reporting, not to let events come and go before their impact can be fully understood. Certain stories demand follow-up. What became of that proposal to reduce acid rain? Has anything else been learned about that apparent solar system near the star Vega? Has that drug made from a fungus had any effect on organ transplants?

Four years after the accident at Three Mile Island, Jim Detjen returned to investigate how the cleanup of radioactive contamination was going and why it was taking so long. His story began this way:

When Larry King came to work at the crippled Three Mile Island reactor in June 1980, he felt confident the cleanup would be done in a thoroughly professional manner.

"This was one place where I figured there wouldn't be any shortcuts," he said recently. "After all, the eyes and ears of the world are on this place."

But now, almost three years later, King says he is a disillusioned man . . .

The Philadelphia Inquirer

Additional Reading

A Passion to Know, American Association for the Advancement of Science, 1984.

Frontiers of Science, National Geographic Society, 1982.

Reflections on Science and the Media, June Goodfield, American Association for the Advancement of Science, 1981.

The Lives of a Cell, Lewis Thomas, Bantam Books, 1974.

The Soul of a New Machine, Tracy Kidder, Avon, 1981.

The Techno/Peasant Survival Manual, The Print Project, Bantam Books, 1980.

"Environmental Reporters: Prisoners of Gullibility," *Washington Monthly,* March 1984.

"Why Is Science Writing So Uncritical of Science?" *SIPIscope,* Scientists' Institute for Public Information, January/February 1984.

▪ A. Research Assignments ▪

ONE

Using research materials or interviews with scientists, write explanations that could be used in a newspaper article for the following terms.

1. White dwarf

2. Chemotherapy

3. Greenhouse effect

4. Local area network

5. Messenger RNA

6. Heavy water

7. Electromagnetic spectrum

8. ROM

9. Restriction enzyme

10. Halogenated organic compound

TWO

Write explanations for the following that might be used in a newspaper article on the subject. Draw on reference books and interviews with local scientists and science teachers.

1. How does an airplane get off the ground?
2. What causes sleet?
3. How do cats purr?
4. How does a breeder reactor work?
5. Why do stars appear to twinkle?
6. How does a battery produce energy?
7. How does photographic film work?
8. How do bats fly in the dark?
9. What causes a total solar eclipse?
10. What does an antihistamine do?

▪ B. Writing Assignments ▪

Write articles based on the following collections of information. In each case you are writing for a newspaper dated tomorrow and read in the town where the events occurred.

ONE

Dr. Eric Vandenberg, a research orthopedist who has headed a team of six scientists at Wellfleet University Medical Center, a leading center in San Francisco in rehabilitative medicine, in speech today: "Ladies and gentlemen, friends. We are pleased to announce today that we have invented an artificial kneecap so flexible and durable that we think it will be possible, as soon as the federal Food and Drug Administration reviews our work, to implant it in growing children. We consider this a significant breakthrough for two reasons, really. The first is this: Nearly 2,000 children in the United States are born each year with a damaged kneecap. About 500 of these children have no kneecap at all and must walk stiff legged. The condition eventually leads to stunted growth in the impaired knee and life-long difficulties with walking. Secondly, about 1,200 children under 12 each year suffer serious and debilitating injury to one or both kneecaps. Through the demands of sports medicine, artificial kneecaps with the flexibility and movement of real kneecaps were invented about 15 years ago and have been used widely to replace the damaged kneecaps of athletes. Although these athletes can no longer compete professionally, they usually are spared a lifetime of pain and repeated operations. They recover about 85 to 90 percent of the mobility of a person with a sound kneecap. But until now, no artificial kneecap has been implanted in the knee of a growing child.

"There are, as you will see, a number of reasons for this. As we grow, our bones grow and the ligaments attaching our bones grow. We get bigger, we get stronger. More pressure is placed on a natural kneecap as we get bigger, but of course the kneecap is growing as well. In the past we did not have a material flexible and adaptable enough to in a sense 'grow' at the same rate as the rest of our body. We also had to figure out what on average that growth was, how much the stress on a kneecap increases during natural growth and how we could construct a material that would respond to the expected increase in stress the same way a natural kneecap works. Five years ago we began experimenting with a material called Synflex-T. It is light, malleable and flexible when pressure is applied in certain ways over a period of time, but it also is durable and strong. Through four years of trials with chimpanzees we discovered ways to construct a kneecap that, we believe, will 'grow' at the same rate as the components of the leg attached to the kneecap grow. Two years ago the FDA gave us permission to operate on five toddlers at the hospital suffering from severe lesoitis, which is the name given the condition in which babies are born without a kneecap joining the upper and lower leg. We are now prepared to announce that all five of these children, who are now 4, are walking and running as well as their peers. Though they've grown an average of 8 inches, their ligaments and bones have not destroyed the kneecap because it has grown too, and at the right rate. . . . The FDA has asked us to continue following the progress of these children for two more years. If, as we suspect, the Synflex-T kneecap continues to keep pace with their growth, we will ask to make this operation available to the 3,200 children each year who would benefit from it. The operation optimally should be done on children before age 2 so that bone structure and muscular development are not dwarfed by the birth disability. But it could also be done on older children who suffer a debilitating knee injury."

Call to Dr. Signor Vanderschmidt, who wrote a recent article on advances in artificial parts for the *Mid-Atlantic Medical Monthly,* a respected journal. Dr. Vanderschmidt is Dean of the Medical School at Weibolt University in Boston: "You know, I've been watching Eric's work eagerly for some months now. He is a brilliant young medical researcher who has already published widely in this field. This new kneecap should be a great step forward. It is even more important in my mind because it should give some children, born with serious disabilities, a chance to lead a normal life."

TWO

Alfred Gigli, director of environmental protection for the county Health Department, at a press conference today: "We've had some complaints of late from the families on Pawanett Road off of Western Highway here in Altoona. They've expressed concern for a few weeks now that their drinking water smells like gasoline. As you know, the homes along Pawanett used to be summer cottages and date back to before the time when the town started a central water system. All 17 homes draw their water from wells ranging from 50 to 125 feet deep. Anyway, we acted as quickly as possible and took samples of water at all the homes earlier this week. Our analysis at Tuckahoe Laboratories shows that the water had benzene in it. The house with the shallowest well belongs to Keith McBurney. That's number 14. We found 3 parts per million of benzene in his water sample. The other samples show a range from somewhere in the area of 850 parts per billion of benzene in the water to 2 and a half parts per million.

"Just to be on the safe side, we've asked the fire department to take a pumper out to Pawanett to provide drinking water to residents until we can get to the bottom of this. We're also asking residents to boil their water before using it for cooking . . .

"How high is 3 parts per million? Well it means there are three parts of benzene for every 999,997 parts of water. That's not a whole lot. But it also means that somehow benzene got into the underground water table, which is a cause for concern. We aren't sure where it got in, where it came from or how fast it's moving. There isn't any state regulation for benzene — it just isn't in water that much, but no one wants to drink water that smells like gasoline. Yes, the state does have a recommended level. It says no one should drink from a water supply with anything more than 5 parts per billion of benzene.

"Where did the benzene come from? We're looking into that now. We've asked the Arcon Gas Station on Faraquat Street to run a test on its underground gas tank. It's a good quarter mile from Pawanett but it's uphill and it's straight east. Another possibility is the Chemtron Industrial Products plant, which is no more than 100 yards to the north. The company makes dyes and plastics and synthetics, and it's our understanding a good bit of benzene is used in making these things. We've written to the company asking whether it uses benzene and in what quantities . . .

"One thing you really should understand though. Benzene is one of the most common chemicals around. Up until a few years ago it was in paint removers, rubber cement and artists' supplies and you still get a pretty good hit anytime you gas up your car . . . You are likely to breathe a few parts per billion of the stuff just standing by a busy highway and breathing in. And workers are allowed to be exposed to up to 10 parts per million every day . . . Still nobody wants to drink gasoline and you always want to be careful with benzene. We know that it's been strongly linked to leukemia, or blood cancer, in workers exposed to levels slightly above that workplace limit. We don't know whether any amount of it is okay to smell or drink. It's always smart to be careful."

Call to McBurney. "Tell my wife this stuff is harmless. She's been getting headaches for a couple of months now, bad ones, right between the eyes, and the doctor don't know where they come from. It smells like we're standing in a gas station when we take a shower sometimes. I got two kids, 8 and 10, and you've got to wonder what this will mean for them in 20 or 30 years. Who knows? I've been asking around and no one seems to know . . . My wife's name? Naomi, she's 33. Kids are Douglas, he's the 8-year-old, and Sarah, she's 10. It's been roughest for Naomi though. The kids are at school and me, I work for the town Department of Public Works, but Naomi's home all day. Gigli may say this stuff is harmless but then why does the state say 'don't drink it'? And why does my wife get excruciating headaches she never got before?"

Call to Arcon gas: Attendant says: "We have nothing to say. The boss has been called and we're looking into it. All I do is pump gas, friend. Talking to reporters isn't in my contract."

Call to Chemtron Public Affairs Officer Dori Prentice: "Chemtron is a good neighbor. We've been at this site seven years. We hire people from the community. We contribute to charity. If there is a leak, and we certainly don't think we're responsible, it would come as a shock to us. Yes, we do have a benzene storage tank. It holds 2,000 gallons underground, but we doubt it leaks. Still, we'll do everything we can to cooperate with the investigation."

Call to Judy Goodman, professor of occupational health, Winston University: "Yes, we've done a lot of retrospective studies on benzene exposure. If the figures you're quoting me are right, I'd be a lot more concerned than Mr. Gigli. Benzene is like a lot of toxic chemicals; we know they're not good for us, but we can't be sure at what point they become dangerous. Still the state didn't set those standards for nothing. There's so much benzene in that water that a lot of it must be evaporating into the air. There may not only be danger in drinking that water but in breathing the air in those houses. They shouldn't even be running the water for any reason . . . if, again, those numbers are correct. I wouldn't even flush the toilet, or open it for that matter, with a couple of parts per million of benzene in the water. Is Gigli right about the state recommended levels? Yes."

Call to Raymond Barry, lab superviser for Tuckahoe Laboratories: "Well, yes, we did those tests. Those are the numbers all right. And we ran three tests on each well just to make sure we didn't have sampling error."

■ C. Story Assignments ■

1. Assume that temperatures in your area have dropped to well below freezing and a severe cold wave is predicted for the next week. Write a sidebar on what causes frostbite and how to protect against it.

2. A drifter is charged with killing a local grocer. He is arrested after he fails to pass a lie detector test. Write a sidebar on how lie-detector tests work and on how reliable they are.

3. An earthquake, measuring 3.8 on the Richter Scale, shakes buildings in your area but causes little damage. Write a sidebar explaining what causes earthquakes.

4. Try to find the latest article on scientific research at a nearby research center or university by using the local newspaper files and the help of the facility's public relations staff. After learning as much as possible about the research, set up an appointment with the scientist who supervised the work. Then write an article concentrating on one of the following:
   a. The scientist. Write a profile. How did the scientist become interested in that particular area of research and what led him or her to the line of inquiry followed?
   b. The process. What steps were involved in achieving the scientific progress or discovery mentioned in previous articles? How long has the scientist been working in this specific area? Did the research team have any false starts? What inspired the team to design the experiments the way it did? What efforts were made to insure against false results?
   c. The future outlook. What obstacles remain to be overcome in the particular line of research? What efforts will the research team make to overcome these obstacles?

5. Write a news story based on an article in the latest issue of the *New England Journal of Medicine.* At the end of the article, write down what questions you would have liked to have asked before writing the article and of whom you would have asked them.

Appendices

Format

Every newspaper has a set of rules for preparing and presenting stories on the page. These rules have only an indirect relationship to how a story will actually appear in print. They are a kind of newsroom shorthand, designed to enable different people in different parts of the paper to examine and work with copy quickly and efficiently.

This is essential since anything non-standard in the look of these pages or anything difficult to decipher could lead to confusion, delay or, worse, a mistake in the product—the newspaper.

Newspapers are in many ways tradition-bound institutions. Many of their rules for format have been developed over decades, even centuries. But the majority of those old rules have been completely rewritten in recent years by an invention most newspaper publishers, no matter how loyal to tradition, decided they could not do business without—the computer.

The computer revolution in newspaper formatting rules leaves this appendix with dual responsibilities. First it will present the format used under the old regime of typewriters, pencils and paper. These primitive tools are still used in some newsrooms and in most journalism classrooms. They have not been purged completely from even the most modern newsroom. This appendix's second task will be to introduce the beginning reporter to the clean, quiet world of the electronic newsroom, where reporters and editors sit hunched in front of their individual *video display terminals*—or *VDTs*—"processing" words on a central computer.

Traditional

If each reporter in the newsroom adopted a different format for typing a story on a page; if each experimented with a different system for naming a story; if some editors circled the words they wanted deleted, some crossed them out and some drew a line through them; a daily newspaper might have to become a weekly. The rules of format are designed so that once they have been memorized, journalists should not have to spend time worrying about copy format again.

Slugs

When reporters begin typing a story, they write one or two words in capital letters in the upper-left corner of the page—about one inch from the top. This notation—called the *slug*—identifies what a story is about. A story about the migration of hawks, for example, might be slugged *HAWKS*. One about inflation might be slugged *INFLATION*.

Slugs are essential because they enable reporters, editors and anyone else who handles a story before it appears in print to identify that story and find it quickly. Speed can be critical in a newsroom as deadline approaches. If a reporter, for example, needs to add new information to a story minutes before the printing presses roll, the reporter or the editors match that insert with the main story by means of its slug.

Here are some rules for choosing and using slugs:

1   Avoid redundancy

Since the slug is the story's label, no two slugs on the same day can be the same. That's why *ACCIDENT* makes a lousy slug—there are too many stories that could go by that name. Instead use *BUS CRASH*. Similarly, *MURDER* wouldn't work as a slug in a big city, where there are a couple of murders a day, but *MURDER* might be fine as a slug on a small town paper where stories on the subject are significantly less common. Two slugs deserve special attention: *Never* use the slugs *KILL* or *SPIKE*. In newspaper jargon, they mean the entire story should be deep-sixed, eliminated.

2   Keep it clean

The slug is designed for newsroom use only. It should not be confused with the headline that will be written later by an editor and will appear above the story in the newspaper. Sometimes, however, slugs inadvertently appear in print. Reporters, therefore, just to be on the safe side, should refrain from using any slug that might offend readers. A profile of the mayor should not be slugged *JERK*. Profanity and derogatory characterizations, such as *FROGS* for a story about the French, are also unacceptable.

3   Your name

Reporters take credit for authorship of a news story by typing their last names, all lower case, two or three lines directly below the slug on the first page of a story. Again, this is just for newsroom use. If a *byline,* giving the reporter's full name, is to appear in print above the story, it will be added, like the headline, by editors later.

4   Additional pages

A story's slug, but not the reporter's name, must appear on the upper left of every additional page in the story. The page number should be typed, using numerals, right next to it. (It's wise to repeat each number a few times to diminish the significance of a potential typing error.) Thus, the second page of the hawks article would be slugged *HAWKS—2,2,2,* the tenth page *HAWKS—10,10,10.*

Takes

Pages in a newspaper story are often referred to as *takes.* So if an editor asks for "four takes" on that demonstration, that means the reporter should write a story four pages long.

Here are rules for typing those pages or takes:

1   The first take

Editors will need room at the beginning of each story to add information about the byline and the headline to be used with the story. Therefore, writers should begin typing the first paragraph of their stories halfway down the first page. That will give the editor a significant amount of space between the slug and the body of the story in which to scribble. Subsequent pages should begin in normal fashion, about an inch from the page's slug or almost two inches from the top of the sheet of paper.

2   More

Type the word *more* at the bottom of each page of a story except the last page, and circle it. This tells anyone reading the story that there are *more* pages to read.

3   Endit

Type one of the following symbols at the bottom of the last page—*endit,* the numeral *30* (a remnant of an old telegraph code) or the numeral sign #. All three mark the end of the story.

4   Triple-space

Some reporters may double-space their copy on the typewriter, but it's wiser to triple-space. That way there's ample room for corrections and editing.

5   Margins

Copy should be centered on a page with room to type about 60 characters on each line. That will leave margins of almost an inch on either side of the page.

6   Indent

The first word of each paragraph should be indented five spaces from the margin.

7   Dateline

Stories that are written outside the town in which the newsroom is located should begin with the name of the city in which they are composed. The city's name should be typed in capital letters. If the story is from another state, the state name should be added, unless the city is well known. (See Appendix B, Style, for rules on abbreviation.) Thus, it is *LOS ANGELES* for a story from one of California's best-known cities, but *MENDOCINO, Calif.,* for a story from that northern coastal town. Follow the dateline with a space, a dash and another space, and then start the story. Datelines should be indented, like any paragraph. Never use phony datelines. If the story is reported from the newsroom, it shouldn't have a dateline, no matter where it took place.

8   Don't overstrike

Never strike over a letter on the typewriter to correct a misspelling or a mistake. Other newspaper staffers shouldn't be asked to guess whether you meant that to be an *o* or an *e*.

9 Cut and paste

If an entire paragraph has to be moved in a story, it should be neatly cut out and pasted where it belongs on the page. Never use arrows to indicate that material must be moved—they're too confusing.

10 Complete grafs

Each page must end with a complete paragraph—or *graf.* (That means, obviously, that each page also will start with a new graf.) This rule makes it easier to edit a story by cutting out paragraphs and moving them around. It requires the writer to question, when beginning a graf near the bottom of a page, whether there is room to complete that entire paragraph. If there isn't, start a new page.

11 Circle

Circle in pencil all words and numerals on the page that are not part of the story—including the slug, the reporter's name, *more, endit, 30,* or #. This is to advise the paper's production department not to set these things in type.

Copy Markings

Few of us type perfectly. Reporters therefore rely on a set of symbols to make changes neatly, clearly and economically. Few of us, alas, write perfectly either. Editors will use the same set of symbols to edit reporters' copy.

All of these symbols, along with anything else not typed on a page of copy, should be written in *pencil.* That way, if even the correction itself proves imperfect, you can still change your mind.

A page that requires too many of these editing symbols may begin to resemble a work of abstract art. If copy starts getting too sloppy to read easily, it must be retyped.

Here are the symbols:

Punctuation

The period. ⨀   This ~~is~~ ^was^ a short session⨀

The comma. ⌃   The man, who was tall⌃said . . .

The hyphen. =   The $40⹁million appropriation.

The colon. ⌄⌃   His firm had six clients⌃John

Foster & Sons, . . .

The semicolon. ⌃⁏   Surviving are his wife,

Margaret; two sons, John and

Stephen, at home⌃a brother . . .

The apostrophe. ⌄   It⌄s a new concept.

Quotations. ⌄⌄   ⌄⌄   "I can't believe it⌄⌄he exclaimed.

The dash. ⌄/ₘ   She said⌃quite loudly⌄⌄balderdash."

Parentheses. ( )   The gauer(pronounced power)

is found in Africa.

Deletion

A letter. ⸜   The bill was⸜ approved.

A letter in a word that   Po⌀lice.
   must then be *closed.* ⌒

A word. →   He ~~said~~ said that he was tired.

A line.

The survivors were taken to
Low Hospital. (Note: check on
their conditions) They were
identified as . . .

An entire paragraph
or block ("X" out
and draw lines to
where the story
picks up again)

Before the school was built the
land was occupied by Joe's
Pharmacy. Joe was a nice man,
still remembered for the lollipops
he would hand out to kids.

Addition

Insert space.   #

Frenchhorn

Let stand (after an accidental   (stet)   deletion).

The man said . . .

Insert letter.   ∧

Tree blind mice . . .

Insert word or phrase.

It was the third time she had won . . .

Other

Paragraph.

Sen. Bill Bradley yesterday
announced that a coalition of
senators from both parties would
propose . . .

Capitalize.   =

north Dakota

Lower case.   /

TEXAS

Italics.   —

She ate 17 hot dogs.

Spell out.   ◯

Ind.

Abbreviate.   ◯

General William Westmoreland

Transpose letters.   ∿

hockey

Transpose words.   ⊓

He briskly walked to school.

Here is what the first page of a story would look like, written in proper format and edited with proper symbols:

(HEALTH SPA)

(jones)

WASHINGTON, D.C. — Disgruntled ~~customer~~ consumers may soon receive more than a sympathetic hearing from goverment officials to their complaints over the use of high pressure sales practices by the health spa industry.

Next week, the City Council is expected to begin consideration of ~~a bill~~ an ordinance that if adopted, would enable consumers to cancel contracts with health clubs at any time and still receive partial refunds for unused services.

Similar provisions are ~~included in more extensive~~ being considered by the Federal trade Commission.

(more)

Electronic

Esther Davidowitz of *The Record* in Bergen County, N.J., had been trained on typewriters in journalism school. She had spent years at a weekly and now a daily newspaper learning to express herself with a beat up old manual, yellow paper and a pencil. The typewriter, paper and pencil, she was convinced, were part of her thinking process. Besides, what did she know about computers? Wasn't a *cursor* someone with a foul mouth?

Davidowitz, to put it mildly, was not anxious to confront one of the metal boxes with green screens that began appearing in *The Record*'s newsroom, as her newspaper, along with most major American dailies, entered the computer age. "I was convinced that I wouldn't be able to handle it," she remembers. "I saw the inch-thick manuals they were handing out — full of computer jargon — and I knew it was beyond me."

But her turn to sit behind a VDT quickly arrived. Davidowitz received about a day's training. "Within a week after I began using the computer I had decided that I never wanted to use a typewriter again," she recalls.

Computers save newspapers money because they allow reporters and editors to work on one electronic copy of a story, preserved in the computer's vast memory — a copy that comes out perfectly clean no matter how many corrections are required and that can be set in type electronically. But the biggest beneficiary of the computer's magic, as Davidowitz learned, is the person who writes the story.

It is impossible in these pages to offer detailed instructions on using VDT systems. The keyboards and coding of these systems are different at different newspapers; each has its own complexities. This section will be limited to an overview of the major components such systems have in common and an introduction to the tricks they can perform.

The VDT

Newspaper VDT systems are specially designed for the function that computer makers call *word processing*. They use a large central computer, which can allow perhaps hundreds of reporters and editors simultaneously to *process* the words that will fill the next day's newspaper. Beginning reporters who have used personal computers at home, in school or on the job will find most of the workings of these VDT systems familiar.

The keyboard

The keyboard of a VDT includes all the keys on a regular typewriter—placed so that they will be comfortable to users of electric typewriters—plus several rows of additional keys. Since, unlike a personal computer, the VDT will not be used for computing taxes, doing business statistics or playing PacMan, these additional keys can be *dedicated* to the special word-processing functions required in the newsroom. One, for example, allows a reporter to send a story to the terminal of an editor across the room. Another deletes entire lines of copy, like a high-speed, built-in eraser. A third will instantly rearrange sentences or whole paragraphs in a story.

The cursor

A small, blinking rectangle of light, called the *cursor,* controls where in the story material will be added or removed. If the cursor is placed at the beginning of the story, for example, any word typed into the system on the keyboard can be inserted as the first word of the story. If the cursor is moved to a line, and the *delete line* key is pressed, the line will disappear.

The cursor normally is controlled by a set of special keys on the keyboard. Four of these keys have arrows on them pointing up, down, right or left. When pushed, they move the cursor in the indicated direction.

The screen

The VDT's screen, or monitor, looks like a small television set. Most of its space is used like an endless electronic piece of paper: The words the reporter types on the keyboard appear on the screen as they are typed. The touch of a key will allow the reporter to change the display on the screen to show another page, or perhaps another story.

What It Can Do

Esther Davidowitz types *LO Esther* on the keyboard of the VDT in front of her. That tells the computer at *The Record* that she wants to *log on,* or begin using it. The computer screen displays a request for her password. She types it, hits another key and her *queue*—a list of all the articles and notes she has stored in the computer's memory—flashes on the screen. She wants to begin writing a new story, however, so in the appropriate place at the top of the

screen she types in a new story name or slug: LAWYER. (To enable the computer to find its way around, everything typed into the VDT must be given a slug similar to those introduced in the first part of this chapter. Many computers can handle only eight-letter slugs, though.)

The screen goes blank, except for the flashing cursor, and Davidowitz begins to write:

In Montvale, the hub of corporate development in Bergen County, the borough attorney is also the lawyer for the planning board, which is illegal.

Wait a second, she thinks, the *planning board* itself isn't illegal. She moves the cursor back to the *w* of *which* and types:

a dual role that violates the law.

As she types in the new words, the letters that had occupied those spaces on the screen disappear one by one. But Davidowitz has thought of another problem with that phrase: The interpretation of the law involved could be controversial. It would be wise to indicate where she got that interpretation. She moves the cursor to the space after the word *that* and presses the *insert* button on the keyboard, so that the letters she types will be inserted in front of the other letters instead of replacing them:

, legal experts say,

Now her first paragraph is complete:

In Montvale, the hub of corporate development in Bergen County, the borough attorney is also the lawyer for the planning board, a dual role that, legal experts say, violates the law.

She will want a quote from a legal expert high up in the story. Earlier she had typed her interview notes into the computer. Now she calls up her queue, spots LAW NOTES, presses a few buttons, and the screen suddenly splits in half (a capability not all VDT systems have). On the right is the story she is writing; on the left the notes from her interviews. By moving the cursor, she *scrolls,* or moves, through the notes. When she finds a quote she wants, she can *block* it off and then *move* it whole into the place in the story where it belongs.

Davidowitz struggles with the story, a tough one, for the rest of the day. When she is done she scrolls through it a few times to check for errors, then she's ready to send it to her editor. The word *SEND* is waiting at the top of the screen in an area called the *header.* She moves the cursor there, types *RGN 5*— for region five—and a perfectly clean copy of her story automatically becomes available to her editor. He'll find *LAWYER* listed in his queue.

▪ **A** ▪

After each of the following story descriptions write a slug that could be used to identify the story.

1. The local school board has decided to stop selling ice cream in the high school cafeteria.

2. Forty-thousand dollars worth of diamonds were stolen from a safe at a downtown jewelry store.

3. The coach of the local university's football team, Terence Howard, has been fired by Athletic Director Rand Dumont after three straight losing seasons.

4. Local bakery workers have voted to strike tomorrow.

5. Three people, including an 11-year-old boy, were killed when the car in which they were riding smashed into a tree in Lakeville.

6. The mayor has announced a new plan to widen a two-mile stretch of Main Street in the downtown business district.

7. A local computer company, Micro Technology, has announced that it will soon be selling a portable desktop computer that can handle advanced engineering projects.

8. A group of mothers, whose eligibility for child support payments has, the mothers say, been challenged by the city's Human Services Department, staged a demonstration in front of the department's offices.

9. Georgina Albert was found guilty of armed robbery following a two-month-long trial.

10. The city Board of Aldermen voted at the end of a long meeting last night to change its name to the Board of Alderpeople in deference to its newest member—Alderwoman Jane Piccalo.

▪ **B** ▪

Correct any errors in the following sentences using proper copy-marking symbols.

1. Councilman Ewdards saidhe decid ed to support the bill after a discussion with mayor;

2. By the tme the firefighters were able to put out it the fire, it had destroyed two three story buildings.

3. Here is the list of contributers Thomas Belfry Robert Jones Sarah Humphrey and Elizabeth Hjersttrand.

4. Car skidded to a top about 40 feet from the edge off the cliff police said, but th boody was founded but the body was found at the bottom of the ravine.

5. "We will not bargain under the trheat of a strike, said Dr. Frank lombardi the shcool boards president

6. According to police the suspect was from Los Angeles, Calif., and hda never seen the Woman befre,

7. The returned jury with a a verdict.

8. Janice madison alsso attended the meeting attended the meeting, but she did did not speak on the ammendment.

9. Traffic will blocked be on Culpepper Ninth and Tenth streets for two weeks forcing cars to use hopkins Road of Eigth street when diving through business district

10. Lumpkin mantained he was not three when happened it he had never scene that women before and he had know interest in the fortunes of Anderson Plumbing

11. There fire companies were called the scene one from the twon it self and one from each neighboring comunity.

12. The land was overgrown with weds, still it asw the towns and it wasa rsponable sight for a was a reasonable sight for a swimming pool.

13. The judge had bbeen been sceen with woman shortly before dey both

   disapeared. He known was for his antiabortion views

14. Each division of the cmpany was xsd considered a seperate entity with own

   management and sails staffs.

15. "It took alot of work on our paart," Howard said. "But man oh man did it

   ever But mnomn did it ever seem worthwhile on sunday when; we saw that

   kids face."

▪ C ▪

Retype this story using proper format, slug and copy-marking symbols.

A 14-year-old student at Brookville Junior High School died yesterday after a freak accident in the school's gymnasium, where she was walking on the balance beam.

Albert W. Rommel, the school's principal, said the student, Nancy George, an eighth grader, slipped on the beam and then hit her head on the beam while falling.

George was first treated at the school by a paramedic team and then was flown by a police helicopter to the Logan Institute for Emergency Medicine at University Hospital, where she was pronounced dead on arrival.

A hospital spokeswoman said the girl died from the head injury, but refused to specify the exact cause of death until after an autopsy is conducted.

Rommel said George was participating in a physical education class with 21 other students when the accident occurred. He said the instructor, Jennifer O'Brien, had just demonstrated how to walk on the balance beam and had asked the students to try. George was the second student to try to walk on the beam, Rommel said.

The principal said he was told that the girl's right foot seemed to slip off the beam, causing her to fall forward and hit her forehead against the beam. She fell to the mat, bleeding from the head and apparently unconscious, Rommel said.

According to Rommel, this was the first serious accident at Brookville Junior High School, which opened two years ago. He said he will conduct a thorough investigation.

George was the daughter of Ralph and Dr. Rita George of 12 Hill Road in Brookville. She had a brother, Jon, 13, who also attended Brookville Junior High School.

Style

When newspaper editors talk about style, they usually don't mean the kind that distinguishes a Hemingway novel from one by Faulkner. They mean the basic rules that tell a reporter which words to abbreviate, which to capitalize, which spelling to choose or how to write numbers.

Without these rules to provide consistency, newspaper copy would be a mess.

UNACCEPTABLE:
With three-hundred, eighty-three-thousand, 365 votes counted, Guevara had 143-thousand, 4-hundred, 40 votes, or thirty-seven percent. Second with 105,410 votes, or 27 percent, was Mario Sandoval Alarcon of the National Liberation Movement.

These returns from a Guatemalan election are, in fact, correct. But the manner in which they are presented is as disconcerting as a businessman wearing one blue sock and one red sock would be. That businessman might have trouble gaining the trust of a potential client. A newspaper without a consistent style would have trouble gaining the trust of potential readers.

ACCEPTABLE:
With 383,365 votes counted, Guevara had 143,440 votes, or 37 percent. Second with 105,410 votes, or 27 percent, was Mario Sandoval Alarcon of the National Liberation Movement.

The (New Orleans) *Times-Picayune*

A consistent style makes stories more readable.

UNACCEPTABLE:
Senator Bill Bradley, Sen. Kennedy and Senator Patrick Leahy supported the bill.

ACCEPTABLE:
Sen. William Bradley, Sen. Edward Kennedy and Sen. Patrick Leahy supported the bill.

And a consistent style helps the writer, too. A reporter on deadline who had to stop each time to puzzle out the best way to write *142 E. Ninth St.* would be lost.

All newspapers use a *stylebook* which lays out the rules of style the paper will follow. That reporter on deadline simply has to turn to the section in the paper's stylebook on addresses to learn how *142 E. Ninth St.* should be written. After a while it will no longer be necessary to consult the stylebook—the rule will have been memorized.

The rules in these stylebooks are determined in part by tradition—newspapers have been abbreviating the word *Captain* as a title before someone's name *(Capt.)* for more than a hundred years. The rules are also based on taste: Some stylebooks call for *damn* to become *d——*. But, fortunately, the justifications for most style rules are efficiency and readability: *383,365* is easier to read and easier to write than *three-hundred, eighty-three-thousand, three-hundred, sixty-five.*

All newspaper styles certainly are not the same. More formal papers, such as *The New York Times,* use more capitalization and less abbreviation. They may also append a courtesy title — Mr. — to a man's last name.

Most newspapers, however, have adopted style rules very similar to those set out in *The Associated Press Stylebook and Libel Manual* . . . and with good reason: More than 1,400 newspapers in the United States run stories by AP, and it would be time-consuming indeed to make all those little style changes after these stories arrived in the newsroom.

Most larger papers have their own stylebooks — manuals with special rules on everything from the names of local institutions and neighborhoods to the preferred spelling of *Hanukkah.* Smaller papers often accept the AP's rules and stylebook wholesale.

Reporters will refer to their stylebooks frequently to check on more obscure matters, and they will memorize the rules that come into play regularly.

To avoid confusion, the examples in this book, including those from *The New York Times,* have been printed in accordance with the rules of *The Associated Press Stylebook.* (We do, however, use yesterday or today in place of the day of the week in discussing when an event occurred. We also add italics to many of our examples to clarify points.)

The exercises throughout are best completed with the help of a stylebook. (*The Associated Press Stylebook and Libel Manual* can be ordered through bookstores or directly from the Associated Press, at 50 Rockefeller Plaza, New York, N.Y. 10020.) Some of the most commonly used style rules, in line with those set out by AP, are outlined below:

Abbreviations

1   Acronyms
The first time an organization is mentioned, spell it out — *National Aeronautics and Space Administration, Organization of American States, Environmental Protection Agency.* The second time, its initials can be used — *NASA, OAS, EPA.* Unless the second reference follows closely upon the first, the initials (or acronym) should be introduced in parentheses after the full name in the first reference — Organization of American States *(OAS).* The acronym of organizations widely known by their initials — *FBI, CIA, NATO, AFL-CIO* — can stand alone on first reference.

2   Addresses
Abbreviate Boulevard *(Blvd.),* Avenue *(Ave.)* and Street *(St.) only* when giving a complete address. All other synonyms for road are always spelled out. It is 64 *W. 85th St.* (but she lives on *West 85th Street)* and 28 Amherst *Road.* (The numbers in a street address

are always numerals; the street names below 10 are written out — *1 Fifth Ave., 8 12th St.)*

3   Dates
Abbreviate *Jan., Feb., Aug., Sept., Oct., Nov.* and *Dec.* when used in a specific date. Always spell out all the other months — *Aug.* 5, 1949, *July 11,* 1954, *August* 1985.

4   States
The names of eight states — *Alaska, Hawaii, Idaho, Iowa, Maine, Ohio, Texas* and *Utah* — should never be abbreviated. The names of all other states should be abbreviated only when used after the name of a town or county. Spell out the names of states when they stand alone.

Here is a list of proper abbreviations:

Ala.	Md.	N.D.
Ariz.	Mass.	Okla.
Ark.	Mich.	Ore.
Calif.	Minn.	Pa.
Colo.	Miss.	R.I.
Conn.	Mo.	S.C.
Del.	Mont.	S.D.
Fla.	Neb.	Tenn.
Ga.	Nev.	Vt.
Ill.	N.H.	Va.
Ind.	N.J.	Wash.
Kan.	N.M.	W. Va.
Ky.	N.Y.	Wis.
La.	N.C.	Wyo.

5   Proper names
In giving the formal name of a company, abbreviate *Co., Inc., Corp.,* and *Bros.* It is *St. Paul Fire and Marine Insurance Co.,* but the *insurance company.* Also abbreviate *Jr.* and *Sr.* when given as part of someone's name — *Thomas P. O'Neill Jr.*

6   Titles
Many titles are abbreviated when they appear directly before a name — *Gov. Mario Cuomo.* Abbreviate *Dr., Gov., Lt. Gov., Rep., Sen., The Rev., Gen., Lt., Capt., Sgt., Cmdr.* and *Prof.* when they precede a name. But it is *President Reagan.* And all titles are written out when they appear alone or after a name — it's *John Jones, a sergeant,* and *Mario Cuomo, governor of New York.*

Capitalization

1   Proper names
Use capitals to start each of the principal words in the formal names of people, places, regions, trademarked products, organizations and companies. Titles of

books, plays and movies also are capitalized. So are the days of the week and the months of the year. It's *Army, China, Ryan O'Neill, Mideast, the South, Republican, Democrat, World War II, Yosemite National Park* and *Koblin's Pharmacy.* It is *Coca-Cola* and *Coke* for the real thing but *soda* for general references to the fizzy stuff we drink. And the book and movie by the same name are *"One Flew Over the Cuckoo's Nest."*

2   Government bodies
Capitalize the full proper names of governmental entities — the *New Jersey Legislature,* the *Brockton City Council,* the *Denver Police Department.* Capitalization should be retained if the dateline or context of a story make clear *which* city council or police department is being referred to. It would be, "NYACK, N.Y. — The *City Council* last night . . ." Without such a clear reference, make it lower case — the *legislature,* the *city council,* the *fire department.*

3   Titles
Formal titles are capitalized before a name — *Republican State Chairman* Chet Upham, but not after a name — Chet Upham, *Republican state chairman,* or standing alone — *the Republican state chairman.* But this holds only for a person's formal title. It is *Republican leader* Chet Upham and *center fielder* Mookie Wilson, not *Center Fielder* Mookie Wilson.

Names and Courtesy Titles

The first time a name is used in a story, use the full name, except for that handful of leaders famous enough so that their last name and their title alone will do — *French Foreign Minister Claude Cheysson, Judge Lawrence N. Martin Jr., Jane Fonda,* but *President Reagan.* For a New York City newspaper, *Mayor Koch* would be sufficient; elsewhere it would be *New York Mayor Edward Koch.* The AP makes a distinction between its handling of men and women the second (third, fourth, etc.) time their names are mentioned in a story (a distinction that because of its implicit sexism, we find unfortunate). After a man has already been introduced in a story, his last name alone is enough — *Cheysson, Martin, Reagan.* But a woman, the AP says, gets a courtesy title — Miss, Mrs. or, if she prefers, Ms. — in front of her last name after she has already been introduced. So after she's introduced it's *Ms. Fonda* or *Mrs. Reagan.*

Numbers

In general, spell out numbers below 10 and use figures for 10 or above — *five* persons were killed, *23*

injured. (Very large numbers use numerals and words — 3 million people.) Here are some exceptions:

1   Ages
Whether someone is *3* months or *86* years old, use a numeral.

2   Beginning a sentence
Spell out a number when it begins a sentence — *Fourteen* people were injured yesterday. Years are an exception — *1985* was a very good year.

3   Dollars and cents
Again, always use a numeral. It's *5* cents and *$1.* When amounts exceed $999,999, use the $ sign and combine a numeral and a word. It is *$3 million* and *$4.25 billion* (never carried beyond two decimal points).

4   Fractions
Only those fractions below one should be spelled out — *two-thirds, 1½, 2.2.*

5   Percentages
Always use numerals — *6 percent, 2.3 percent.*

6   Time
Use numerals except for noon and midnight. It is *4 a.m.* and *11:45 p.m.* (Use a colon to separate hours from minutes; a.m. and p.m. are lower case.)

7   Weight and dimensions
Use numerals (and spell out pounds, ounces, feet and inches). It is a *6-foot-5-inch* shark that weighed *350 pounds,* and it snowed *3 inches.*

Punctuation

We will not attempt to address the many complexities of punctuation common to all writing here. For that, we recommend the AP Stylebook *and* one of the grammar books suggested in Chapter 3, Spelling and Grammar. Here we will address three broad punctuation problems that trouble many journalists:

1   Commas
AP style normally does *not* use a *serial comma* — no comma is placed before a conjunction that ends a series. It would be, "He bought carrots, milk and ice," *not,* "He bought carrots, milk, and ice." (The exception is in a series of long, complicated phrases. Then a comma before the conjunction ending the series may make things clearer.) Otherwise, the rules for the use of commas are standard. If there's no natural pause in a sentence, usually there is no need for a comma. Make sure, however, you remember the comma on

both sides of an interjection or apposition—The movie's star, Sean Penn, was there.

2   Possessives

In general, add an apostrophe and an *s* to the end of a singular or plural noun to form a possessive unless the noun ends in *s*. It is the *school's roof,* the *man's suit* and the *men's problem.* For plural nouns ending in *s* and singular proper nouns ending in *s,* simply add an apostrophe at the end to form a possessive—*Jones' car,* the *Joneses' house,* the *United States' debt.* Common singular nouns ending in *s* take an extra *s* after the apostrophe—*the hostess's invitation.*

3   Quotation marks

These should go around a speaker's exact words (See Chapter 11, Quotations). They are also used around the titles of books, movies, plays, songs and articles—*"For Whom the Bell Tolls"*—and around nicknames introduced in a full name—*Leon "Bull" Durham.* For quotes within quotes use a single quotation mark around the material within the quote to be set apart —He said, *"Have you read 'The Right Stuff'?"* A comma or a period at the end of a quote belongs within the quotation marks—*"I couldn't believe the whole thing,"* she said. The question mark, dash and exclamation point should be within quotation marks only when they apply to the quoted material; otherwise they belong outside. It is: "He asked, 'Why are you being so mean?'" But: "Why do you think he called you 'mean and callous'?"

Spelling

A dictionary will answer almost all spelling questions (See Chapter 3, Spelling and Grammar). The AP recommends *Webster's New International Dictionary.* Here are some examples of the preferred spelling of words where two spellings are accepted by dictionaries: *percent, goodbye, employee, whiskey, Vietnam, Taipei, Teheran, kidnapped.*

Sexism

Some writers still persist in stereotyping. In a world in which women operate jackhammers on construction crews and men stay home with their children, this is not merely insulting; it's wrong. Doctors are not *he*s, and nurses are not *she*s. One way of overcoming subconscious stereotyping is to use the plural rather than the singular.

UNACCEPTABLE:
Day care *worker* is best prepared for the job if *she*. . . .

ACCEPTABLE:
Day care *workers* are best prepared for the job if *they* . . .

Additional Reading

"All the Obscenity that's Fit to Print," Mitchell Stephens and Eliot Frankel, *Washington Journalism Review,* April 1981.

▪ **A** ▪

Edit the following sentences to correct style errors.

1. The Gov. invited the 2 senators to visit the four Army bases scheduled to close January 15.

2. Twenty-three people, including a four-year-old girl, were on the bus when it skidded to a stop on Franklin Ave.

3. The Federal Bureau of Investigation is still investigating the kidnapping, but the Atty. Gen. announced that the family does not wish to press charges.

4. 40 percent of the county's population of forty-six thousand lives in redwood city.

5. The Reverend William Howard and Fred Neal, Chairman of the Church Finance Committee, were there, but Mr. Neal left early.

6. The injured included three employes of Franklin Locks: Mrs. Allison Hampton, thirty-two, of three Lakeview Road; Mr. Eliot Harms, twenty-three, of Seven Pinetree Street; and Ms. Julie Harrison, twenty-eight, who also lives with Mr. Harms on Pinetree Street.

7. Most Legislators in the state opposed the Equal Rights amendment.

8. Mrs. Norman's first child was born on Jan. 11, 1981, and her second child was born in Feb. of the next year.

9. The NAACP has scheduled 2 demonstrations for the month of Dec. in Atlanta, Georg. plus 13 demonstrations in March in other areas of the State.

10. John Marshall, President of the state's lottery, announced that 2 people would share the $3,700,000 pot.

11. The President of one local Computer Company said that 8 per cent of the settlers came from the East.

12. The House Ways and Means committee approved the Bill sponsored by Representative Clark.

13. He has played Bridge every friday night since he was sixty-two years old, and he ends each game with a bottle of sprite.

14. The Des Moines fire department fought the blaze for nineteen hours, calling in 120 firefighters, twelve pumpers, and 3 hook-and-ladder trucks.

15. Superintendent Rayoff said there was no doubt the schools roof needed repair but added that it might not need to be replaced.

16. Andrews, a captain in the police force, and lieutenant Richard Stole, were both seen in the Tavern.

17. Perhaps half the americans who served in viet nam never went near Saigon.

18. Haley's Canned Goods Company announced quarterly earnings of twenty-five million dollars, about ⅓ more than last year.

19. Nineteen eighty-four was the first year in which the mayor did not get a popularity rating of at least sixty percent.

20. According to Harry P. Swenson Junior, chairman of the communist party in the country, the conflict in the Mideast threatened to embroil much of Europe.

■ **B** ■

Edit this story to correct any style errors.

FLOOD RELIEF

perkins

Governor Arthur Montgomery toured flooded areas of Lewiston yesterday in the wake of the worst rainstorm in the city in more than fifty years.

"I've been in public office 25 years but I've never seen anything like it", the Governor said as he was paddled in a rowboat down Main St., which is still under four feet of water. "We will do everything possible to help the people here.

Junetta Diaz, Assistant Director of the state's Disaster Relief Agency, estimated that the damage to Lewiston alone would be two- to three million dollars. She added that the total damage to property in the county could surpass 10 million dollars.

Montgomery, a democrat was accompanied by Republican representative Carl Peters, who counted himself among the flood victims. "My house is on the hillside," he said, But I had 20 head of cattle grazing in a feedlot near the river. It rose so quickly that most of them drowned."

8 inches of rain fell in 3 hours friday, sending the Joscinta river over its banks and flooding areas that normally are bone dry. Geologists for the state already have identified the storm as a 100 year flood, or one that has one chance in 100 of occurring in any given year. Five people drowned when the storm hit at about 6:00 P.M. The water level rose to seven ft. on Elbow Rd., right next to the river before it began receding Sunday.

The flooding was compounded by the soggy Apr. weather which already has dumped 13 inches of rain in the area in the past twenty days. The last major flood in Lewiston occurred on August thirteen and fourteenth, 1926, when 6 people drowned and 13 were injured in a flood that followed eleven inches of rain over two days.

Ethics

Reporters, out on the town for a night together, often regale each other with tales of their adventures in gathering the news. But as the evening wears on, the bragging and joking may be replaced by soul searching: Was it wise to accept that free trip to Detroit to see that new car? Was the newspaper right to pay that prisoner a little something for that interview? Was I justified in getting the mayor's assistant to talk without identifying myself as a reporter? Was it fair to print that story about the mayor's drinking?

Unlike doctors, lawyers and certified public accountants, journalists do not have to pass licensing exams. The only rules they are bound by are their newspaper's policy, a handful of state and federal laws (See Appendix D, Law) . . . and their own consciences.

Some of the ethical decisions faced by journalists are straightforward: They should never pass off even a sentence of someone else's writing as their own. They must stick to the facts. They should never attack without solid proof. They should not distort the meaning of the quotes they use. They should struggle to be fair. They should honor their pledges to sources. Most of these principles of responsible journalism are outlined in previous chapters (See Chapter 6, Objectivity; Chapter 11, Quotations; Chapter 16, Facts; Chapter 19, Sources).

Beyond these basic principles, however, the ethical calls get tougher. Many large newspapers and journalism associations have drawn up codes of ethics. Some have been around for the better part of this century.

When closely scrutinized, however, these codes tend to dissolve into a pool of platitudes. Most, for example, speak reverently of the "public's right to know." But the right to know what? How? Does the public have the right to know that the governor frequents massage parlors? Does that right to know give journalists the right to disguise themselves as patrons of a massage parlor in an attempt to find out what the governor is doing there? These noble-sounding pronouncements, when applied to the real world, solve few ethical issues. They leave journalists disagreeing, sometimes vigorously.

What follows are some guidelines that we hope will help untangle, if not resolve, some of these arguments.

Freebies

Lunch time and Christmas are two tempting occasions for reporters. At lunch they are vulnerable to check grabbers; before Christmas, to gift givers. Picking up a tab or dropping off a bottle of scotch are common and accepted practices in the business world. Reporters interviewing the health and safety officer of a chemical plant over lunch are likely to be greeted with "Don't be silly!" when they reach for the check. Reporters covering the courts may find a nicely wrapped bottle of Chivas Regal at their doorstep around December 18th with a little card saying, "Seasons Greetings from Flannery, Rivera and Blumenthal" — a local law firm.

Good meals and good scotch aren't cheap. Is there anything wrong with accepting these gifts? Many top editors say, "Yes."

Few reporters are so hungry or thirsty that they can be bought by these relatively minor kindnesses. It is not that these editors fear that their people will suddenly decide to leave out all quotes from the union about working conditions in that chemical plant or will write a piece extolling the legal skills and good taste of Messieurs Flannery, Rivera and Blumenthal. Rather these editors fear the subtle effects small favors may have on reporters—perhaps an inclination to give the gift giver a call on a story, when a number of other equally good sources would do. And these editors also fear even the hint that the news columns of their paper are for sale.

The safest strategy for any reporter, no matter what the paper's policy, is either to split the bill or to pick up the tab the first time and allow the source to return the favor the next time around. As for that Christmas gift, it should be returned with a gracious note: "Thanks for your thoughtfulness, but I'm sorry, I am not able to accept any gifts from a source."

Resisting the temptation becomes a bit tougher when the gift is an all-expense-paid trip to Palm Springs to preview the opening of the Sunswept Inn or to Mexico to observe filming of Movie Inc.'s latest feature. Reporters, particularly on smaller papers, ask, "How else can we afford to go to these places to write these stories?" The answer is that maybe there is no other way but that reporters who accept such *junkets* clearly are allowing them to affect their decisions on what is news. They are also leaving themselves vulnerable to a subtle pressure: They may feel a touch uncomfortable panning the resort or movie after being treated so kindly by its sponsors.

Readers deserve to be assured that the stories they are reading were selected because they were newsworthy, not because they came prepaid. And reporters must try to eliminate as many as possible of the slightly "uncomfortable" feelings that might slant, or give the appearance of slanting, their work.

Reporters are given freebies for a reason, and that is exactly the reason they should be turned down.

Checkbook Journalism

Money, of course, can change hands in either direction. News organizations, striving for a competitive edge, have more than once paid for news. Some of the returning American hostages from Iran were showered with gifts in the hope they would agree to exclusive interviews. Convicted mass murderer Charles Manson and H. R. Haldeman, who was convicted of Watergate-related crimes, both received five-figure payments from networks in exchange for interviews. Though the price tag will be lower, such propositions are made in local reporting as well. Police informants, for example, are just as happy to sell their information to reporters as to police. Is there anything wrong with slipping them a couple of twenties? We think plenty.

Money distorts both the news and the news judgment of reporters and editors. Sources who know they can hold out for cash before telling their stories will ignore all but the wealthiest news organizations and may be tempted to embellish their story a bit to up the ante. Editors and television producers who have paid for news may feel compelled to promote the story and to play it prominently—even if the story turns out to be a dud.

Perhaps there may come a time when the public's interest in learning something is so overwhelming that a news organization must decide to pay for it. But when someone asks journalists for money, their first inclination should always be to say, "No."

Conflict of Interest

A newspaper's consumer reporter writes an investigative series on local supermarkets. A leading supermarket, among the largest advertisers on the paper, rings the publisher and threatens to withdraw its advertising unless the series is stopped. The series is stopped.

A young reporter, on his first full day at work, is handed a press release from a major local retailer announcing that the company has filed for bankruptcy, but artfully avoiding the uncomfortable word "bankruptcy." The reporter dutifully fills in the holes in the press release and clarifies what is going on. He is fired for not following orders to run the press release exactly as written—the newspaper had apparently agreed to do that as a favor to the retailer, one of its biggest advertisers.

These stories both are true. The supermarket investigation was killed in the *New York Post* (before Rupert Murdoch took over). The young reporter was fired by the *Trenton* (N.J.) *Times*.

Newspapers are major local businesses, depending on advertising from other local businesses to survive at the same time as they report on issues that will affect those local businesses. Those publishers who care to maintain the integrity and reputation of their papers learn early politely but firmly to say "No," when friends and advertisers ask them to tinker with the news. However, there are publishers, particularly on struggling newspapers, who will place their advertisers ahead of the integrity of the news columns. Reporters on such papers have little choice but to protest loudly and to move on if their protestations are ignored. Fortunately, many do take a stand. After the supermarket series was stopped in the *Post,* most of the paper's reporters went on a "byline strike" — they refused to allow their bylines to appear in the paper. After that *Trenton Times* reporter was fired, a quarter of the news staff quit.

Reporters also run the risk of getting entangled in their own webs of conflict. A reporter is a citizen with political and economic interests who will report on issues with political and economic impact. Like their publishers, reporters must be strong enough to resist the tug of any interest that might compromise their paper's commitment to unblinking coverage.

Reporters must resist the *appearance* of conflict as well. A police reporter should not be an honorary member of the PBA. A political reporter should not be helping to plan strategy for one of the candidates. A business reporter should not be moonlighting by writing press releases for a local corporation. And a city hall reporter should not be having an affair with the mayor's press secretary.

No matter how committed to fair and objective reporting these journalists may believe themselves to be, they owe it to their readers and to their papers to avoid — that phrase again — *even the appearance of* bias. *New York Times* editors demoted their wine critic when they learned he had written a book that was sponsored by a wine company. The critic had written nothing that compromised his integrity, but this business connection with a company he would have to write about gave the appearance of a conflict of interest. That was enough for *Times* editors.

Misrepresentation

This is a classic "gray area," one in which the end is frequently held as justifying the means. The rule seems simple: Reporters should always introduce themselves as reporters *before* they begin an interview. But there are rare occasions when that rule will be violated.

The (Chicago) *Sun-Times* once had its reporters actually open a bar — "The Mirage," they called it — to expose the under-the-table payments that saloon owners were asked to pay inspectors in Chicago. The reporters manning the bar certainly did not warn every corrupt inspector that walked into the place that they were about to speak to journalists. Other reporters have posed as assembly-line workers, nurses in mental hospitals and college students.

So back to that simple rule: Reporters must introduce themselves as reporters before they begin interviewing someone except . . . when? Many editors who have confronted this question have settled on this not-entirely-satisfactory answer: First, they say, it is rarely ethical to make believe you are someone else. But it may be justified if the story is of overriding interest and importance to the public and if there is *no* other way to get it. (Some editors wouldn't agree here; the *Sun-Times* didn't get a Pulitzer, reportedly because some members of the prize's jury questioned the ethics of the whole "Mirage" operation.)

Certainly, it would have to be an awfully important story, and a carefully thought out situation, before reporters should allow themselves to start playing make believe. It might be acceptable to sidle up to some assistant to the mayor in a bar without revealing who you are if that seems the only way to check on reports that the mayor has been accepting kickbacks from contractors. It wouldn't be acceptable to pull that subterfuge in search of a mere scoop on the mayor's upcoming speech to the city council.

On those rare occasions when they are hiding their true identities, reporters must go out of their way to protect the innocent people they are duping into giving them information. No reporter should print the admissions, confidings or tips of any person interviewed under false pretenses without, at a minimum, returning under their true identities as reporters to get the reaction and comments of the people they've tricked. And innocent people surreptitiously coaxed into participating — the honest nurse in a crooked abortion clinic, the inspector who doesn't take bribes but tells of those who do — should not be quoted without their agreeing. It would not be fair to use their names, perhaps costing them their jobs, in passing on loose talk they had presumed was being shared with a co-worker or bartender.

Television programs and movies might make it appear that "undercover" journalism is glamorous and commonplace. Occasionally it is necessary, but were it more common, the country would be facing, in effect, a secret police of undercover journalists waiting to trap people into mistakes. As a rule, people deserve to know when what they're saying could wind up on the front page of a newspaper. It requires truly extraordinary circumstances to warrant depriving potential sources of that basic right.

Private Lives

Our personal secrets do not belong in the newspaper unless they somehow become newsworthy. The problem, again, is defining when that is. Should a reporter write that a congressman has a penchant for brunettes and martinis after work? The courts would probably protect the reporter's right to print that information. They accord public figures little right to privacy (See Appendix D, Law). But most journalists would say that ethically the information should *not* be printed if the brunettes and martinis are not interfering with the congressman's work . . . even if he's married. But if those women had no-show jobs on the congressman's payroll or if his drinking began keeping him out of the office for days at a time, the answer would change. The private lives of public officials *should* be discussed in public *if* their outside activities affect how they are serving their constituents.

People who have *not* accepted positions of trust should get more protection. A profile of an up-and-coming young businesswoman should not mention the fact that she has a gambling problem. That aspect of her private life is not the public's business. However, should that businesswoman be arrested for embezzlement, her gambling becomes newsworthy and would, if it can be proven, be mentioned.

Rules such as these, of course, can be difficult to apply. What if that congressman just misses a few days of work a month and seems somewhat foggy, not clearly disoriented? What if that gambling businesswoman gets appointed head of the local Chamber of Commerce?

In this appendix we have tried to present, where possible, guidelines for journalistic behavior. We won't pretend that these guidelines will solve all the specific problems with which journalists will be confronted. When puzzling out these specific problems, journalists should err, if they're going to err, on the side of the people about whom they are reporting. If it's unclear whether the public needs to know, it's better to lose the scoop and save the person's reputation. In all these ethical decisions, there is no substitute for a healthy conscience.

Additional Reading

Playing It Straight, John Hulteng, American Society of Newspaper Editors, 1981.

The Messenger's Motives, John Hulteng, Prentice-Hall, 1976.

Reporters' Ethics, Bruce M. Swain, Iowa State University Press, 1978.

"Prize and Prejudice! The Journalism Awards Racket," Eliot Frankel and Mitchell Stephens, *Washington Journalism Review,* July/August 1981.

Law

If laws affecting the press make many journalists uncomfortable, it may be because they are aware that in too many countries, for too many centuries, such laws have been used to prevent the press from challenging or even disturbing the powerful. Reporters only have to stare across borders, or look into the early histories of their own countries, to see journalists operating in a legal straitjacket. The wording of the First Amendment—the guarantor of a free press in the United States—makes clear how concerned some of the country's first leaders were with protecting the press from legal restraints. It reads, in part: "Congress shall make no law . . . abridging the freedom . . . of the press."

The courts responsible for applying such 18th century pronouncements to the modern world have usually interpreted the First Amendment as a shield against *prior restraint* of the news media. Recent arguments invoking national security have nudged the courts back a bit from this interpretation, but, in general, the first principle of our free press is that the government cannot *in advance* stop anyone from publishing.

However, the First Amendment has not been interpreted as preventing legislatures and courts from surrounding journalists with an intricate web of laws that affect their ability to gather information and that establish their liabilities *after* material has been published. The majority of journalists probably would agree that most—though not all—of these laws and interpretations of laws are consistent with the pre-

cepts of responsible journalism. Some help define those precepts.

Whether journalists agree with these laws or not, they must live with them. It is risky and foolish to try to function as an aggressive journalist in this country without first gaining some familiarity with the laws affecting journalists. They will rarely be in the foreground as reporters go about their business, but they will often be in the background.

This book has room for only a brief overview of the subject. We encourage you to turn to the additional readings at the end of this appendix for a more complete briefing. And local libraries and press associations should be approached for copies of relevant state and local statutes.

Libel

The news can hurt. A front-page story reporting allegations that a doctor has had patients die because of negligence can cost that doctor her practice; a report that a teacher is a member of the Nazi party can lead to the loss of his job; the printing of a charge that a local housewife is a prostitute can permanently damage her reputation. All these charges are "defamatory," to use the legal term. They may cause their subjects to be, again using legal terminology, "shunned or avoided" or "exposed to public hatred and contempt or ridicule" or "injured in their occupation."

Some words are almost automatically defamatory. Anyone who has been publicly labeled a burglar, drunkard, gangster or plagiarist presumably has been exposed to public contempt. Bigamist, crook, drug addict, fascist and Mafia member are but a few of the other words that would fall into this category.

Still other words may prove defamatory if leveled against certain people in certain circumstances. There would appear to be little sting in the charge that a minister was driving a car, but if that minister belongs to a religious group that does not believe in driving cars, the charge may in fact be defamatory.

Potentially defamatory stories must be handled with extreme care. People who believe that they have been injured in print may sue for *libel.* Nonetheless, it is crucial to remember that there is nothing wrong with defaming somebody in a newspaper if proper care has been exercised in reporting and writing the story. If that doctor *has* had patients die because of negligence, if that teacher *is* an avowed member of the Nazi party, if that homemaker *was* convicted of prostitution, then fine. As a reporter you can say, "I defamed you and I'm glad. What I wrote is true."

Truth is always the best defense in libel cases. If the story can be proven true — and the burden of proof is on the news organization — then the newspaper and reporter should win. Reporters should be aware, though, that the courts set particularly high standards of proof. With complex stories — a day-care worker accused of child abuse, perhaps — "truth" can be hard to prove and be very much open to interpretation. Typically, lawyers are consulted before highly sensitive stories run to minimize the risk of a libel suit.

Regrettably, even the most responsible and thorough reporting is not a guarantee against being sued. Anyone can sue for libel and the cost of mounting a defense can be high, regardless of the outcome, unless the case is thrown out at a very early stage. Some legal experts fear that a recent spate of expensive libel judgments against the press has begun to inhibit sound investigative reporting. It can be hoped that the best newspapers, instead of being cowed by the number of libel cases and the size of libel judgments, will redouble their efforts to establish truth.

But the point for beginning reporters to remember is that incomplete and sloppy reporting of stories can attract libel suits as icy sidewalks attract negligence suits. And if someone's reputation *has* been hurt, and if the facts are *not* on the reporter's side, newspapers may lose those suits. It's not acceptable to ruin that doctor's reputation on the basis of just a few complaints by disgruntled patients. The reporter also had better not confuse Dr. Althea White with Dr. Doria White in writing the story. Such inaccuracy invites a libel suit and demands the printing of an immediate and prominent retraction.

However, if the reporter handles the facts carefully and bases the story on interviews with dozens of patients and colleagues and on death certificates and other hospital documents — in short, if the reporter has found proof — then the story has to be printed and the lawyers trusted, if necessary, to demonstrate its soundness in court.

There are three other, less noble, defenses against libel actions. The first is *privilege.* In general, reporters are responsible for the accuracy of everything in their stories, including direct quotations. Reporters can't base a libel defense on the fact that they merely quoted a colleague calling that teacher a Nazi. Careful attribution is little help here. But the law does give reporters the *privilege* of reporting on some events without fear of losing a libel action as long as the reporting is considered full, fair and accurate. Statements made in court or by public officials during official proceedings fall into this category.

Such a privilege exists because of the belief that people need to be able to talk freely in court or in other governmental proceedings and that the public has the right to know what was said. If that teacher was accused of being a Nazi in court or by the mayor at a city council meeting, the allegations could be printed. (The charge in court will be scrutinized by the justice system; the reporter's obligation is only to keep up with the proceedings. The mayor's charge, even though it was privileged, still should be checked out and the teacher given a chance to respond. Reporters' failure to check out privileged charges made during the 1950s by Sen. Joseph McCarthy on the floor of the U.S. Senate helped spread his wild accusations about Communists in government.)

The courts also protect journalists who in the course of writing reviews or opinion pieces level what is called *fair comment and criticism* against the people they are discussing. This is another possible defense against libel. A critic can write that "a windup doll programmed to deliver lines on cue would have given a more satisfying performance," although such a statement obviously cannot be proved true. Placing yourself in the public eye, as an actor does, means subjecting yourself to such criticism, the courts have ruled. It would not, however, be defensible to charge that actor, without proof, with being drunk on stage. Such substantive allegations about the person's life go beyond fair criticism of a public performance.

The courts also have ruled that public officials, along with some public figures, should not be able to collect damages for libel as easily as private citizens. In order to win libel suits, these well-known people are required to demonstrate not only that they've been defamed and that the charge was false, but also that either the journalist knew the charge was false or that the journalist acted "in reckless disregard" of whether the charge was true or false.

This final libel defense, which the courts have recently been rethinking, was intended to protect the press's right to investigate the powerful without being inhibited by excessive fear of libel. Still reporters do not want to have to fall back on the excuse that they were merely wrong, not deceitful or reckless in their reporting.

Libel, with the rarest of exceptions, falls under civil law. No one is likely to go to jail for libeling someone else. Nevertheless, successful libel suits can cost hundreds of thousands, even millions of dollars. Fear of litigation, however, is no excuse for timidity in digging up dirt. What the threat of libel should do is underline the need for care, accuracy and diligence in the excavation of that dirt.

Privacy

The courts have ruled that there is little privacy in news (though journalists might decide to keep some of the personal facts they dig up out of their stories for ethical reasons—See Appendix C, Ethics). Facts publicly obtained about a victim, suspect or witness that are pertinent to a breaking news story are, legally at least, fair game for reporters. Similarly, the courts have ruled that people who have voluntarily injected themselves into the news—politicians, entertainers, athletes—have surrendered much of their right to privacy.

However, the courts have begun to draw the line at *intrusion* into people's homes in search of damaging information, at descriptions of people's private lives that portray them in a *false light,* and at stories that dredge up embarrassing facts about people who have no direct connection to the news. A reporter, for example, might risk being judged liable for invasion of privacy for sneaking into a woman's living room in an attempt to find evidence that she is a bad mother, for misrepresenting the condition of her living room, or for poking into the private affairs of her family for no good, or newsworthy, reason in the first place.

Privacy law is rarely a concern in the daily reporting of news, but it may have to be considered while reporting an investigative piece or an unusually intimate profile.

Protecting Sources

You are working on an article about drug use at the local high school, and some students agree to discuss the situation with you on background (See Chapter 19, Sources). You agree not to use their names, but when the piece appears you find yourself asked to appear before a grand jury investigating drug sales in town. The prosecutor wants names. You explain that you can't violate your pledge not to reveal those

names. The judge responds that you have the same legal responsibility to testify about potential crimes as any other citizen and that you can be held in contempt of court if you refuse. Still, you won't break your word to your sources. Can the judge hold you in contempt of court?

Maybe. The Supreme Court has ruled that the First Amendment gives reporters *no* special right to avoid testifying in court. In response, a number of states have passed laws, called *shield laws,* bestowing on reporters the right to shield their sources in court. Sometimes, however, these laws turn out to provide less than perfect protection when challenged in court, and they don't apply in federal courts. Even in states with shield laws reporters have spent time in jail for protecting their sources.

Two basic needs of a democratic society are in conflict here. On one side is the need for a system of journalism in which reporters can investigate the underside of society without being used as surrogate police who will tattle on their sources at the drop of a subpoena. On the other side is the need for citizens to cooperate with the criminal justice system and the right of the accused to have a fair trial based on a full review of the evidence.

Without assurance of protection, journalists argue, sources aware of wrongdoing in government or in society would be less likely to come forward, inhibiting the journalist's role as a watchdog on government. In support of their argument, journalists point to the First Amendment.

But how, counter lawyers, can prosecutors build a case or defense attorneys assure their clients a fair trial when journalists are allowed to withhold evidence that bears on the case? They cite the Sixth Amendment, guaranteeing everyone the right to a fair trial.

Judges, for the most part, have sided with those who believe the press has no special right to withhold potential evidence. And when forced to choose between their promises of anonymity to sources and the risk of going to jail, most reporters have chosen jail. This means that reporters investigating potentially criminal behavior may have to decide *before* they agree to accept information on background, deep background or off the record (See Chapter 19, Sources) whether they are prepared to risk a stay in jail to protect the anonymity of the source of that information.

Access

Reporters need to be at the meeting, to visit the scene, to sit in the courtroom, to read the documents. But on occasion various government agencies put obstacles in their way. Sometimes the reasons are valid: the need to protect a reporter's safety, the need to protect a person's privacy, the need not to jeopardize an investigation or a bidding process. Sometimes the reasons are invalid: a desire to keep the public in the dark, to avoid the inconvenience of public debate or the heat of public anger.

Occasionally reporters get special privileges such as the right to cross police lines or to sit in special sections at meetings or trials. But usually they can attend or read only what the public can attend or read. In recent decades both public and press have been beneficiaries of new laws that expand the right of the public to monitor the activities of its leaders, laws that make some of the obstacles illegal.

Probably the most important of these laws is the federal Freedom of Information Act. This law sets up a process for obtaining access to government documents and restricts the government's right to withhold documents from the public. The final say, when there's a dispute, rests with the courts. The FOI Act, as it is known, is not a *carte blanche* for rifling the files of government, though its opponents like to portray it as such. The law delineates nine categories of information the government can refuse to release, including properly classified documents, files from ongoing criminal investigations, personnel and medical files, and certain inter-agency and intra-agency memoranda. An appeals procedure is built into the act, but reporters must be willing to hunker down for months in many cases in order to gain access to material with which a government agency is reluctant to part.

Still, the act has been used effectively as the basis for more than one investigative series. Jack Taylor, now with *The Denver Post,* filed nearly a thousand FOI requests while working on a series on the Bureau of Indian Affairs for *The Daily Oklahoman* in Oklahoma City in 1980. A thorough explanation of how the FOI Act can be used is contained in *The Reporter's Handbook.*

All 50 states now have their own laws, often called *sunshine laws,* designed to ensure the public access to a wide variety of the papers pushed by state and local governments. The federal government and most states now also have laws requiring that most of the meetings of governmental bodies—city councils, school boards, committees—be open to the press. These laws generally allow officials to close the door to the public and press *only* when discussing personnel matters, business transactions, litigation or investigations of wrongdoing.

Though these laws can help reporters monitor government and uncover corruption or just plain incompetence, they are of little value unless reporters know them well enough to hold officials to them. That's why many reporters carry copies of these laws in their wallets.

The court system, meanwhile, has its own standards of access: trials, hearings and appellate proceedings should be open to the press and public except in exceptional circumstances—perhaps the need to protect the identity of a secret witness. Grand jury hearings and judges' deliberations are closed to press and public.

Upon occasion judges, presumably concerned with protecting defendants from damaging pretrial publicity, have imposed *gag orders,* not only forbidding lawyers to talk, which is the judge's right, but forbidding reporters from reporting. These attempts — essentially efforts to impose prior restraint on the press—would seem to be violations of the First Amendment, and they have consistently been overturned on those grounds when appealed to higher courts. The Supreme Court has ruled that judges should shelter jurors or potential jurors either by denying them access to the news media during a trial or by changing the location of a trial, not by attempting to censor the news.

In combating gag orders, as in other areas in which the law touches their work, the best defense reporters have is a clear knowledge of their rights.

Additional Reading

The Reporter and the Law: Techniques of Covering the Courts, Lyle Denniston, Hastings House, 1980.

The Good Guys, the Bad Guys and the First Amendment, Fred Friendly, Random House, 1975.

Law of Mass Communications, Harold L. Nelson and Dwight L. Teeter, Jr., Foundation Press, 4th edition, 1982.

The Reporter's Handbook, ed. John Ullman and Steve Honeyman, St. Martin's Press, 1983.

The News Media & the Law, published quarterly by The Reporters Committee for Freedom of the Press, Washington, D.C.

Index

DATE DUE

MAY 1 4 2007	
OCT 15, 2010	